MODELLING EARLY CHRISTIANITY

Modelling Early Christianity explores the intriguing and foreign social context of first-century Palestine and the Graeco-Roman East, in which the Christian faith was first proclaimed and the New Testament documents were written. It demonstrates that a sophisticated analysis of the context is essential in order to understand the original meaning of the texts.

This study employs a wide variety of models drawn from anthropology, sociology, social psychology and other social sciences to pose fresh agendas for investigating the New Testament in its context. The contributors examine themes central to this new approach: the fundamental economic, social and religious features of the Mediterranean world; phenomena relating to the formation and maintenance of early Christian groups; the centrality of notions of kinship and honour in understanding a range of material from Paul, Matthew and Luke; the impact of the ideology of war on the New Testament and Jewish texts roughly contemporary with it. They offer a wealth of novel and socially realistic interpretations which make sense of the texts.

At the same time, *Modelling Early Christianity* contains significant new ideas on the relationship between social-scientific and literary-critical analysis, the theoretical justification for model-use, and the way these new approaches can fertilize contemporary Christian theology.

Contributors: Sean Freyne, John J. Pilch, J. Duncan M. Derrett, John H. Elliott, Bruce J. Malina, John M. G. Barclay, Nicholas H. Taylor, Jerome H. Neyrey, Dennis C. Duling, Richard L. Rohrbaugh, Stuart L. Love, Stephan J. Joubert, David G. Horrell, Philip F. Esler, Raymond Hobbs, Vernon K. Robbins.

Philip F. Esler is Dean of Divinity and Professor of Biblical Criticism at the University of St Andrews, Scotland. He is the author of *The First Christians in their Social Worlds* (Routledge 1994).

MODELLING EARLY CHRISTIANITY

Social-scientific studies of the New Testament in its context

Edited by Philip F. Esler

London and New York

First published 1995
by Routledge
11 New Fetter Lane, London EC4P 4EE

Simultaneously published in the USA and Canada
by Routledge
29 West 35th Street, New York, NY 10001

Typeset in Baskerville by Florencetype Ltd, Stoodleigh, Devon

Printed and bound in Great Britain by T. J. Press (Padstow) Ltd,
Padstow, Cornwall

British Library Cataloguing in Publication Data
A catalogue record for this book is available from the British Library

Library of Congress Cataloguing in Publication Data
A catalogue record for this book has been requested

ISBN 0 415 12980 X
ISBN 0 415 12981 8 (pbk)

To James Esler SM

ipse tamquam imbres mittet eloquia sapientiae suae
et in oratione confitebitur Domino.

CONTENTS

ILLUSTRATIONS

The following illustrations of the Flavian Iudaea Capta coins appearing on pp. 249–254 were prepared by Miss Teresa Rickards from the originals in the British Museum. The particular coins are identifed by reference to the Plates in Mattingly 1930 or Hill 1914. Copyright of the drawings is held by the University of St Andrews (School of Divinity).

CONTRIBUTORS

John M. G. Barclay is a Lecturer in the Department of Biblical Studies, University of Glasgow, Scotland.

J. Duncan M. Derrett is Emeritus Professor of Oriental Laws, University of London, living in Blockley, Moreton-in-Marsh, England.

Dennis C. Duling is Professor of New Testament, Canisius College, Buffalo, New York, USA.

John H. Elliott is Professor in the Department of Theology and Religious Studies, University of San Francisco, USA.

Philip F. Esler is Dean of Divinity and Professor of Biblical Criticism, University of St Andrews, Scotland.

Sean Freyne is Professor of Theology, Trinity College, Dublin, Ireland.

Raymond Hobbs is Professor of Old Testament Interpretation, McMaster Divinity College, McMaster University, Hamilton, Canada.

David G. Horrell is Research Tutor, Wesley House, and Chaplain and Fellow of Fitzwilliam College, Cambridge, England.

Stephan J. Joubert is Professor in the Department of Biblical Studies, University of Pretoria, South Africa.

Stuart L. Love is Professor of New Testament, Pepperdine University, Malibu, California, USA.

Bruce J. Malina is Professor in the Department of Theology, Creighton University, Omaha, Nebraska, USA.

Jerome H. Neyrey is Professor of New Testament, University of Notre Dame, Indiana, USA.

John J. Pilch is visiting Associate Professor of Biblical Literature, Department of Theology, Georgetown University, Washington, DC, USA.

Vernon K. Robbins is Professor of New Testament in the Department and Graduate Division of Religion, Emory University, Atlanta, Georgia, USA.

Richard L. Rohrbaugh is Professor of Religion, Lewis and Clark College, Portland, Oregon, USA.

Nicholas H. Taylor is Lecturer in Biblical Studies, Department of Theology and Religious Studies, University of Swaziland, Kwaluseni, Swaziland.

PREFACE

The essays in this volume are revised versions of papers presented at *Context and Kerygma: The St Andrews Conference on New Testament Interpretation and the Social Sciences* held in St Andrews from 29 June to 3 July 1994. A number of those who attended are members of the (largely US) Context Group: Project on the Study of the Bible in its Cultural Environment, and there were further participants from Scotland, England, Ireland, Belgium, Spain, Italy, Germany and South Africa.

The usual *modus operandi* of the Context Group (on which see Esler 1993b), consisting of collegial yet forthright discussion of papers to assist their authors prepare them for publication, was adopted at this Conference and, as a result, most of the essays have been modified to take into account views expressed by a particular nominated respondent or in discussion following their delivery. So although the reproduction of these views themselves would not have been possible here, they flavour the essays which follow.

I am grateful to my colleagues Dr R. A. Piper, the Principal of St Marys, and Professor R. Bauckham for the help they gave me before and during the Conference. I am also particularly indebted to Ms Helen-Ann Francis, a Senior Honours student in the School of Divinity at St Andrews, for having been a cheerful and efficient administrative assistant during the course of the Conference and also for the long hours she spent in helping to get the manuscript ready for submission to the publisher, especially in the preparation of the composite List of References and Indices, and in proof-reading. Mr Scott Hastings, a postgraduate student at St Andrews, also assisted with proof-reading.

The Routledge staff, especially Mr Richard Stoneman, have encouraged this project from its inception and have seen to the publication of the manuscript with their usual professionalism and good humour.

The dedication to my cousin Fr James Esler SM, of Sydney, Australia, represents a small acknowledgement of a much older debt.

Philip F. Esler
St Andrews
1 May 1995

ABBREVIATIONS

ABD	D. N. Freedman (ed.) *The Anchor Bible Dictionary*
AnBib	Analecta biblica
ANRW	*Aufstieg und Niedergang der römischen Welt*
BA	*Biblical Archaeologist*
BAGD	W. Bauer *et al.*: *Greek–English Lexicon of the New Testament*
BASOR	*Bulletin of the American Schools of Oriental Research*
BBB	Bonner biblische Beiträge
BEvT	Beiträge zur evangelischen Theologie
Bib	*Biblica*
BR	*Biblical Research*
BTB	*Biblical Theology Bulletin*
BZ	*Biblische Zeitschrift*
CBQ	*Catholic Biblical Quarterly*
ConBNT	Coniectanea Biblica, New Testament
CRINT	Compendia rerum iudaicarum ad novum testamentum
CurTM	*Currents in Theology and Mission*
ETL	*Ephemerides theologicae lovanienses*
ETS	Erfurter theologische Studien
ExpTim	*Expository Times*
FRLANT	Forschungen zur Religion und Literatur des Alten und Neuen Testaments
HDR	Harvard Dissertations in Religion
HR	*History of Religions*
HTR	*Harvard Theological Review*
HTS	*Harvard Theological Studies*
ICC	International Critical Commentary
IEJ	*Israel Exploration Journal*
Int	*Interpretation*
IRT	Issues in Religion and Theology
J. A.	Josephus: *Jewish Antiquities*
JAAR	*Journal of the American Academy of Religion*
JAC	*Jahrbuch für Antike und Christentum*

JBL	*Journal of Biblical Literature*
JJS	*Journal of Jewish Studies*
JQR	*Jewish Quarterly Review*
JR	*Journal of Religion*
JRA	*Journal of Roman Archaeology*
JRH	*Journal of Religious History*
JRS	*Journal of Roman Studies*
JSNT	*Journal for the Study of the New Testament*
*JSNT*Sup	*Journal for the Study of the New Testament*, Supplement Series
JSS	*Jewish Social Studies*
JSSR	*Journal for the Scientific Study of Religion*
JTS	*Journal of Theological Studies*
J. W.	Josephus: *Jewish War*
Neot	*Neotestamentica*
NICNT	New International Commentary on the New Testament
NJBC	R. E. Brown *et al.* (eds) *The New Jerome Biblical Commentary*
NovT	*Novum Testamentum*
*NovT*Sup	*Novum Testamentum*, Supplements
NTS	*New Testament Studies*
OBT	Overtures to Biblical Theology
PEQ	*Palestine Exploration Quarterly*
PG	Migne's Patrologia Graeca
PW	Pauly–Wissowa, *Real-encyclopädie der classischen Altertumswissenschaft*
RSR	*Recherches de science religieuse*
RSV	Revised Standard Version
SBLDS	SBL Dissertation Series
SBLMS	SBL Monograph Series
SBLSP	SBL Seminar Papers
SBS	Stuttgarter Bibelstudien
SBT	Studies in Biblical Theology
SJLA	Studies in Judaism in Late Antiquity
SNTSMS	Society for New Testament Studies Monograph Series
TDNT	G. Kittel and G. Friedrich (eds) *Theological Dictionary of the New Testament*
TS	*Theological Studies*
TToday	*Theology Today*
TWNT	G. Kittel and G. Friedrich (eds) *Theologisches Wörterbuch zum Neuen Testament*
VT	*Vetus Testamentum*
WBC	Word Biblical Commentary
ZNW	*Zeitschrift für die neutestamentliche Wissenschaft*
ZTK	*Zeitschrift für Theologie und Kirche*

INTRODUCTION

Models, context and kerygma in New Testament interpretation

Philip F. Esler

EMMAUS

In one of the most distinctive incidents in his Gospel, Luke relates how two disciples who had met Jesus on the road to Emmaus, although without recognizing him, invited him to stay with them overnight and discovered their evening meal took an unexpected course:

> When he was at table with them, he took the bread and blessed, and broke it, and gave it to them. And their eyes were opened and they recognised him; and he vanished out of their sight. They said to each other, 'Did not our hearts burn within us while he talked to us on the road, while he opened to us the scriptures?'
>
> (Luke 24:30–32; RSV)

Since the time of Aristotle, literary theorists have referred to an incident such as this as a 'recognition' (*anagnorisis*), meaning a change from ignorance to knowledge, in this case leading not to tragedy (as when Oedipus discovers that he has killed his father and married his mother) but to good fortune and enlightenment.[1] There are parallels to this account in Graeco-Roman literature, as in Plutarch's description of how Romulus, after his death, appeared to a friend on a road outside Rome, told him he was the god Quirinus and vanished.[2] Yet to appreciate how Luke has employed this literary *topos* and to establish the bearing which the Emmaus incident has upon the nature of New Testament interpretation, we need to consider its setting within the entirety of Luke 24:13–35.

The evangelist has developed his narrative through a series of four possible moments during which the recognition might occur: first, in the initial meeting on the road, when he expressly says that the disciples did not recognize Jesus; secondly, while one of the two disciples, in answer to Jesus' question, 'What matters are you discussing as you walk along?', describes what has just happened in Jerusalem; thirdly, when Jesus rebukes them for their dejection and explains from scriptures why it was necessary for the Messiah to suffer and enter his glory; and, fourthly, during the meal. The disciples observe later that their hearts burned within them as Jesus talked to them on the road (24:32), yet no recognition accompanied such excitement at the time, if indeed they did experience it.

These four moments mark off stages in the deepening social interaction between Jesus and the disciples which climaxes in one of the most integrative occasions between unrelated males in first-century culture – a meal. It is only at this final stage that the stranger sitting at the table reveals his identity. Only in a paradigmatic ceremony of social harmony in the Mediterranean world of the time, the breaking of bread, does God's power in the world become apparent. But the epiphany is short lived, since Jesus promptly vanishes. Nor does the story end there. For its closure only comes when the two disciples, having returned to Jerusalem, relate to the others 'what had happened on the road, and how he was known to them in the breaking of the bread' (24:35). The explanation offered refers not only to the revelation of their companion's identity, but to the extended social interaction which led up to and even embodied it – the everyday human experience of shared journey and shared meal.

We should not miss the wider implications of this ending. Just as the other disciples are at one remove from the events, needing to rely on a report of a numinous disclosure of Jesus' identity within an explicitly social context, so too do readers of the New Testament share this experience, as we seek to discern flashes of the divine momentarily irradiating the social realities in which they are experienced. The large issue thrown up by this is the connection between social setting and theological affirmation, between context and kerygma.

Luke is by no means the only evangelist who explicitly raises this question of the social embodiment of the divine presence. Matthew, for example, can say 'For where two or three are gathered in my name, there am I in the midst of them' (Matt. 18:20) and again 'Lo, I am with you always, to the close of the age' (Matt. 28:20). Furthermore, when John states in his Prologue that 'The word was made flesh and dwelt among us' (1:14a), the second part of this affirmation plainly acknowledges the importance of the social dimensions of God's presence among us, even though early christological controversies have caused most attention to be fixed on the first part. The Synoptic accounts of Jesus calming the storm on the sea of Galilee (Matt. 8:23–27; Mark 4:35–41; Luke 8:22–25) also offer a striking example of the contextualization of the kerygma, with the power of Jesus blazing out among a group of the disciples in the one boat, leaving them to wonder at his identity. Yet in Luke's Emmaus narrative we have the most graphic and compelling presentation of the insight that context, in its ordinary and everyday aspects, and kerygma are intimately connected. Generations of European artists who have portrayed the supper at Emmaus, Caravaggio and Rembrandt in particular,[3] bear witness to the evocative power of Luke's insight.

What holds for Luke holds for the rest of the New Testament. To appreciate the character of the transcendental affirmations communicated in the twenty-seven documents of which it is comprised we must comprehend their contexts, the particular social scenarios of the first-century Mediterranean world in which the sacred manifested itself. This inevitably means that New Testament interpretation will be historical in nature. All of the contributors to this volume share an interest in this historical task of situating the meanings communicated by the New Testament texts within their first-century contexts. They wish to understand New Testament scenarios for the sacred.[4]

Yet what distinguishes their work from other types of research into these texts is that they consider it necessary explicitly to enlist help from the social sciences, anthropology, sociology and social psychology in particular. The methodology of social-scientific interpretation, in general terms, has been explained in a number of places recently by some of its practitioners and I will not repeat it here,[5] although I will take up the critical issue of models below. Thus, the work of the contributors to this volume is avowedly inter-disciplinary in nature. They recognize the truth of Vernon Robbins' observation (p. 275 below) that the defensive perimeters erected around 'properly historical method' by critics who oppose the importation of social-scientific ideas into biblical criticism are really social constructs, purity restrictions of the type described by Mary Douglas (Douglas 1966).

We may go further and assert that traditional disciplinary boundaries are unnecessary and unfortunate limitations on our understanding of Christian beginnings and must not be allowed to impede our investigations. Perhaps we should adopt in relation to them the attitude once expressed by a great British jurist towards old forms of action which were impeding the development of principles suitable to the needs of the present, namely, 'when these ghosts of the past stand in the path of justice clanking their medieval chains, the proper course for the judge is to pass through them undeterred'.[6]

By and large, the essays which follow emphasize context rather than kerygma. Moving to a kerygmatic focus means shifting from the historical question of what the texts meant to their original audience, to the contemporary one of what they might mean today. In many quarters one now hears the cry that New Testament scholars should be doing just that, although such a view underestimates the distinctiveness of historical enquiry and the confusion which results if we too easily blur the character of the New Testament texts as documents from the past with the role they may play in the present. On the other hand, it is sometimes even suggested that historical method is unable to contribute to the development of contemporary meaning (Watson 1994). Against views such as these, in the fourth and last section of this introductory essay I will set out with assistance from the theology of George Lindbeck how I envisage that the type of historical research represented in this volume can play a role in helping contemporary readers appropriate New Testament meanings. Indeed, I will go beyond this to argue that such a process cannot proceed apart from an appreciation of the historical dimension of these texts. As we will see, however, the appropriation which I have in mind is something which can only take place in the context of a believing community. Although New Testament critics may be able to unveil the nature of the original connection between text and context and even advocate, at a general level (as I will do below), how such connections might be brought into dialogue with contemporary experience, the contextualization of the kerygma can only be achieved by a community. To anticipate Lindbeck's theory for a moment, only the faithful themselves can make the New Testament story their story.

MODELS

The essays in this volume employ a number of areas of social-scientific enquiry. At a very general level, all of them can be regarded as exercises in the sociology of knowledge to the extent that they seek dialectically to relate social realities with cognition and symbolism, in other words, context with kerygma.[7] More particularly, however, the sociology of sectarianism is employed by Elliott. Social psychology forms the framework of the essays by Malina and Pilch. David Horrell adopts the structuration theory formulated by Anthony Giddens. Mediterranean anthropology is utilized by Duling, Joubert, Love, Neyrey, Rohrbaugh and, to an extent, myself.

All the essays are notable for their deliberate use of social-scientific ideas and perspectives, especially in the form of explicitly formulated models and perspectives.[8] John Elliott has rightly pointed out that this approach is characteristic of social-scientific criticism and differentiates it, for example, from a social history which attempts to investigate social aspects of early Christianity without availing itself of help from anthropology, sociology or social psychology (Elliott 1993a: 7). In this context a model may be described in an admittedly broadbrush way as an 'abstract, simplified representation of some real world object, event or interaction, constructed for the purpose of understanding, control or prediction' (Malina 1983: 14).[9] Models are heuristic tools, not ontological statements. Accordingly, they are either useful or not, and it is meaningless to ask whether they are 'true' or 'false'.

Unfortunately, not everyone is yet convinced of the value of using models in New Testament interpretation. One objection sometimes taken (although usually in the form of laconic grumbling, rather than reasoned discussion) is that the use of models constitutes the imposition of alien and inappropriate frameworks on first-century data and that, therefore, they should be avoided.[10] The short (and to my mind irrefutable) answer to this is that we all use models in our work; the only question is whether or not we acknowledge them and bring them out into the open for critical scrutiny. Whenever New Testament critics discuss textual features in terms such as 'family', 'class', 'politics', 'power', religion', 'personality', 'conscience', or 'boundary-markers' they are employing models, although usually implicit and unrecognized ones deriving from modern experience quite remote from biblical culture, with the inevitable risk of ethnocentric and anachronistic readings.

A more interesting criticism of models has been made recently by Susan Garrett (1992), in which she defends 'sociological' interpretation but proposes that it be 'interpretive' rather than model-oriented in nature.[11] Garrett seeks to relate discussion over the use of models in New Testament criticism to an ongoing debate in the human sciences themselves.[12] Her initial point is whether social-scientific inquiry should be seen as science or a humanistic discipline. Following Marcus and Fischer (1986) and Peacock (1986), she contrasts a scientific or quasi-scientific methodology adopted by social scientists who 'assume that social groups follow laws or law-like patterns' which consists of testing a model or hypothesis against empirical data to produce 'objective' or 'valid' results (a method she calls 'nomothetic', 'hypothetico-deductive' and 'positivist'), with an approach which recognizes that human social discourse is always expressed in symbolic forms whose meaning is relative to particular sets of social and cultural circumstances. This relativity and the multivalent quality of symbolic forms 'resist the abstractions of the scientist'. The latter approach is 'interpretive' and does not claim 'objective' validity for its findings. In particular, she proposes the symbolic perspective of Clifford Geertz as the clearest case of the interpretive approach, in its focus on the analysis of cultural systems through symbols and their power to constitute reality. This approach has ample room for subjectivity, since the aim is to produce an interpretation which has been filtered through the experience and worldview of the interpreter. She claims that the total immersion in a foreign culture by an ethnographer is a classic method for accomplishing symbolic interpretation and that in practice many ethnographers find a rigorous model-testing approach inappropriate. Accordingly, while agreeing with John H. Elliott that exegetes must make 'intentional and well-documented decisions about their methodological perspectives', such explicitness does not necessitate model-testing. She alleges that the interpretive method constitutes a more adequate treatment of the continual problem of how one can ever translate the discourse or social script of one culture into another ('incommensurability'), since it sticks closer to the natives' point of view, to cultural particularity, whereas the 'positivist' approach – which employs cross-cultural comparison and gives credit to law-like patterns despite superficial cultural differences – is less concerned with this issue. Yet she acknowledges that even interpretive researchers such as Geertz employ 'etic' categories, that is, those of trained outsiders, and that it is always necessary to strike a balance between insider ('emic') and etic categories, although without being too specific about just what type of etic perspectives are permissible.

In anthropological terms, it is clear that there *is* a tension between the ethnographic discernment of what native people think – in all its particularity – and the formulation of models or theories which can be employed cross-culturally. The issue is how to reconcile the experience and conceptualizations of actor and observer. Until recently the former aspect seems to have been regarded as the privileged partner (Kuper 1992: 2). In recent years, however, there has been a growing realization that cultural anthropology needs both aspects. The influential figures whose essays appear in the collection edited by Kuper (such as Fredrik Barth, Philippe Descola and Maurice Bloch) are united in the view that 'together, ethnography and theoretically informed comparison constitute a single plausible enterprise' (Kuper 1992: 2). All human groups, however diverse, are capable of communicating with one another. Merely to entertain the possibility of one culture seeking to understand or even translate another presupposes the necessary foundations in human nature and human sociality which transcend ethnographic particularity (see Carrithers 1992).

These writers are careful, however, to specify the type of models they have in mind to ensure a reasonable degree of contiguity between emic and etic perspectives. Thus Bloch calls for researchers not to base models on the assumption that natives (or observers!) think in terms of propositions linked by logical inferences in a single lineal sequence, but rather on the recognition that thought relies on clumped networks of signification organized in multi-stranded, non-lineal ways (Bloch 1992: 129–130). Similarly, Descola, rather than defending the grand universals of older theory, advocates that research be focused on local systems of variants that exist in a particular series of landscapes and within a specific historical period (Descola 1992). Both Bloch and Descola recognize the importance of ecological factors in cultural differentiation.

Heavily interpretive approaches, on the other hand, are riddled with difficulties. Destabilizing the whole interpretivist project is a fundamental paradox. As Descola has pointed out, excessive concentration on particularity results in the failure to produce an interpretive framework necessary to discuss cross-cultural differences, resulting in a kind of 'cognitive apartheid' (Descola 1992: 108). This is the problem of the radical relativism of strongly ethnographic research. To seek to know and to describe other cultures only in their own terms means both that one has embraced a fundamental relativism and, moreover, that those other cultures are largely unknowable to us in the later twentieth-century West. For this reason, Garrett's view, noted above, that the adoption of native viewpoints involved in the interpretive method provides a more adequate method for cross-cultural translation is regrettably misconceived.

Another problem with interpretivism for New Testament research is that it is largely incompatible with historical method. In seeking to understand the complex web of meaning in a particular culture at a given time interpretivists may find it relevant to address the extent to which folk history or folk memory features in that web, but they have no role for the techniques of historical analysis, for the etic or model-driven investigation of diachronic developments which may be crucial to our understanding of the phenomenon. The sectarian model set out by John H. Elliott in this volume, for example, could not be accommodated within an interpretive view of early Christianity, nor could the model fixing on the transition from reform movement to sect which I have developed with respect to early post-Easter Christianity (Esler 1987: 47–70).

Perhaps the ultimate danger with the heavily interpretive and ethnographic approach is that it falls prey to a radical post-modernism. The advocates of models and theory retain a belief in the duty of the social scientist to communicate and they recognize that this means imposing some order on reality. The post-modernist antipathy to such 'meta-narratives' seems to leave social scientists only two possibilities – either Stephen Tyler's wildly unhelpful notion that the meanings of the other can only be evoked, through poetry for example (Tyler 1986), or the notion that, at the end of the day, all that matters is the researcher's own experience. Even Geertz has acknowledged the 'epistemological hypochondria' (in part a product of post-modernist deconstruction) which is inducing many ethnographers to despair of being able to say anything at all about other forms of life (Geertz 1988: 71–72).[13]

Finally, at the practical level, in the case of research dependent on ancient texts like the New Testament documents, although one would certainly not wish to say that interpretive criticism is impossible, plainly the customary total immersion in another culture by a trained observer is out of the question and this suggests that a model-oriented approach is less problematic.

As far as New Testament criticism is concerned, the main problem with Garrett's analysis is that its image of 'positivist' model-using is a stalking-horse having no resemblance to social-scientific interpretation as it is actually practised. New Testament critics who employ this method, including the authors represented in this volume, certainly do not claim that there are social laws, or that their results are 'objectively valid' (although since they certainly reject the view that one historical opinion is as good as another, they may well claim that their views are more plausible than some). No ontological status is accorded to the models; they are seen merely as heuristic tools. Either they throw up a set of new and interesting questions, which the texts themselves must answer, or they do not. Models which do not have this result will be discarded and replaced with others. Social-scientific modelling yields insight rather than necessarily embodying truth. Garrett herself, somewhat inconsistently, approves of interpretation in which the 'models are used as heuristic devices, to prompt questions and highlight possible connections among the data' (Garrett 1992: 95–96), and that is overwhelmingly the approach taken in social-scientific criticism generally and in the essays which follow.

Models will have built into them certain modern assumptions and perceptions, but these are essential if we are to address cultural experience different from our own in terms we can comprehend. The debate is really about what assumptions we should adopt, not whether we model or not. The necessity of making sense of the strange world of the first-century CE as manifested in the New Testament becomes even more important when we seek to move beyond the historical analysis of the original meanings of the texts to the appropriation of those meanings within the experience of contemporary communities.

Moreover, like the authors in the Kuper volume mentioned above, the authors represented here are committed both to ethnographic observation and to the use of models and other perspectives. Many of them have even been influenced by Geertz. They have been at pains to bring emic data into dialogue with the etic categories employed. This does not mean that some are not more rigorously systematic in their use of models than others.

On the other hand, as already noted, the danger with an avowedly interpretive approach to biblical criticism is that its practitioners, if they find that post-modernist criticism actually leaves them with anything to do, since they lack the aid of models and theory generally they risk slipping into a morass of relativism. Without a methodology which highlights cross-cultural similarities and differences, they are likely to read the biblical texts in terms of twentieth-century Western culture. Hence the necessity, for example, of employing the perspectives generated by recent anthropologists concerning the contemporary Mediterranean region to provide an alternative set of scenarios to those we would otherwise unconsciously employ. In its regional and ecological emphasis, this project fits nicely into the type of approach advocated by Descola and mentioned above. Anyone familiar from recent anthropological research with the centrality of honour in the Mediterranean area today, for example, will find that the Bible is replete with references to it, yet two decades ago (before Bruce Malina began pointing it out) there was virtually no recognition of this.[14] The exegetical essays below by Neyrey, Duling, Rohrbaugh, Love and Joubert, for example, amply demonstrate the significance of Mediterranean attitudes to family honour for understanding a wide range of New Testament texts. Rohrbaugh is even able to show not only that a convincing reading of Luke 4:1–30 requires a familiarity with Mediterranean culture, but that in some cases pre-modern commentators actually understood issues opaque to modern critics. Accordingly, Garrett's brusque resistance to the use of Mediterranean cultural anthropology in biblical criticism (Garrett 1992: 97) is ill-advised.

CONTEXT

The world of first-century Palestine

Christianity came to life in the world of first-century Palestine. Yet this world – and the Mediterranean generally – diverges widely from our modern experience in terms of many significant social variables. The essays by Sean Freyne, John Pilch and Duncan Derrett explore bedrock features of New Testament context in areas such as economics, primary religious experience, magic and witchcraft, the configurations of which are quite foreign to the world of Northern Europe and North America.

Freyne adopts two models from the area of economic anthropology drawn from T. F. Carney, the first relating to a stable economy and the second to a developing one, and applies them to a rich set of data derived both from recent archaeological research and literary evidence to investigate economic development in Antipas' Galilee. The particular foci of his investigation are markets, monetization and the way in which insitutions and values changed in response to developments in both. His presentation of economic issues in Galilee has important consequences for the quest for the historical Jesus, since he is able to relate aspects of the Jesus tradition to the dynamic forces unleashed by the evolving Herodian market economy.

Pilch is concerned with altered states of consciousness, an aspect of human experience foreign to most Northern European or North American readers of the Bible, except those in contact with the more genuinely uninhibited forms of Pentecostalism, yet common human experience in the majority of the world's cultures, including 80 per cent of circum-Mediterranean societies. Interpreting the transfiguration of Jesus as a typical experience of alternate reality carries a strong measure of cultural plausibility in the Mediterranean world and enables Pilch to offer an explanation for the event very different from those normally proposed.

Derrett's essay on the Evil Eye (a social feature of fundamental importance in the region for several millennia) represents a response to a proposal made in recent research that the Evil Eye was connected with illness. He seeks to differentiate the ways in which Greeks and Jews understood the phenomenon, arguing that in the Jewish sources, and in the New Testament, the Evil Eye is related to envy and grudging, rather than witchcraft and illness. Derrett ends by raising the possibility that the absence of a connection between the Evil Eye and sickness in the New Testament may be related to the implementation of the love commandment, which puts to an end the envy which is the source of the Evil Eye.

Early Christian group formation and maintenance

A fundamental aspect of inquiry into early Christianity, covered in the next four essays, is how to interpret the ways in which the social entities which formed around those who followed Jesus and later acknowledged him as Messiah established and maintained their distinctive identities. This remains an area of lively debate. A productive line of research has been the sociology of sectarianism, beginning with Max Weber and Ernst Troeltsch and developing in the hands of Richard Niebuhr and Bryan Wilson. One of the earliest proponents of this approach, John Elliott (1981; 1991c) has returned to the theme in this volume to propose and employ a diachronic model which characterizes the growth of the Jesus movement before and after Easter in terms of a development from faction to sect.[15] Elliott focuses on a number of variables relating to the conditions favouring the development of a sectarian group, the characteristics of such a group and the strategies it might adopt. These variables allow one to interrogate the evidence for any first-century Christian group with a high degree of penetration and detail to see where it lay on this issue. The sharply nuanced profiles of different groups which emerge under such analysis provide a challenging answer to critics who have reservations about the appropriateness of sectarian theory for New Testament criticism.[16]

Bruce Malina proposes a quite different way of envisioning early Christian social organization. His aim is to develop a model of the formation of small groups which might fit the data we have of the first generations of Christians. He focuses on three issues: (1) why small groups form at all; (2) the five distinctive stages through which they develop – forming, storming, norming, performing and adjourning; (3) the reason for joining groups – to achieve change, either intrapersonal, interpersonal, intragroup or extragroup. Broadly speaking, he sees the Christians as members of 'face-to-face' groups in a 'face-to-mace' society. An important theme is to contrast the task-oriented group which formed around Jesus (focusing on intergroup change with political implications for Israel) from the social activity groups ('elective associations') which eventually formed after his death and resurrection (focusing on the cosmic rescue of the person, with strong bonds of fictive kinship, in a household setting).

John Barclay addresses another issue bearing upon the manner in which early Christian groups established and maintained a distinct social identity, in particular with respect to Judaism and the phenomenon of internal dissent. In each case he fixes upon the notion of deviance as developed by sociologists like Becker (1963) and Schur (1971) as a product of social interaction, rather than as an objectively definable entity. In this perspective the critical questions are who defines someone as 'deviant' (or 'apostate'), in what circumstances, from what perspective and in whose interests. The process can be seen at work with respect both to its external and internal aspects in Paul's treatment as an 'apostasizing' Jew in Jewish communities and in his labelling of certain persons as 'deviants' in his churches.

The conversion process itself is the topic of Nicholas Taylor's paper. He applies to early Christianity a scheme formulated by Shaye Cohen (1989) which distinguishes seven categories of increasingly intimate association between a gentile and neighbouring Jews which might result in a complete conversion to Judaism. This leads him to opt for a model of conversion as resocialization (based on Snow and Machalek 1983), which identifies four critical elements as: (1) autobiographical reconstruction of the convert; (2) the assumption of a comprehensive attribution scheme, which means that phenomena are accounted for within the framework of a newly acquired belief system; (3) suspension of analogical reasoning, which means the adoption of the view that the new faith is unique and all others are categorically distinct from it; and (4) the assumption of a master role, whereby the convert comes to identify totally with the new affiliation and seeks to represent it to outsiders.

Family and honour in Matthew and Luke

Four of the contributions address issues in the Gospels of Matthew (Neyrey and Duling) and Luke (Rohrbaugh and Love) connected with critical Mediterranean realities of the honour attached to one through family membership. Neyrey and Duling demonstrate how both pre-Matthean tradition and Matthew may be understood within a process of the fraught replacement of natural kin by the fictive kinship of the Jesus faction and early Christian groups.

Neyrey's thesis is that the Q tradition underlying the Matthean beatitudes is directed to assisting disciples to come to terms with the loss of honour and material resources they suffered *within their families* when they decided to follow Jesus. He proposes that the four original makarisms which formed the basis of Matt. 5:3–12 describe the unfortunate fate of a disciple who has been ostracized as a 'rebellious son' by his family on account of his loyalty to Jesus. On this view the beatitudes function to honour the dishonoured.

Yet the severing of ties with real kin highlighted by Neyrey is compensated by incorporation into the fictive kinship of the group(s) which formed around Jesus and continued in various ways after his death. Duling's essay deals with a central aspect of this process, by arguing that the Matthean *ekklesia* should be regarded as a fictive kinship group or, more particularly, a fictive brotherhood association. Building on Gerhard Lenski's treatment of the Roman empire as an advanced agrarian society in which small fictive kin groups emerge when natural families are in decline, he proposes that the Matthean community developed into a social entity best comparable with the voluntary associations of the first-century Graeco-Roman world. His thesis is that Matthew and his audience represented a well-educated, self-sufficient scribal group dominating a mixed community but who were marginal in the sense that they existed on a margin between two competing normative schemes, the old Jewish one and the new one of Christian brotherhood and discipleship.

The proper honour of a son comes to prominence again in Rohrbaugh's essay on Luke 4:1–30. With a firm grasp on recent anthropological research (strengthened by his own experience on the West Bank), Rohrbaugh interprets this text (and Luke 3:23–38) in the context of Mediterranean village understanding of family honour in a way which offers incisive solutions to several questions traditionally misunderstood. He proposes that the genealogy of Jesus (3:23–38) is naturally placed to establish a claim to his ascribed honour as son of God, which is then tested in challenge-and-response interactions, first on a cosmic plane with the Devil (4:1–13), and then with the people in his own village. In this perspective Jesus' change in mood at 4:23 is not virtually inexplicable (as so many modern commentators find it), but a natural response to the blunt insult of the villagers' question 'Is this not Joseph's son?', which presupposes that it is a serious breach of local conventions relating to family honour for the son of a mere carpenter to speak like this in public. Rohrbaugh is able to underline the ethnocentric nature of modern misreadings of this verse by referring to pre-modern interpreters who saw the point.

Stuart Love turns to a different aspect of the way in which family honour was reshaped within one section of early Christianity – the issue of whether women should attend banquets. Normally courtesans, not wives, dined with men, although the Romans were somewhat less strict on this than the Greeks. Having demonstrated the male-centred nature of banquets in the Graeco-Roman world of the time and the shamefulness involved in women attending, Love argues that Luke reshapes prevailing social conventions by presenting a picture of the incorporation of outcast women into Christian fellowship meals.

Paul, kinship and ideology

Joubert's essay on Paul's Corinthian correspondence fuses theoretical perspectives deriving from anthropological research into Mediterranean family life and the quasi-kinship involved in patron–client relations with a detailed survey of the Roman institution of *paterfamilias*. He advocates the particular relevance of the Roman experience by reason of the status of Corinth as a Roman colony founded by Julius Caesar in 44 BCE after having lain in ruins for a century. Joubert demonstrates with reference to a large amount of textual data how Paul functions both as a broker moving between the 'heavenly patrons' (Father, Son and Holy Spirit) and the Corinthian 'clients' and, even more noticeably, as a *paterfamilias*, establishing a particular kind of affective relationship, correcting behaviour and dealing with conflict.

Whereas Joubert employs social anthropology to set Paul within a first-century context, David Horrell, approaching from a sociological direction in the form of Anthony Giddens' structuration theory, unmasks the ideological structures which may be discerned in the family imagery (including *paterfamilias*) employed in certain letters by Paul or written in his name. Horrell focuses in particular on the role of ideology in Giddens' theory to refer to the cognitive, symbolic or linguistic systems by which the powerful justify their methods of domination. The most common forms of ideology occurring in relation to religion are the representation of sectional interests as universal ones and the naturalization (or 'reification') of the present. Horrell notes that legitimation of dominating structures may be intended or unintended and that texts may 'escape' from the intentions of their creators, to have a range of entirely unanticipated results, a phenomenon also noted by Peter Berger and Thomas Luckmann. Horrell next applies this theory to a sample of Pauline and pseudo-Pauline texts to investigate the extent to which Paul is involved, either deliberately or unintentionally, in the ideological maintenance of power. His findings that Pauline and pseudo-Pauline texts have the potential for the theological naturalization or reification of first-century patterns of domestic domination raise disturbing questions both for exegesis and for the modern appropriation of biblical experience.

Oppression, war and peace

At a high level of generality my own essay pursues a sociology of knowledge approach to the interpretation of three Jewish apocalypses written after and in response to the destruction of Jerusalem by Rome in 70 CE by seeking to discern the connections they reveal between this experience and their theology. Adopting a view of Michel Foucault on the way in which power, ideology and discourse cluster together, I propose that these texts respond to the Roman ideology of imperial subjugation expressed in the discourses of ritual, coinage and monumental architecture, an ideology explicable within the honour/shame value system of Mediterranean society. In the case of 2 Baruch this involves the development of a counter-ideology and counter-discourse focusing on the fate of the Temple vessels.

Mediterranean warfare is also taken up by Ray Hobbs, who discusses the extent to which the language of war has found its way into the New Testament and the implications of the choice of such imagery. He differentiates his approach from that of numerous commentators on this subject by exploring the socio-cultural context of this semantic field rather than its literary 'background'. His central concern is with the extent to which metaphors such as warfare function to define the social values of a group and as a means of self-definition. His particular (social-psychological) model is the 'Masada Syndrome', a state in which members of a group have a central belief that the rest of the world has highly negative behavioural intentions towards them. In contrast with other imagery, such as that of the household, Hobbs shows that the military metaphor reflects and promotes certain aspects of behaviour, such as boundary control and heroic suffering. Finally, he raises the disturbing question of the appropriateness of the warrior as an image of the disciple – then or now.

Since war is the focus of the penultimate two contributions, it is perhaps appropriate to end the collection with one devoted to the establishment of peace – in the form of Vernon Robbins' essay on the prospects for cooperation between social-scientific and literary-critical approaches. As one of the very few commentators at home in both, Robbins offers a diagnosis of the current (generally unfriendly) state of relations between the two, sets out a particular type of accommodation and urges reasons for greater cooperation. His starting-point is the issue of disciplinarity in biblical research. He rightly observes that disciplinary limits are really social constructs, purity boundaries of the type explained by Mary Douglas, which their proponents use to keep at bay 'impurities' which would otherwise intrude – like mud tramped into one's living room by an unwelcome visitor. His answer is not eclecticism, with its essential abandonment of disciplinarity, but inter-disciplinarity, where the methods of various disciplines are employed to interrogate a set of data and the results are then brought into fruitful dialogue. Robbins views rhetoric as central to the integration of social-scientific and literary-critical approaches and his own nuanced socio-rhetorical model has the potential to open up numerous lines of enquiry. While acutely pointing out the difficulties which proponents of either methodology have with the other, he argues that they do have certain features in common worth building on. In particular, in ascribing to the need for the conscious application of theory they both stand in stark opposition to the post-modernist rejection of method.

KERYGMA

As already noted, to bring out the kerygmatic dimensions of the New Testament texts means bridging the gap between history and theology, between what the texts meant and what they might mean. But here we need to ask 'mean for whom?' We need to distinguish between a present meaning for the Christian faithful, immersed in the various forms of Christian ecclesial life, and a rather different meaning for the Christian theologian, who is seeking to make intellectual sense of the processes. Some theologians see the main issue as the critical evaluation of Christian truth claims. An example in point is Francis Watson, who, in a major contribution on the hermeneutical question (Watson 1994), seems primarily interested in addressing those for whom such claims, especially his primary one 'Jesus is Lord', are problematic. His target audience seems to be Christian thinkers limping along with suspect ontologies, or agnostics, post-modernist or otherwise, kind enough still to be interested in the topic – the Porphyries of the twentieth century. Either way, we are talking mainly about a few thousand academics in Europe, North America and their colonial off-shoots. The danger of emphasizing this audience is that of theology giving way entirely to apologetics. This would be especially unfortunate in Watson's case, given his dedicated interest in the socio-political impact and function of Christian theology.

While the vigorous exposition of Christian doctrine within the canons of contemporary discourse is an important task, we should not forget all those believing Christians for whom Christian truth claims are not really an issue. There are about one billion of these. The challenge is to enable the New Testament to speak to them in the present – to empower, to provoke, to activate. We must expose the original meanings of the texts in a way which will facilitate their recontextualization by present-day Christian groups. Georg Gadamer's notion of the fusion of the horizons of the past and the present, their mutual co-existence in creative tension, offers the beginnings of a path forward (Esler 1994a: 2–3). The dynamic nature of this dialogue is fostered by the strangeness of the biblical world as revealed by Mediterranean anthropology which emerges in so many of the essays below.

Yet to speak of a fusion of horizons in this way is to operate at a fairly high level of abstraction. To investigate more precisely how such fusion might occur it is necessary to attend to the nature of the historical investigation under discussion. The type of original meaning of interest here is that which emerges from the integration of social-scientific ideas and perspectives into historical analysis. Historical interpretation infused with social-scientific insights focuses on New Testament documents as written from and for early Christian communities in the throes of creating new social worlds for themselves. It treats them as texts which integrate context and kerygma. Only with this method is it possible to penetrate the critically important social dimensions of early Christianity, above all the inter-relationship between social context and the theologies of New

Testament texts, which is the target of a sociology of knowledge mode of analysis, as outlined for example by Peter Berger and Thomas Luckmann (see Esler 1987).

The theological appropriation of this form of historical research requires an understanding of contemporary Christian theology with which the historical results might be brought into conjunction, or, in Gadamer's perspective, creative tension. In other words, a style of New Testament exegesis which focuses on the texts as written for early Christian communities in the process of creating new social worlds (in which context and Gospel traditions are brought together beneath an overarching symbolic universe) is more likely to speak to the present Christian situation if the latter can be construed in reasonably analogous terms.

Among contemporary Christian theologians, George Lindbeck has come closest to an understanding of Christian theology which satisfies this requirement in *The Nature of Doctrine: Religion and Theology in a Postliberal Age* (Lindbeck 1984), a work inspired by his deep commitment to ecumenical dialogue. In Lindbeck's model of religion, as a kind of cultural framework which shapes the entirety of life and thought, I find a way of construing the present Christian situation in workably analogous terms.[17] It is worth stressing that since I am treating Lindbeck's proposal as a model, as a heuristic tool productive of insight, not as necessarily being an expression of ontological truth, my interest lies in whether it is useful, not in whether it is 'true'; this distinction seems lost on those who criticize Lindbeck for the philosophical underpinnings of his theory (Phillips 1988).

Lindbeck distinguishes three contemporary theories of religion and doctrine, with respect to which he proposes an alternative. The first, which he labels 'cognitive', stresses the ways in which church doctrines function as informative propositions or truth claims about objective realities.[18] The second theory, which he calls 'experiential-expressive', interprets doctrines as noninformative and nondiscursive symbols of inner feelings, attitudes or existential orientations. He associates this theory with liberal Christianity stemming ultimately from Schleiermacher. The third theory, represented by Karl Rahner and Bernard Lonergan, embraces both the cognitive-propositional and the experiential-symbolic (p. 16).

In contrast to these theories, Lindbeck utilizes perspectives from anthropology (Max Weber, Emile Durkheim and Clifford Geertz), sociology (Karl Marx and Peter Berger) and philosophy (Wittgenstein, Ninian Smart and William Christian), perspectives which have hitherto had little impact on theology, to develop a theory of religion as resembling a language or culture. In this theory, which he describes as 'cultural-linguistic', religions constitute reality and value systems, or idioms for the construing of reality and the living of life. For Lindbeck, church doctrines function not as truth claims or expressive symbols, but as 'communally authoritative rules of discourse, attitude, and action' (p. 18).

According to Lindbeck, a religion can be viewed as a kind of cultural and/or linguistic framework or medium which shapes the entirety of life and thought:

> It is not primarily an array of beliefs about the true and the good (although it may involve these), or a symbolism expressive of basic attitudes, feelings, or sentiments (though those will be generated). Rather, it is similar to an idiom that makes possible the description of realities, the formulation of beliefs, and the experiencing of inner attitudes, feelings and sentiments. Like a culture or language, it is a communal phenomenon that shapes the subjectivities of individuals rather than being primarily a manifestation of those subjectivities.
>
> (p. 33)

The extent to which religion is understood as a communal phenomenon highlights the way in which this perspective meshes with approaches to the New Testament which focus upon the relationship between social context and theology.

At a general level, the cultural-linguistic model of religion treats the internal experience of its adherents as deriving from external realities; it sees human experience as shaped, moulded and, in a sense, constituted by cultural and linguistic forms. In this respect it reveals its indebtedness to the internalization of human social productions as described by Berger and Luckmann. Of particular interest, however, is the precise mode by which Lindbeck sees this internalization process occurring. For Lindbeck, this occurs through the appropriation of the primal stories of a religious tradition by subsequent generations:

> To become a Christian involves learning the story of Israel and of Jesus well enough to interpret and experience oneself and one's world in its terms. A religion is above all an external word, a *verbum externum*, that moulds and shapes the self and its world, rather than an expression or thematization of a preexisting self or preconceptual experience.
>
> (p. 34)

Again, however, it should be noted that the community is seen as the locus for the appropriation of the story:

> The proclamation of the Gospel, as a Christian would put it, may be first of all the telling of the story, but this gains power and meaning insofar as it is embodied in the total gestalt of community life and action.
>
> (p. 36)

Yet, in spite of criticism which has frequently been levelled at him,[19] Lindbeck does not suggest that cognitive claims are excluded from the picture, rather that the emphasis is no longer on them. He sets out his position on this issue very clearly in a section entitled 'Excursus on Religion and Truth'. He begins by acknowledging that to do justice to the actual speech and practice of religious people we must allow for the possible propositional truth of a religion. If we take a statement such as 'Jesus Christ is Lord', it is clear that the great strength of a cognitive-propositional theory of religion is that it admits of the possibility of the truth of such a claim, whereas an experiential-expressive one does not. His primary point is that a cultural-linguistic theory can also do so.

To explain how this is so he distinguishes between the 'intrasystematic' and the 'ontological' truth of statements. The first is the truth of coherence to some relevant system and the second the truth of correspondence to reality which, according to epistemological realists, is attributable to first-order propositions. According to Lindbeck, religious utterances can have an ontological truth, can correspond to reality in and of itself, but they do so in a distinctive way, as part of a wider conformity of self to God. Thus when a religious person affirms 'Jesus Christ is Lord' the words not only convey the objective reality of Christ's Lordship (although that is also something that they definitely do convey) but they are implicated in the subjective disposition of those who utter them. Thus Luther frequently states that I cannot genuinely assert that Jesus is 'the Lord' unless I also make him 'my Lord' (p. 66). For this reason it is appropriate to treat religious utterance as propositional only to the extent that it is also performative; that is to say, the assertion of religious truths necessarily involves a personal commitment to the consequences of their truth. Lindbeck is careful to explain that 'this performatory conformity of the self to God can also be pictured in epistemologically realistic fashion as involving a correspondence of the mind to divine reality' (p. 66).[20] He applies the same reasoning to the statement 'Jesus Christ rose from the dead', since here 'the claim that Jesus truly and objectively was raised from the dead provides the warrant for behaving in the ways recommended by the resurrection stories even when one grants the impossibility of specifying the mode in which those stories signify' (p. 67).

Lindbeck's conclusion on this issue is worth noting:

> a religion can be interpreted as possibly containing ontologically true affirmations, not only in cognitivist theories but also in cultural-linguistic ones. There is nothing in the cultural-linguistic approach that requires the rejection (or the acceptance) of the epistemological realism and correspondence theory of truth, which, according to most of the theological tradition, is implicit in the conviction of believers that when they rightly use a sentence such as 'Christ is Lord' they are uttering a true first-order proposition.
>
> (pp. 67–68)

The theory of religion set out by Lindbeck paves the way for the integration of the results of historical criticism of the New Testament, at least to the extent that it is informed by the social sciences, into a new style of New Testament theology. One qualification must be made, however. Although Lindbeck's theory operates by speaking of religion as analogous to a culture or a language, when he proceeds to details in the latter part of the work the cultural aspect seems to be overwhelmed by the linguistic or textual one. He introduces the notion of 'intratextuality' (p. 114) as a way of speaking of the immanent location of meaning and goes so far as to assert that 'An intratextual reading tries to derive the interpretive framework that designates the theologically controlling sense from the literary structure of the text itself' (p. 120). As Wayne Meeks has observed (1986b: 180–181), this view seems to pick up Hans Frei's argument against all forms of 'referential' hermeneutics and is inimical to the diachronic investigations of the historical critics. The answer to Lindbeck's view on this issue, which should be seen as an unnecessary and unfortunate modification of the broad thrust of his theory, is that, as amply revealed by the essays in this volume, texts can only be understood in context.[21] Thus, in adopting Lindbeck's model, I take 'story' to mean not a decontextualized narrative, but rather to convey the existential sense of a biographical or autobiographical account relating or reflecting actual human experience.

We should acknowledge, however, that there will be occasions when we must question aspects of the way the early Christians retold the story of Jesus as their story. As Horrell and Hobbs have pointed out in their essays, even at the earliest stages of the Christian movement there are signs of the incorporation of ideology and imagery which seem at odds with the bedrock of our tradition – the subversive memory of Jesus. Accordingly, there will be times in assimilating their versions of the primal story when we will need to recognize and excise distortions which have crept in with the telling.

Although we share with these early Christians (then not even bearing that name) the kerygmatic utterance 'Jesus is Lord', to see what that kerygma meant for them we need to understand the symbolic universes created when it was taken up in particular social settings. Accordingly, social-scientific New Testament interpretation becomes theologically relevant within Lindbeck's theory to the extent that it, and it alone, provides paradigms, the oldest available, of Christian ways of living in the world.

The goal of a New Testament theology based on a cultural-linguistic theory of religion is neither the defence of propositions alleged to be ontologically true nor the unreflective iteration of biblical ideas and symbols. Rather, it is the formation of contemporary communities whose identity has been informed, within their own local situations, by a critical appropriation of the 'story' of the first Christians, that is, by the assimilation of the experience they had of shaping the story of Jesus, and of God's presence in the world which he represented, to the diverse exigencies of their own contexts. Sharing the foundations of their faith, yet within our own contexts and with our own self-understandings, we make their stories our story. As we continue on our journey through time and space, we draw inspiration and guidance from our deepening appreciation of how our first predecessors began that journey, of the goals they set, the ways they moved, and the hopes they nursed in their hearts.

Then we too may reach Emmaus, having had the experience described in the words from the Scots version of Luke's Gospel as read at the liturgy concluding the Conference where the essays below were first delivered: 'Wisna the hairts o us lowin in our breists, as he spak wi us on the gate and expundit the Scripturs til us?'

NOTES

1 Aristotle, *On the Art of Poetry*, 11.

2 Plutarch, *Life of Romulus*, 28.

3 Caravaggio painted two versions of the scene, in c. 1600–1601 and c. 1606 (see Moir 1982: 102 and 132), the second of which is reproduced on the cover of Esler 1994a, and Rembrandt painted three, one an early work from c. 1628 done in potent chiaroscuro, where the silhouette of the transformed Jesus creates a disturbingly numinous effect, and two more in 1648. Rembrandt also produced a number of etchings and pen and ink drawings on the theme (Hoekstra 1990: 422–429).

4 I am indebted to John H. Elliott for the phrase 'scenarios for the sacred'.

5 Esler 1987 and 1994a; Holmberg 1990; Elliott 1993a; Morgan and Barton 1988: 133–166. Explanations of the method by those who do not practise it are of less value.

6 Lord Atkin (1867–1944), in *United Australia Ltd v. Barclays Bank Ltd* (1941) AC 1, at 29.

7 The earliest work explicitly utilizing Berger and Luckmann's sociology of knowledge known to me is Wayne Meeks' superlative 1972 essay on the descending and ascending son of man motif in John's Gospel (Meeks 1972).

8 John Barclay prefers to regard the perspective he employs from the sociology of deviance as a 'sensitizing concept' suggesting an angle of enquiry rather than a theory or model generating predictive hypotheses. Similarly, David Horrell prefers to describe Giddens' notions as a 'theoretical framework' rather than a model. At a general level, however, it is clear that both approaches are indebted to social-scientific theory and that virtually everything said of models in what follows applies to them as well.

9 For an admirably detailed recent discussion of models, see Elliott 1993a: 40–48. For a briefer treatment, see Esler 1987: 8–9.

10 See Elliott 1993a: 94–95 for an effective (and amusing) critique of the 'Procrustean bed' or 'cookie-cutter' objection to models.

11 *The Anchor Bible Dictionary*, oddly, has an entry for the sociology of early Christianity, but not one on anthropology, even though it has articles on both for the Old Testament. This results in the curiosity that the ever-burgeoning and productive New Testament research utilizing Mediterranean cultural anthropology inaugurated by Bruce Malina is left to be briefly treated by Garrett in her article on sociology. The lamentable omission of an article on this subject constitutes a serious deficiency in the general usefulness of the *Dictionary*. It should be rectified at an early date in a supplementary volume.

12 I am grateful to my colleagues Dr David Riches and Dr Nigel Rapport, of the Department of Social Anthropology in the University of St Andrews, for discussing this issue with me.

13 Vernon Robbins (p. 288 below) sees the adherence to theory in the face of post-modernism as an important characteristic shared by social-scientific and literary-critical approaches.

14 This is not to say that honour means exactly the same then as it does now, only that there is an abiding core of meaning.

15 For a somewhat similar diachronic model, tracking certain strands of *post-Easter* Christianity in terms of a development from reform movement to sect, see Esler 1987: 46–70 and 1994a: 13–17.

16 Bruce Malina prefers small group theory to sectarianism and Stephen Barton (1993: 158) fears it is too blunt a tool in this context.

17 Wayne Meeks pointed out Lindbeck's significance as providing a contemporary style of theology which meshed with social-scientific interpretations of the New Testament, especially those pursuing sociology of knowledge approaches, as long ago as 1986 (Meeks 1986b).

18 On this view religions are seen as similar to philosophy or science as traditionally conceived.

19 Michael Jackson has spoken of his 'relative insouciance about ontological truth claims' (cited by Michalson 1988: 111). Also see Phillips 1988. Much of the criticism takes up philosophical issues while downplaying the critical cultural ones. An important discussion is found in Marshall 1990.

20 To explain this view he employs the type of modest correspondence proposed by Thomas Aquinas. For Aquinas, although in statements concerning God the human mode of signifying does not correspond to anything in the divine being, the signified (*significatum*) does (*Summa Theologiae* I.13.3; *CG* I.30). In other words, if we say 'God is good' we do not mean that God is good by human standards of goodness, but rather that there is a standard of goodness, God's own, which does apply. Thus what 'we assert, in other words, is that " 'God is good' is meaningful and true," but without knowing the meaning of "God is good" ' (p. 66). Despite its informational vacuity, the statement 'God is good' is highly significant in the context of the performative function of religious utterances just described 'because it authorizes responding as if he were good in the ways indicated by the stories of creation, providence, and redemption which shape believers' thoughts and actions' (p. 67). Conversely, to commit oneself to thinking and acting as if God were good in the sense described in the biblical stories involves asserting that he is good in himself, even though the meaning of this latter claim is beyond human understanding (p. 67).

21 This seems preferable to Meeks' own answer — that sociology of knowledge readings of the New Testament are not so much interested in the determination of what really happened, the enterprise so decried by Frei, but rather in the meaning of what the actors did and said within their culture and their unique subculture — since this seems too closely associated with interpretive readings of the texts.

Part I

THE WORLD OF FIRST-CENTURY PALESTINE

1

HERODIAN ECONOMICS IN GALILEE

Searching for a suitable model

Sean Freyne

INTRODUCTION

One of the occupational hazards of ancient historians must surely be the temptation to draw a complete picture of whatever segment of life interests them, irrespective of the adequacy of their data for such a task. Few of us are happy to acknowledge the many gaps in our knowledge of the ancient world, no matter how sophisticated the modern retrieval systems are. This dilemma, the need to present a coherent hypothesis (often disguised as the definitive description) despite the absence of sufficient information, poses important hermeneutical questions which scholars are sometimes reluctant to address. For instance, when I reread my own previous work on Galilee I find myself repeatedly asking why precisely I had opted for a particular understanding of the data (Freyne 1980, 1988, 1992). The answer, hopefully, is because in my judgement the evidence pointed in that direction, even when other possible interpretations could and should be considered. The question becomes more acute still on comparing one's own views with those of others writing about the same topic. Why is Martin Goodman's (1983) description of Galilee very like my own – a predominantly peasant Jewish village culture? Why is it that D. Edwards (1988) and J. D. Crossan (1991), J. Strange (1992) and A. Overman (1988) can speak so confidently about the urbanization of Galilee, particularly lower Galilee, with all the attendant consequences for social and religious life in the region? Is this due to the bias of the sources which may be selectively chosen, or are there deeper methodological or even ideological issues at play and how might one rationally adjudicate among the competing views?

One important new tool in the repertoire of the ancient historian is the use of the social sciences, whose critical application can mean an end to what has been described as 'the intuitivist approach', with its 'hit or miss' aspect. By carefully choosing an appropriate model and applying it as rigorously as possible many mistakes can be avoided and it becomes possible to assess the validity of one's initial intuitions and to compare the results with those of others in a more critical and rational manner. In a previous paper I attempted to develop and apply a model to do with the cultural role of cities to Galilean social life (1992), basing myself primarily on the writings of Josephus. Though reasonably pleased with the exercise another challenge emerged, namely, how best to integrate the findings of the rapidly growing corpus of archaeological work on the region with the literary evidence. How is one to bring spade and text together in view of the fact that the one (texts) are tellings, not showings, whereas the other (archaeological data) are showings in need of tellings which are largely dependent on those very texts? Unlike the earlier concentration on isolated sites or on particular types of buildings such as synagogues, the more recent archaeological work is informed by insights from landscape, ethno- and socio-archaeology, as findings at individual sites are being integrated with the results of regional and inter-regional surveys (Meyers, Strange and Groh 1978; Urman 1985; Barker and Lloyd 1991; Rich and Wallace-Hadrill 1991). In these developing branches of the new archaeology, there is considerable input from the social sciences also, as researchers attempt to develop adequate models for understanding and interpreting the data so painstakingly acquired.

Models will not of course obviate the need for on-going critical assessment of one's procedures, nor will they fill in the gaps in our information where these exist. There is the initial task of choosing a model appropriate for the task to which one wishes to put it. Even then models can never encapsulate the whole of life in all its complexity, but rather select and highlight certain key aspects, which after careful reflection are deemed to be crucial in understanding the whole. Inevitably, therefore, there is an element of personal judgement involved as one attempts to match the model based on typical features with the particular aspects of a given society. Despite this subjective dimension, the value of model-building is that it assists in making one's presuppositions explicit. There will be less likelihood that essential aspects will be overlooked and such abstract notions as power, elites, etc. can be dissected analytically by asking more detailed questions like: to whom; for what purpose; in whose interest; who decides what the problems are, etc. (Carney 1975; Elliot 1986a, 1993a). Finally, the application of a model helps in assembling and organizing the scattered pieces of data at our disposal and in uncovering the missing links. Thus within the the overall frame of reference which the model represents it is possible to predict the direction which changes are likely to take by having a clearer perception of the role which individual items play within the whole system.

MODELLING AN ECONOMIC SYSTEM

The number of serious analytical studies of ancient economies by biblical scholars is few, and in this respect the discipline contrasts unfavourably with that of ancient history generally, where much more attention has been given to the question by historians of Greece and Rome. The omission is all the more surprising in view of the fact that economic issues figure so prominently in the recorded sayings of Jesus. There have been various attempts to describe the economic realities of first-century Palestine and the Gospels (Grant 1923), but with rare exceptions the question of how deeply economic issues were at the heart of Jesus' own experience and ministry, as well as that of the early Christians, has not been adequately addressed (Oakman 1986; Moxnes 1988). There are undoubtedly many reasons for such an oversight. The fact that economic issues in antiquity are seen as embedded in, and therefore inseparable from, political ones is certainly a factor. However, this should not be overstated. While it is true that abstract thinking on economics as we know it today is a product of the industrial revolution, this does not mean that 'rational' economic thinking never occurred in pre-industrial societies. There is enough evidence ranging from fifth-century BCE Athens to fourth-century CE Egypt to indicate that there was a general awareness of issues such as the maximizing of resources, the need to keep production costs low and the possibility of manipulating market demand in order to achieve higher prices (Osborne 1991; Rathbone 1991).

Among ancient historians the work of Moses Finley has dominated much of the recent discussion. His theory of the ancient city being parasitic on the countryside in a highly exploitative way set a very definite landmark that is only gradually being modified, but which is never likely to be entirely abandoned (Finley 1985). Finley's model, like that of Weber on which it was based, sharply contrasted the ancient 'consumer' city with its medieval 'producer' counterpart. It stressed the inequality of the relationship between town and country by maintaining that control of the land, the most important ancient resource, was essentially in the hands of a wealthy elite, who for *political* reasons dwelt in cities and had little interest in re-investing into the economy of the countryside, provided their own relatively luxurious life-style was maintained. The resulting stagnation meant the increased impoverishment of and pressure on the remaining small land-owners, as well as precluding the emergence of an urban merchant or entrepreneurial class. In this view of the city as the village 'writ large' in terms of economic realities, relating to its hinterland in the way that a village relates to its fields, the wealthy land-owner shares the peasant's passion for self-sufficiency, without any qualitatively different view of the possibilities of greater production (Osborne 1991: 120). Little account is taken of the manufacturing and commercial potential of ancient cities in terms of the production of goods such as household wares which are not directly related to agriculture. On this understanding, therefore, ancient cities are primarily administrative centres where the wealthy land-owners reside and play a full part in the civic and political life of the *polis*. It is the honour and prestige attached to such activities rather than the maximizing of resources in commercial enterprises that determine their conduct of affairs.

Several modifications of these ideas have been suggested, particularly in view of the fact that in the wake of Alexander's conquests the city itself as institution had been transformed from the free-standing entity of the classical period, the main focus of Finley's typology. It was now put to the service of the commercial, cultural and administrative policies of the Hellenistic monarchies and later the Roman empire. In particular, the opening up of new and lucrative trade routes changed the whole commercial balance of the Middle Eastern world, several of which touched directly on Galilee. Both local and international trade developed in a manner and scale never before experienced as the demands for goods and services increased among the wealthy elites of the West. In this changed climate it has been suggested that cities and towns were 'organizers' of the countryside in that they paid for their consumption needs through profits from the increased trade that they were engaged in. Thus, it is claimed, cities should be seen as production centres, giving rise to a commercial class who were able to pay the rural population for their produce, thereby enabling the peasants to pay their taxes in money rather than in kind (Hopkins 1978, 1980). Archaeological evidence is seen as crucial in establishing this changed picture. On the one hand, it is argued that the evidence from Pompeii and even Rome itself suggests a much greater diversity of commercial activity, even in the elite residential areas, than might have been expected (Wallace-Hadrill 1991). In support of Finley, however, it has been claimed that coinage is relatively scarce in the countryside until the third century CE and the evidence on the ground from Roman Britain and elsewhere in the Western provinces does not support the notion of cities as manufacturing centres (Whittaker 1990). Of course this debate is by no means settled and there is no reason why different local circumstances may not have prevailed in different contexts. A lot seems to hinge on what size town we are talking about, whether upwardly towards the *polis/civitas* end of the spectrum or downwardly towards the *kome/vicus* end. This is a large topic which cannot be dealt with adequately here. What the debate highlights, however, is the need for a model that will encompass economic issues dealing with manufacture, exploitation and redistribution of wealth. We must not reduce the undoubted urban/rural differences as these were perceived in antiquity to a meaningless tautology, yet we must equally avoid setting up rigid oppositions that fail to capture, however imperfectly, the many-faceted dimensions of that relationship.

All of which brings us neatly back to Galilee, and more specifically to the Galilee of Antipas. I am especially interested in the situation in the northern region generally at that particular period, since it is possible to detect a pattern of change in terms of the development of urban settlements, not only in Galilee but also in Perea as well as in the territory of Antipas' brother, Herod Philip (*J. A.* 18.26–28). These developments were not concerned merely with the honouring of their Roman patrons as evidenced by the names given to the new foundations, and it may be indicative that Josephus mentions them in the context of the new arrangements in Judaea by the Roman procurator Quirinius, who had been appointed on the deposition of Archelaus in 6 CE. It is the working hunch of this essay that some more far-reaching and rapid forms of change were occurring that had a strong economic component built into them. This would provide the most immediate context in which to understand the ministry of Jesus with its strong emphasis on wealth and poverty, money, debts, etc. and the value system related to such matters. Of course these realities were not new on the Palestinian landscape, but the conjunction of the proposed developments for Galilee in the reign of Antipas and the concern of the Jesus movement with such issues points to a growing preoccupation at just that time that would explain many features of the Gospel narratives, not least the total silence with regard to Sepphoris and Tiberias among the places in which Jesus conducted his ministry.

In order to verify (or falsify) such a hunch we need an appropriate model that could register and highlight rapid economic change, since this is the claim that needs to be tested. T. F. Carney's study, *The Shape of the Past: Models and Antiquity* (Carney 1975), has proved to be a helpful resource for others engaged in this task of model-building with a view to studying various aspects of the ancient world, since it displays an unusual grasp of both the social world of antiquity and modern theory from the social sciences. Carney contrasts the different procedures involved in, on the one hand, profiling a stable economy, and on the other, plotting change within a developing one. In the former instance it is simply a matter of capturing a 'still life' view of the various component parts of the total system and presenting them in a manner which portrays their inter-relationships (Figure 1, p. 30). Profiling change (Figure 2, p. 31) is a more complex task, however. Here, according to Carney, the challenge is one of selecting and highlighting key elements or probe zones, as he terms them, which are essential for rapid change to occur. These elements affect (1) the relations between production and distribution (i.e. the market itself); (2) the social structures and institutions controlling the market; and (3) the values and decision-making process which determine what the dominant priorities are. In each of these crucial areas it is necessary to concentrate on certain aspects which act as spurs to change within the total system. These are attitudinal changes with regard to production and consumption, leading to increased specialization within the productive sector, which in turn calls for a more sophisticated exchange mechanism associated with the more widespread use of money. When there are clear signs of all three elements – attitudinal changes, specialization and monetization – occurring simultaneously, then, according to the model's underlying assumptions, rapid changes are taking place throughout the whole system. These call for careful handling by the steering political control group through *adaptation* of the institutions to meet the new situation, *maintenance* of the stability of the social order through military, law-courts, policing, etc. and *integration* of the new insights in technology, values etc. through education and other means of dissemination of ideas. In other words, the changes need to be politically inspired, controlled and channelled if the body politic is to survive and social chaos avoided.

The stimuli for change are both external and internal, but since no political system exists in isolation, the external factors are inevitably seen to be the more important, especially in dealing with a merely regional situation such as Galilee. The external factors which Carney lists can certainly be shown to have been operative to an unprecedented degree throughout the whole Mediterranean world, and not least in Palestine, in view of Herod the Great's active propagation of the values of 'the new age' of peace (Zanker 1988). The temple of Roma and Augustus, set on a high podium overlooking the magnificent harbour of his foundation, Caesarea Maritima (*J. A.* 15.339), was a symbol of Herod's intentions to introduce a new climate of thought, new international alliances of power and new technology into his kingdom as the officially designated King of the Jews. Inevitably these factors were to percolate downwards to the whole of Palestinian society as the building programme developed, calling for specialization of labour, a more widespread use of money and changes in attitudes with regard to traditional values, despite his best attempts to placate Jewish religious opinion. In applying the model to Galilee, therefore, the main focus of attention will be on the internal changes there, always keeping in mind the backdrop of the wider, international changes of which these were a symptom.

APPLYING THE MODEL TO GALILEE

Antipas inherited a territory which, like the rest of the kingdom of Judaea, had been grossly over-taxed in order to support the many undertakings of his father, Herod the Great, both at home and abroad. This situation emerges clearly from the delegation sent to Rome to complain to Augustus on Herod's death, as well as by Archelaus' withdrawal of some of the taxes (*J. A.* 17.204–205, 304–308). More sober evaluation of Herod's reign has, however, come to acknowledge the good aspects of his domestic policies as far as stimulating the economy, particularly his many building projects. He could also show himself to be a benign dictator, imitating his Roman masters in providing for a supply of corn from Egypt on the occasion of a famine (Stern 1974; Schalit 1969). The development of the port of Caesarea as a rival to the more northerly Phoenician cities of Tyre and Sidon shows his recognition of the value of having direct access to a larger foreign market as well as to the income derived from tariffs and similar charges. This achievement in terms of economic forward-planning can be contrasted with the reluctance of both Augustus and Tiberius to build a proper port at Ostia for the grain imports to Rome, a task only completed at enormous expense by the emperor Claudius (Carney 1975: 285–306). Roads were also developed and hitherto under-occupied agricultural lands were planted with veterans from his own army (Gaba in the Great Plain) or with Babylonian and Idumean settlers (Batanea and Trachonitis). It is against this background – easily documented from both literary and archaeological evidence – of a rapidly developing economy already under Herod the Great that we should evaluate the performance of Antipas in this regard also, especially in view of the fact that Herod seems to have concentrated most of his energies in the south and in the territories of the pagan cities. In a very real sense it was only with Antipas that the full effects of the Romanization of the Augustan age were felt directly in Galilee.

The market

Carney describes the market as an exchange arena wherein goods and services are bartered in order to maximize the returns to buyers and sellers alike. This description immediately calls to mind the agora or market-place which was so central in the layout of Roman towns. This public space was, however, only a sign of the larger and more complex arena where supply and demand meet to the mutual benefit of buyers and sellers. The question to be explored with the aid of the model is whether the reign of Antipas represented a particularly significant moment for Galilee in the development of this demand/supply network which, all are agreed, had received a major boost with the emergence of the Principate after the civil wars of the previous half-century.

What had Galilee to offer? In the sixth century BCE the prophet Ezekiel was aware of its role as supplier of agricultural products to Tyre (Diakonoff 1992). The plain of Gennesareth was extolled by Josephus for its rich and varied fertility (*J. W.* 3.35–38), and both Strabo and Pliny describe the natural resources of the lake. Galilee was relatively better endowed than other regions in terms of soil and moisture, thus ensuring good annual yields – wheat in the rich alluvial valleys running in an east/west direction in lower Galilee and olives and vines in upper Galilee and in the Carmel region (Avi-Yonah 1966: 201–206; Bosen 1985: 44–52). In terms of the model, it was well positioned, therefore, to be developed, when demand for basic products called for greater exploitation of resources. Nor did it lack the human resources in terms of population, even though the figures of Josephus are generally accepted to have been exaggerated (Hoehner 1972: 291–297; Byatt 1973). His mention of 204 settlements in his own day can be corroborated to some extent from the findings of recent regional surveys, which suggest an increase in the overall number of settlements from the Hellenistic to the Roman periods (Aviam 1993).

Peter Garnsey has documented the repeated food crises which appear to have been endemic to Roman society throughout the Republican period. The causes were complex, but essentially stemmed from the fact that the Italian peninsula was not able to produce sufficient grain to meet the needs of a rapidly expanding city population, largely dependent on wheat for its staple diet (Garnsey 1988). Piracy at sea, fluctuations in terms of yields from one year to another due to human inefficiency and natural causes, all contributed to the unstable situation, not to mention the increased demands to supply the various armies that had to be maintained. Pompey had succeeded in stabilizing the situation, especially with his victory over the pirates, but it was only during the reign of Augustus when Egypt emerged as a major supply centre that the situation was finally regulated with the *lex Iulia de annona*. This measure whereby the state guaranteed an annual corn dole to the citizens of Rome itself, effectively meant a state mobilization of the exchange in terms of the model in Figure 1, since 'the grain that found its way to Rome was, in the first place, state grain, coming in the form of taxes in kind from tribute-paying provinces, or of rents in kind from

THE MARKET		MODES OF EXCHANGE				VALUES AND ATTITUDES		
Resources		**Types**				**Dominant Systems**		
Natural	*Human*	*Barter*	*Redistribution*	*Markets*	*Mobilization*	*Internal*		*External*
Land, water, minerals	Skilled and unskilled labour	Non-organized	Centralized	Free trading	State controlled	Kinship	Jerusalem religious system	Roman imperial ideology
Supply–Production		**Personnel**				**Key Values**		
Agricultural produce: grain, olives, vines	Manufacturing: pottery; oil and wine; fish products	Peasants; day labourers	Estate managers	*Negotiatores: navicularii*	*Agoranomoi*; tax-collectors	Sharing limited goods	Appeal to patrimonial values for support	Political control of production and supply
Distribution		**Modes of Exchange**				**Institutions**		
Roads	*Ports*							
Beasts of burden	Shipping	In kind	Corvée: share cropping	Money (accounting/ banking)	Tribute in kind and in cash	Household, clan, village	Temple and pilgrimage	The *polis* institutions; patron–client relations; gymnasia
Needs and Demands		**Social Types**				**Behavioural Patterns**		
Subsistence	*Elite*							
Food, clothing, shelter	Luxury items; glassware; ornaments; spices	Village and clan leaders; elders, householders	Military personnel and religious hierarchy	Entrepreneurs, money lenders and bankers	Herodian client kings and their retainers	Petty feuds; violence	Social discrimination on purity grounds	Ostentatious life-style and lack of concern for lower strata

Figure 1 A cross-sectional model of socio-economic factors in Roman Palestine (adapted from Carney 1975)

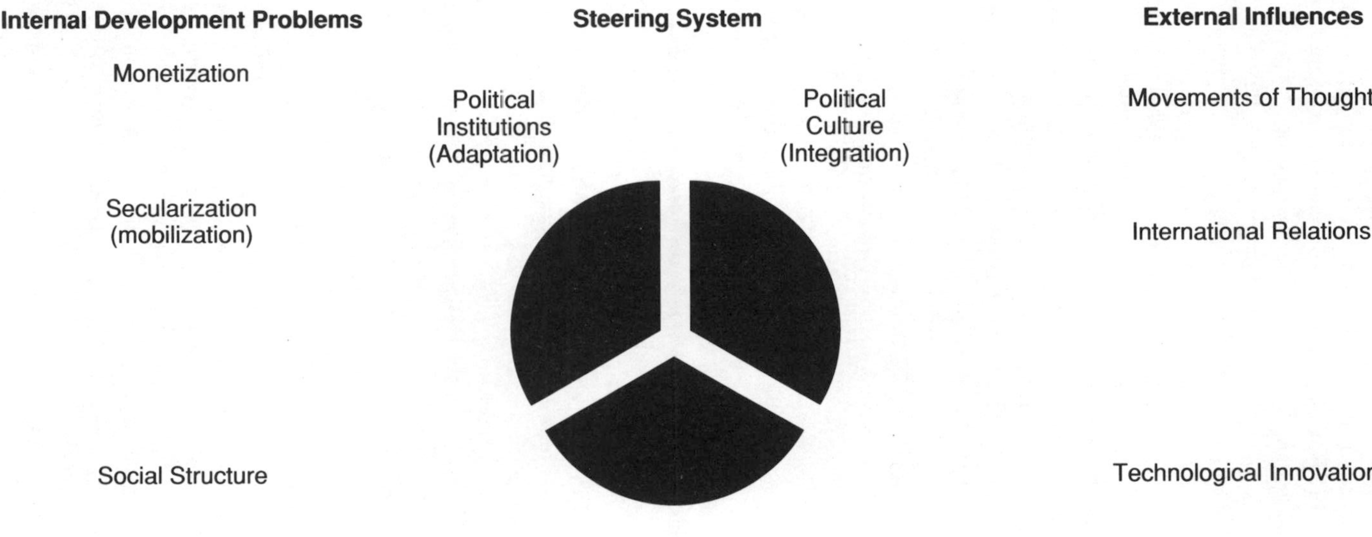

Figure 2 A general transformation matrix model for socio-economic change (adapted from Carney 1975)

tenants of the *ager publicus* or of imperial estates' (Garnsey 1988: 120). It is not absolutely clear to what extent this provision and the arrangements that had to be put in place to support it allowed for the free market of grain to continue. In all probability it was greatly restricted. The absence of a state fleet meant, however, that private ship-owners were encouraged to ply the routes between Alexandria and Puteoli and on to Ostia, and the presumption must be that these *navicularii* were also *negotiatores*, or middlemen merchants, who could make a handsome profit from the grain trade with prices guaranteed by the state and with protection against shipwreck and other hazards of transport.

While Galilee could certainly not compete in terms of grain production with Egypt or Syria as a major supplier for Rome and Italy, the fact that these latter sources were likely to have been fully stretched to meet imperial demands only meant that lesser suppliers had the opportunity to meet more local needs. The exact amount of tribute in land and poll tax that Antipas had to pay to Rome is not known, even though Josephus does inform us that he was allowed 200 talents in personal income from his combined territories. The wording of Caesar's decree would seem to suggest that a payment in kind had been stipulated: 'and that in the second year they shall pay the tribute at Sidon, consisting of one fourth of the produce sown, and in addition they shall pay tithes to Hyrcanus and his sons, just as they paid to their forefathers' (*J. A.* 14.203). Despite the well-known problem of how the reference to the second year is to be understood, the general tenor of this decree assumes a payment in kind similar to the Jewish religious system. There is no evidence that this was changed subsequently under the Principate and in this instance the argument from silence would seem to support the view that it was not.

This would merely bring the situation in Galilee into line with that which obtained elsewhere as cited above from Garnsey, namely, that in order to meet the needs of the *annona* in Rome the imperial administrators were happy to receive payment in kind in terms of the grain produce of the various provinces. This would also explain the term *ton Kaisaros siton*, the imperial corn, used by Josephus for the corn stored in the villages of upper Galilee, which John of Gischala had hoped to confiscate (*Life* 71). On the other hand, Josephus also mentions explicitly corn stored at Besara (in lower Galilee) collected from the neighbouring villages which belonged to Queen Bernice, the wife of Agrippa II. Since this area of lower Galilee was not in the king's territory at that time it must mean that the Herodian house retained private estates in this region, close to Gaba where Herod the Great had settled some veterans, as previously mentioned (*Life* 118–119). Admittedly this evidence comes from some thirty years after Antipas' reign, but it does give us some insights into the situation with regard to wheat production in Herodian Galilee. The surplus corn would have been used both to pay the tribute to Rome in accordance with the decrees of Caesar, which were still operative, and presumably also to supply market needs for the personal income of the Herodian family. Their agents would have functioned as estate managers and *negotiatores*, ensuring that whatever surplus could be obtained would reach the most lucrative markets either in Rome itself or nearer still in the Phoenician cities. The fact that seafaring operated close to the coast, something we know also from Paul's journey to Rome (Acts 27:1–3), meant that a considerable amount of trading was done at intermediate rather than long-distance range (Duncan-Jones 1990: 48–58). As we shall presently see, there are very good reasons for thinking that the pattern of trading with Tyre suggested by Ezechiel was maintained into the Roman period.

According to the proposed model, increased international pressure inevitably leads to internal changes also. In an agrarian economy specialization would mean a shift in land-owning patterns from small, family-run farms to larger estates in which the tenants work the estate, often for an absentee land-owner under a manager, receiving a subsistence living in return for their labour. In a developing economy where surplus production is necessary in order to maximize profits such estates make it possible to have increased production and specialization in various crops and to develop a rational and monetized economy (Rathbone 1991: 116–149, 318–330). It is difficult to be definitive on land-owning patterns on the basis of the evidence available. The Jewish ideal of private ownership in small holdings as expressed in such texts from the Persian and Hellenistic periods as Neh. 5:1–11 and 1 Macc. 14:10 seems to have persisted into the Roman period despite pressures to the contrary, which can be documented for Galilee as early as the third century BCE from the Zenon papyri (Freyne 1980: 156–169). The problem is that there is no way of distinguishing between private and leased holdings even when settlement data from archaeological surveys suggests nucleated villages rather than the centralized villa-style settlements, some of which have been identified in Samaria (Applebaum 1986). A recently excavated site near Caesarea Maritima (Byzantine over Roman period) would appear to be typical of the kind of settlement which the Mishnah describes as an ᶜ*ir* (*m. B. Bat.* 4.7). Here the remains of water cisterns, wine and olive presses, a threshing floor and residential quarters for as many as 100 people suggest a more intense form of production than that of the family-run farm of 6–9 acres which has been estimated as the average size (Hirschfeld and Birger-Calderone 1991; Fiensy 1991: 92–95).

On the basis of the evidence from Egypt and elsewhere there is nothing improbable about the two types of ownership and the two modes of production side by side in Galilee also. The better land would belong to the wealthy elite, either through forcible expropriation or default in payments of taxes by smallholders, and in some cases also through bequests of larger tracts of land by the central administration. Such a picture would fit in well with Herodian land-owning patterns already alluded to: the settlement of veterans in Gaba and Babylonian Jews in Batanea, Trachonitis and Auranitis by Herod the Great, as well as the ownership of private estates in the great plain and presumably also in the better lands of lower and upper Galilee.

We shall have to await detailed publication of survey findings before the archaeological evidence can be adduced as confirmation of the land-owning patterns and the consequent styles of agricultural production. Nevertheless, the refurbishment of Sepphoris and the founding of Tiberias in a short space of time by Antipas surely point in this direction also. In the case of Tiberias allotments of land were granted in return for residence in the new city (*J. A.* 18.36–38). Later in the first century when Josephus is describing the social classes in the city, among several of the leading class having the *praenomen* Herod, one Crispus is also mentioned. He happened to be absent on his estates across the Jordan when the city revolted against Josephus, thus pointing to the pattern of residence in the city while owning property in the country, typical of urban elites everywhere in antiquity (*Life* 33). In the case of Sepphoris equally, Josephus can chide it for its pro-Roman stance at the outbreak of the revolt, alleging that had it so wished, it could have made a brave stand against the Romans, 'surrounded as it was by many villages' (*Life* 346). The reliance of the people of Sepphoris on these outlying villages for provisions presumably indicates a similar ownership pattern to that of Tiberias for the fertile land of the Netofa valley, since elsewhere we hear of the Galileans (i.e. the independent land-owning class) showing hostility to the inhabitants of Sepphoris, storming the city and forcing the leading citizens to flee to the acropolis (*Life* 372–378). Nothing that archaeology has so far uncovered at either site goes against the suggestion that these foundations of Antipas fit into a pattern of Herodian land-ownership which was concerned with maximizing production, and some of the finds point positively in that direction. Apart from the many underground storage silos at Sepphoris, an inscribed lead weight found there mentions two generations of *agoranomoi* or market inspectors, and another ostracon has the Greek word *epimeletes*, or manager, inscribed on it (Meyers 1992). Equally, two lead weights from Tiberias have been published with the names of *agoranomoi* and the rulers, Antipas and Agrippa II, the one dating from 29/30 CE and the other from 61/2 CE. According to the editor it is quite unusual to have the names of both rulers and managers on these weights, possibly linking the Herodian rulers with the market in a special way, or at least suggesting their tight control of the institution (Qedar 1986–7).

Thus far we have concentrated on changing land-ownership patterns associated with Antipas' two foundations as symptomatic of economic changes in Galilee. However, there are other significant indicators also which can be positively evaluated in the light of the model. In particular Galilee is famed in the rabbinic sources for its olives (Avi-Yonah 1966: 202f.). Climatic and soil conditions in upper Galilee seem to have been particularly suited for their cultivation, though they were cultivated in lower Galilee also. While the notorious incident of John of Gischala availing of the higher prices for oil among the Jewish community in Caesarea is used by Josephus to vilify his opponent (*Life* 74–76), it does in fact indicate a ready market among the observant Jews in Syria and beyond for this product, so essential for cooking in the Mediterranean culture generally and therefore so integral to Roman trading patterns (Mattingly 1988). Thus the association of the olive oil industry with Galilee can certainly be dated to the first century already. The many discoveries of olive presses at various sites is ample archaeological testimony to corroborate the literary evidence. What is most significant for our present purpose, however, is the concentration of various types of olive presses with various sub-regions of the Galilee (Frankel 1992). In particular, the fact that in western lower Galilee a type characteristic of the Phoenician littoral is consistently found while in eastern Galilee and the Golan typological affinities with Judaea can be demonstrated, is significant in trading terms also. The Phoenician cities must have provided the natural market for much of the oil produced in its immediate hinterland, irrespective of cultural or religious diversity that may have existed between town and rural hinterland.

Land was not the only natural endowment of Galilee. The pagan writers and Josephus are all conscious of the lake and the fertility of its environs, features that are at least implied in the Gospels also. In describing the lake Josephus mentions a special type of fish, the *coracin*, that otherwise was only found in the Nile (*J. W.* 3.506–508, 520). This may well point to the development of the fish industry as early as the Ptolemaic period. Both Bethsaida and Migdal Nun (Magdala) have been associated with fishing on the basis of their names, and the latter has been identified with Taricheae of the Hellenistic period, a name which is believed to be associated with the salting of fish. This technique was itself symptomatic of the market economy, allowing for export of Galilean produce to centres as far away as Rome. Closely associated with this industry was the production of various fish sauces, especially one called *garum*, made from fish entrails, which was very popular in Rome, and which would have required jars or amphorae if in fact it was produced at the fishing centres of Galilee also (Peacock and Williams 1986: 35–37). Archaeological surveys around the lake have uncovered the remains of many breakwaters, anchorages, harbours, storage pools and the like from the Roman period, not to mention the famous 'Galilean boat', all confirming the high level of commercial activity that went on (Nun 1988; Wachsmann 1990). The fact that Jesus recruited his first followers from those who were engaged in such an enterprise shows that his message was not addressed solely to the peasant farmers in the villages, something that needs to be borne in mind in evaluating its alternative value system, as we shall see. It is surely significant that in leaving their nets, families and hired servants, the first followers of Jesus were actually rejecting the values of the market economy as these operated in Galilee then, and that they were highly commended within Christian circles for doing so (though see Neyrey's essay below for the reactions of their families!).

Discussion of oil and fish products inevitably turns attention to the pottery industry which of late has been receiving special consideration due to the scientific analysis of David Adan-Bayewitz in particular. Guided by the literary evidence he has sought to identify the sources of supply and the range of distribution of the common household wares found at various northern sites from the Hellenistic to the Byzantine period, using modern techniques of chemical analysis of sherds recovered from various sites. Six types of standard wares (with a number of sub-types) have been identified and tentatively dated to different periods. What is most significant for our purposes is that two important production centres in Galilee, Kefar Hanania on the borders between upper and lower Galilee and Shihin near Sepphoris, have been identified, each with its own specialization, the former in household wares and the latter in storage jars and different household wares. The extent of the distribution of the Kefar Hanania pottery is significant also, since this centre provided all the household wares in use at important sites in the Galilee, especially Sepphoris, and a considerable percentage of that in use in a number of Golan sites sampled, as well as being represented in the wares of Akko/Ptolemais and Susita/Hippos (Adan-Bayewitz 1993; Adan-Bayewitz and Perlman 1990).

This pattern of considerable specialization at various centres based on the locally available raw material (black clay is mentioned in the rabbinic sources) or produce (as in the case of the fish industry) confirms the impression that larger market conditions rather than purely local needs were operative in Galilee and that many Galileans, not just the inhabitants of the two main Herodian centres, had adapted to the changes. It is important not to exaggerate the extent of the pottery industry which was on the whole confined and could not be compared with the African Red Slip ware, for example, which was widely distributed. Apart from the two sites mentioned whose wares have been studied in detail there is archaeological evidence for other pottery manufacturing centres in Galilee (Vitto 1983–1984). In particular the oil trade and the fish industry would have required the manufacture of amphorae in order to realize their potential for export. Thus the pottery industry has been described as parasitic and dependent on routes established for other purposes (Tomber 1993). This makes Adan-Bayewitz' findings all the more significant in terms of our model, since it suggests trade within a wider region than political Galilee, while corresponding to the general pattern in the ancient world, namely, that with a few notable exceptions, long-distance trade was not a highly significant factor in the economy (Duncan-Jones 1990: 48–58).

In applying the first element in our model to Herodian Galilee the focus of attention has been on specialization in production as an indicator of increased market awareness. Inevitably the discussion has touched on other aspects of the model also, particularly the modes of exchange and the emergence of personnel, exchange centres, etc. that would have been necessary to implement such a development. In using the archaeological evidence it is difficult to be precise to the point of dating developments to the reign of Antipas, even when dealing with sites such as Sepphoris. Nevertheless, the changes to the economic conditions involved in the building of two new centres such as Sepphoris and Tiberias should not be underestimated, since these projects involved demand for labour, materials, development of roads, water systems and the introduction of some skilled craftsmen into the region. These in turn must have acted as further spurs for attitudinal changes. The new settlements increased the demands for basic food supplies for their inhabitants, thereby stimulating the rural economy also. It remains to be seen how all these changes affected different strata of the population and who stood to benefit from them. In terms of the earlier discussion of the consumer/producer debate there is nothing in the evidence from Galilee so far examined to challenge the basic assumption of Finley's model, however. The increased activity among the village culture both in production and manufacture does not of itself imply escaping the net of patronage, control of resources and channelling of profits. Perhaps the exploration of other probe zones from Carney's model may help in deciding how far those changes which we have been able to document were for the benefit of the few or the many in Galilee.

Monetization

Various types of exchange, ranging from reciprocal (i.e. barter) to redistribution (state controlled) were operative in antiquity, often side by side within the same region. This has given rise to the question of how far it is proper to speak of a free market, especially under the Principate. Certainly the *annona* was an outstanding example of state intervention, but it should be recalled that this operated only in regard to corn and only for the city of Rome. The absence of a state fleet meant that there was a reliance on *navicularii* and *negotiatores*, as we have seen, so that it is a moot point as to whether these are to be regarded as private traders or agents of the state. It is scarcely adequate therefore, to consider, as some have done, that free-market exchange was confined to very local trading, irrespective of the amount of political control that operated in all ancient economies (Peacock and Williams 1986: 59–63). Admittedly, in the case of long-distance trading there are problems in distinguishing between what is free and what is state controlled, since both will follow the same distribution patterns. On the basis of all the available evidence, however, it does seem more probable that some free trading did occur, at least on an inter-regional basis, and that the emergence of the Principate was a considerable stimulus to more long-distance trading also.

This suggestion inevitably raises the issue of the diffusion of money throughout the empire generally. The proposal has been made that increased long-term trade meant a much greater diffusion of coins by the central imperial administration, giving rise to 'a single monetary economy', with the resulting insistence on payment of taxes in cash rather than in kind (Hopkins 1980). However, as noted above, this conclusion has been challenged on the basis of insufficient evidence apart from the indirect taxes levied on the monetized elements of the economy, such as the traders (Duncan-Jones 1990: 187–198). The use of money for paying the army was, it seems, still the primary method of diffusion of the imperial, as distinct from city, coinage, and that occasioned by inter-regional and long-term trade was never great. At first sight this might appear to put Galilee of Antipas' day at a distinct disadvantage in terms of cash flow, since at that time there was no Roman division stationed there, unlike Judaea to the south where a procuratorial guard was present, or Syria to the north, where the nearest Roman legion was stationed. The mention of chiliarchs among the guests at Antipas' birthday party (Mark 6:21) reminds us, however, that he must have maintained some standing army, especially in view of his troubles with the Nabateans, and that it would have had to be paid.

Why is monetization so important in terms of a developing economy? According to Carney (1975: 142) money can be defined as 'any type of object that has generalized value allowing exchange for goods and services'. It is vital for the development of the market economy since it functions as a legitimate and recognized unit of value which can be stored, to be used subsequently in the purchase of goods or services as required from a supplier other than the person with whom the original transaction took place. It thus allows for a far greater range of exchange possibilities than would be feasible if one were dependent on repayment in kind, as in a reciprocal exchange system. Since the wealth that is generated can be stored in a non-perishable form of coinage, payment can be deferred, provided an accounting system is in operation, whereby debts and other promises are recorded. Meanwhile goods and services can be availed of and used to generate further wealth before repayment takes place, and money itself can be used to gain more money by lending at a price, thus becoming an end in itself. Such developments obviously benefited those who owned the wealth-generating resources and who could protect their income against thieves if required, either through policing or well-protected residences. Inevitably also there were major shifts in values as the wealthy were in a position to increase their status through the acquisition of luxury goods, often in an alienating fashion that radically changed the ways in which people interacted in home, village and region.

As a medium of exchange money had been in operation in Palestine at least from the Persian period, as is evidenced by the famous *yehud* coins. Succeeding overlords, Ptolemaic and Seleucid, as well as the Hasmonean rulers, had minted their own coins, in part for personal propaganda reasons but also to facilitate intra- as well as inter-regional exchange. While the ban on human representation may have somewhat inhibited the former aspect, Jews, like other peoples, certainly took advantage of the trading possibilities that money offered. Moreover cities such as Tyre, Ptolemais and Scythopolis struck their own coins from the Hellenistic age and these were current in Palestine also. The large Jewish Diaspora in Egypt, Syria, Asia Minor, Mesopotamia and the western Mediterranean cities meant that there was bound to be a steady flow of people to and from the homeland, requiring goods and services, inevitably contributing to a greater supply of money in the economy generally. As already noted, John of Gischala showed his entrepreneurial spirit by benefiting from the much better prices for oil among fellow Jews in Caesarea than were available in his home town. He was scarcely an exception among a certain level of Jewish inhabitants in the land in first-century Palestine.

Its status as the national cult-centre meant that the Jerusalem Temple was undoubtedly a source of foreign revenue for the Palestinian economy generally with the various rituals of pilgrimage, offerings and festivals, all requiring service from caravaneers, inn-keepers and money changers. In particular the half-shekel offering which every adult male Jew was expected to pay annually for the upkeep of the Temple ensured a steady inflow of the much sought after Tyrian coinage to Palestine. No greater tribute could be paid to the stability of this currency than the fact that, despite bearing the image of Melkart/Heracles, it was described as the 'coin of the sanctuary' according to a later halachic decree (Ben-David 1969). The city of Jerusalem undoubtedly profited most directly from this source of revenue, yet given the difficulties of overland travel many Galilean centres must also have benefited from those travelling along the more important routes, especially those from the East who would require shelter and sustenance on their journey.

The internal monetary situation in Antipas' Galilee must also be explored, even when coin finds are not as useful as pottery sherds in tracing commercial transactions. Not enough is known about the numbers of coins minted at various centres to allow definite conclusions to be drawn about trading patterns on the basis of coin finds at different sites. Since coins are an extremely portable item and since in the ancient world in particular they remained in circulation for a long time after their issue, their intermediate usage cannot be determined, but only their point of origin and final deposit (Adan-Bayewitz 1993: 247f.). Despite these reservations some things can confidently be asserted about the monetary situation in Galilee that are relevant to the present discussion. Neither Tiberias nor Sepphoris minted their own coins until much later, thus indicating their inferior status in comparison with other nearby cities that were 'free and autonomous'. They both operated within the overall constraints of the regional economy, thus underlining their retainer status within an overall agrarian situation. This does not mean that they played an insignificant role locally, however. Justus of Tiberias bemoans the fact that with the transfer of his native city to the territory of Agrippa II by Nero, it had lost its status as capital of Galilee, which had now reverted to Sepphoris. This meant that the royal bank and the archives were now located in that city (*Life* 38). This complaint is revealing in that it points directly to a situation in which money could be stored, and presumably borrowed also, and where records of such transactions were kept. The fact that Justus sees the loss of this facility as damaging to his native city, suggests that for him and his ilk control of banking offered possibilities for the generation of wealth, presumably by charging of interest on loans. This also provides the context for the action of the destitute class of Tiberias, who, together with some Galileans, stormed Herod's palace, ostensively for religious reasons, and confiscated luxury items together with a considerable amount of uncoined silver (*Life* 68).

We must remember that Antipas himself operated under constraints in terms of his fiscal policy. Not even Herod the Great was allowed to strike silver coins, presumably because of the greater financial independence this would have given him. Only three strikings of Antipas' coinage can so far be documented: one for the year 19/20 CE, another for 26/27 CE and a third for 38/39 CE. All three strikings were minted at Tiberias, bear his name as ethnarch and are of a large denomination (c. 16 grammes). They bear no human or animal representation, unlike the palace at Tiberias (*Life* 65), but have various decorations of a palm branch or a reed, a wreath, and on the final striking a bundle of dates as well. These latter also have the inscription: 'To Gaius Caesar Germanicus' – ironically, considering that it was this emperor who deposed him in that very year (Meshorer 1967: nos 63, 64 and 65). One can detect in these coins somebody who is caught between the religious conservatism of his largely Jewish population and his subordination to imperial fiscal policy, and who nonetheless is anxious to honour his patron, make a personal statement and facilitate local trade, possibly between the two diverse parts of his territory.

In view of these signs of the development of the internal market under Antipas, it is striking but not altogether surprising that Tyrian coins should have had the widest currency in Galilee, on the basis of the archaeological finds. The evidence for upper Galilee is clear and is in line with what we might expect in light of the literary sources already mentioned. Apart from Hasmonean coins of smaller denomination than the Tyrian didrachma and therefore, presumably, used for smaller transactions on a local base, coins from Tyre represent the largest percentage of all coins found at Meiron (4.7 per cent compared with 1.9 per cent of Herodian – mainly of Herod the Great). A similar percentage is reported for other upper Galilean sites – Kh Shema (3.5) and Gush Halav (4.5). More surprising still is the fact that a similar percentage of Tyrian coins (4.5) is reported for Sepphoris as compared with only 0.5 Herodian coins for the same site (Hanson 1980: 51–54; Raynor and Meshorer 1988: 83–85). Although this figure is based on earlier excavations and does not take account of recent and ongoing digs at this site, it is nonetheless quite significant. It certainly points to the importance of trade with Tyre for all of Galilee and could be seen to confirm our suggestion concerning the subordinate role of Sepphoris within the total economy of the northern region, despite its pre-eminence internally in Galilee. Confirmation of this appears to be the fact that very few coins from Tiberias have been found in the upper Galilean sites. By contrast Tyrian coins predominate in hoards found in lower Galilee. Thus in the Migdal hoard of coins dating from Titus to Elagabulus, 74 of a total of 188 bronze coins were from Tyre. This has been explained by the fact that the mint at Tyre produced many more coins than those from other competing mints (Barag 1982–1983: 7–13). Even more significant perhaps, in view of the latest date (52/3 CE) is the Isfija hoard of almost 5000 Tyrian silver coins of various denominations found in 1960 in the Carmel range. Several theories as to the significance of such a large find have been suggested, none totally convincing (Ben-David 1969: 33–36). Whatever the circumstances in which they came to be hidden it is clear that they indicate the continued dominance of Tyre as the major trading centre for the whole of Galilee, despite the development of Caesarea to the south as a possible rival port, thus underlining Galilee's regional independence from the south in trading terms.

The Synoptic Gospels testify, in their different ways, to the fact that money was widely used in everyday transactions, even by the poor. This would point to the fact that the use of money had penetrated right through the society and was now the standard form of exchange even among the day-labourers, widows and other marginalized people. Did the fact that all male Jews had to make an annual contribution of a half-shekel to the Temple mean a higher degree of monetization in that culture than in similar societies in antiquity? In this regard it should be noted that according to the Mishnah (*Sheq.* 1.3) tables for money changers were set up outside Jerusalem before the great feasts in order to assist the pilgrims. Likewise Josephus' colleagues from Jerusalem are said to have 'amassed a large sum of money' from the tithes owing to them as priests from the Galilean country people before returning to Jerusalem (*Life* 62). It is interesting also to note that apart from one Q saying (Luke 6:38; Matt. 7:2) about the measure one gives determining the measure one receives and the parable of the unjust manager (Luke 16:1–9), there is not a hint of barter exchange in any of the sayings of the Jesus tradition. People are presumed to have money for purchasing necessities or to meet other emergencies (Mark 6:36–38; Luke 10:35). However, Jesus' own attitude towards money appears to have been one of suspicion, if not of downright hostility. The practice of hoarding is described as futile, the disciples are not to rely on money in their travels and the tables of the money changers are overturned. We can enquire about the reasons for this attitude in view of the fact that Jesus and his followers accept the reality of money. But this question brings us to the third element in the model, that of changing values and institutions. The results of the present probe, however, point firmly towards a monetized economy which is dominated by trading links with Tyre, even though local trading within Galilee and with the Golan region was also thriving.

Institutions and values

Carney insists that for rapid change leading to a full-blown market economy to occur value changes had also to take place which would affect the existing institutions and give rise to new ones – values relating to kinship and family, entrepreneurship, status maintenance and other determinants of honour and shame, those two pivotal Mediterranean values. Elsewhere he speaks of this as a process of secularization, whereby the masses are no longer controlled by the dominant belief-system, but have to be persuaded or coerced (mobilized) to achieve public goals (Carney 1975: 149–152, 334f.). Sectional interests surface as more individualistic modes of thinking emerge. Thus in fifth-century BCE Athens the rise of rationalistic and 'atheistic' thinking went hand in hand with monetization and the development of markets, which were subsequently made to serve the interests of the redistributive/mobilized economies of the Hellenistic monarchies. A similar pattern can be seen with the rise of the Principate in the first century CE, putting an end to rationalistic debates among the elites of late republican times and leading to a growth in superstition, re-enforcement of traditional values and the promulgation of a new ideology, namely the victory of Rome and the emperor that ushered in the age of peace. Herodian policies in Palestine have to be evaluated in the light of these developments. With the aid of both the multivariate, matrix model (which should help in seeing all the factors that were operative within the situation) and the transformational one (which suggests where and how rapid change can affect the whole system) we shall attempt to explore the extent to which the ethos of Galilee was undergoing dramatic changes in the early first century CE.

It would be patently wrong to suggest that prior to the aggressive Romanization process of the Herodians, Palestinian society had not experienced the effects of rapid economic changes and their related attitudinal shifts. The Zenon papyri give us some insights into these changes for Galilee as well as for other regions in the Ptolemaic period (Tcherikover 1937). The process would appear to have been accelerated under the Seleucids with the emergence of the extreme Hellenizers at the time of Antiochus Epiphanes, who are described as being lawless men, and who complained that traditional Jewish isolationism precluded them from availing of the economic advantages of the new era (1 Macc. 1:11). It is scarcely an accident that these ideas were beginning to be expressed at a time when a Greek-style gymnasium had been established in Jerusalem. Despite their appeal to ancestral pieties in re-establishing the cult and legimitating the conquest of the land, the Hasmoneans did nothing to reverse the social trends that had been occurring for centuries, as some recent archaeological evidence for the first century BCE from Samaria would appear to suggest (Dar 1986). The extreme pressure on traditional values may be seen in the fact that such levelling mechanisms as the Jubilee and Sabbatical Year institutions were increasingly employed as images for the eschatological future in the literature of the period, rather than as currently functioning institutions. True, the *prosbul* arrangement points to a situation in which the need for a cash flow was recognized as being essential in order to maintain the stability of the society, and hence the stipulation of cancellation of all debts every seventh year could not be adhered to. In addition the Pentateuchal and prophetic ideal for Israel of 'every man under his own olive or fig tree', that is, individual ownership of land in traditional holdings (1 Kgs 5:5; Mic. 4:4; Zech. 3:10), was at least part of Hasmonean ideology also (1 Macc. 14:10). Even Herod the Great's land policy comprised of smaller lots for his veterans side by side with the development of royal estates. It was in the interests of the Hasmoneans to maintain such a pattern since the system of tithes and pilgrimages was in effect a functioning mobilization exchange system, legitimated by shared religious values, but which could be both punitive and exploitative as far as the country people were concerned (*J. A.* 20.181, 206f.; *Life* 63). It was this ambivalence that caused the political rebellion against Rome to be turned into a full-scale social revolution in 66 CE when the country peasants of Judaea joined with the lesser clergy in Jerusalem in ousting those who had lived the double standard and established in their place an egalitarian alternative (*J. W.* 2.242–247; 4.147–148).

During the ministry of Jesus, however, matters had not yet come to such a pass. The emergence of the Herodians and the alliance established between them and the retainers of the Jerusalem priestly aristocracy (Mark 3:5; 12:18), must, however, have helped in unmasking the inequalities of the situation. While the latter could use religious categories based on the purity system as a way of maintaining their social elitism, the former had no such inhibitions. An ostentatiously luxurious life-style is hinted at in Jesus' encomium on John the Baptist (Matt. 11:9; Luke 7:25; *Gos. Thom.* 78), giving rise to a sense of alienation and resentment on the part of the ordinary people (*Life* 67, 118f.; cf. Mark 12:7). The emergence of banditry as a social phenomenon is another consequence of such an ethos in which inequalities are no longer disguised, and people have a heightened awareness of being unfairly treated (Horsley and Hanson 1985; Freyne 1988. 163–166). Indeed, Josephus' as distinct from the Gospels' account of the death of John the Baptist hints at the fact that it was his critique of the life-style of the affluent, particularly his call for the practice of justice to one another, that had led to Antipas having him removed from the scene because of the danger of a revolution (*J. A.* 18.118; Hoehner 1972: 136–146). This makes the relative freedom of Jesus all the more surprising, though it may explain his strategy, as we shall presently see.

Carney argues that the institution that is central to the redistributive system but wholly unsuited to the market economy is the extended family. It operates on and is held together by values that are not suited to the requirements of a market situation. The specialized skills required are not necessarily available within the family unit and bonding is for reasons other than the maximization of profits from the available resources. Accordingly, the market worked in favour of the privileges of the few rather than to the advantage of the many, and maintenance of status became a primary concern for those who controlled the resources. Nor was there any incentive or motivation to improve the lot of the peasants or lower classes. Thus the market economy, far from producing an improved situation for all was highly exploitative in a way that led to social stratification and fragmentation. In a system based on kinship this could be disguised more easily through the shared acceptance of other, non-economic values.

In such a situation traditional institutions invariably come under severe pressure and the values that have held them together are easily eroded. In this regard it is noteworthy how Josephus repeatedly appeals to the value of *homophylia*, kinship, as a way of maintaining harmony among the various factions in Galilee during his sojourn there. Justus of Tiberias is charged with violating these bonds by acts of violence on the Galileans (*Life* 302) and Sepphoris is blamed for its refusal to support the Temple 'which is common to us all' (*Life* 348) when it was in danger. These appeals highlight the ambivalent situation that Josephus found himself in as governor of Galilee. As a wealthy Jerusalem land-owner he certainly shared the economic values of the wealthy Galileans, including the Herodians of Tiberias such as Justus, whose education in the Greek manner he acknowledges and, one suspects, admires also (*Life* 40). Yet the native nobility resented his appointment as governor in their own territory. In this situation Josephus needed the support of the peasants and played on their loyalty to Jerusalem and their hostility towards the aristocratic elites within the region. At the same time he had no desire to foment a full-scale social revolution against those elites, such as occurred in Jerusalem, as noted earlier. The fact that he was able to maintain his position successfully prior to the Roman advance speaks volumes both for the strength of the peasants' religious convictions and their loyalty to the Jerusalem cult-centre, and his ability to mobilize them for his own purpose (Freyne 1987).

Such were the competing values and loyalties in Galilee at the outbreak of the first revolt. It was not a new situation then, nor had it come about overnight. We must surmise that some thirty years earlier this situation was beginning to emerge, as both Sepphoris in its refurbished state and Tiberias were recent establishments. What was new about them was that they had introduced into the heart of lower Galilee in a relatively short space of time people whose values clashed directly with those on which the Jewish peasants' lives had operated. It was not that they were encountering these values for the first time, but now in their midst they had received visible expression in stone and through an institutional presence, often in the person of fellow Jews. It was this complex of factors that generated the tensions which surface so clearly thirty years after Jesus.

JESUS AND HERODIAN ECONOMICS

The rapid change of basic values symbolized in the two new foundations helps to explain both the values and the strategy of Jesus, and a critical correlation between his stance and the demands of the new situation would appear both possible and plausible. Both Sepphoris and Tiberias were avoided not necessarily because Jesus shared the alienation of the peasants towards those centres, but rather because he rejected the value system on which their position of power was based, and the treatment of the Baptist undoubtedly cast its own shadow. Jesus' ministry was rural based, but did not exclude the lesser officials, such as the tax-collectors in the villages, who were positively welcomed. Thus the Jesus movement was not one other protest movement, venting its anger on the elites in violent actions. Neither did it espouse the kind of social and personal withdrawal that were associated with various forms of Cynicism which have recently found favour as the most suitable analogue in some contemporary studies of Jesus (Crossan 1991 and Mack 1993). He proposed an alternative way of life that both adopted and adapted the kinship and familial values which were being eroded in the larger culture represented by Antipas' foundations. Drawing on the ethical insights of the prophetic motif of the restoration of Israel, and combining these with common wisdom, he sought to give these values concrete expression in a new style of community living. Family feuds must have occurred as the direct result of the social changes taking place and the invitation to join an alternative family would have resonated particularly with those who had become alienated or excluded in the prevailing social upheaval.

My proposal is that Jesus and his renewal movement is best understood as offering another set of values in addition to the two competing ones which we have seen within the social world of Antipas' Galilee. Insofar as it might be expected to have had a widespread appeal in that particular setting it was potentially threatening to both. The very radical nature of its social programme challenged the values that the Herodian market economy espoused, and the revision of the traditional religious categories of Temple, Torah and land which it demanded would have undermined the centrality of Jerusalem and the unqualified loyalty that it was able to foster among its rural adherents. The fact that Jesus' message proved as unacceptable to the latter as to the former is perhaps indicative of the reserve with which the Galilean peasantry viewed its radical social agenda, despite the sense of alienation from the dominant system that must have been experienced, and the seeming inability or unwillingness of the cult-based system to stop the drift towards penury. The wandering charismatic/healer/holy man, Jesus, may well have fulfilled a definite social need in the villages of Galilee, but in a climate in which people clung precariously to some things though all was in danger of being lost, his call to freely abandon all would appear to have been too demanding and too utopian. That same message propagated by those who passed on the Q tradition, albeit adapted in the light of new experiences, would appear to have still been equally unattractive to the fishermen and farmers of Capernaum, Bethsaida and Corazain some decades later (Kloppenborg 1991). If Josephus is to be trusted they regarded it as less disruptive to support Jerusalem and its Temple while venting their anger against the Herodian centres than to follow the millennial dream. Thus when he took over as governor there in 66 CE the two systems, Herodian and theocratic, were still firmly in place and to an extent competing with each other, while forming an alliance of convenience in order to maintain their privileges. Nowhere can we detect any trace of the Jesus movement or its agenda in the social world of *Life*. Instead that movement and its alternative value system had found more fertile soil in the cities of the Mediterranean world, where its appeal for many, though muted because of the political realities, was still based on the challenge it posed to the mobilized economy that was Rome.

CONCLUSION

In applying the model to the Galilee of Antipas' day I have concentrated on those elements which Carney has suggested should be selected and highlighted for special treatment, namely attitudinal changes in production and consumption, increased organizational specialization and monetization of transactions. Under all three headings we have been able to identify clear signs of such movement within the society of Jesus' day. The values of a market economy with all the attendant signs of exploitation of the weak and ostentatious living of the wealthy are easily documented; specializations in terms of more intensive harvesting of produce both from the land and lake, as well as production of goods for inter-regional trade in addition to domestic use were occurring; and there are clear signs of the extension of monetization as a means of exchange with the production of native Galilean coins for the first time, however subordinate these remained to the Tyrian money. It seems possible to link these developments with Antipas' foundations of Sepphoris and Tiberias, as symptomatic of the more complex changes occurring within the whole region. It is not a case that with Antipas these developments occurred for the first time, but rather that his attempts to emulate his father and his desire to convince Augustus of his right to kingship meant that there was a particular intensification in Galilee of processes that had generally been in train in Palestine for a considerable time.

The use of Carney's model seems to have more than justified itself, therefore. Not merely has it assisted in clarifying the changes that were taking place, but it has also brought more sharply into focus the most immediate historical context for the rise of the one Galilean renewal movement known to us from the first century CE and the reason for the particular set of values which that movement espoused.

NOTE

1 This essay picks up and amplifies one aspect of the material covered in my paper 'The Geography, Politics and Economics of Galilee and the Quest for the Historical Jesus', in Bruce Chilton and Craig A. Evans (eds) *Studying the Historical Jesus: Evaluations of the State of Current Research*, Leiden: E. J. Brill, 1994.

2

THE TRANSFIGURATION OF JESUS

An experience of alternate reality

John J. Pilch

INTRODUCTION

In his article, 'What Really Happened at the Transfiguration?', Jerome Murphy-O'Connor proposes that Jesus was troubled by contradictions in the will of God as he understood it. According to Luke, whose report includes the original tradition, Jesus resolved his difficulties in prayer and his face lit up. The glory that Peter and the others saw (Luke 9:32) was the radiant joy that accompanies the resolution of a terrible perplexity (Murphy-O'Connor 1987: 18).

As a true Westerner, Murphy-O'Connor turns to science, 'which offers the best illustrations'. Jesus' flash of insight can be compared with scientific insights like those of Newton. No one can explain them; they just happen (p. 19). And the face lights up! How curious that biblical scholars who object to relying upon contemporary Mediterranean cultural information to shed light on the ancient Mediterranean world apparently find no difficulty using modern Western experience to illuminate ancient Mediterranean experience.

Murphy-O'Connor's literary analyses and conclusions inspired a doctoral dissertation at the Catholic University of America (Washington, DC), revised and recently published by Barbara Reid. Her source and redaction-critical study traced the history of the tradition behind Luke and sought secondarily to discover 'what kind of event, if any, in the life of the historical Jesus gave rise to it' (Reid 1993: 29).

Reid's research isolated a primitive tradition preserved by Luke (9:28–36b), who embellished it with personal composition and redaction of Marcan tradition:

> Eight days [later] taking with him Peter and John and James, he went up the mountain to pray. The appearance of his face was altered. And behold, two men who appearing in glory spoke of his 'exodus' which he was about to fulfil in Jerusalem. But Peter and those with him saw his glory and the two men standing with him. And when they parted from him Jesus was found alone.
>
> (From Luke 9:28–36b, translated by Reid 1993: 33–34, from her version of the Greek at 73–74).

On the basis of Judaic tradition, the two men are probably anonymous angels. Form-critically, then, this passage is a predictive angelophany, that is, an instructive message from heavenly figures for earth-bound listeners about forthcoming events. The Lukan redactor equated the angels with Moses and Elijah in the Marcan tradition and by adding other elements from Mark into the final text transformed the report into a pronouncement story.

Since the primary intent of this narrative is to make a theological statement rather than present historical or biographical information about Jesus, Reid is sceptical about any attempt to discover what really happened in the life of Jesus. 'Because of the fragmentary nature of the evidence, the methods of historical criticism cannot provide scientifically certain results [about the historical events of Jesus' life]' (Reid 1993: 147).

Reid (1993: 1) concurs with Fitzmyer:

> Given the diversity of the way in which the incident is reported, no real historical judgment can be made about it; to write it all off as mystical is likewise to go beyond the evidence. Just what sort of an incident in the ministry of Jesus – to which it is clearly related – it was is impossible to say.
> (Fitzmyer 1981: 796)

Other modern scholars deny facticity to the transfiguration *a priori* because 'such an event does not harmonize with what we know about the earthly ministry of Jesus and of the naturalistic laws that govern all existence' (reported by Stein 1976: 89 and Ramsey 1949: 104–105). Even the ancients heatedly debated whether epiphanies actually occurred or not (see Dionysius of Halicarnassus, *Antiquitates Romanae* 2.68), and Aristotle denied that God communicated with humans in 'waking' dreams (*On Prophecy in Sleep*, 462b).

Yet despite her scepticism, Reid admits that if Murphy-O'Connor is correct in considering that the special Lukan transfiguration tradition is closer to the actual event in Jesus' life than what is reported in the final Synoptic texts, that tradition gives a good 'glimpse into the process by which the earthly Jesus came to understand more completely God's intent for his "exodus" to be the fulfilment of his mission' (Reid 1993: 147). In other words, Jesus experienced a flash of insight in prayer that lit up his face.

Reid excels in literary analysis of texts, and her critical survey of literary interpretations of the transfiguration based on the resurrection-appearance approach, the mythological approach, approaches from Old Testament background and Jewish Apocalyptic, and the redactional-critical approach (pp. 7–30) is well executed. Her objections to the historical approach (pp. 3–7), generally shared by the majority who favour literary-critical studies, are less successful. Effective rebuttals can be made to each objection. For instance, one weakness of the historical approach that she lists is that scholars disagree about the possibility that supernatural, transcendent experiences can break into the natural sphere of human experience (p. 6). This disagreement is hardly different from disagreements among literary critics in their own specialties. Even so, scholars who deny that 'supernatural' experiences can occur in 'natural' human experience demonstrate Western cultural myopia rather than scientific astuteness. Saler (1977) has demonstrated that a distinction between 'supernatural' as opposed to the 'natural' is a Western, culturally determined concept. Evans (1987), whom Reid cites without critique, describes this myopia very well.

Given the Western cultural bias inherent in any concept of science and scientific certitude (Malina 1978), the scepticism of historical critics like Reid and Fitzmyer and their preference for theological interpretations are perfectly intelligible (see Chilton 1992 for a summary). Yet humanists argue that adequate and culturally plausible explanations are just as valid as scientific certitude. This essay, therefore, proposes a Mediterranean-culturally plausible scenario for understanding and interpreting the transfiguration whether in the life of Jesus or as reported in biblical tradition.

This essay selects insights and models from the social sciences (Pilch 1993a; 1991; Pilch and Malina 1993; Elliott 1993a; Esler 1992 and 1994a: 37–51) to shape new strategies for understanding and interpreting the transfiguration as an actual event in the lifetime of Jesus (Ramsey 1949: 107), irrespective of whether or not it occurred exactly as described (see the relevant comment by Esler (1992: 137–138 and 1994a: 40–43) explaining the value of Goodman (1972) to analyse glossolalia in the New Testament). In Part One, I propose and design a *reading scenario* that is culturally appropriate to the report of the transfiguration. From psychological anthropology, I propose and describe altered or alternate state of consciousness ('ASC'), or an experience of alternate reality as the central element of this reading scenario. Specifically, the ASC known etically as trance or waking dream and emically as vision seems to be the scenario best suited for reading and interpreting the transfiguration accounts with respectful sensitivity to their cultural setting. In Part Two I adapt a model to map phenomenologically the transfiguration as an ASC so as to explore how this reading scenario sheds fresh light upon the interpretation of the Synoptic transfiguration accounts.

PART ONE: READING SCENARIO FOR TRANCE/WAKING DREAM/VISION

Reading scenarios in general

All language derives its meaning from the social world. The language used by the evangelists, namely koine Greek, derives its meaning from the first-century, eastern Mediterranean social world. Since these authors and their original readers (or listeners) shared this social world and were intimately familiar with it, there was no need for an author to spell out the obvious. Readers or listeners could even be counted on to supply quite reliably and correctly any data that was missing yet necessary to understand and interpret correctly what the author wrote. It is important to realize that we are dealing with literature from a 'high-context' culture (see Malina 1991e: 19–20), where far more was left unsaid than in a modern Western context.

Western readers, of course, do not share the social world of the ancient authors they read. Unless they take careful pains to avoid doing so, Western readers will bring to these ancient Mediterranean texts inappropriate reading scenarios drawn from their Western cultural experiences. Even the Greek words they read will usually be understood in the target language into which they are translated, such as English. Technically, this is known as ethnocentrism and eisegesis. Thus, 'the goal of the social-scientific approach is to outfit the contemporary reader with scenarios that befit the alien texts that he or she seeks to understand' (Malina 1991d: 255).

Reading scenarios are not unfamiliar to traditional biblical scholars, but they tend to understand such scenarios rather narrowly. As noted above, the scenario that Murphy-O'Connor (1987: 18) proposes for the transfiguration is rooted in Judaic tradition (prayer) and his Western cultural experience (insight), particularly Western science. But Western culture has a very limited range of categories for states of consciousness other than waking, sleeping and pathological ones (Walsh 1993: 740). This explains the tendency of Western scholars to conflate or pathologize (or 'theologize?') altered and alternate states of consciousness that form the core experiential component of cultures in which the spirit world is an integral part of the worldview.

Yet cross-cultural research indicates that more than 90 per cent of world cultures possess institutionalized forms of ASCs (Pilch 1993a: 233). The percentage for contemporary circum-Mediterranean cultures is 80 per cent, and it is very likely that these ASCs were similarly frequent in the ancient Mediterranean world (Dodds 1951: 116; Hankoff 1991: 395). Indeed, it is 'reasonable to conclude that the states [of consciousness] described by the ancient and the modern observers are, if not identical, at least analogous' (Dodds 1951: 297; see also Esler 1992 and 1994a: 37–51).

Only the contemporary, secular West appears to have successfully blocked out access to these otherwise pan-human dimensions of the self (Pilch 1993a: 233). More than this, Western readers typically declare all such experiences 'unreal' or a clever deceit (Luck 1989: 214) because they do not tally well with so-called scientific habits of thought (Stein 1976: 89; Ramsey 1949: 104–105). Luck (1989: 217) is correct in urging scholars to seek improved understanding of these phenomena in terms of modern psychology, psychic research and anthropology (see also Inglis 1977; 1989; and Evans 1987). That is the tack taken in this essay building on the author's previous research.

The ASC 'trance' or 'waking dream' or 'vision'

The ancient Greeks recognized that human beings live in two worlds: the waking world and the dream world. The Greek word *hypar* describes a waking vision and its adverbial usage means 'in a waking state, awake', or 'in reality, actually' (Liddell and Scott s.v.). The word *onar* means dream and generally stands in contrast to the waking world. A common phrase in ancient literature, *ouk onar, all'hypar*, paints the contrast: 'not an illusive dream, but a reality!'

Aristides (*Oratio* XLVIII, 31–35 = test. 417) appears to report a waking dream or waking vision during his visit to an Asclepian temple:

> It [the remedy] was revealed in the clearest way possible, just as countless other things also made the presence of the god manifest. It was like seeming to touch him, a kind of awareness that he was there in person; one was between sleep and waking, one wanted to open one's eyes, and yet was anxious lest he should withdraw too soon; one listened and heard things, sometimes as in a dream (*onar*), and sometimes as in waking life (*hypar* = waking vision); one's hair stood on end; one cried, and felt happy; one's heart swelled, but not with vainglory. What human being could put that experience into words? But anyone who has been through it will share my knowledge and recognize the state of mind.
>
> (translated by Dodds 1951: 113)

Aristides' conviction that a person must have this experience in order to appreciate reports of it is shared by modern researchers (Walsh 1993: 748; Goodman 1972: 5).

Contemporary cross-cultural experts who study the world's cultures classify a waking dream or a trance as an altered or alternate state of consciousness (ASC). Bourguignon defines ASCs as:

> conditions in which sensations, perceptions, cognition and emotions are altered. They are characterized by changes in sensing, perceiving, thinking, and feeling. They modify the relation of the individual to the self, body, sense of identity, and the environment of time, space and other people.
>
> (cited by Pilch 1993a: 235)

Figure 3 displays side by side an emic (insider) and etic (outsider) arrangement of some alternate states of consciousness. From an emic perspective, for example, that of an evangelist or some other first-century Middle Eastern native, the disciples' experience of Jesus' transfiguration could be classified as a vision (*horama* – Matt. 17:9) very broadly understood (Pax 1955: 177). A vision is a normal and ordinary means of communicating with the spirit world that takes place in a 'mystic' state (Lambek 1981: 50). The word 'mystic' on this side of the model is probably etic, but it conveniently captures the richly diverse emic experience (but see Walsh 1993: 759).

From an etic, or contemporary *non*-Middle Eastern perspective on Middle Eastern experience, the emic vision is roughly equivalent to a trance or waking dream. The etic perspective believes such experiences derive very likely from hypnosis, most often self-induced, resulting from intensely focused attention. In the accounts of dreams reported by those who sought healing from Asclepius

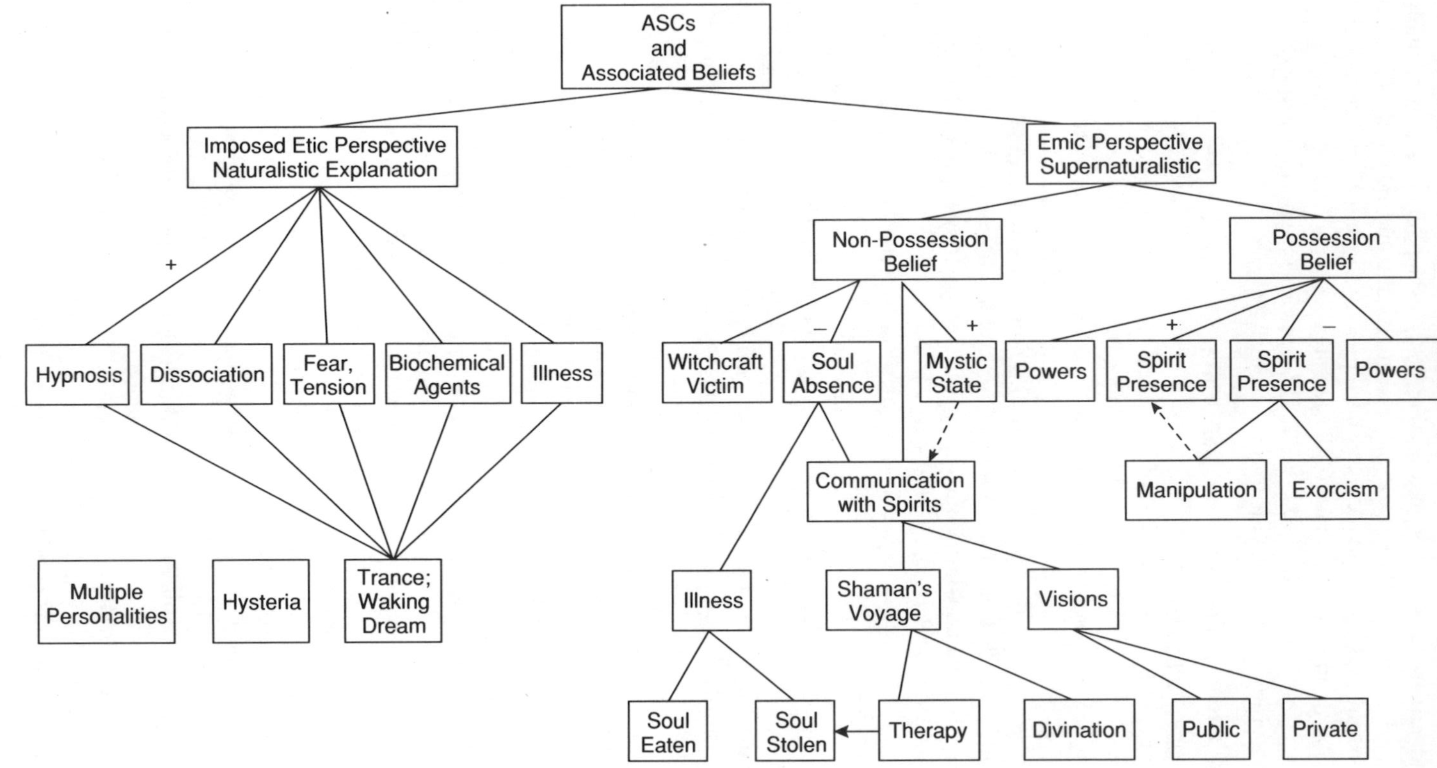

Figure 3 Emic and etic perspectives of some alternate states of consciousness (adapted from Bourguignon and Pattison, cited in Pilch 1993a)

in his temples, commentators believe that the dream-trances of the suppliants were very likely self-induced. The patient had a strong sense that the god was present in the temple and eventually heard his voice. The more detailed prescriptions recorded in the testimonies were very likely received by petitioners in this state of consciousness rather than in actual dreams (Dodds 1951: 113).

As Walsh (1993: 745) notes, trance is a term that is widely used but imprecisely defined in modern contexts. The key defining characteristic of a trance is its intensely focused attention which reduces awareness of the experience-context, namely, objects, stimuli or environment outside the specific focus. The object of intensely focused attention can be internal or external. In the transfiguration, Jesus' focus may have been on something internal (for example, communication with God) while the disciples (unless they were sleeping, as in Luke) were focused on him, his face and garments.

In a trance, contact with self and others is modified in a distinctive way. This modification can range from total unconsciousness to a very mild distraction. Trance is externally manifest to observers whether native or trained specialists. It can be induced in a variety of ways, including hypnosis, dissociation, fear or tension, biochemical agents (such as incense, aromatic scents etc.) and illness. Dissociation can also produce multiple personalities, and some may argue for this feature in trance, though that does not seem to be the case. Nevertheless, because of this possibility, I retain that box on the model in Figure 3.

Lambek's research on possession trance among the Mayotte of the Comoro Islands in the Indian Ocean highlights yet other characteristics of this ASC (Lambek 1981: 50–53). Trance behaviour follows definite cultural role types which make cultural sense. The role must be internally coherent, that is, it must be available in the culture. As a result, there are constraints on individual behaviour in trance. The spirits who appear in trance are also constrained, for example, by consideration of rank and deference among other things. Though also bounded by time and space during the apparition, visitors from the 'other' world exist outside of time, a purely human creation. Moses and Elijah, whose lives were separated in human time, meet Jesus in the Synoptic report of the ASC which is not constrained by human time. It is the region of the timeless. Truly this ASC is a rich area of human experience (Peters and Price-Williams 1983).

Trance and ecstasy

The ancient world also developed a technique or set of techniques called 'theurgy' (Luck 1989; Dodds 1951: 283–311) intended to bring on trance or facilitate the opportunity for encountering the spirit world. These techniques were codified as *Oracula Chaldaica* in the reign of Marcus Aurelius (121–180 CE). Theurgy was considered a form of worship and a path to salvation. The techniques included silence, fasting, praying, lack of sleep over a long period of time, self-mutilation, sleeping on a skin of a sacrificed animal, or in contact with some other holy object, or sleeping in a holy place (= incubation, as in the Asclepian temples). Each of these techniques and more often a combination of them induced altered states of consciousness. One of these was 'ecstasy'.

What the Greeks called ecstasy, contemporary Westerners call trance, but not every trance is *ekstasis* in the Greek sense of the word (Luck 1989: 194). It is the religious context of the experience that determines ecstasy. In the New Testament, Luke reports that Peter fell into an ecstasy or trance during prayer (Acts 10:10) and saw a vision in this ecstasy (Acts 11:5) wherein God disclosed to him that 'all foods are clean'. Luke also reports that Paul fell into an ecstasy or trance as he was praying in the Temple after returning to Jerusalem (Acts 22:17), and in this ecstatic vision Jesus advised him to flee. The other four occurrences of *ekstasis* in the New Testment (Mark 5:42; 16:8; Luke 5:26; Acts 3:10) are not combined with vision and are more appropriately translated 'amazement', 'astonishment', 'awe', meanings peculiar to the New Testament and Septuagintal Greek use of *ekstasis* and *existemi* (as at Gen. 43:33; 1 Sam. 11:7 etc.). Paul uses *existemi* of his own religious experience at 2 Cor. 5:13.

The Greeks were convinced that not all so-called philosophers experience ecstasy but only one who is 'beloved by the gods' and whose soul is 'god-loving' (Luck 1989: 195). If this conviction reflects part of the cultural pattern of ecstatic vision, it helps us to appreciate that the 'voice from heaven' identifies Jesus as a 'beloved or chosen' son (Mark 9:7; Matt. 17:5; Luke 9:35).

It is difficult to say whether any Gospel-personages explicitly engaged in what the ancients termed theurgy. Their encounters with the spirit world may have been only a coincidental result of the use of the strategies later codified by theurgy, such as fasting or prayer. Whatever the case, these insights provide a modern, Western reader of ancient documents with culturally appropriate data which can serve to make sense of high-context literature better than Western imagination alone might do. This answers Reid's suspicions concerning the role of imagination (Reid 1993: 6).

Cultural beliefs

E. R. Dodds proposed that waking visions or waking dreams in general have the same origin and psychological structure as dreams and that both reflected traditional cultural beliefs and culture patterns (1951: 116). In the popular imagination, the dreamer passively receives an objective vision (1951: 105). Thus the Greeks always spoke of 'seeing a dream' rather than 'having a dream' as Westerners do.

Kinds of dreams and visions

The ancients distinguished between significant and non-significant dreams (Sir. 34:1–8). Non-significant dreams included visions that occurred to some persons in the stage between sleeping and waking (Aristotle, *On Dreams* 462a, 11) and nightmares. They also distinguished three kinds of significant dreams

(Artemidorus, *Oneirocritica* I.2). First was the symbolic dream full of metaphors which needed interpretation, such as Joseph's interpretation of the dreams of the chief butler and chief baker in prison (Gen. 40). Secondly, the vision or *horama* which pre-enacts a future event, for example, Peter's *horama* in Acts 10:9–16. Thirdly, the oracle or *chrematismos* in which the dreamer's parent, a priest, a god, or some other respected person reveals clearly what will or will not happen, or should or should not be done, as in God's reply to Elijah (1 Kgs 19:10, 18, reported by Paul in Rom. 11:4).

Plato (*Laws* 909E–910A), who was sceptical of the supernatural nature of dreams or waking visions, notes that many dedications were made on the basis of such dream experiences particularly by 'women of all types' and 'men who are sick or in some danger or difficulty'. Plato's comment, though sceptical, nevertheless serves to highlight the frequency of such experiences in antiquity. It also points out one function of a waking vision, namely consolation in danger or difficulty, for example the debated verses in Luke 22:43–44 that speak of an angel comforting Jesus during his agony in the garden.

Local culture patterning of dreams and visions

Most significant, however, is the strong conviction among anthropologists that the manifest content of dreams and waking visions is determined by a local cultural pattern, a socially transmitted pattern of belief (Dodds 1951: 103). These beliefs are accepted by the visionary or dreamer and everyone in the environment (recall Lambek's comments cited above). The culture pattern determines how the dreamer or visionary will identify figures or other elements in the dream. According to Reid (1993: 39–40), who follows Murphy-O'Connor (1987: 15), the dreamers or visionaries in the transfiguration account (Jesus and the disciples) very likely saw two men and interpreted them as heavenly figures, messengers, angels, as indicated by Luke's source reflected in 9:30a. This tallies well with Judaic tradition such as 2 Macc. 3:26. The Evangelist or redactor, drawing once again on Judaic tradition, later identifies the two men as Moses and Elijah rather than Zeus and Apollo.

The 'voice from the cloud' is likened to the *bat qol*, another element presented and interpreted by the culture. In the transfiguration story, context indicates that the 'voice from the cloud' belongs to the Father ('my Son'). In John 12:28–29, the narrator identifies a 'voice from heaven' as the Father responding to Jesus, while some in the crowd thought they heard thunder, and others thought that an angel had spoken to Jesus.

The pervasive Mediterranean belief in a densely populated spirit world and the regular and ready interference of those spirits in human life is certainly an integral part of the culture pattern of dreams in that world. The cloud as a sign of God's presence, tents or tabernacles, gleaming garments, changed appearance – all these are part and parcel of the socially transmitted pattern of beliefs characteristic of epiphanies (Pax 1955; Lentzen-Deis 1970).

Dodds (1951: 109) makes a very insightful observation confirmed by the group-centered nature of Mediterranean culture. Commenting on Macrobius' phrase that key figures in Greek dreams often are 'a parent or some other respected or impressive personage' he says: 'And we may further suppose that so long as the old solidarity of the family persisted, such maintenance of contact in dreams with the father-image would have a deeper emotional significance, and a more unquestioned authority than it possesses in our more individualized society.' Given the enduring influence of Mediterranean fathers in the lives of their sons, it is easy to appreciate the classification of the transfiguration as a commissioning vision or text (Neyrey 1993c: 172). All these various elements constitute the culture content of dreams or waking visions in the Mediterranean world in which the Bible originated.

Culture-based experience and literary form

Of special significance is the fact that culture pattern dreams and visions are an integral part of the religious experience of a people (Dodds 1951: 108). The relationship between belief and vision or dream is somewhat circular. What the visionary believes is what the visionary sees or dreams, and what the visionary sees or dreams the visionary automatically believes. This is how the dream and vision reports become increasingly stylized. Literary critics need to note that the stylization of these dreams, therefore, is not purely literary. In other words, literary forms are stylized in part because the experience itself is stylized. As Dodds notes, poets from Homer on down have adapted these experiences to their purposes and used them as a literary motif (1951: 108). And when the dream or revision is retold, secondary elaboration takes place. 'In this case the secondary elaboration will have operated, without conscious deception, to bring the dream or vision into closer conformity with the traditional culture-pattern' (Dodds 1951: 114). In many instances in the Asclepian dream reports, for example, a tertiary elaboration seems to have been contributed by priests or fellow patients. Granted the influence of literary tradition on the creation of a stereotyped form for reporting visions and dreams, Dodds concludes that experiences of this kind were real and fairly frequent in antiquity and still occur.

Psychological anthropology supports and documents his conclusion (Pilch 1993a; Hsu 1972). Dodds (1951: 131, n. 84) observes: 'As Pfister (in Pauly–Wissowa, *Epiphanie*) says, we cannot doubt that the mass of ancient epiphany-stories corresponds to something in ancient religious experience, even though we can seldom or never be quite sure that any particular story has a historical basis.' Luck (1989: 214) concurs: 'Visions such as the theurgists claimed to have experienced are rejected instinctively by the modern mind because of our scientific habits of thought, but it seems impossible, considering the evidence we have, to declare all these experiences 'unreal', or call them cleverly orchestrated deceit.' Anthropologists like Bourguignon and Kleinman (cited by Pilch 1993a: 233) confirm Smythie's conclusion that 'the decision to call only ordinary sense-experience real is an isolated phenomenon of our more recent type of Western European culture' (cited by Luck 1989: 216).

Conclusion

Research drawn from psychological anthropology suggests that the altered or alternate state of consciousness variously described as 'trance', 'waking dream', 'vision', 'waking vision', 'ecstasy', among others provides the appropriate scenario for reading and interpreting the Synoptic account known as the transfiguration. One must remember that the concept of a 'state of consciousness' is 'an arbitrary and static crystallization of what is, in living experience, a multidimensional dynamic flow of experience' (Walsh 1993: 745). Analyzing such experiences requires a specialized model to which we now turn attention in Part Two.

PART TWO: INTERPRETING THE TRANSFIGURATION STORY

The ecstatic experience of Jesus and the disciples

The variety of modern terms for the ASC under discussion (trance, ecstasy etc.) has a parallel in classical Greek and biblical literature as well. In his study of epiphanies, Pax (1955: 174) points out that though the Greek word *epiphaneia* in the ancient world was a technical term for this experience, Christians seldom used that word to describe that experience. He suspects that *epiphaneia* carried content which early Christians did not want to accept, hence they used various other words.

Michaelis (1964: 351) is convinced not only that there are no theophanies at all in the New Testament apart from Acts 7:2, but also that:

> The transfiguration of Jesus in Mark 9:2ff. and parallels is not to be regarded as an ecstatic experience of Jesus himself. . . . If so the participation of the disciples would have to be very different from that recorded, or, in fact, non-existent. Account must be taken of the appearance of Moses and Elijah and the voice from the cloud when we try to decide whether the whole event was a real experience of Jesus or a visionary experience of the disciples.
>
> (1964: 354)

Michaelis (1964: 354) disagrees with Behm (1964: 478) who seems to think this is not a vision, but a real change in Jesus perceived by the disciples. But Behm is positive that the event has nothing to do with metamorphosis in the Hellenistic sense 'but suggests the context of apocalyptic ideas' (1964: 758).

These floundering discussions rooted solely in philology demonstrate the sorry results of failing to realize that all language derives its meaning from the social system. Without an adequate knowledge of the social system, interpretation based on philology alone is bound to fail.

A very relevant Asclepian testimony strongly suggests that the transfiguration account is quite likely reporting ecstatic or trance experiences by Jesus and the three disciples (Edelstein and Edelstein 1975: test. 331). Here is the summary of an account in which the same divine figure was perceived simultaneously by one person in a dream and by another in a waking vision:

> The translator of a book recording healings by Asclepius was struck ill by a pain in his right side and sought relief from Asclepius. His mother, herself recently healed by Asclepius, was with him. She, in a waking vision ('it was no dream (*onar*) or sleep (*hypnos*) for her eyes were open, immovable, though not seeing clearly, for a divine and terrifying vision (*phantasia(n)*) came to her. . .') saw someone 'clothed in shining raiment' look her son over two or three times and depart. When she came to, she woke her son to tell him, but 'I (said the son) anticipating her told her all myself; for everything that she saw in vision (*dia tes opseos eiden*) appeared to me in dreams (*di'oneiraton ephantasiothen*)'.
>
> (P. Oxy. IX.1381.91ff. = test. 331)

Rather than repeat a traditional, exegetical comparison of the Synoptic accounts of the transfiguration to highlight the Greek words they use, do not use, or change (Ramsey 1949; Stein 1976; Moessner 1983; Reid 1993 and the like), I propose instead to explore the ASC of trance as reported in these accounts as a 'multidimensional dynamic flow of experience' reflective of cultural beliefs.

Mapping the ASC in the transfiguration story

Jung notes that 'all human beings are bad observers of things that are unfamiliar to them' (1976: 307). In a ground-breaking study of ASCs that moves the pioneering work of Bourguignon and her associates significantly forward (see Pilch 1993a for bibliography), Walsh proposes a model for multidimensional description, mapping and comparison of alternate states of consciousness in shamanism (1993: 751–752). It was developed on the basis of research and ten years of personal experience. Though the transfiguration is not an instance of shamanic trance or journey, Walsh's model appropriately modified to address the biblical data can serve as an appropriate tool for analyzing the ASC of trance.

As in the Asclepian testimony, the transfiguration story reports Jesus and three select disciples (Peter, James and John) experiencing an ASC of trance or waking vision. Jesus is probably focused on an internal object (communion with the Father), the disciples are focused on him (face, garments etc.). I will now relate the transfiguration story to the nine elements from Walsh's model outlined in Figure 4.

Dimension	*Matt.*	*Mark*	*Luke*
1. Awareness of environment	J= ↓ 3= ↑	J= ↓ 3= ↑	J= ↓ 3=sleep
2. Ability to communicate	J=Yes (with Moses and Elijah) 3=Peter to Jesus	J=? (Moses and Elijah to him) 3=Peter to Jesus; did not know what to say	J= Yes (with Moses and Elijah) 3=Peter to Jesus
3. Concentration			
fixed	Jesus ↑	Jesus ↑	Jesus ↑
fluid	3; Jesus?	3; Jesus	3; sleep
4. Control			
ASC – enter and leave at will	?	?	?
ASC content	partial*	partial*	partial*
5. Arousal	J= ↑ face shone like sun 3= ↑joy; then extreme fear	J= ↑ 3= ↑ joy; then extreme fear	J= ↑ appearance was altered 3= ↑ joy; then extreme fear
6. Calm	?	?	3=sleep; then wake
7. Self-sense	J= ↑	J= ↑	J= ↑
8. Affect	+	+	+
9. Content	organized and coherent *bat qol*	organized and coherent *bat qol*	organized and coherent *bat qol*

* content consistent with learned cosmology and traditions that shape culture-pattern waking dreams or trances

Figure 4 Mapping the alternate consciousness in the transfiguration accounts (adapted from Walsh 1993: 751–752)

1 Awareness of the experiential context or environment

All three accounts indicate the experience took place on a mountain. In 348 Cyril of Jerusalem identified Tabor (c. 1,950 feet) as the place, though earlier tradition also included Hermon (c. 9,232 feet) and the Mount of Olives (330 feet). Hiking up a mountain like Tabor would physically and psychologically predispose the hiker for an ASC. Dodds (1951: 117) observes that the visions of Hesiod, Philippides and Pindar all occurred in lonely mountainous places, and the psychological influence of such solitude ought not be underrated.

It is difficult to assess how far up the mountain this quartet hiked, but the hike up, the ASC experience, and the hike down probably would entail more than a day's time. Luke's reference to the apostles 'heavy with sleep' could indicate the exhausting nature of the hike or night-time, and either is favourable to experiencing an ASC (even if this element has been transferred by the redactor from the Agony in the Garden as Reid (1993: 40–42) and Murphy-O'Connor (1987: 15–16) propose).

In the experience itself, the disciples in Matthew and Mark (and the Lukan tradition) are focused exclusively on Jesus in the environment (up-arrow in Figure 4). In Luke, they are asleep and definitely unaware of the environment. Luke alone indicates Jesus was praying which entails intense focus on God. Modern research indicates that in the meditative experience 'consciousness of one's physical positioning and environment rapidly fade away' (Forman 1993: 716; down-arrow for Jesus).

2 Ability to communicate

In all accounts, Jesus communicates with the two men (angels or Elijah and Moses) but does not speak with the disciples. Of the three disciples, Peter alone speaks to Jesus. The evidence does not allow a conclusion about whether Jesus heard or could respond to Peter, though these are normal possibilities in ASCs. In all accounts, the cloud envelops the group and a voice from the cloud responds to Peter (and presumably the others). Traditional interpretation identifies the voice from the cloud as a *bat qol*, and the context indicates it is the Father's voice. In ASCs the subjects sometimes change voices, and it is possible that the Father spoke through Jesus or one of the other disciples.

3 Concentration

Two things must be considered: the degree of concentration, and whether it is fixed or fluid. Jesus appears to be intensely concentrated, especially in Luke's context of prayer. The disciples are less focused in Matthew and Mark, and not at all in Luke (sleep). It would also seem that Jesus' concentration is initially fixed immovably on a single object, the Father. Did Jesus experience the two men as angels or Moses and Elijah? Were the two men (angels) or Moses and

Elijah only in the ASC of the disciples? This is impossible to answer with a direct report from Jesus. If these figures were in his ASC, then his attention is also fluid, that is, it shifts between selected objects, as most certainly is the case with the disciples in all accounts.

4 Control

Two elements of the ASC enter into the consideration of control. First, can the subjects enter and leave the ASC at will? If Luke's prayer context is original, as the Lukan tradition suggests, then one might conjecture that Jesus was able to enter (and presumably leave) the ASC at will. The other accounts give no clue about Jesus in this regard, and the disciples seem to slip easily into the ASC, a common experience documented in cross-cultural research.

Second, can the subjects control the content of the ASC? In Walsh's model, this question seeks to determine whether the one experiencing an ASC is able to seek answers to specific questions. Peter's willingness to make tents for Jesus and the visitors could be interpreted as an attempt to manipulate or control the ASC. This interpretation takes on greater likelihood in Luke's account, where the disciples awake from sleep. It is plausible that they are in the in-between state, not a dream but not fully awake either. In contemporary ASC experience, this is the realm of 'waking dreams', guided meditation and similar visualization strategies which a trained person can manipulate to suit personal interest.

At another level, it is also plausible that the ASC was 'brought on' by these four by the nagging concern over Jesus' true identity raised just prior to the transfiguration ('Who do people say I am?'). Such a question would weigh heavily on the dyadic mind-sets of people who live in group-centered rather than individualistic cultures. A trance ASC like the transfiguration account would bring enlightenment and relief.

5 Arousal

In all accounts Jesus seems to experience heightened arousal reflected in the change of facial appearance (Matthew and Luke) and glistening garments (all three). This sounds similar to the contemporary experience of a person's 'aura'. Some people believe that every person emanates an aura that is visible to those who know how to see it. The aura glistens or changes colours as that person becomes stimulated or aroused. This phenomenon occurs, for example, when a member of an audience resonates very positively with a speaker and the message being delivered. It happens even if others, including those involved, do not see it.

The disciples similarly experience heightened arousal in all three accounts: joy ('it is well that we are here') followed by extreme fear.

6 Calm

In Luke's account, the disciples are presumably calm during their sleep. It is possible that Jesus experiences calm in prayer (Luke).

7 Sense of self, or identity

In Walsh's model, this question seeks to discover whether someone in ecstatic vision loses self-identity, takes up an 'out of the body' posture or becomes enveloped in the ALL or something similar. That is not true in the transfiguration story. Rather, Jesus' distinctive identity is clearly spelled out by the voice from the cloud: 'My beloved or chosen son'. He is not to be confused with Moses or Elijah, or the Baptist or any of the prophets. He deserves full attention and obedience ('listen to him').

8 Affect

Was the experience pleasurable or painful? The three accounts indicate that the experience was pleasurable for all involved, even if partially frightening for the disciples. Yet these are normal patterns of reaction (Walsh 1993: 785). People often confront frightening experiences, only to find them followed by pleasant, ecstatic and blissful sensations.

9 Content of the experience

Is the content formless or with form? The content of the transfiguration experience does not seem to be formless, that is, an experience of undifferentiated light, colour, sound etc. On the contrary, the content has differentiated form: people (Moses and Elijah and Jesus), discussions, gleaming garments etc. The ecstatic vision as reported in the Synoptics is well organized. The modality of the predominant objects (Jesus, two men/Moses + Elijah, cloud, voice from cloud) is mixed: that is, there are somatic, visual and auditory dimensions to this ASC. The objects appear to have equal intensity (sound, colour, appearance), and the imagery of the vision is personal rather than archetypal.

In conclusion, this overall phenomenological analysis of the Synoptic transfiguration reports confirms that the etic categories of Walsh's model have sufficient breadth to encompass the emic descriptions presented by the Synoptics and the special Lukan source. What does this analysis contribute to the interpretation of the accounts?

PART THREE: INTERPRETING THE TRANSFIGURATION AS ECSTATIC VISION

People in the Mediterranean world of past and present slip readily and easily into various altered states of consciousness. They do so for a variety of reasons, a major one being the need to find an answer to a question or a resolution to a problem. The Bible is replete with examples of dreams that serve this purpose. From a Mediterranean cultural perspective, it makes plausible sense to interpret the Synoptic account of the transfiguration of Jesus as the report of altered or alternate states of consciousness experienced by Jesus and three disciples. Jesus has his vision; the three disciples have theirs. We have no way of telling what Jesus saw, or heard or said, but the changes in his appearance and his garments strongly suggest he was indeed experiencing an altered state of consciousness, and his silence in the event suggests a trance.

The Gospels report chiefly what the disciples experienced, saw and heard. They witnessed Jesus experiencing an altered state of consciousness. In their own ecstatic visions, they saw Jesus conversing with two figures from the tradition (Moses and Elijah), saw an indication of God's presence (the cloud), and heard a voice from the cloud proclaim Jesus' identity ('My beloved or chosen son') and issue a command ('Listen to him').

What function does this ecstatic vision perform for Jesus? It is a key vehicle of revelation which confirms his status as beloved or chosen son and authorizes his role to proceed to Jerusalem, the cross and ultimate honourable vindication (Neyrey 1993c: 172). Surely an honourable or chosen Mediterranean son will obey the destiny determined by his father.

What function does it perform for the disciples? The ASC is also a vehicle of revelation for them that lessens confusion about Jesus' identity: not Elijah, nor Moses, nor one of the prophets, nor the Baptist, but rather chosen or beloved son. It calms them down in the face of the frightening destiny that awaits Jesus but already begins to emerge ominously in the growing number of powerful enemies made by Jesus' victories in challenge and riposte encounters.

What is the pay-off from using a social science like psychological anthropology to interpret a biblical passage like the transfiguration? The pay-off is most clear by comparison with the results of literary-critical studies. Reid concludes that the literary form of the transfiguration is a predictive angelophany. Chilton believes that the transfiguration is 'a vision-literary metamorphosis of the genre of *bat-qol*' (Chilton 1992: 641). Any Bible reader would appreciate knowing what all this means in terms of actual human experience.

Thus the immediate pay-off from using social sciences as an interpretive tool is a new awareness of the need to pay close attention to the social system that gives all language meaning. This should precede any literary analysis. For instance, claiming that Luke avoided the word *metamorphoo* because of its association with pagan myths is less persuasive in the light of the cultural and psychological anthropological background presented in this essay (e.g. Plummer 1903: 251). Or claiming that *doxa* in Luke 9:32 reflects an 'inner quality of Jesus' (Fitzmyer 1981: 799) is in patent contradiction with the meaning of honour and shame as core, Mediterranean cultural values that are public by definition. The people who populate the pages of the New Testament were more deeply embedded in their culture than modern interpreters recognize (Pilch 1991).

In summary, the social sciences reduce the number of plausible interpretations of texts like the transfiguration, but the choices that remain have a high degree of Mediterranean cultural plausibility and would make good sense to illiterate peasants who constituted 90 per cent of population of first-century Palestine. The ASC is undoubtedly an epiphany or theophany for Jesus and his select companions, even if these words are not used. For people who have no control over their lives and who believe that God alone is in charge of life, ASCs like ecstatic visions are as essential to well being as aspirin or Tylenol are to modern Westerners.

3

THE EVIL EYE IN THE NEW TESTAMENT

J. Duncan M. Derrett

THE EVIL EYE AS A CAUSE OF ILLNESS IN THE NEW TESTAMENT

George P. Murdock summarizes a quantity of anthropological data on the causes which pre-scientific peoples have attributed to illness, and he attempts to account for the major causes so imagined (Murdock 1980).[1] It is known that the perception and diagnosis of illness differs even in Western Europe from territory to territory (Payer 1990). To Murdock it was clear that witchcraft and the Evil Eye were recognized as the prime cause of illness in Babylonia (Murdock 1980: 38, 58, 62) and that the latter was and is a witchcraft technique in the circum-Mediterranean region (Murdock 1980: 40). Not rare elsewhere, this technique for causing illness in others is significantly perceived in the very region to which our New Testament authors belonged. The Evil Eye is attested in 88 per cent of the societies of the region, but witchcraft is outranked by spirit aggression, which rates as important in 96 per cent of the constituent societies, the imaginary supernatural aggressors being major deities and gods (Murdock 1980: 49; cf. Derrett 1985: 99–103, Gerasenes/Girgashites). Spirit aggression figures even more largely in East Asia (Murdock 1980: 51, Table 3). Mystical retribution as a cause of illness, if found in the Mediterranean region (Murdock 1980: 52, 90), is proportionately less well represented there than in North America, where the native societies provide the largest number of instances.

Murdock does not examine ancient Jewish sources exhaustively, nor does he use the New Testament as an anthropological source. Since the New Testament authors knew that Greek was understood from Spain and North Africa in the West to the eastern extremities of Afghanistan, to the Oxus and north-western India in one direction and to Ceylon in another, we can be sure they expected their own style and its implications to be grasped by the most diverse social groups, manifesting the widest variety of theories of illness. They were as well informed as Murdock.

There is no reason to surmise that Mediterranean societies have undergone fundamental changes, removing or replacing superstitions within the relatively short interval of two millennia. The ubiquity of the superstition of the Evil Eye from Italy to Istanbul is known to any traveller who has been surprised by the common wearing of amulets, and by the scowls of parents noticing that one has admired their children (see Esler 1994a: 19). That Jews were aware of the Evil Eye in ancient times is certain, and they will remain so as long as Yiddish-speaking parents say *kein ayin ra* ('let there be no Evil Eye') whenever their children are mentioned.[2] Elliott's papers provide exhaustive information on the Eye.[3]

It is strange therefore that, while there is abundant and emphatic evidence of demons as imagined causes of illness in the New Testament, an idea familiar to its presumed audience and, naturally, to Jesus himself – Jews traditionally acknowledged the damaging desires of demons and their hurtful powers (Strack and Billerbeck 1969: Exkurs 21: 501–535 at 521, 524–526; Foerster 1935: 13, 19) – there is no evidence of the Evil Eye being treated as a cause of any illness by Jesus, his disciples or other miracle-workers. A zero is an impressive numeral. The apparent conflict between Murdock and the New Testament calls for an explanation.

THE EVIL EYE IN GREECE AND ROME

The nature of the Evil Eye has been considered seriously by Plutarch, so that literary material on the phenomenon is available.[4] It is clear from anecdotal evidence, and anthropology has confirmed,[5] that the Eye has power, that it figures in relationships and motivation, and that a *look* may cause harm (Deonna 1965; Distasio 1981).[6] It need not be voluntary, and the Evil Eye may be possessed independently of the looker's intention (Dundes 1984; Rheubottom 1985: ch. 5). However, an evil intention is not excluded: one can wish to harm by a glance. The Evil Eye is a sub-category of witchcraft in that a 'specialist' uses it, even if unconsciously. Some peoples were said to have the Evil Eye, including a group of mythical magicians who interfered even with the weather, and blighted crops.[7] But not only strangers were suspected.

The Romans were clear that steps must be taken to avert the Evil Eye from whatsoever source it came. The Phallus, and indeed anything eye-catching, could be used to avert this Eye (Kee 1986: 103; Elliott 1988: 48–49), and similarly amulets were and are used to distract it. Analyzed by contemporaries, the Evil Eye demonstrated jealousy, and a person could be jealous of his own family and even of himself (so Plutarch). It was not isolated as a moral fault; rather it was seen as an invisible disability in the possessor, such as could often be inferred but was mostly secret and incapable of proof. One took general steps to avert such malign influences. There was no direct link between the jealousy (or envy) of *A* and the illness of *B*.

The Latin *fascinum* is related to Greek *baskaino*.[8] Drawing a stemma of the word-cluster *bask-*, we find that that nebula of meaning has *witchcraft* as its centre. Meanings then bifurcate into (1a) bewitch,[9] (1b) sorcery[10] and (2) be jealous, envious,[11] itself branching into (2a) malign, disparage[12] and (2b) begrudge, be miserly.[13] It is the last which we meet in Jewish use of the root *bask-*, and one wonders whether one ought to define *ᶜayin raᶜa* in Graeco-Roman terms. *Baskainomenoi* (the victims) are not defined in Jewish sources. However that may be, the Greek stemma suggests *baleful jealousy* as the emotion at its root. (So Plutarch, *Quaest. Conviv.* 5.7.681D–F, 5.7.682D.) Since the emotion of *X* can affect the welfare and balance of *Y*, jealousy, via envy, could be invested with malign power (Elliott 1992: 57–58). Amulets, or prayers, may distract envious glances (Plutarch, 681F). Are there other shields against undeserved malignity? Romans and Greeks shared these notions, as Elliott explains, but did Jews in Palestine share the whole scope of them? (Elliott 1991a: 151).[14]

Murdock's thesis is supported to the extent that the Evil Eye was generally supposed to cause evils, mishaps and illness to cattle, crops and even the more susceptible members of the family. Strangers, neighbours, even relatives, were able to envy good fortune or prosperity.[15] To the best of our knowledge no one claims to have been *cured* specifically from having been struck by the Evil Eye. And which of these ideas did Jews share?

THE EVIL EYE IN JEWISH SOCIETY

We have seen that the expression, as the fear, persists as a Jewish superstition. The term in the New Testament, *ophthalmos poneros*, 'wicked, or evil, eye', equates with the same expression found in the Septuagint, where it renders the Hebrew *ᶜayin ha-raᶜa* or *ᶜayin raᶜa*. The idea itself is well documented.[16] We cannot demonstrate that it covers the whole semantic area of *bask-* (see above), but it certainly corresponds to *bask-*(2b). Evil eye as 'hostility' is not identical with Evil Eye as 'meanness' (Elliott 1988: 57–58).[17]

The eye is thought of, not as a sense organ subordinate to the brain, but as an agent in its own right (Matt. 5:29). It manifests emotion and motive. Hence, one said, eyes have no pity (Deut. 7:16, 13:8, 15:9 – grudging; Deut. 19:13, 21; 25:12; 28:54, 56 – envy; Isa. 13:18; Ezek. 16:5; Ps. 10:8; *Test. Ben.* 4:2 – lurking malignity); one can cast desirous eyes upon a person (Gen. 39:7; Matt. 5:28; 2 Pet. 2:14; 1 John 2:16; Job 31:1; Ps. 119:37; Ezek. 23:16); an enemy sharpens his eyes upon one (Job 16:9); and, correspondingly, there are bountiful, generous and kind eyes (an *ophthalmos agathos* is bountiful: Prov. 22:9; Sir. 35:7, 9 LXX; Prov. 28:27. And capable of expressing pity: Ezek. 20:17; Is. 1:15). It was admitted that enemies rejoiced at their victims' illnesses (Ps. 41:7–8). It is no surprise that the eye conveys hatred, and should be thought to cause harm. At 1 Sam. 18:9 Saul begins to look menacingly at David (he 'eyes' him: Hebrew *ᶜoyen*, Greek *hypoblepomai*), obviously out of jealousy. At Ps. 35:19 we read of enemies wrongfully rejoicing over the psalmist, and of those that hate him without a cause 'winking with the eye'. At Babylonian Talmud, Berakot 58a, Rav Sheshet (c. 300 CE), who was blind, and had learned rabbinical tractates by heart, was annoyed by an impudent 'Sadducean', who asked impertinent questions, and so 'cast his eyes' – though sightless – 'upon him, and reduced him to a heap of bones'. Nevertheless the Evil Eye in Jewish sources is virtually a metonym for envy (Strack and Billerbeck 1969 I: 883–884; Schöttgen 1733: 67–68).[18] Envy was harmful indirectly, not directly. Amulets may combat it (Isa. 3.20; Judg. 8.21), in part.

In particular 'Evil Eye' expresses the idea of niggardliness, or meanness, in contexts where society expects, and rewards, generosity (Sir. 31:13; Prov. 23:6–7; 28:22 – miser; Sir. 14:3, 8–10; 18:18; 37:10 – miser, skinflint).[19] The whole subject of generosity (including hospitality) is ambivalent. Those who rate reciprocity highly (as Jews in ancient times did) welcome the good (i.e. generous) eye in others, provided they are not expected to imperil their own welfare. They are correspondingly hostile to an 'Evil Eye', which promises a shortfall in contributions to common causes, and to exchanges. Unlike the Evil Eye of witchcraft one can soon detect which of one's neighbours and relatives have the 'evil eye' of meanness. It is not a permanent characteristic, and can be remedied by either a change in fortune or a change in attitude. Hence the ancient moralists were not wasting their time, exalting solidarity and reciprocity by ridiculing the Evil Eye.

It is all too likely that the possessor of an Evil Eye will envy his neighbour's prosperity – but that is a secondary attribute. The primary fault is meanness, want of an open hand (Deut. 15:8, 11).[20] Such a person would have a low prestige-rating. There lies a powerful reason why he/she should exert him/herself to avoid a reputation for stinginess.

THE EVIL EYE IN THE NEW TESTAMENT

If it is true that Jesus was a typical Mediterranean peasant (Crossan 1991), that he worked with and for such, and that stories about him circulated among them and were written down for them, then he must have been aware of the Evil Eye. It was notorious in the Graeco-Roman world, itself heavily represented on the Palestinian coastline and in the Decapolis, adjacent to Galilee. Whereas demonization, in various forms and with various implications, figured dramatically in the Gospels,[21] and had probably done so in the original (oral) gospel, and whereas Jesus is seen overcoming the 'spiritual powers', and receiving their recognition and their surrender, no conflict between him and the Evil Eye, or with that department of witchcraft, is hinted at. Let us look at the very few cases where the expression itself occurs.

At Matt. 6:22–23 we hear that the eye is the 'light of the body' (Derrett 1989: 53). It is clear that, in this part of the Sermon on the Mount, Jesus is pointing out the effect of meanness, the 'Evil Eye', upon the personality of the one who has it. If one's outlook is mean no part of one can be generous (Hatch 1889: 80). Many virtuous acts, for example alms-giving, (Tob. 4:7, 16) would be precluded. It is part of a sermon in favour of the generous treatment of the fellow human being.

Again at Matt. 20:15 a workman is accused of manifesting an 'Evil Eye'. His judgement is warped, and he has no right to criticize the generosity of a third person. The circumstances were peculiar (Derrett 1977: 48–75; Elliott 1992:

57–58). An employer hired workers at various points through the working day and paid them all the same wages at the close of work. Those who had worked hardest complained at being paid the same as those who had worked least. The lesson intended by this parable seems to be that merit is not to be calculated quantitatively, or indeed calculated in natural human terms at all. Only workmen with an 'Evil Eye' (and there is nothing to suggest that any of the early workers had a 'good eye') would regard with hostility the generous employer's arbitrary decision not to reward effort proportionately. Being jealous of those who had worked least, those who manifested a grudging demeanour were disqualified from judging their employer's discretion. An economist's view of the matter would be irrelevant. That group were 'wicked' (*rasa*: Mishnah, *Avot* V. 13). Were they disloyal to God? Perhaps.[22]

We have no further information on the Evil Eye, save at Mark 7:22, where it figures as a vice analogous to fornication, greed, deceit, sensuality, cursing and pride. No doubt it was found, by experience, to co-exist with some or all of these habits. People who are mean towards others are commonly generous towards themselves: indeed they would claim that the latter positively requires the former. Thus the Evil Eye is an antisocial disposition, capable of being detected and reprehended in any individual within his own society. Its cure, if any, lies in a religious conversion, perhaps a 'rebirth'. All those vices, in the idiom of the Gospel, desecrate the individual who evinces them (Mark 7:23) (Derrett 1992: 69–78).

Thus there is nothing in the New Testament to confirm Murdock's emphatic finding that the Evil Eye is feared as a cause of illness in the circum-Mediterranean region.

THE ARGUMENT OF SILENCE

Whereas Jesus conflicts with demons, and wins, and thereby demonized persons are cured, we are told of a range of diseases which he cured, the causes of which are not mentioned, though some are *not* due to what Murdock would call 'spirit aggression' (Matt. 4:24; 14:35; Mark 1:32, 34; Luke 4:40; 6:17; 9:1; John 6:2; Acts 19:12, 28:9). We find, for example, that the cure of certain medical or psychological conditions is linked with the sufferers' faith, or with their sins being forgiven.[23] The former may be somewhat ambiguous, but the latter clearly confirms Murdock's report that mystical retribution is known, though not dominant, as a perceived cause of illness in the circum-Mediterranean area. It could well be that guilt, personal or by association, was in the first century widely accepted as a cause of illness, or was *notionally* accepted by reason of the prominence of the idea in the Hebrew scriptures (Exod. 15:26; Deut. 7:15; 28:60; 2 Chron. 21:15, 18–19; Ps. 38:3–18), which had a dominant position in Jewish culture. Where an idea was enshrined in scripture it could easily be foisted upon a Jewish community (by mimesis) as a virtual fact, whether it was known in practice or not.

Are we to infer from the New Testament's silence on the Evil Eye as a cause of illness that Murdock's information is misleading, or that the superstitions of the Levant have changed through time? Neither is likely. So fundamental a change would require some evidence, and there is none to hand. What significance shall we attribute to silence?

Let us consider the difference between demonization and the Evil Eye. Demons were thought hostile to men's and women's welfare. They made themselves felt dramatically, and could have been suspected to be present even when the symptoms did not demand such a diagnosis. On demon possession and its bizarre symptoms there is plenty of anthropological evidence, confirming continuity of ideas and practices, including exorcisms (see n. 21). Hence a healer's direct attack on a demon (as at Matt. 17:18) made, and makes, good sense.

The Evil Eye, however, being a disposition expressed in physical terms, does not masquerade as a call for exorcism, either of the possessor or his/her victim. The Jews' inclination to witchcraft is evidenced, though scripture inveighed against it, and sorcery likewise (Exod. 22:18; Deut. 18:10; 1 Sam. 15:23; 2 Chron. 33:6; Gal. 5:20; Mishnah, *Shab.* VI 10; *Sanh.* IX. 6; *Avot* II.7).[24] There is no evidence that possessors of the Evil Eye were themselves witches – but that idea is not to be ruled out *a priori.*

If any illness could be attributed to the Evil Eye it could not be cured by tracing the possessor of that eye, the envious or jealous person, or treating him/her, since proof of the connection was wanting. The only way in which such people could be reached would be by tackling the root causes of jealousy. The teaching 'Love thy neighbour as thyself' (Matt. 22:39), or, more relevantly, 'Love your enemies' (Matt. 5:44), reaches jealousy directly. As soon as one identifies with a person of whom one is, or may be, jealous, the prime cause of jealousy ceases. Solidarity and sharing offer an arena for jealousy and also for its cure.

Hence the silence of the New Testament does not falsify Murdock's findings. He raises a presumption that Jesus' contemporaries did accept that envy, manifested by meanness, could undermine prosperity and affect, invisibly, the welfare of exposed members of the community. Nothing in the New Testament denies this. It makes the teaching of loving the neighbour, and also of the dispersing of guilt through a unilateral forgiveness by the offended party, especially relevant and commendable.[25]

NOTES

1 I owe this reference to Prof. Bruce J. Malina, also sight of articles of John H. Elliott in the field.

2 Elliott 1988: 45, 50 and G. Janner, *Sunday Telegraph*, 24 Oct. 1993. Cf. the Latin *praefiscine* (Plautus, *Rudens* 2.5.4) and *praefiscini* (Petronius, *Sat.* 73.6).

3 Elliott 1988: 42–71; 1990a: 262–273; 1991a: 147–159; 1992: 52–65.

4 Plutarch, *Moralia: Quaestiones Conviviales* (Table Talk) 5. 7: 680C–683B (Loeb edn, Plutarch, *Mor.* 8). He deals with *baskanos ophthalmos*, which some 'had'. Those who

are said to harm children by looking at them are wrongly blamed, for the children themselves are the cause!

5 Johannes 1675; Jahn 1855; Story 1877; Rolfe and Ingleby 1888; Elworthy 1895; Maclagan 1902; Encyclo. Brit. 10:21–22; Seligmann 1910; Macfarlane 1985: 65. Both *epophthalmo* and *epopthalmizo* ('look upon', 'eye') imply *envy*.

6 C. Z., 'Zauberei', *Kleine Pauly*, vol. 5, 1465, lines 37–60.

7 Pliny, *Nat. Hist.* 7.16; Ovid, *Met.* 7.366; Diodorus Sic. 7.55–56 (Loeb edn, Diod. 3, 244–250); Strabo, *Geog.* 14.2.7. *Kleine Pauly* cited above, n. 6.

8 Francis Bacon notes the only affections to 'fascinate' or bewitch are Love and Envy; *Oxford Classical Dictionary*, 56a, 637b (Apollonius Rhodius, *Argon.* 4.1638ff.), 638a. K. Delling, *baskaino*, *TWNT* 1: 595–596.

9 Aristotle, *Probl.* 34, 20, 926b24. (On Dt. 28:56 see n. 13 below.) Herodian 24.4, 5. On spitting to ward this off: Theocr. 6:39; Gal. 4:14. Elliott reads too much into Gal. 3:1, 1988: 63–64; 1992: 56.

10 Wisd. 4:12; Plato, *Phaedo* 95B; Menander, *Perik.* 279/406; Strabo, 14.2.7; Philo, *Flacc.* 29; Josephus, *J. A.* 6.59; Testament of Issachar 3:3 (meaning not quite certain); Martrydom of Polycarp 17:1; Plut. *Quaest. conviv.* 5.7.682D; Gal. 3:1 (on which see n. 9 above). For the fascination of wickedness (?) see various renderings of Wisd. 4:12 (above).

11 Josephus, *Life* 425; *Against Apion* 1.72; Sir. 14:6, 8; Ignatius, *Rom.* 3:1, 7:2. G. W. H. Lampe, *Patristic Greek Lexicon*, s.v. *baskania*, p. 293b. At 4 Macc. 1:26 *baskania* is coupled with greed, vanity, competitiveness; at 2:15 (malignity/jealousy) it is coupled with love of rulers, vanity, arrogance.

12 Aristophanes, *Eq.* 103; *Pl.* 571. Strabo, 14.1.22. Plutarch, *Fab.* 26.

13 Dio Chrysostom, 78.25, 37; Philostratus, *Life of Apollonius*, 6. 12; Lucian, *Nav.* 17; *Philops.* 35. The correct translation of Deut. 28:56 is given by G. B. Caird 1968: 463 (niggardliness).

14 Elliott says, 'From Hebrew to Greek to Latin the constant associations of eye–look–hostility–envy become increasingly explicit'. But this does not tell us what *damage* the eye can do.

15 See the parable at Matt. 13:24–28, cf. 39. Bacon says envy observes no holiday. See Targum ps. Jonathan, Num. 33:55 at next note. Francis Bacon, 'On Envy', *Essays* IX, notes that envy strikes most hurtfully when the party envied is beheld in triumph; and he at once speaks of the eye.

16 See the biblical passages referred to in the next paragraph of the text (also Job 16:9). Strack and Billerbeck 1969, I: 432 on Matt. 6:22–23, and I, 833. See Mishnah, *Avot* (Aboth) II.9, 11; V.13, 19. Avot de Rabbi Nathan 40. Babylonian Talmud, B.B. 64b; B.M. 84a with many parallels. The man said the Evil Eye had no power over him, meaning (?) he could watch girls coming out of the bath without being accused of damaging them (or their keepers?) with his admiration. The Evil Eye implies jealousy (with a definite fear of inflicted harm) at Targum ps. Jon., Gen. 42:5; Exod. 33:8; Num. 33:55. The Palestinian Targum has a chance of being older than the rabbinical tale of the Dirty Old Man, the meaning of which is admittedly not certain. At any rate, Jews were aware that the Evil Eye could inflict harm. The note of Hugo Grotius in his *Annotations* on Matt. 20:15 needs correction.

17 Elliott does not make this distinction. The meaning of Evil Eye cannot be assumed (as it seems to be by Murdock) to have the same value throughout the Mediterranean area.

18 Schöttgen (1733), like John Lightfoot (1823: 150–151), saw the idea simply as 'non-generosity' in the matter of alms. Cf. Sir. 37:10.

19 This was recognized by Caird, but not in Liddell–Scott–Jones' *Greek–English Lexicon*. The gift of the one who grudges wears out the eyes, Sir. 18:18.

20 Sifre Deut. 116 (there are some who first extend their hand but then withdraw it and shut it). For the phrase: Prov. 31:20; Sir. 40:14; cf. Ps. 104:28.

21 The materials are comparable with Josephus, *J. A.* 8.48; Obeyesekere (1977).

22 See Elliott 1988: 61, although Elliott may go too far.

23 The major discussion at Mark 2:1–12. On the factor of forgiveness see Derrett 1986: 145.

24 *Avot* II.7 (more women, more sorcery) – cf. Murdock's idea (1980: 61) that polygyny helped to account for the Evil Eye. Strack and Billerbeck 1969, IV: 523–525, 532–533. For Jacob of Kefar Sama, a (?) Christian wizard, see Babylonian Talmud, *A.Z.* 27b, etc.; Urbach 1975: I, 116; II, 730.

25 Owing to his being unwell at the time, Professor's Derrett's paper was read at the Context and Kerygma Conference with his permission *in absentia* by Ms Helen-Ann Francis.

Part II

EARLY CHRISTIAN GROUP FORMATION AND MAINTENANCE

4

THE JEWISH MESSIANIC MOVEMENT

From faction to sect

John H. Elliott

INTRODUCTION

In recent decades it has become customary, in fact, fashionable, to refer to early Christianity as a 'sect'. Only occasionally, however, does one encounter any sustained attempt to explain this category, to justify its use as an analytical model for the study of early Christianity and to consider its implications from a social-scientific perspective. The sociologist Bryan Wilson, in summarizing the features typical of sects and the supportive environment they provide, has noted:

> A sect serves as a small and 'deviant' reference-group in which the individual may seek status and privilege and in terms of whose standards he may measure his own talents and accomplishments in more favourable terms than are generally available in the wider society. It alters the context of striving, puts a premium on attributes different from those counted significant in the world, and provides the reassurance of a stable, affective society whose commitment and value-structure claim divine sanction and divine permanence. Its ideological orientation and its group cohesion provide a context of emotional security so vital to the adherent that its teachings necessarily become, for him, objectively true. It is for the individual an adjustment and an accommodation, offered even at the cost of institutional maladjustment.
>
> (1961: 354)

To study the sect as a total social entity, Wilson has observed in a further study (1988: 231–232), involves providing an account of, among other items, its teachings and their provenance, the movement's origins as a separated body, the course of its development, the character and transmission of its leadership, the source of its appeal, its methods of recruitment, the nature of 'conversion', the social composition of its constituency, the maintenance of social control, its economic structure, the extent to which children are retained in the movement, its capacity to motivate and mobilize its members, the relationship of ideology to organization, the movement's social ethos and its relation to the wider society and to other movements.

This essay represents a revised and expanded version of part of a larger paper[1] in which I have attempted to identify some of these issues as they apply to the analysis of early Christianity as a messianic Jewish sect. This larger study surveys the seminal work of Ernst Troeltsch and Max Weber, its contribution and limits; the more recent utilization of the sectarian model in exegetical examinations of early Christianity including the work of Robin Scroggs, Wayne Meeks, Philip Esler and my own analysis of 1 Peter; the exegetical use of the sectarian typology presented by Bryan Wilson in his work on pre-industrial tribal societies; and it offers a comprehensive listing of the sectarian features and strategies of early Christianity.

In the current essay I focus upon the various features of early Christianity which reflect sectarian characteristics. My aim is not only to show that the study of early Christianity as a Jewish sect is justified and profitable, but also to present material which might serve as a basis for further reflection and research.

An initial question requiring clarification is the stage at which the early Christian movement appears to adopt the features and strategies of a Jewish sect. Recent work by my colleague Bruce Malina and Norwegian scholar Torrey Seland has led me to conclude that before the Jesus movement took on the character of a Jewish sect it first operated during Jesus' lifetime as a Jewish faction still embedded within the structures and norms of its corporate body, the House of Israel. Only following the death of Jesus and under changing social conditions did this Jesus movement gradually begin to adopt the features and strategies of a Jewish sect.

Seland (1987), in an article prompted by the work of Bruce Malina, has argued that the model of the sect is an inadequate and anachronistic model for analyzing early Christianity. This is so, he claims, because the sect model, as developed by Troeltsch, assumes a symbiotic relationship between the church as a dominant institution and the sect as a movement emerging within, deviating from and opposed to the established church. Seland's rejection of Troeltsch's model of the sect and its relation to the church is certainly on target. But the fatal weakness of his critique is his apparent unawareness of the extensive modification of the sect model since the seminal work of Troeltsch, and particularly his unfamiliarity with the research of Bryan Wilson on pre-industrial, tribal communities. This work of Wilson which redirects attention away from the relation of church and sect to the relation of sect and world and the nature of a sect's 'response' to the world has provided a much more apposite model for a cross-cultural examination of the conditions, developments and strategies of early Christianity. Thus Seland's chief objection to the sect model is itself anachronistic. This is not to say, however, that Seland's study is totally without merit. For what his study has suggested to me is that distinctive phases of the Jesus movement must be taken into consideration and that in its earliest phase, during Jesus' lifetime, the Jesus movement is best analyzed as a Jewish faction interacting with other Jewish factions and coalitions.

These concepts of coalition and faction have been adopted from the research of anthropologist Jeremy Boissevain. In his study of modern Mediterranean collectivities and networks, *Friends of Friends: Networks, Manipulators and Coalitions* (1974), Boissevain defines a *coalition* as 'a temporary alliance of distinct parties for a limited purpose' (1974: 171); cf. Malina (1988b: 29): 'a collection of people within some larger, encapsulating structure consisting of distinct parties in temporary alliances for some limited purpose'. Coalitions emerge within, and distinguish themselves from, a 'corporate group'; that is, 'a corporate body with a permanent existence; a collection of people recruited on recognized principles, with common interests and rules (*norms*) fixing rights and duties of the members in relation to one another and to these interests' (Boissevain 1974: 171). Coalitions are temporary, unstable alliances formed by individuals intent on attaining certain common goals:

> The *ad hoc* nature of coalitions makes them ideally suited instruments to exploit new resources in changing situations. Coalitions may thus reflect changing circumstances, they may bring about change and, by their very nature, are constantly subject to change. They may disappear as certain goals are achieved, or they may evolve into social forms of a different structural order, such as more permanent association, often transforming their social and cultural environment in the process.
>
> (Boissevain 1974: 170)

A *faction*, in turn, is one of several types of coalitions including also cliques, gangs and action-sets (cf. Boissevain 1974: 170–205). It is 'a coalition of persons (followers) recruited personally according to structurally diverse principles by or on behalf of a person in conflict with another person(s) with whom they [the coalition members] were formerly united over honour and/or control of resources' (Boissevain 1974: 192) and/or 'truth' (Malina 1988b: 24). The distinguishing feature of the faction is its central focus on 'the person who has recruited it, who may also be described as the leader' (Boissevain 174: 192). What unites a faction is the relation of each of its members individually to the faction leader. Recruitment occurs along personal lines, involving kinship and neighbourhood links; 'sometimes some followers in their turn will also mobilize the support of members of their own networks. The links may thus range from single-stranded transactional relations, to many-stranded moral relations' (Boissevain 1974: 192).

The social relations which these categories of coalition and faction describe, Malina and Seland cogently argue, demonstrate a close fit with the New Testament data concerning the Jesus group and other rival groups of Palestinian Judaism. The nation of Israel, they show, rooted in Torah and Temple, constituted the 'corporate group' within which various Jewish coalitions and factions emerged. These coalitions were formed over against the dominant Temple aristocracy and the control it claimed and exerted over all aspects of the social, economic and cultural life of Jewish Palestine. These coalitions, such as the Herodians, Pharisees, Essenes/Qumranites, Jesus group and John the Baptist group, while constituting parts of the corporate group of Judaism and maintaining ideological allegiance to the dominant traditions and values of this society, organized in distinctive forms of temporary alliance in order to achieve specific and contrasting goals.

The groups associated with Jesus and John in particular constituted factions, person-centered coalitions. As factions, their members were recruited personally by a core leader who assumed the role of patron or broker providing access to desired goods, services or goals, such as access to healing, food, material support, acceptance and belonging, forgiveness, and the favour of God the ultimate patron and benefactor. As factions, they came into existence because of rivalry and competition with controlling elites and other Jewish coalitions and factions over honour and/or resources or access to resources, honour and the 'truth' (Malina 1988b: 25). As structurally simple and unstable entities, their duration was determined by the ability of the leader to fulfil the expectations of the members and by the degree of intensity of relations of the members to the leader and to one another. The size of these factions was limited by the personal links which the leader was able to maintain with all members of the faction. Given the central importance of Jesus and John as leaders and recruiters of their respective groups, it is more appropriate to regard these groups as factions rather than as mere moral collectivities or 'movements' or 'parties'. During the lifetime of Jesus, all conflicting Palestinian coalitions, including the Jesus faction, and even the Qumran dissenters, remained inseparable parts of and ideologically bound to the *ethnos* of Israel. Though their specific group interests, goals, strategies and ideologies vary in their rivalries with one another, they nevertheless all remained social entities within, and not separated from, the corporate body of Israel. Thanks to Malina and Seland it now appears more accurate and more productive to view diverse Palestinian Jewish groups *prior to the death of Jesus* as various types of coalitions (Herodians, Sadducees, Essenes, bandits) or factions (John the Baptist faction; Jesus faction) embedded within the social, economic and political institutions and culture of the House of Israel. For this period, the classification 'sect' does not apply and should no longer be used. For both the features of this social phenomenon and the conditions under which a sect emerges are not in evidence. It is only after the death of Jesus when there is a change in the geographical, social and cultural conditions pertaining to the Jesus faction that this faction gradually assumes the features and strategies of a Jewish sect. Of paramount importance in this shift is a gradual *dissociation* of the faction from the parent body, socially and ideologically, and its perception by the parent body, the larger society and its own members as a social entity that is related to and yet distinct from its parent body in terms of the central identifying characteristics of the House of Israel.

THE SHIFT FROM FACTION TO SECT

Following the death of Jesus, under a particular constellation of conditions, the Jesus movement ceased to be regarded by the corporate body of Judaism as a Jewish faction in social and ideological allegiance with Judaism, and in a process of differentiation and dissociation gradually began to assume the character and strategies of a Jewish sect.

The changing conditions under which this shift from Jewish faction to Jewish sect gradually occurred include the following developments.

(1) An increase in the quantity and intensity of social tension and ideological difference between the Jesus faction and the corporate body of Israel, especially over Jesus as Messiah, Torah observance, Temple allegiance and purity rules and boundaries.[2]

(2) A recruitment by the faction of groups and classes of persons previously excluded from membership in Judaism according to conventional interpretation of Torah.[3]

(3) A claim on the part of the faction that it alone, in contrast to the parent body, embodies exclusively the authentic identity of Israel and the realization of its expectations – a claim involving the expropriation of traditions and marks of identity coupled with a judgement concerning the obsolescence or termination of previously valid norms and sanctions.[4]

(4) A replacement on the part of the faction of major institutions of the parent body, such as Jesus or the community as a replacement for the Temple,[5] critique of calendar observance (Gal. 4:10) and inclusion of the 'Lord's Day' (Rev. 1:10), and a shift in the rituals of incorporation (baptism for circumcision) and solidarity (Lord's Supper for Temple worship).

(5) A view held by the faction that the parent body is distinct from itself. They constitute 'the Jews/Judaeans' (John 7:13; 9:22, 28; 19:38; 20:19) or are even included among the 'gentiles' as a term for all non-believers (1 Pet. 2:6–8, 12). Reference is made to 'their synagogues' (Matt. 4:23; 9:35; 10:17; 13:54 and Synoptic parallels) or to the 'synagogue of Satan' (Rev. 2:9; 3:9); see also the distinction between the perishable inheritance of the Jews and the imperishable inheritance of the Christians (1 Pet. 1:4) and the numerous contrasts in Hebrews (Jesus as son of God vs. angels, Joshua, Moses, High Priest, Levites; old/new covenants; city below/above etc.).

(6) A move on the part of the corporate body to differentiate and dissociate itself from the erstwhile Jewish faction with the claim that this movement is no longer representative of, or consistent with, the core values and commitments of the parent body of Israel (*Birkat ha-minim*; exclusion of the Jesus movement from synagogues: John 9:22; 12:42; 16:2).

(7) A perception on the part of the society at large that the erstwhile Jewish faction has assumed a distinctive social identity within Judaism, a perception expressed in the application of a distinctive label: *Christianoi* (Acts 11:26; 26:28; 1 Pet. 4:16).

(8) A mode of interaction between the faction and groups previously condemned by the parent body that violates previous social boundaries and norms of the House of Israel, such as physical and social contact with women, the infirm and impure, Samaritans, gentiles (Acts; Pauline mission); and disregard for restrictions on meals and table fellowship (Gal. 2).

As these conditions begin to develop and accumulate, eventually a stage of differentiation and dissociation is reached in which the erstwhile Jesus faction assumes the features and strategies of a sect within Judaism. This shift from faction to sect is marked primarily by the tendency of the Jesus faction to redefine the marks of social and cultural identity and boundaries and to be engaged in a process of social dissociation, reorganization and ideological expropriation of the identity and traditions of the parent body.

This sectarian stage of the Jesus group's development, I suggest, is implied in numerous writings of the New Testament and is accompanied by a recognizable set of typical sectarian strategies.

To pursue this thought, I shall first list some twenty-one salient features of a sect as summarized from sociological research. The correspondence of aspects of early Christianity to each feature is mentioned, along with illustrative (rather than complete) references from the New Testament and selected relevant secondary literature which takes note of these features. The New Testament references document aspects of sectarian mentality and strategy typical of much of the New Testament corpus and hopefully will stimulate more detailed analysis of particular writings in their entirety.

SALIENT SECTARIAN FEATURES AND THEIR MANIFESTATION IN VARIOUS WRITINGS OF THE NEW TESTAMENT

(1) The sect in its earliest phase emerges as a faction or coalition within a corporate body or as a minority group within a specific society.

By comparison, within Palestinian Judaism, a Jewish faction centered in Jesus of Nazareth comes into being during the reign of the Roman emperor Tiberius, Rome's puppet king Herod Antipas, and the high priesthood of Caiaphas.[6]

(2) The sect in its earliest stage as faction arises under general societal conditions of stress and tension, instability, and social change.

By comparison, in Palestine, conflicting interests of Roman colonial control, Herodian hegemony, Temple-based aristocracy and peasants had resulted in a situation of tension and instability and had occasioned the formation of rival coalitions with contrasting programmes, strategies and ideologies for perpetuating or ameliorating prevailing conditions.[7]

(3) This situation involves a protest against perceived economic and societal disparity, deprivation and repression; lack of access to goods, services, honour and status and the media of salvation; methods of political and ideological

control; issues of the teaching and interpretation of the tradition; issues of ritual observance and moral conduct.

In Palestine, the Jesus faction, like other Jewish coalitions (Qumranites; Pharisees; bandit groups) and factions (John the Baptist) mounted protest against various aspects of Roman, Herodian and Temple-aristocracy control and exploitation.[8]

Later in its spread throughout the Diaspora, the protest of the messianic faction (developing from Jewish faction to dissociating Jewish sect) shifts to protest against 'unbelievers' (including, besides gentiles, now also Jews, Pharisees – now articulators of the dominant Jewish ideology), who are *tout court* responsible for the oppression and suffering of the Messiah and his followers; protest also against contamination/pollution by alien beliefs, values and codes of behaviour which threatened the cohesion of the group and the commitment of its members.[9]

(4) The sect is critical of and rejects the view of reality taken for granted by the establishment, thereby being labelled and treated as a group deviating from fundamental societal norms and values.

In Syria–Palestine and the Diaspora, the messianic group expressed such critique and rejection and was so treated as a Jewish group deviating from both prevailing Jewish as well as pagan norms and values (messianic group vs. Temple and Torah Israel and *kosmos* (i.e. 'unbelieving society'; RSV: 'world').[10]

(5) The sect is a clearly defined community perceived by both its members and others as an identifiable social, organized entity. It is differentiated from its parent body in its voluntary and inclusive membership, organization, roles, social relations, behavioural norms, cardinal values and ideology.

In the Diaspora, the Jewish messianic sect which first identified itself as 'the Way' (Acts 9:2; 19:9, 23; 22:4, 14), an inner-Jewish group following the 'way of the Lord' (Acts 18:25–26), appears as such a clearly defined community and eventually its members, as adherents of Jesus as the Messiah/Christ, are identified by the parent body as deviants from the Mosaic Law (Acts 18:12; 20:20–21; 24:5–6; 25:8) and by gentiles with the distinctive and opprobrious label *Christianoi* (Acts 11:26; 26:28; 1 Pet. 4:16); cf. also *hairesis Nazoraion* (Acts 24:5, 14; 28:22). The messianic sect, for its part, identified itself variously as a, or the, *ekklesia (tou Theou, Christou)* (Matt. 16:16; 18:17; Acts 20:28; Rom. 16:16; 1 Cor. 1:2 and *passim*); the 'body of Christ' (1 Cor. 6, 12 etc.); the 'household of faith' (Gal. 6:10), 'household of God' (1 Pet. 2:5; 4:17); the 'Israel of God' (Gal. 6:16) etc.[11]

(6) The sect develops as a voluntary association where membership is gained through personal decision, and commitment to the values and norms of the community.

Admission to the messianic sect likewise occurs through voluntary repentance, confession of faith and baptismal conversion.[12]

(7) The sect is open to adherents from all sectors of the society, but is particularly attractive to the deprived (relatively and absolutely) and dissatisfied, the socially depressed, marginated and out-groups.

Admission to the messianic sect, in contrast to the Jewish parent body, is also open to all classes, genders and strata, including the marginated and gentiles.[13]

(8) The sect offers social acceptance and material support within the community; improved access to material and social resources, safety, security, stability, personal and social empowerment; escape from shameful conditions; a supportive environment within which one can survive with honour and can experience some degree of coincidence between aspirations and experience.

The messianic sect similarly offered such hope of social and divine acceptance, support and love through incorporation in the brotherhood of faith, the household of faith, the family of God, the *ekklesia* of God (Christ).[14]

(9) The sect promotes equity or is egalitarian in its orientation.

The messianic sect, in contrast to its Jewish parent body stratifed along purity lines, is egalitarian (so Scroggs) or seeks to establish equity (so Meeks) or generalized reciprocity (so Elliott) among its members as typical of family relations, claiming undiscriminated access to God and equal reception of the divine Spirit.[15]

(10) The sect conceives of itself as an elect, gathered remnant of the parent body, possessing special enlightenment.

The messianic sect likewise identified itself – over against the parent body of Judaism – as the faithful 'remnant chosen by grace' (Rom. 11:5), the 'Israel of God' (Gal. 6:16), the elect and holy covenant people of God (1 Pet. 2:4–10), called into existence by God, and enjoying God's special revelation, favour and spiritual endowment, appropriating to itself the honour and epithets of the parent body.[16]

(11) The sect requires of its members termination of and separation from previous associations and loyalties; it insists on exclusive allegiance and total commitment.

Membership in the messianic sect through faith, repentance and conversion likewise required termination of previous alliances and allegiances, separation from evil and the 'world' (unbelieving society), resistance to outsider influences and pressures to conform to non-Christian standards and values, maintenance of its purity and exclusive faith in Jesus Christ, fear of God and love of the brotherhood.[17]

(12) The sect develops and seeks to maintain a distinctive and coherent pattern of values, belief and behaviour.

The messianic sect appropriated, combined and modified the cultural (religious) and ethical traditions of its parent body and of Greece and Rome in conformity with its distinctive kerygma of the unique Lordship of Jesus Christ, his death and resurrection.[18]

(13) The sect develops distinctive rituals of inclusion, association and communal identity reinforcement.

The messianic sect, in contrast to its parent body, substituted baptism (replacing circumcision) as the ritual of admission and incorporation, and the

Lord's Supper (replacing Temple worship) as the chief ritual of association and solidarity.[19]

(14) The sect is small in size (relative to the parent body and macrosociety) and political influence, thereby permitting only a minimal range of diversity of conduct while simultaneously being vulnerable to external pressure for conformity.

The messianic sect likewise constituted in its early development a small movement (in contrast to the size of Judaism, its parent body) spread over a wide area of the Mediterranean world. Its small size and negligible political influence made it vulnerable to extinction as a result of external pressure for conformity as well as of manifold internal diversity and division.[20]

(15) The sect insists on personal perfection and integrity as the expected standard of aspiration, in whatever terms this is judged.

In the messianic sect also, the expectation of personal perfection/integrity is linked with purity, wholeness and imitation of the perfection and holiness of God or Jesus.[21]

(16) The sect expels from its midst those who contravene doctrinal, moral or organizational precepts.

In the messianic sect, expulsion (excommunication) resulted from violation of God's will and the standards of purity, from false teaching and from disrupting the unity of the community.[22]

(17) The sect must maintain its social cohesion and the emotional commitment of its members, especially under conditions of hostile external pressures and internal conflict.

In the face of internal ethnic and social diversity and external hostility, the messianic sect was required to develop a variety of strategies and rationales for securing the solidarity of the community and the commitment of its members.[23]

(18) The sect is an ideological unit with a specific ideology involving extraordinary legitimation and warrant for its contested structure of values and its contested system of beliefs and codes of behaviour.

The messianic sect also utilized various theological claims to provide divine warrant for its patterns of values, beliefs and behaviour, including assurance of divine favour, election, sanctification; realization of divine promises and eschatological fulfilment; illumination by and endowment with the Spirit; and participation in the death and resurrection of its Lord; and the imminence of divine judgement.[24]

(19) The sect may manifest one of several types of assessments of and responses to the world, society and the human condition.

The Christian faction/sect, generally eschatological and adventist in its early orientation, under varying social and political conditions, could exhibit features of varying sectarian types, such as those of the conversionist sect ('supernaturally wrought transformation of the self', Wilson 1973: 22), the revolutionist sect (divine destruction and restoration of the social order, 23) or the introversionist sect (insulation of a separated, holy community, 23–24).[25]

(20) In its general 'response to the world', the sect seeks to insulate itself from the effects of external social change and the influence of the wider society; it seeks to reduce the need for compromise with the changing social pattern.

The Christian sect, on the whole, likewise attempted to insulate (but not isolate) itself from the pressures of the larger society by employing a concept of fictive kinship and brotherhood along with a modification of traditional codes of purity and pollution to establish a distinctive group identity, internal cohesion and clear lines of social and moral boundaries.[26]

(21) Though critical of outsider beliefs and behaviour, the sect nevertheless shares many of the values of the parent body and the macrosociety and must accommodate its ethic to the changing needs of its members and to the changing nature of the challenge of the wider society.

The Christian sect criticized conventional Jewish and pagan institutions and morality as inferior to its own, but it simultaneously adopted and adapted values, beliefs and moral standards wherever compatible with its understanding of its Christ mythos and the will of God.[27]

From the foregoing comparison of typical sectarian features with the portrait of the Jesus movement in the New Testament it thus becomes clear that the Jesus faction, after the death of its leader and as a consequence of its conflict with its parent body and the macrosociety, eventually assumed the features and strategies typical of a sect. These sectarian characteristics of the Jesus group distinguish it from other Jewish groups, coalitions and factions (Sadducees, Pharisees, Essenes and Zealots) which, whatever their peculiar features and programmes, remained incorporated within the parent body of Judaism. Accordingly, among the various Jewish groups or coalitions of the first century, it is only the messianic group centered in Jesus which is accurately classified and profitably analysed as an eventual Jewish sect.[28] This leads us to a closer examination of some of the sectarian strategies employed by early Christianity and reflected in its writings.

EARLY CHRISTIAN SECTARIAN STRATEGIES

In its sectarian phase, early Christianity employed a variety of typical sectarian strategies, both social and ideological, to establish itself and advance its goals. These included the following.[29]

(1) The establishment and promotion of group consciousness. See Sectarian Feature 5 above. Examples include:

– the reinforcement of group consciousness through terms, metaphors for communal identity: brotherhood, family of God; *ekklesia*; body of Christ; flock; vine-branches etc.); through communal assemblies and rituals; the 'we' form of communication and appeal; through personal contact via visits and communication through letters etc.

(2) The establishment and fostering of a distinctive social identity. See Sectarian Features 10–13 above. Examples include:

– promotion of a self-understanding of eliteness and superiority conferred by God: 'elect and holy people of God'; God's special people; covenant people; holy people (saints) united with their holy God; solidarity with Jesus Christ; animated by the Holy Spirit of God (NT *passim*);

– claim of embodying exclusively 'in Christ' the fulfilment and realization of ancient sacred promises, expectations and hopes (in contrast to the parent body) (Gospels; Acts; Galatians; 1 Tim. 2:5–6; Hebrews; 1 Peter; Apocalypse);

– claim of being the subject of God's reversal of social status (in contrast to a perceived inferior status in society at large); claim of new honour and dignity before God who stands over and above society (NT *passim*);

– reinterpretation/replacement of main institutions of parent body: the place of God's presence shifted from Temple to body of Jesus (John 2:13–22) or community of the faithful (1 Cor. 6:19–20); rite of initiation and incorporation shifted from circumcision to baptism (Gal. 5:2–12; Col. 2:11–14); calendar and purity rules of parent body transcended (Gal. 4:8–12; 6:15; Col. 2:20–23; faith in Christ replaces observance of the Law (Galatians; Romans).

(3) The establishment and enforcement of clear and non-porous social and ideological boundaries. See Sectarian Features 10–13, 15–18 above. Examples include:

– conceptual and ideological distinctions and demarcations within four correlated realms: the cosmological (heaven/earth); the temporal (this age/the age to come); the social (the righteous/unrighteous); and the personal (double-minded/whole);

– distinction and contrast of realms and groups through use of concepts and metaphors contrasting earth/heaven (Matt. 6:10; Phil. 3:21; Hebrews *passim*), demonic/divine (Jas. 4:7), wisdom from above (= divine)/from below (= devilish) (Jas. 3: 13–18); this age/age to come (Gal. 1:4); then/now (1 Pet. 2:10; 4:2–3); darkness/light (1 Pet. 2:9); death/life, rebirth (Rom. 6:1–5; 1 Pet. 1:3, 22); impure/pure (1 Cor. 5–6; 1 Thess. 4:1–8; Jas. 1:26–27; 4:7–8); flesh/spirit (Gal. 3:3; 5:16–26); sinners/righteous (1 Pet. 4:17–18); old nature/new nature (Col. 3:9–10); doubleminded/integral person (Jas. 1:4–8; 4:8); non-believers/believers (1 Pet. 2:4–10); inside(rs)/outside(rs) (Matt. 8:12; 22:13; 25:30; Mark 4:11; 1 Cor. 5:12, 13; Col. 4:5; 1 Thess. 4:12; 1 Tim. 3:17; 1 John 4:1; 2 John 7; Rev. 22:15); afflicters/afflicted (1 Thess. 3:3–5; 2 Thess. 1:6; 1 Pet. 3:13–16; 4:12–19);

– differentiation of Christian sectarians from 'negative reference groups' (Pharisees (as 'hypocrites'): Matt. 5–7, 23; Sadducees: Mark 12:18–27 and Synoptic parallels; Gentiles: Matt. 5:47; 6:7; 18:17; Mark 10:42–45 and Synoptic parallels; 1 Cor. 5:1; 1 Thess. 4:5; 1 Pet. 2:12; 4:3; Rev. 16:19; 18:23; 20:8; 'synagogue of Satan' (Rev. 2:9; 3:9); the 'world' (John, 1–2 John; Jas 1:17);

– insistence on termination of and separation (conversion) from previous associations, allegiances (social and religious), and way of life; explicit imperatives:

('abstain', put off, 'resist' e.g. Rom. 13:12; Eph. 4:22, 25; 6:11–13; Col. 3:8; Jas. 1:21; 4:7; 1 Pet. 2:1, 11; 4:2–4; 5:8–9). See Sectarian Features 11 and 20 above;

– criticism and vilification of the parent body and 'others', i.e. outsider, non-group members as 'hypocrites' (Matt. 6:1–18; 15:7; 23:1–36; Luke 12:56), 'snake bastards' (Matt. 23:33); 'blind leaders' (Matt. 15:14; 23:16, 24; John 9:41); inaccurate interpreters of Torah (Matt. 9:13; 12:1–8; 19:3–9; 21:16, 42; 22:29–33); 'fools' (Matt. 7:24–27; 1 Pet. 2:15); 'impious' (1 Pet. 4:18). Identification of 'impure' outsiders with Satan, Devil who is/are to be resisted (John 8:29–34; Jas. 4:7, cf. 1:26–27; 1 Pet. 5:8–9; 2 John 7); with the 'synagogue of Satan' (Rev. 2:9; 3:9; cf. 12:1–18; 20:1–10); with the impurity or darkness of the 'world' (unbelieving society) (John 1:10–11; 16:18; Jas 1:27; 1 John; 2 John);

– adoption and modification of the Jewish purity/pollution code for the demarcation of boundaries and the distinction of the socially pure and impure (1 Cor. 6:11; 18–21; 2 Cor. 6:14–7:1; 1 Thess. 4:1–8; Jas 1:27; 4:8; 1 Pet. 1:14–16; Rev. 21:8; 22:11). See Sectarian Feature 13 above.

(4) The assertion of social legitimacy and moral superiority. See Sectarian Features 10–12, 15, 18 above. Examples include:

– attribution of the cause of rupture between parent body and faction to the machinations and envy of the parent body: their leaders rejected Jesus and instigated his execution (Mark 3:6/Matt. 12:14; John 11:47–53; Passion Narratives; Acts 2:22–23; 3:12–17; 4:8–12, 27–28; 10:39; 13:27–29). They likewise opposed and persecuted Jesus' followers (Acts 3–4; 6:8–8:3; 12:1–23; 13:45–50; 14:5, 19; 16:16–40; 17:5–9; 18:5–6, 12–17; 19:8–9; 20:3; 21:11, 27–36; 22:4–5, 20, 22–24; 23:12–15; 24:1–9, 18–21; 25:2–7, 24; 26:7, 9–11, 14, 21; 28:17–20; 2 Cor. 1:3–9; 11:24; 12:10; Gal. 1:13, 23; Phil. 1:7, 13, 17; 3:6; 1 Thess. 2:1–2; 2:14; 3:4, 7; 2 Thess. 1:4–5; Jas 5:6);

– claim of the origin of the sect by divine initiative, its Messiah as sent by God, its community as sustained and legitimated by divine favour; claim of being divinely foreknown, called and elected as God's special covenant community of the endtime (Rom. 8:29–30; 1 Pet. 1:1–2, 3–12, 14–16; 2:4–10), the object of divine favour, and the recipient of special revelation (1 Cor. 2:6–10; Gal. 1:11–12, 16; 2:2; 1 Pet. 1:12, 25), of the divine Spirit (Acts *passim*; 1 Cor. 6:19–20), and of spiritual gifts/charisms, including spirit-endowed leaders) (1 Cor. 12; 1 Pet. 4:10–11);

– claim of its antiquity, with its roots in and continuity with ancient Israel; its appeal to ancient scripture and claim of its eschatological fulfilment in the sect's experience (NT *passim*) and its identity as the progeny of Abraham (Gal. 3–4; Rom. 4), and Sarah (1 Pet. 3:1–6), and its solidarity with other traditional Jewish heroes of faith (Hebrews 11);

– appropriation-cum-modification of the corporate identity, honorific epithets, and tradition of parent body and claim of now embodying that identity most fully as the 'Israel of God' (Gal. 6:16), the elect and holy covenant people of God (1 Pet. 1:14–16; 2:4–10), the faithful 'remnant' (Rom. 11:5), the 'household of faith' (Gal. 6:10) etc.;

– claim of its superiority to the ancient prophets in reception of the Christ and the gospel (Hebrews; 1 Pet. 1:10–12); claim of the obsolescence of previous covenants, sacrifices, modes of worship (Hebrews); claim of the superiority of Jesus Christ to prophets, angels, Moses, Joshua, high priest, priests, sacrifices (Hebrews);

– claim of the moral superiority of its members in contrast to the parent body and other outsiders (Matt. 5:20; Jas 1:4); 1 Pet. 1:3–5, 10–12; 2:4–10; 2:11–17; 3:15–16; 4:14–16); the 'new [and superior] creation' (Gal. 6:15; cf. 5:1–7).

– an eschatological warrant claimed for its reinterpretation of the tradition (Rom. 15:4; 1 Cor. 10:1–13).

(5) The reordering of internal social roles, relations and criteria of status. See Sectarian Features 4, 6–9, 12–13, 15, 17–18 above. Examples include:

– role and status alterations (in contrast to outsider arrangements) based on claim of divine reversal of status (exemplified in Jesus' crucifixion/resurrection, rejection by men/acceptance by God) (Matt. 19:30; 20:16 and Synoptic parallels; Luke 1:52; 1 Pet. 2:4–10, 18–25) and special favour towards the poor and powerless (Luke 1:53; Jas. 2:5); roles and relations involve subordination to the will of God (in imitation of Jesus Christ) (1 Pet. 2:18–25); mutual humility (1 Pet. 3:8; 5:5); familial reciprocities (christological modification of household codes); equity of access to the grace of God (Gal. 3:28; 1 Pet. 3:7); mutual service rather than domination as criterion of leadership (1 Pet. 4:10–11; 5:1–5).

(6) The maintenance of internal social cohesion and management of internal conflict. See Sectarian Features 13, 15–17, 20–21 above. Examples include:

– establishment and enforcement of norms and sanctions governing conduct within the community through appeal to the will of God as clarified in the teaching and experience of Jesus Christ; the use of the Decalogue, the *oikonomia* tradition, lists of virtues and vices, with the additions of christological rationale; explications of the christological, ecclesiological and moral implications of baptism (1 Cor. 1:10–16) and Lord's Supper (1 Cor. 10:14–22; 11; 14); and the providing of christological (1 Pet. 2:18–25; 3:13–22; 4:1, 12–16) and eschatological rationales (Rom. 13:11–14; 1 Cor. 10:1–11; Gal. 6:16; 1 Pet. 4:7–11) for behaviour;

– insistence on the personal and social integrity and wholeness of members (Matt. 5:48; James *passim*; see Sectarian Feature 4 above);

– stress on reciprocal forgiveness (Matt. 18:15–18); brotherly love (1 Pet. 1:22; 3:8); unity of mind and spirit (Phil. 2:1–11; 1 Pet. 3:8); building up of the community via love (1 Cor. 8:1; 10:23; 12–13); order (1 Cor. 14:40); equity (Gal. 3:28; 1 Pet. 3:7: 'co-heirs of the grace of life'); mutual respect (1 Cor. 7:4); mutual service (1 Pet. 4:10–11); mutual humility (1 Pet. 3:8; 5:5); mutual subordination (1 Pet. 5:5); hospitality (1 Pet. 4:9; 3 John);

– stress on the divine impartial judgement of living and dead (Rom. 14:10–23; 1 Cor. 4:5; 1 Pet. 1:17; 4:6, 17–19);

– exclusion of violators of norms and disrupters of cohesion (Matt. 18:15–17; 1 Cor. 5:1–13).

(7) The maintenance of members' confidence and emotional commitment. See Sectarian Features 8–10, 17–18 above. Examples include:

– stress on God's benevolence, fidelity, love, mercy and providential care as the basis of trust, faith, obedience and hope (NT *passim*);

– stress on solidarity with the experience of Jesus Christ (rejection, suffering and divine vindication) (Gospels; Pauline epistles; 1 Pet. 2:18–25; 3:13–22; 4:1, 13–14) and the experience of the larger Christian brotherhood (1 Pet. 5:8–9);

– stress on the personal experience of the Spirit of God (Luke–Acts; Gal. 3:2–3; 5:25);

– stress on personal growth and maturity (Gal. 3:23–4:7; Eph. 4:1–16; 1 Pet. 1:22–23);

– stress on God's transforming and resurrecting power (1 Cor. 15:51–52; 1 Pet. 1:3–12);

– stress on imminence and impartiality of divine judgement (1 Pet. 1:17; 4:5, 7; 17–19) and divine compensation for steadfastness and fidelity (Jas 5:7–11; Revelation *passim*).

(8) The establishment and enforcement of norms and sanctions governing interaction with outsiders and society at large. See Sectarian Features 9, 11–12, 14–16, 18, 20–21 above. Examples include:

– establishment and enforcement of boundaries separating insiders/outsiders, especially through concept of purity/pollution (Jas 1:26–27; 1 Pet. 1:14–16); see Sectarian Feature 15 above;

– insulation from outsider pollution by keeping oneself separate, holy and unstained (Jas 1:26–27; 4:8; 1 Pet. 4:2–4);

– urging of good conduct towards outsiders to gain their respect, silence their slander, and possibly win their adherence (1 Thess. 4:11–12; Col. 4:5; 1 Pet. 2:12, 15; 3:1–2);

– in situations of tension and conflict, turning adversity into assets, e.g. finding a positive meaning to suffering; accentuating the impression of external hostility and conflict as a motivation for increased external resistance and internal social cohesion (Mark 13 and Synoptic parallels; Pauline letters; 1 Peter); acceptance of the opprobious label imposed by pagans, *Christianoi* (lit. 'Christ-lackeys', Acts 11:26; 26:28; 1 Pet. 4:16) as badge of honour of those suffering in Christ's name (1 Pet. 4:12–16; cf. suffering because of the 'name' of Christ, Mark 13:13/Matt. 24:9/Luke 21:17; Matt. 10:22; Luke 21:12; Acts 9:16, 21:13).

(9) Provision of a plausible, coherent worldview/symbolic universe integrating values, goals, norms, patterns of belief and behaviour and supplying ultimate (divine) legitimation for the sect's self-understanding, interests, programme and strategies. See Sectarian Features 4–13, 15–21.

A coherent symbolic universe, as developed in the Jesus movement, involved an attempted integration of views of space and time (cosmology, eschatology), a doctrine of God, of humanity and the human condition, of evil, of salvation, of the messianic saviour, and of renewed human community, its self-understanding, morality and relation to the world (natural and social). In the literature of the messianic sect the following well-known features of this symbolic universe may be noted:

Cosmology: a universe under the sway of demonic powers vanquished by Jesus' death and resurrection;

Eschatology: approach of the end of the age, appearance of the Messiah, fulfilment of expectations, imminence of divine judgement;

Human condition: alienated from Creator God and under the control of demonic, satanic forces;

Evil: alienation from God, creatures and created order; transgression of the Creator's will;

Salvation: liberation from demonic control and reunification with Creator God through the death and resurrection of Jesus the Messiah; transformation of society;

Human community: humans reconciled with God and one another in covenantal community in Christ through divine action and response of trust and faith active in love;

Morality: maintaining exclusive union with God, Jesus Christ and one another through trust, fidelity, mutual respect and love and remaining unpolluted by unregenerated society;

Relation to society: defensive protection of its holiness and wholeness coupled with an external mission anticipating personal and social transformation wrought ultimately by God.

In this worldview, eschatological and apocalyptic beliefs served conceptual, social and ideological functions in demarcating incompatible realms of reality; providing warrant for social boundaries, the maintenance of internal cohesion, and innovations in teaching and norms deviant from that of the parent body and society at large; legimitating leadership; and in providing sanctions for normative behaviour within the sect and resistance to disruptive pressures from without (Meeks 1983a).

CONCLUSIONS

In first-century Palestine, in a period of social and political conflict and instability with various forces vying for control and allegiance, conflicting perceptions, experiences and assessments of prevailing conditions led to the formation of rival coalitions and factions protesting current power arrangements and seeking improved access to scarce goods and resources. Among these rival coalitions was the Jesus faction which, though initially weakened by the execution of its leader, later reconstituted itself as a group-centered faction within Palestinian Judaism. Over time, however, its protest, programme, strategies and ideology came to be perceived as sufficiently deviant from and dangerous to the House of Israel, its central institutions and its ruling class so as to warrant censure, punishment and eventually exclusion. As a deviant movement at odds with and censured by the corporate body of Judaism, the Jesus faction gradually dissociated from the parent body first ideologically and then socially and gradually assumed the attitudes and actions of a sect, an erstwhile Jewish movement which because of its inclusion of gentiles had deviated from Jewish norms and violated Jewish social boundaries to such an extent that it could no longer be regarded as merely another Jewish faction.

In this conflict with its Jewish parent body, the Jesus faction adopted the strategies and ideology of a sect, claiming to embody in superior fashion the identity and dignity of covenantal Israel. It sought to provide, apart from its parent body, an exclusive and all-embracing environment for its members. In this social environment, persons of all classes, race and gender were offered acceptance, communal support, enhancement of honour, equal dignity before God and the certainty of salvation in return for their unswerving trust in God, adherence to the norms and traditions of the sect which envisioned itself as the elect and holy people of God and their steadfast commitment to God, Jesus Christ and the brotherhood of faith. An inclusive policy of membership was accompanied by an exclusive intolerance to polluting influence from outside society including Jews and gentiles. Steadfastness in commitment, even in the face of suffering due to external hostility and internal tension or division, would be evidence of solidarity with the suffering of the vindicated Christ and would be rewarded by God who was soon to judge the living and the dead and transform the world. In the sect, its adherents were offered both a place of social belonging and a plausible and coherent symbolic universe integrating experience and aspiration.

Thus the Jesus movement assumed different social forms and strategies at different stages of its development and social interaction. From its inception as a Jewish faction it assumed after the death of its leader the features, strategies and ideology of a Jewish sect in conflict with its parent body over fundamental issues concerning the identity, boundaries, norms and projects of the eschatological people of God and its role in the world. Although within the Hellenistic society of the Roman imperium it may have been viewed as another novel Oriental cult, the movement consistently regarded itself as the culmination of ancient Israelite promises and hopes and maintained its roots in the history, sacred traditions and self-understanding of Israel. Accordingly, in the terminology of the social sciences, it is best conceived and studied as a Jewish faction which in the course of time assumed the features and strategies of a Jewish sect.

A close social-scientific scrutiny of early Christianity as first a Jewish faction and then a Jewish sect is yet in its initial phase. But this social-scientific perspective on the factional and sectarian features of early Christianity has already yielded fruitful results unattainable through conventional analysis.

First, in general an advance has been made in sharpening the perspectives and the categories necessary for examining emerging Christianity as a social phenomenon. This includes both synchronic and diachronic perspectives; that is, the conditions, relations and strategies relevant to each phase of its formation and those factors also relevant to its development and modification over time.

Second, tested models from cross-cultural research – the faction and the sect (as refined above to meet the criticisms of Seland (1987) and Holmberg (1990: 108–117) – have provided useful heuristic tools for conceptualizing the specific and varying forms of the messianic movement in its early stages of development and for indicating factors requiring detailed analysis. These factors include the varying social, economic, political and cultural conditions bearing on the emergence of the messianic faction and its transformation from faction to sect; the particular issues under contention and the contending parties (dominant groups, factions) involved; the differing interests, strategies and ideologies of contending parties; the changes in the interests, organization, strategy and ideology of the messianic group as it developed from faction to sect; and the impact these changes had, in turn, on the interaction of the Christian faction/sect with both its erstwhile parent body and the larger society.

Attention to this constellation of factors provides precision in the analysis of formative Christianity as a developing social phenomenon in interaction with its social environment. As a heuristic device, the faction/sect model suggests what data to look for. As an explanatory mechanism, it indicates how these data are related and constitutes a more coherent picture of Christian beginnings.

Third, analysis of the Jesus group as a Jewish faction and then Jewish sect facilitates attention to its fundamentally Jewish character and orientation and to both the conceptual issues and social strategies which played a determinative role in its engagement and conflict with its Jewish counterparts. This allows the investigator to take the Jewish roots of Christianity with radical historical seriousness. Accordingly, Christianity is analyzed not as a *novum* on the stage of world history but as an offspring of the House of Israel and the result of an initially inner-Jewish struggle.

Fourth, it also has helped identify the dilemmas faced by the Jewish messianic sect in its relations with the larger Graeco-Roman society, especially as a conversionist sect intent on attracting recruits to its inclusive community while simultaneously keeping itself 'unspotted by the world', together with the strategies and ideology developed for meeting these dilemmas.

Fifth, analysis of the Jesus group as first faction and then sect has helped to envision and then explain changes which took place in its perception of and response to its environment, its self-definition and organization, and its interests, social strategies and ideology.

Finally, viewing the emergence of the Christian community through these lenses has begun to provide social scenarios according to which the early Christian literature can be more perceptively read and interpreted as expressions of factional or sectarian consciousness and purpose. As a result, a clearer sense is gained of the pragmatic dimension of these writings and of the factors determining their content, organization and rhetorical aims and strategies.

Retrospect and prospect

In sum, New Testament evidence of the social and ideological features of early Christianity indicates that within a generation of Jesus' death the Jewish messianic faction centered in Jesus of Nazareth eventually began to assume the character of a Jewish sect. Under the reigns of Augustus Caesar and Tiberius, it originated as a Jewish faction alongside other Jewish factions in Roman-controlled Palestine. It consituted not a new social phenomenon outside Judaism but an inner-Jewish faction rooted in the history, organization and traditions of the House of Israel, critical of prevailing administrative policies and cultural values incompatible with the will of God and calling for reform and renewal of commitment to the reign of God.

Following the execution of its founder and its reassessment of the meaning and social and moral implications of his death as Messiah, the faction reorganized as a group-centered messianic faction which saw in itself the eschatological and authentic embodiment of Israel and in its Messiah the mediator of an inclusive access to the holiness and power of God (salvation). Conflict with authorities of the Jewish parent body over fundamental issues of the identification of Jesus as Messiah, interpretation and observance of the Law and association with gentiles eventuated in the gradual distinction and dissociation of parent body and messianic faction and the latter's transformation into a Jewish sect. This process, as Esler (1987: 65–70) has noted, is most graphically detailed in the double volume of Luke–Acts.

In contrast to the one other coalition within Judaism which also assumed sectarian tendencies, the community at Qumran, it did not espouse a policy of vicinal isolation but rather, like the Pharisaic coalition, advocated a strategy of social, moral and ideological insulation. In contrast to the Pharisees, who eventually gained political ascendency, however, its smaller size, minimal political influence and vulnerability to the charge of moral and ideological 'deviancy', coupled with its aggressive recruitment of gentiles, worldwide 'mission' and its reordering of values, norms and social boundaries, resulted in the gradual marginalization and sectioning off of the messianic faction from the parent body and its adoption of the role and strategies of a Jewish sect.

The sectarian struggle with the parent body was intense precisely because it was a family conflict. Eventually members of this Jewish sect would be labelled pejoratively by outsiders as 'partisans of the Christ', or 'Christ-lackeys' (*Christianoi*), a label which would eventually supplant all others and preserve forever the group's Jewish origin but distinctive identity. Such is the course of the faction/sect's development suggested by the foregoing discussion.

As I indicated at the outset, the aim of this essay has been to lay the basis for a more consciously social-scientific examination of the sectarian nature and development of early Christianity. As a start in this direction, I have discussed eight features of the changing conditions fostering the development of the Jesus-oriented group from messianic faction to Jewish sect, along with twenty-one characteristics and nine selected strategies of early Christianity as a messianic sect. The textual evidence provided was illustrative, not complete. What now remains for a future agenda is further analysis of each of these areas: first, what more can and must be said about the environmental, economic, social, political and cultural conditions affecting the shift from faction to sect? Secondly, how might the inventory of sectarian features be expanded and more extensively documented so that we attain a fuller picture of the range and variation in sectarian strategies? Thirdly, further attention might be directed to specific documents, as I have done with 1 Peter, James Wilde with Mark, and Philip Esler with Luke–Acts, in order to achieve a clearer understanding of the social aims and effects of specific writings. Here is a fertile field for future doctoral dissertations!

NOTES

1 The larger paper will appear in due course in the series *Emory Studies in Early Christianity*, edited by Vernon Robbins and David Gowler.

2 For harassment/punishment by Jewish authorities, frequently in collusion with Roman authorities, see Matt. 10:17–23; 24:9; Mark 9:13 and Synoptic parallels; Luke 12:11–12; John 9:22; 12:42–43; 15:18–16:4; Acts 2:23; 3:14–15; 4:25–29; 5:17–40; 6:12–7:60; 8:1–3; 12:1–11; 13:27–29; 14:1–5, 19; 17:1–9; 18:12–17; 20:3; 21:11–14, 27; 26:32; 1 Thess. 2:14–16; 2 Thess. 1:6; *diogmos*, *thlipsis*: Mark 4:17 and Synoptic parallels, 10:30; Acts 8:1; 13:50; Rom. 8:35; 2 Cor. 12:10; 1 Thess. 2:14–16; 2 Thess. 1:4; 2 Tim. 3:11; cf. *dioko*: Matt. 5:10; Gal. 1:13; Phil. 3:6; Heb. 12:4; 13:3; Rev. 2:13 and *passim*.

3 The two main types are Samaritans and gentiles. See the NT *passim*, e.g. Matt. 28:19; Mark 13:10; Luke 2:32; 9:52 (cf. Matt. 10:5); 10:29–37; 17:11–19; 24:47; John 4:1–42; 7:35; 10:16 (?); 12:2–21; Acts 10:1–11:18; 13:46–48; 21:25; 28:28; Rom. 1:5–6; 9:24; 15:18–21; Gal. 1:16; 2:7; Eph. 2:11–3:6; Col. 1:27; 1 Thess. 1:9–10; 1 Pet. 2:12; Rev. 5:9; 7:9; etc.

4 See John 1:17, 47–49; 3:1–15; 4:23–24; 5:22–24, 39–47; 6:30–40, 57–58; 8:21–26, 31–59; 9:39–41; 10:7–13; 12:44–50; 14:6; 15:21–25; 16:3; 19:13–16; Gal. 2:14–21; 3:16, 26–29; 6:16; Hebrews *passim*; 1 Pet. 1:4, 10–12; 2:4–10); see data below on 'Strategies'.

5 See John 2:18–22 (on Johannine replacements see Brown 1979: 48–51; Brown 1966, 1970: 1.lxx–lxxv, cxliii–cxliv, 201–204; Neyrey 1988a: 131–137) 1 Cor. 6:19–20.

6 Relevant primary texts include the earliest strata of the Gospels and Josephus. The secondary literature on this point includes Malina 1986a, 1986b; Seland 1987.

7 Primary texts: the earliest strata of the Gospels; Josephus. Secondary literature: Scroggs 1975; Brown 1976; Theissen 1978; Belo 1981; Hollenbach 1983; Horsley 1987; Borg 1984; Oakman 1986, 1991: 151–179; Elliott 1986a, 1991b; Füssel 1987; Goodman 1987; Malina 1991a: 97–122; Moxnes 1988; Rohrbaugh 1991: 125–149.

8 Primary texts: the earliest Jesus traditions of the Gospels; early traditions in Acts. Secondary literature: see n. 7.

9 Relevant texts include the redactional strata of the Gospels and Acts; Pauline epistles; 2 Cor. 6:14–7:1; Hebrews; James; 1 Peter; 1–3 John; Rev. Secondary literature: Meeks 1972, 1983a, 1986a, Scroggs 1975; Belo 1981; Elliott 1981, 1991b; Rensberger 1988; Stanley 1986; Esler 1987, 1994a; Füssel 1987; Neyrey 1986, 1988a, 1988b, 1990; Malina and Neyrey 1988.

10 Primary texts: redactional material of the Gospels, e.g. Luke 4:28–30; John 9:22; 12:42; 16 (cf. the *birkath ha-minim*); John (contrasts of above/below, this world/not this

world; truth/falsehood, e.g. 8:23, 42–47; 14:17, 19, 30; 15:19; 16:8–11, 33; 17:14–19); Acts (13:50; 17:10, 17; 18:7; 19:9; 28:23–29); Pauline letters; Hebrews; Jas. 1:27; 5:6; 1 John (we/world, light/darkness); 2 John 7; Rev. Secondary literature: see n. 9.

11 Primary texts: redactional strata of Gospels and Acts; Pauline letters; Hebrews; James; 1 Peter; Apoc. See texts in n. 6. Secondary literature: Scroggs 1975; Elliott 1981; Meeks 1983a, 1986a; Esler 1987, 1994a.

12 Primary texts: Gospels; Acts; Pauline letters; Hebrews; James; 1 Peter; 1 John; Rev. Secondary literature: Scroggs 1975; Brown 1979; Elliott 1981; Meeks 1983a; Stanley 1986; Rensberger 1988.

13 Primary texts: redactional levels of the Gospels and Acts (esp. chs 10–11, 15); Pauline letters (esp. Rom. 10:12; Gal. 3:28); Col. (3:11); James; 1 Peter; Rev. See further data under n. 7. Secondary literature: Brown 1979; Elliott 1981; Meeks 1983a.

14 Primary texts: numerous throughout the NT. Secondary literature: Scroggs 1975; Elliott 1981, 1991b; Meeks 1983a, 1986a.

15 Primary texts: Matt. 23:8–12; Luke–Acts; Rom. 12:3–8; Gal. 3:28; Eph. 2:11–22; 4:11; 1 Cor. 7:4, 17–24; chs 12–13; Col. 3:11; Jas. 2:1–16; 4:13–5:6; 1 Pet. 3:7; 4:10–11. Secondary literature: Scroggs 1975; Meeks 1986a; Elliott 1991b.

16 Primary texts: these are numerous throughout the NT, e.g. Mark 13:2–27 and Synoptic parallels; Luke–Acts (community led and infused with the Spirit); John ('born of God' 1:12–13; 3:3–8; cf. 1 John 2:29–3:10; 4:7; 5:1–5, 18–20); Rom. 8:31–39; 11:5; Col. 3:12; 1 Thess. 1:4; 2 Tim. 2:10; 1 Pet. 1:1, 2:4–10; 5:13; 2 Pet. 1:10; 1 John 2:20; 2 John 1:13; Rev. 17:14. See also texts referred to in n. 8. Secondary literature: Elliott 1966, 1981; Malina 1981; Meeks 1983a, 1986a; Neyrey 1986, 1988b, 1990, 1991a.

17 Primary texts: Matt. 22:21 par; Acts 4:12; Eph. 4:17–5:20; 1 Thess. 4:1–8; Col. 3:1–17; Jas. 1:27; 4:7–8; 1 Pet. 2:17, 4:1–4; 5:8–9; 1 John; Rev. Secondary literature: Scroggs 1975; Elliott 1981, 1990b; Malina 1981; Meeks 1983a, 1986a; Stanley 1986; Neyrey 1986, 1990; Esler 1987, 1994a.

18 Primary texts: these are numerous throughout the NT. Secondary literature: Elliott 1981; Meeks 1983a, 1986a; Esler 1987; Neyrey 1990.

19 Primary texts: Matt. 28:19; Mark 16:16; Acts 2:38 and *passim*; Rom. 6:3–4; 1 Cor. 1:13–17; Gal. 3:27; Eph. 4:5; Col. 2:12; 1 Pet. 3:21; Mark 14: 22–25 and Synoptic parallels; 1 Cor. 11:17–26. Secondary literature: Meeks 1983a, 1986a; Malina 1981, 1986c; Esler 1987; Rensberger 1988; Neyrey 1990, 1991a.

20 Primary texts: Acts; 1 Cor.; James; 1 Peter; 1–3 John; 2 Peter; Jude; Rev. Secondary literature: Elliott 1981, 1986b, 1991b.

21 Primary texts: Matt. 5:48; Rom. 12:2; 2 Cor. 6:14–7:1; 1 Thess. 4:1–8; Eph. 5:1–20; Jas. 1:26–27; 4:8; 1 Pet. 1:14–16; 2:4–10; 3:1–6; 1 John (linked to imitation of God or Jesus: 1:6–7; 2:19; 2:29–3:10; 3:11–24; 4:7–12, 16–21; 5:16–18). See also the texts referred to in n. 17. Secondary literature: Elliott 1981, 1990b; Malina 1981; Meeks 1983a; Neyrey 1986, 1988b, 1990, 1991a.

22 Primary texts: Matt. 18:15–17; 1 Cor. 5:9–13; 1 Tim. 1:20; 6:3; 2 John 10–11. Secondary literature: Meeks 1983a; Neyrey 1990.

23 Primary texts: Mark 13 and Synoptic parallels; John 15, 17:11–12, 20–23; Pauline letters; Hebrews; James; 1 Pet.; 2 Pet.; 1–3 John; Jude; Rev. See also below, 'Strategies'. Secondary literature: Elliott 1981; Meeks 1983a; Esler 1987.

24 Primary texts: these are numerous throughout the NT. Also see the data referred to in nn. 16, 18 and 21 above. Secondary literature: Elliott 1981; Meeks 1983a, 1986a; Esler 1987.

25 Primary texts: conversionist: Synoptics, Acts, Pauline letters, 1 Pet., 2 Pet., Jude; introversionist: John, James, 1–3 John; revolutionist: Rev. Secondary literature: Wilde 1978; Elliott 1981, 1991b; Stanley 1986; Esler 1987, 1994a; MacDonald 1988.

26 Primary texts: these occur throughout the NT, esp. Gospels; 2 Cor. 6:14–7:1; James, 1 Pet., 1 John; Rev. Secondary literature: Elliott 1981, 1990b, 1991b; Malina 1981; Meeks 1983a, 1986a; Neyrey 1986, 1988b, 1990, 1991a; Rensberger, 1988.

27 Primary texts: these occur throughout the NT, especially parenetic sections (vices/virtues, *oikonomia* tradition etc.). Secondary literature: Elliott 1981, 1986b; Malina 1981; Balch 1986; Meeks 1983a, 1986a; Neyrey 1990, 1991a.

28 My intention here has not been to trace specific phases leading up to consolidation as a sect. For that purpose the three-phase pattern of events outlined by Kenelm Burridge (1969: 105–116; 170) in his study of millennarian movements, a process leading from an initial phase of awareness of disenfranchisement to a culminating stage of sect formation, offers a useful model.

29 Illustrative texts in addition to those cited below are provided in the material above on sectarian characteristics and therefore will not be repeated.

5

EARLY CHRISTIAN GROUPS

Using small group formation theory to explain Christian organizations

Bruce J. Malina

MODELLING SMALL GROUPS

In his recent book, *What is Social-Scientific Criticism?* John H. Elliott with his usual perspicacity provides a rather detailed chart of desiderata for the understanding and analysis of early Christian groups (Elliott 1993a: 110–121). This essay is a contribution towards filling in but a small segment of those desiderata. By group here I mean any collection of persons who come together for some purpose (see Elliott 1993a).[1]

I believe it fair to say that early Christians formed groups that were essentially small, face-to-face groups within an incipiently face-to-mace (agency controlled) society.[2] (Whether Christians were aware of belonging to a wider social entity extending beyond their small group is not my question here.) As a contribution to scenario building, my concern here is with developing a model of the formation of small groups and their development that might fit the data we have from the first generations of Christians. Although this essay touches on many different aspects of early Christian groups, the discussion of these separate topics could be subsumed under one or another of several generalizations that summarize the major ideas in contemporary, cross-cultural group study. A fundamental presupposition in social-scientific criticism of the Bible, duly outfitted with historical and cross-cultural lenses, runs: if something actually exists, then it could possibly exist (the old Scholastic bromide: *Ab esse ad posse valet illatio*). Thus generalizations about small groups deriving from empiric, cross-culturally validated contemporary models could possibly apply to group formation in the past. Some of these generalizations will seem rather obvious. They are structural-functionalist observations, based on the axiom that if things were any different, they would not be the way they are. I set out three of these generalizations that I find pertinent to an initial understanding of early Christian groups.

First generalization

To begin with, why small groups at all? My first generalization addresses this question (see Zander 1985; Ross and Staines 1972):

> Small groups emerge because some person becomes aware of a need for change and that person shares this vision with others who mutually nurture a hope of success in implementing the change in a cultural context in which group formation is expected.

Second generalization

Groups develop according to distinctive and predictable stages. This is my second generalization (see Tuckman 1965, synthesized by Moreland and Levine 1988):

> Small groups develop through the following five stages: forming, storming, norming, performing and adjourning. During forming, storming and adjourning, all group members are in the same phase of group socialization, while such is not the case for the norming and performing stages.

Third generalization

Change is the desire for social satisfaction. A motive is a person's capacity to find satisfaction in a given state of affairs and a disposition to seek that satisfaction. Motives may be self-oriented or other-oriented, group-oriented or societally oriented. Consequently, a group's sought after change may be a change within a person, between persons, within a given group or within society at large. Hence my third generalization:

> Small groups form to support and advance intrapersonal, interpersonal, intragroup or extragroup change or a combination of these.

Each of these focuses, alone or in combination, gives rise to distinctive types of groups.

A question which has occupied historians since the eighteenth century has been the reasons for the spread of Christianity. Those telling the story of early Christianity have frequently sought to describe why Christianity spread about the ancient Mediterranean. They did so and continue to do so, as a rule, with the aid of implicit models of the nature of social movements, social movement groups, group formation, conversion psychology and the like. The purpose of this presentation is to suggest a set of explicit models that might serve to clarify some aspects of early Christian group formation. I will develop the topic with reference to the three generalizations just mentioned. The first part of what follows presents a number of observations concerning why groups form at all, the second looks specifically to small group development, while the third part considers types of groups depending on their social focus.

WHY DO SMALL GROUPS FORM?

A social-scientific approach to early Christian groups, their formation and development, requires that the interpreter define the terms, models and goals of investigation as clearly as possible, and this from the outset. It is such definition that is lacking in traditional studies that invariably demonstrate a competent command of the data set (for example, see Judge 1960a, 1960b; Riches 1991; Barton 1992; and the excellent survey by Praet 1992–1993). Scholars devoted to biblical interpretation or to the history of early Christianity do not seem to have been trained in the need to define the focus of their investigation. The meanings of the main features under discussion are taken for granted. It is presumed that people intuitively know the subject of their disquisition. Recent studies of urban Christians presume everyone knows what 'urban' meant in antiquity and what it means today. Studies of early Christian morality presume everyone knows what morality means. Recent studies of early Christian communities or conversion presume that community and conversion are self-evident concepts. The simple fact that every such study describes the behaviour of collectivist selves should be sufficient to skew perceptions based on contemporary experience away from the peoples and period under investigation (see Malina 1994).

From the perspective of structure (and story), the New Testament evidences concern for two general types of groups: Jesus movement groups and Christian groups. The fact that it is these latter that are our main evidence for Jesus movement groups would lead one to expect traces of Christian group concerns in descriptions of Jesus movement groups as well. The study of the Jesus movement group and of early Christian groups is much like studying two trains moving in one direction at varying rates of speed while sitting in a third passing train that moves in the opposite direction. I say this because of the temporal confusion inherent in the Gospel documents, a confusion that is generally acknowledged in biblical studies. It is well known that the groups founded by Paul and other Christian groups as well antedate the composition of the Synoptic Gospels. In other words, the Gospel story of the early Jesus movement group mirrors a period before the foundation of early Christian groups, yet that story was set down in various forms after the foundation of those Christian groups. These are like two trains often moving past each other in either direction. And we who stand apart from the Gospel story and the Christian story have to move to get a focus on the dimensions of either story. How can we be fair in discussing both without too much distortion from the Doppler effect? Distortion there must be. In the study of early Jesus groups this distortion is generally called 'the interests of the community' that told the story. While in biblical study in general, further distortion derives from the interests of interpreters and their audiences.

Be that as it may, early Christian groups were organized at all, putting it simply, because they were useful and meaningful for the organizer as well as for those who became members, and/or for bystanders. As a result of their experience with some early Christian group, individuals who had a stake in them became concerned about the group's fate. This brings us to our first concept about why early Christian groups form at all.

All groups derive from some person who sees the need for change. Obviously not every instance of awareness of the need for change results in a group. Rather the person aware of the need for change must share this awareness with others. These others then compare existing situations, options, obstacles and the like. Should these others agree with the shared awareness after comparing alternatives, they join the group and declare its purposes to others. Hence at the bottom of every group is the sequence: aware – share – compare – declare (see Ross and Staines 1972).

The positive response of others at the compare stage points to some societal trigger state. The trigger state arouses individuals to join a group and work to maintain it. A trigger state converts a social situation into motivational material, such as some unjust act into striving for a just social order; a grievance against some authority into desire to eliminate the grievance. The existence of the Jesus movement indicates that Jesus believed a specific situation should be changed and that one person acting alone could not create that change. We are not informed of what the trigger state was, but the situation to be changed was some sort of behaviour prevailing 'in Israel'. The Synoptic tradition indicates that in this he shared the awareness of John the Baptist. Both proclaimed the need for 'getting one's life in order' and the onset of God's running Israel ('Repent for the kingdom of heaven is at hand'). Individuals joined the core group of the Jesus movement by invitation. Invitation was required to underscore the honour of those asked to join (Malina 1993a: 29–54). And since they did in fact join, they too believed some specific situation should be changed and that Jesus acting alone could not create that change.

What of Christian groups? It seems that the awareness of the need for change derived from 'experiencing the Risen Lord', that is from an altered state of consciousness experience (see Pilch 1993a and Ch. 2 above). All traditions that mention the point trace the rise of Christian groups to the experience of the Risen Lord (Matthew's edict in 28:18–20; Luke's final vision of Jesus in Acts 1:6–11; Paul's personal insistence on having seen the Risen Lord in Gal. 1:16; 1 Cor. 15:8, and his knowledge of five hundred-plus group members who saw the Risen Lord also in 1 Cor. 15:3–6). For these persons, it was an altered state of consciousness experience interpreted through a shared story of Jesus that led them to believe some specific situation should be changed. The situation here dealt with that cosmic rescue called 'salvation'. The change sought was something that would guarantee salvation. And the guarantee was accepting the group rooted in Jesus as Messiah.

At this point, I will unpack the four dimensions of my first presupposition. To repeat, the presupposition states: Small groups emerge because some person becomes aware of a need for change and that person shares this awareness with others who mutually nurture a hope of success in implementing the change in a cultural context in which group formation is expected (Zander 1985; Ross and Staines 1972). In other words, for a small group to emerge, there must be (1) conditions favourable for change; (2) along with a vision of a new situation; (3) coupled with hope relative to implementing that situation successfully; (4) and all this in a social system that has problem-solving groups. These are facilitating circumstances for the creation of any group. Since groups emerged both with the Jesus movement and with the Christian communities, obviously all four of these dimensions were present. I will consider each in turn.

Presence of change conditions

Conditions in the environment or in the behaviour of influential persons (1) were unsatisfactory or (2) offered an opportunity for favourable change. Particular conditions are taken to be unsatisfactory or suggest an opportunity for favourable change.

The formation of any group is always rooted in some person's desire for change perceived as feasible due to the presence of conditions favourable for change. A potential organizer such as Jesus in Galilee obviously realized that a situation was not what it might be and that something ought to be done about it. In the Synoptic story, it was John the Baptist who presumably suggested this realization to Jesus (clearly articulated by Matt. 3:1–4:17, presumably thanks to Mark 1:1–14; Luke 3:1–5:11 unpacks it differently). Upon John's arrest, Jesus proceeds to recruit a faction to carry out the programme suggested by John. This was a political programme premised on the need for Israelites to get their lives in order in face of God's impending takeover of the country.

On the other hand, organizers of Christian groups believed something ought to be done largely because of their experience of the Risen Jesus and what this implied for the cosmic rescue of interested persons – first in Israel then among foreigners. The strategy was not political, but of a kinship sort, hence naturing through recruitment and nurturing through group attachment and support.

Vision of new situation

A subsequent satisfactory state of affairs was conceived by organizers. A potential group organizer does not simply perceive something to be wrong, hence a potential need for change. Rather a group developer foresees how things could be improved and successfully transmits this vision to others. These better possibilities are often envisioned by one person or a few persons, and others are then invited to improve on the plan and to join its activities. Jesus' plan, rooted in John's activity, was clearly in mind as he recruited a number of core associates, but we are given details of the plan only when he sets his coalition into performing his own chosen task of proclaiming and healing (Mark 6:7–13; Matt.

10:1–11; Luke 9:1–5). In turn, those who created Christian groups believed not only that something was amiss with Israel and the cosmos, but also that something could readily be done to improve matters. Their assessment was rooted in the resurrection of Jesus. The New Testament documents portray these organizers as developing their vision of the new situation while they recruited group members as fictive kin, prior to formulating the group's charter (creed).

Hope for success

Organizers and group members believed their joint actions would succeed if they tried to achieve the proposed better state of affairs. Members join because they believe that they will achieve a satisfactory state of affairs.

The organizers' efforts will be empty unless they trust that the group's activities will create the desired end and get adherents to believe the same. The leaders of a group are responsible for building confidence in the organization. Often, they can do this best by making it possible for members to build their own faith in the group's fate (e.g. 'love the church', a strong group abstraction; e.g. 1 Corinthians 13). Jesus got his core group to successfully proclaim and heal along with him. Their successes pointed to the group's achievement potential (Mark 6:12–13). Paul's Christian groups witnessed a range of alternate states of consciousness enforcing confidence in the achievement of the group's purposes of naturing and nurturing one another (1 Corinthians 12). Participants then developed confidence in their unit by their active participation and success in realizing the group's objectives.

Cultural context

Conditions in their society encouraged persons to establish a unit and to take part in its activities. Societies must offer their members the option of group formation if groups are to be formed. Societal conditions favouring group formation are called promoters. Persons are more likely to form a group if sources of influence foster such a move or, at the least, offer little resistance to it. Given the presence of the preceding three conditions, interest in creating and joining a group tended to be greatest if the environs were stimulating, that is, if people lived in a complex society where groups were common and valued. For Galilee and Judaea of Jesus' day, the presence of Pharisee, Sadducee, Herodian, Essene and other groups point to such an environment. The circumstances affecting the formation of the Jesus movement group would be quite similar to those affecting similar action groups of a political kind (see Horsley and Hanson 1985).

Similarly, the widespread formation of philosophical schools and clubs (*collegia*) in the Hellenistic world would account for a climate favourable to Christian group formation (see Wilken 1971; Barton and Horsley 1981). The significant issues here include: frequent contact among potential members; similarity among members; personal preference for working with others rather than for working alone; more benefits available to members than otherwise; existing legal requirements for the creation of groups (e.g. the Roman *societas*); and the way of life in a given place supportive of group activity. Conflict would occur in those societies where such circumstances did not exist. Thus the situation described by Pliny the Younger was not triggered by a desire to 'persecute' Christians, but by legal requirements hostile to the creation of enduring groups. Roman history indicates that not only Christian groups encountered such hostility (see Wilken 1971).

In any event, groups develop when people in the society are willing (1) to join groups; (2) to tolerate ambiguity during the early days of a group's life; (3) to favour values in the culture that support a particular group; (4) to forgo interest in keeping things just as they are; and (5) to develop the knowledge and skill needed for being a member.

In contrast, persons who were aware of a need for change did not create a group (1) if they could not conceive of a better state of affairs (hence no vision); (2) if they did not think a group could attain such a state (hence no hope of success); (3) if people were not willing to join any group; (4) if they had no skill in being a group member; (5) if they had values opposed to those of potential members, or had no tradition that fostered formation groups (hence no cultural context). It was perhaps this lack of cultural preparedness that limited the spread of Christianity among the *pagani* of rural areas.

Group organizers must have declared a purpose for the body they organized. In order to establish a purpose, members must desire certain outcomes for their group as a whole or for participants as individuals, and they must be reasonably confident they can attain those ends. When a purpose is known, understood and accepted by many participants, this purpose serves like a word of honour guaranteeing commitment to group activity. In other words, the practical requirements of group behaviour flow from such a 'word of honour' (see Malina 1993a: 43).

There are several reasons why group organizers and members want that group to have a purpose for its activities. The purpose provides a direction for activities, and members are uncomfortable if they do not have this guide. It tells members what they ought to do and what they can expect of colleagues. It offers a criterion for evaluating whether the efforts of members are as effective as they ought to be. It is a focus for the personal commitment a member might make to that unit. It may serve, after the fact, as a rationalization for actions which members take before they have a precise aim for their efforts. It reduces participants' sense of aimlessness in their work for that unit.

For the Jesus faction, the purpose was to have Israelites get their lives in order as preparation for God's forthcoming takeover of the country. The goal was political. For Pauline groups, the prevailing purpose was salvation, cosmic rescue from the present situation. Pauline organizations were formed to attain God's rescue by enduring, persevering and waiting 'in Christ'. Paul's problem, given this purpose, was to inform people how to get 'in Christ', and how to remain 'in Christ'. This goal is characteristic of fictive kin groups.

In sum, groups are organized when some person(s) is not satisfied with a situation, has enough social standing to define the undesirable state of affairs, envisions a successful alternative, gives others hope for success, in a culture that prepares people for group roles. The envisioned better state of affairs is the group's purpose or objective.

By way of appendix, consider the following scenario. If it is a truism that an individual was more likely to join and remain a member of an early Christian group that had a purpose, what happened with the advent of Christendom? Christian group structures were now embedded in politics, with the norms of the political institution serving to channel the values of Christianity. Further, allegiance to a cosmic Christ entailed allegiance to the emperor and his representatives. If faithful imperial subjects were to become members of the empire-wide Christian group now, they must know the group's purpose. But what was its purpose now? If salvation in Christ were available to all, what would be the purpose or objective of the state religion apart from or along with such available salvation? It would seem that in the emerging circumstances, some persons grew aware of problems in a generic, imperial, political Christendom. They envisioned their solutions to these problems in terms of ascetic holiness. They nourished the hope of implementing their solution if only because their social system did indeed have groups devoted to ascetic holiness even before the advent of Christendom. These ascetic holiness groups usher in Christianity's next major phase and mark a major shift in purpose, from salvation to ascetic holiness.

STAGES OF SMALL GROUP DEVELOPMENT

The study of the internal workings of small groups looks to both changes over time in the group as a whole as well as changes in the relationship between the group and each of its members. My second presupposition looks to the changes over time within the group as a whole, that is group development. This presupposition is based on the model developed by Tuckman (1965) and further corroborated by Moreland and Levine (1988). Tuckman's model indicates that over time small groups develop through the following stages: forming, storming, norming, performing and adjourning, with verifiably predictable behaviour at each stage. Consider each of these.

Forming

The forming stage is the period when the group is put together. The faction recruited by Jesus was a group with a task to perform. The task activity of this group is articulated in the Synoptic tradition in the so-called 'mission' charge: to proclaim God's taking over the country soon, to require Israel to get its affairs in order to this end, and to heal those in need of healing. Mark indicates that group members were chosen with healing ability in tow, while Q states that Jesus bestowed this ability on his recruits. During the forming stage, group members discuss the nature of their task and how it might be performed.

Christian groups, on the other hand, were not task-oriented like the Jesus faction. Rather Christian groups were social activity groups. During the forming stage, individuals are invited by a central personage to join the group, while others seek out this central personage with a view to group affiliation. The forming stage develops group dependence.

At this stage, members of both types of groups, that is the task-oriented and the social type, are anxious and uncertain about belonging to the group. They exhibit typically cautious behaviour. Each member cautiously tries to ascertain whether the group will meet his or her needs. The behaviour of group members towards each other is tentative; commitment to the group is low.

Storming

At the storming stage, group joiners jockey for position and ease into interpersonal stances. Members of task activity groups such as the Jesus faction resist the need to work closely with one another. Conflict among members emerges, with emotions getting free expression. Christian social activity groups likewise break out in conflict, with group members arguing with each other and heaping criticism on the leader.

In both types of groups, group members become more assertive and each tries to change the group to satisfy personal needs. Resentment and hostilities erupt among group members with differing needs. Each member attempts to persuade the others to adopt group goals that will fulfil his or her needs. The behaviour of group members towards one another is assertive, and their commitment to the group is higher than it was before.

Norming

The norming stage is marked by interpersonal conflict resolution in favour of mutually agreed upon patterns of behaviour. This phase is one of exchange in task activity groups such as the Jesus faction. Everyone in the group shares ideas about how to improve the group's level of performance. In social activity groups such as Christian fictive kin groups, on the other hand, it is a phase of cohesion. Group members begin to feel more positive about their membership in their particular group.

In both cases, norming involves group members in the attempt to resolve earlier conflicts, often by negotiating clearer guidelines for group behaviour.

Performing

With the performing stage, group participants carry out the programme for which the group was assembled. Performing marks the problem-solving stage of task activity groups. Members solve their performance problems and work together productively. Social activity groups, on the other hand, move into the performing stage by role-taking. Members take social roles that make the group more rewarding to all. They work together cooperatively to achieve mutual goals.

From the evidence provided in the New Testament documents, it is clear that the Jesus faction moved into a performing stage. The sending of the seventy (-two; Luke 10:1–20) points to enlarged activity. This implies further recruitment or forming, with subsequent storming and norming to lead to greater performing.

On the other hand, there is little, if any, evidence for a performing stage in Pauline Christian groups. The problems addressed in the Pauline corpus look to storming and norming. The desiderata listed in the Pastorals concerning group leadership still look like items desired and not yet realized.

Adjourning

With adjourning, group members gradually disengage from both task activities as well as from social activities, in a way that reflects their efforts to cope with the approaching end of the group.

In the gospel story, the adjourning phase is rather abrupt, distinguished by the crucifixion of Jesus. As regards the core Jesus movement group, the post-crucifixion stories liberally attest to this phase. But with the experience of the appearance of the Risen Jesus, a feedback loop enters the process with new norming and subsequent performing, as described telescopically in the final sections of Matthew and Luke, but at length in the opening of Acts. The new norms point to a shift from political concerns to fictive kinship concerns.[3] The ritual of baptism commanded in Matthew and described in Acts points to such fictive kinship focus. The quality of these groups as fictive kin groups is further indicated by the main group ceremony, the common meal (see Esler 1987: 71–109). Thus in the development of Christianity, the adjournment of the Jesus movement group signalled by the crucifixion of Jesus loops back to renewed norming and performing for former Jesus faction members, around whom Christian fictive kin groups emerge. The trigger event for this loopback was their experience of Jesus after his death, an experience understood as the work of God, now perceived as 'He who raised Jesus from the dead' (Acts 3:15; Rom. 8:11).

I should like to note in conclusion, with Moreland and Levine (1988: 164) that 'most theories of group socialization implicitly assume that the group is in the performing stage of development'. This of course is the situation in studies of early Christian groups, whether of 'wandering charismatics' or Pauline communities! Our New Testament documents come from storming and norming situations for the most part and are studied by scholars in performing (or adjourning) phases. Furthermore, the documents are used in churches that are into performing. Obviously inattention to this state of affairs can lead to some distortion due to the Doppler effect signalled previously.

SMALL GROUP FOCUSES

Groups always have a purpose that consists in the perception of some needed and meaningful change. The required and desired change may be seen to inhere in persons, in groups or in society at large. Consequently small groups form to support and advance intrapersonal, interpersonal, extragroup or intragroup change or a combination of these. Extragroup objectives are transitive objectives, directed towards changing non-members or even society at large. Groups with extragroup objectives are also called instrumental groups. Intragroup objectives are reflexive objectives, looking to change members of the group itself. Groups with intragroup objectives are often called expressive groups. I will diagram these options, with some examples:

	extragroup	intragroup
intrapersonal	conversion appeal based on healings	advice to individuals in the group
interpersonal	Jesus movement group organization	Christian movement group organization

The group recruited by Jesus was an instrumental group, a faction with extragroup objectives. The Gospel tradition tells of the Jesus group with a mission to Israelite society as a whole, in Galilee as well as Perea and Judaea. This datum indicates that the Jesus group sought to change Israelite society as a whole. When the change envisioned by a group is societal, the change involved is a social movement. The group supporting and implementing the change is a social movement organization. I will now consider the implications of these small group processes with respect to three different types of organization: social movement, countermovement and elective.

Social movement organization: fictive polity

A consideration of social movements and social movement organizations will indicate the main difference between the Jesus movement and the Christian movement that succeeded him.

> A social movement is a set of opinions and beliefs in a population representing preferences for changing some elements of the social structure

> or reward distribution, or both, of a society. Persons who embrace the opinions and beliefs of a social movement and guide their lives accordingly form a social movement group or organization.
>
> (McCarthy and Zald 1987: 20)

The Jesus movement was a social movement; his group was a social movement organization. On the other hand, the Christian groups founded by those change agents called 'apostles' were not social movement groups since their purpose was not to change 'elements of the social structure or reward distribution, or both, of a society'. Rather Christian groups looked to the cosmic rescue of the person, i.e. the collective selves of the first-century Mediterranean world. For this reason Christian groups were most like clubs and *collegia*, equally concerned with the social well being of collective selves.

Countermovement organizations: Pharisees *et al.*

To return to the Jesus group, it is fair to say Jesus conceived and articulated a social movement in support of social change. The outcome was a Jesus movement organization. Social movements invariably stand along with countermovements, that is 'a set of opinions and beliefs in a population opposed to a social movement' (McCarthy and Zald 1987: 20). And countermovement organizations are equally part of the scenario: Pharisees, Sadducees, Herodians and the like.

Countermovements focus on stability and permanence. These are realized in organizations, in contrast to those we have been examining, whose members make a point of holding to the same purposes indefinitely. Perhaps the easiest way to insist upon such permanence is to make eligibility for membership reside in birth. In that way, prospective members can be duly socialized to fit into permanency patterns. Thus Sadducees rooted in aristocratic families, Pharisees rooted in Abrahamic pedigree and Herodians rooted in a monarchic family, clearly aim at well-guarded permanence. This is an officialdom based on birth, with religion rooted initially in kinship, then in the body politic by means of some ruling kin group.

Such groups normally underscore the value of stability and tend to establish methods that protect against attempts to change objectives. The Sadducees insist on Torah and only applicable Torah. The Pharisees allow for a growing tradition that must necessarily fit the practice of the ancients. The Herodians focus on a single set of properly rooted heirs. In all cases, we have established doctrine, ceremonies that ask participants to revere an unchanging set of beliefs, a society pledging faith to its (implicit) charter, and all with staffs that lay plans that fit respective special systems of behaviour. Each group's firmness of purpose is duly guarded by officials who train members not to doubt the aims of the organization and who punish persons who deviate from the set's objectives. Politically embedded religious bodies were particularly likely to police the behaviour of members in this way.

These groups consisted largely of individuals who felt most comfortable with things as they were. They insisted on interpretations of Torah in terms that were familiar to them. As members of the House of Israel, they would press officials to keep their aims as these have been in the past. While with Roman control a number of monarchic or priestly agencies may have disappeared, interested parties still sought to make sure that their purposes were preserved. The initial objectives were passed on to a body whose life was continuing. The disembodied purposes were thus transplanted and kept vital because Jerusalemite elites who benefited from the government's activities towards those ends pressed their representatives to maintain support for the objectives. The agencies of embedded religion were not immortal, but their purposes appear to have been.

Some objectives in organizations remained unchanged and did not emerge as a source of concern because there was no way to tell whether their group was moving towards desired ends. Does Torah observance in Sadducee or Pharisee style actually please God? Does it produce righteousness among group members? Does scribal study of Torah further Pharisee or Sadducee purity? Do these groups actually help the House of Israel by their way of life? Questions like these were hard to answer, and members could only guess whether their goals were being satisfied. Participants most often estimated that the group's objective was being satisfactorily fulfilled and ought not be changed because looking for success was (and is) more attractive than anticipating failure (Zander 1971).

Elective associations: fictive kin groups

Groups were shaped, of course, in terms of the norms of the social institutions within which they were embedded. The Jesus movement group was a type of political action group, looking to societal change by God's intervention. The Christian movement group, on the other hand, was a type of fictive kin group shaped by norms of the prevailing kinship institution. Thus Christian groups expected the 'birth' of new members and their nurture until the group's ultimate goal of salvation was realized. The institutional quality of groups is normally replicated in the places where such groups gather and/or perform their major activities. Thus regular meeting in quasi-public places and buildings points to political action groups (Jesus faction members on the road, amid crowds, in the Temple); while meeting in people's houses points to fictive kin groups (Christian groups mentioned in Acts and Paul).[4]

Simply put, Christian groups were fictive kin groups rather than social movement groups. The type of group that expresses the common values and solidarity of fictive kinship is the 'voluntary association'.[5] Contemporary US voluntary associations are 'groups seeking to promote the common interest of the membership, affiliation being noncoercive' (Pfuhl 1980: 263). It would seem then that the groups founded by Christian change agents like Paul and others were

Christian voluntary associations. However a first-century Mediterranean voluntary association would not be 'voluntary' by our standards since no one really volunteers in the Mediterranean. To differentiate first-century associations from those of today, I have called the first-century version an elective association. It was an 'elective grouping' as opposed to a natural grouping based on birth and geography.[6] Being based on the common interests typical of collective selves, the elective association would be established for the good of some other larger group (for example, one's *oikos* or *domus*) in order thereby to promote the common collective interest of the membership. Affiliation would be under pressure, hence rather coercive (see Kleijwegt 1994). Such elective associations would form fictive kin in that they presumed mutual loyalty and solidarity among persons presumed to be what they have been labelled.[7] Given the kinship labels used by Paul, for example, his would clearly be fictive kin groups. On the other hand, the social movement organization set up by Jesus was based upon loyalty and solidarity towards Jesus himself and his cause rather than among the recruits. Thus, while the Jesus faction was elective in its recruitment, it did not have the qualities typical of the fictive kin groups of the Christian movement organization.

Perhaps it would help to note some of the distinctive features of this sort of 'elective' association. In the first place, people joined only under pressure, largely in search of benefits for their primary kin group (not in search of benefits for themselves alone). Further, people joined associations because the larger society did not allow their kin group space or voice (not because society did not give them as individuals space or voice). Consider how lepers or other stigmatized persons 'voluntarily' joined together. They did so because they were not allowed in society but needed social support. Once people 'voluntarily' joined a group, interpersonal ties with central personages and the prestige afforded their kin group made it morally impossible for people to leave without great dishonour (witness Judas). While US and northern European persons can leave a team and join another with ease, in the Mediterranean once one joins, it is rather difficult to leave since the unit is the collective self not the individualistic self, and groups cannot see themselves dissolve without dishonour.

Christian associations formed expressive groups. They existed primarily to serve the needs of members: social, informational, support. As expressive groups they were not concerned with issues of the larger society and its social and political problems. They were not concerned at all to reform society, because they awaited the coming of Jesus with power. As expressive groups with intragroup focus, they were apolitical, choosing to foster any of various methods of evading group stigma. Thus they would eject deviants, help the individual to correct his or her faults or defects, adopt socially acceptable life-styles and the like.

So long as Christian associations had an intragroup focus, they formed a 'church' only when its members gathered. There were, indeed, extragroup interludes, notably during the rare and sporadic conflicts with more powerful outsiders. Such rare and sporadic conflicts with more powerful outsiders are often called 'persecutions'. Extragroup interaction produces a more abiding sense of 'church' largely because of the boundaries extragroup persons draw. In this sense, the church owes its existence to opposition, much like Pauline morality owes its norms to outsiders. Paul wishes his groups to win honour acclamations from outsiders, hence to behave at least as well as outsiders did. So too Christian individuals were to hold by their movement, which was highlighted by extragroup opposition.

CONCLUSION

Given the present state of group study in the social sciences, the study of early Christian groups is a rather daunting enterprise. By way of conclusion, I should like to mention that from the viewpoint of time or longevity, groups may be enduring or ephemeral. An enduring group has structural features that assure continuance such as membership requirements, a name, a charter and officers. An ephemeral group lacks these structural features (e.g. coalitions such as factions, gangs, action sets, task forces, crowds, discussion meetings, picnics and the like). The Jesus movement was a faction, personally recruited by Jesus for his purposes for a given time. In terms of the famous nineteenth-century apologetic question: Did Jesus intend to found a 'church'? – if his organization was a faction, then the answer can only be 'No!' In the book of Acts, Christian groups take on the qualities of enduring fictive kin groups, much like the groups described by Paul. It is there that one ought look for the founding of the church. And in the description of Acts and Paul, it was God who founded the church, not Jesus!

The Jesus group was an ephemeral social movement group. Subsequent Christian groups were not social movement groups at all, but rather Mediterranean voluntary associations. The Jesus movement group was well into the stage of performing and adjourned rather abruptly. The sporadic but enduring Christian associations (composed of Judaeans, Judaean creoles and foreigners) was largely at the forming, storming and incipient norming stages.[8] It seems that it was at the incipient norming stages that persons in several of these associations drew up their descriptions of the formation of the Jesus movement group. Perhaps a ready project flowing from the orientations offered by this essay would be to redo the story line of the Synoptics in terms of Tuckman's model of forming, storming, norming, performing and adjourning. The use of such an explicit model would be a notable improvement over the approach to which Bultmann has alerted us with his perceptive observation: 'Conjectures are easy enough' (Bultmann 1963: 161, n. 2).

NOTES

1 Perhaps the fundamental distinction that must be made in this sort of discussion is between a gathering of unrelated people and a gathering of people related in some

way. I call a gathering of unrelated people a collectivity, while a gathering of people related in some minimal way is a group. Others make the distinction otherwise. Thus Halliday notes: 'How does society differ from a group, as we conceive it here? A group is a simple structure, a set of participants among whom there are no special relations, only the simple coexistence that is implied by participation in the group. A society, on the other hand, does not consist of participants but of relations, and these relations define social roles' (Halliday 1978: 14). 'From this point of view, language is the medium through which a human being becomes a personality, in consequence of his membership of society and his occupancy of social roles' (*ibid.* 15).

2 James (1992) notes that the relations that bind communities are of three forms: face-to-face, agency-extended, disembodied-extended. The emergence of each form of relation marks a step level change over the previous mode, while the previous mode continues to exist. Face-to-face characterizes human relations until the emergence of ancient empires which serve as transition to normative agency-extended forms c. 800 CE in feudal Europe. I would call agency-extended relations face-to-mace since here the mass of persons deals with agents of those wielding power (the mace), whom they rarely, if ever, see. Finally, disembodied-extended relations characterize nation states, which emerge only about the time of the Enlightenment (see especially Anderson, B. 1983). Here relations are between individuals and disembodied wielders of power and influence, e.g. via the media; I call this face-to-space. Significantly for biblical studies, face-to-face and face-to-mace always entail communication between actual, physically present persons – prepared texts are performed by a person who recites or reads. With face-to-space, no persons are physically present in communication, e.g. television and film, books read alone, letters read alone, internet etc.

3 Those who theorize about group functions usually omit kinship-based groups, a type crucial to understanding Graeco-Roman *collegia*, guilds and Christian groups as well. For example, Parsons (1960) proposes four types of functions which groups serve: acquiring sufficient resources for that body to operate (as in a small shop) [economic based], implementing goals set by the group (as in a department within a larger organization), preserving smooth collaboration among separate parts (as in a police agency) [politics based] or supporting cultural values (as in a school or museum) [religion based]. Curiously, he has no fictive kin type groups that might nurture individuals in a family-less setting.

Katz and Kahn (1966) name four kinds of organizations: productive or economic (to provide goods), managerial or political (to coordinate resources), maintenance of the organization or society (to train students) and adaptive (to create new knowledge). Thus they list economics, politics and some religion-based organizations, but, like Parsons, no kinship-based groups.

Perrow (1961), in an analysis of large organizations, assumes that such bodies have one or more of five goals: (1) to fill the needs of society as a whole by producing goods, providing services, maintaining order or maintaining cultural values (these are the goals of basic institutions: economics, politics and religion – kinship missing); (2) to provide what the customer or consumer of an organization wants in consumer goods, business services, health care or education (this is economic based); (3) to ensure appropriate functioning of the organization itself, with an emphasis on its growth, stability, profits, control or development (this is management, a branch of economic based); (4) to describe the goods or services provided by that institution, thereby emphasizing their desirable quality, quantity, variety, style, availability or uniqueness (this is advertisement, a branch of economic based); and (5) to indicate proper procedures for the group's activities, such as political moves, community services, training of employees or responses to rules made governing agencies (again, this is politics based). Clearly, this set of categories covers the functions of many organizations. It can be relisted as follows:

(a) Groups' replications of general societal institutions: (1) to fill the needs of society as a whole by producing goods, providing services, maintaining order or maintaining cultural values;
(b) Groups with economic functions: (2) to provide what the customer or consumer of an organization wants in consumer goods, business services, health care or education (this is economic based); (3) to ensure appropriate functioning of the organization itself, with an emphasis on its growth, stability, profits, control or development (this is management, a branch of economic based); (4) to describe the goods or services provided by that institution, thereby emphasizing their desirable quality, quantity, variety, style, availability or uniqueness (this is advertisement, a branch of economic based);
(c) Groups with political functions: (5) to indicate proper procedures for the group's activities, such as political moves, community services, training of employees or responses to rules made by governing agencies.

Once more kin groups, or properly fictive or pseudo-kin groups, are absent.

4 In modern society, home surrogates in a city (such as restaurants and bars = kitchen of a house = commensality; hotels = bedrooms = coition) point to commercialized fictive kinship; business surrogates (such as downtown streets in front of stores = goods for sale = commerce) point to economic relations; while out of bounds places (railroad sidings, bridge abutments, dumps and the like) point to placeless persons.

5 I initially wished to call these Christian associations 'Christian communities'. For 'community', I would follow Pfuhl who takes a social-scientific tack and observes: 'Community refers not to a physical thing, a geographical area having a political identity and name. Rather . . . community is a psychic and social thing, a state of mind and a set of relationships' (1980: 265). Following Pfuhl, I would define community as follows: A community is a set of values, interests and relationships shared by people who are set apart or set off from others (on the basis of ethnicity, sexuality, disability, behaviour or ideology) resulting in a sense of oneness, of brotherhood and/or sisterhood, hence of pseudo or fictive kinship. However, this sort of definition only produced confusion when I shared it with colleagues. On the other hand, the type of group that expresses community and oneness is the 'voluntary association'. Hence in my model I move directly to association.

6 *Elective groupings*, on the other hand, depend upon a person's choices and result from contracts, quasi-contracts, or from competition. However such choices are almost invariably made due to social compulsion and necessity. At times such groupings are called 'voluntary' groupings, even 'voluntary associations'.' Yet Mediterraneans as a rule do not volunteer for anything outside of their natural grouping. If they had their 'druthers,' Mediterraneans would confine everything to natural groupings. Yet given the press of social circumstances and the vagaries of life, at times persons find themselves under compulsion to join groupings outside of their natural ingroups. In elective groupings, the persons involved have no sacred qualities as persons because of who they are in relationship to others. Rather, it is the posts, positions, or offices in such groupings that bear the qualities otherwise embodied by persons in natural groupings. While ingroup opinion as well as general public opinion are at work in natural groupings, in elective groupings public opinion is sovereign. Some such elective groupings in the first century would be trade guilds, municipalities (systems of villages), city-states with republican forms of government, elective

> burial organizations, Palestinian parties such as the Pharisees, Sadducees, Essenes, and the like. Perhaps the early groups of Christians likewise looked upon their groups as elective associations much like the Palestinian parties after whom they often modeled themselves.
>
> (Malina 1993a: 47)

7 Accepting persons simply on the basis of who they are is a function of commitment/solidarity, hence kinship; but accepting persons on the basis of their rank in some hierarchy is a function of power.

8 Since Christian associations as described in the New Testament never got to the performing stage, it would be quite anachronistic to describe them as sects. Further, to explain any first-century CE embedded religion in terms of church and sect typology is to explain first-century carts in terms of internal combustion vehicles or automobile typologies.

6

DEVIANCE AND APOSTASY

Some applications of deviance theory to first-century Judaism and Christianity

John M. G. Barclay

INTRODUCTION

Historians of early Christianity are concerned with the phenomenon of deviance in at least two respects. In the first place, we wish to understand the process by which, over a period of three or four generations, this originally Jewish movement was deemed to have deviated sufficiently from Jewish norms to be regarded by its parent community as a distinct social and religious entity. Secondly, we are intrigued by the ways in which the early Christian communities defined their own boundaries, a process which involved excluding those they considered to have deviated from the norms of Christian practice or belief. This double process of definition is central to the phenomenon of early Christianity: its definition as distinct from Judaism and its internal definition of its own identity. The sort of questions which intrigue us are well illustrated by the case of Paul, who was indeed a pivotal figure in the whole process: we want to know how Paul came to be regarded as an apostate by his Jewish contemporaries and how he, in turn, came to reject some adherents of his churches as 'false brothers'.

Sociologists have long been concerned with the processes by which societies define and maintain their boundaries, and special attention has also been accorded to those individuals or groups which deviate from social norms. The 'sociology of deviance' which has flourished under that name since the 1950s (and under other names before that date) might well hold some promise for research focused on the Christian movement as a deviant form of Judaism and on the definition and exclusion of deviants from the early Christian communities. It will not, of course, provide a magic wand with which to solve the many intricate problems of our subject, but we can at least inquire what light, if any, it could shed on the historical processes we struggle to understand. In recent years some attempts have indeed been made to apply deviance theory to the topic of 'the parting of the ways' between Judaism and early Christianity, notably by Anthony Saldarini (1991) and Jack Sanders (1993). My efforts in this direction will be somewhat more modest than theirs in scope and claim but I hope still fruitful in suggesting avenues for further research.[1]

THE SOCIOLOGY OF DEVIANCE: THE INTERACTIONIST PERSPECTIVE

Many kinds of sociological theory have been employed in the analysis of deviant behaviour, as theoretical approaches go in and out of fashion and as different features of the phenomenon are illuminated.[2] Without making monopolistic claims for its value, I wish here to explore the potential of what has been termed the 'interactionist' or 'societal reaction' perspective (sometimes also, rather loosely, 'labelling theory'). This perspective on deviance suddenly rose to prominence in the early 1960s and became the focus of intense interest (and controversy) through the 1960s and 1970s; the value of its contribution is now widely recognized, though (as we shall see) its limitations are also obvious. Drawing on a theoretical framework known as 'symbolic interactionism' (developed by Mead and Blumer), the interactionist perspective received its programmatic expression in Howard Becker's book *Outsiders* (1963) and fitted the mood of the 1960s so perfectly as to become the new orthodoxy in an amazingly short time.[3] The basic features of the interactionist perspective can be summarized under two headings: deviance as a social product and the consequences of labelling.

Deviance as a social product

The interactionist perspective is essentially a reaction against theories which take deviance to be a particular quality inherent in certain acts or persons; it questions whether deviance is an objectively definable entity at all. If we think we know who or what is deviant and muster quantitative statistics, interactionists insist that the definition of deviance is radically dependent on the societal reaction which behaviour evokes. To quote the now famous words of Becker:

> Social groups create deviance by making the rules whose infraction constitutes deviance, and by applying those rules to particular people and labeling them as outsiders. From this point of view, deviance is not a quality of the act the person commits, but rather a consequence of the application by others of rules and sanctions to an 'offender'. The deviant is one to whom that label has been successfully applied; deviant behavior is behavior that people so label.
>
> (Becker 1963: 9)[4]

The cutting edge of this definition is that deviance cannot be predicated of acts as such, only of acts as they receive a negative social response or reaction. The point here is not simply that in any given society norms and laws define what is or is not deviant (that is true but also trite). The point is that in actual fact societies apply their own norms differentially, selecting and stereotyping those they choose to mark as deviant, so that only some norm-breakers are actually treated as deviant. Moreover, what makes an act socially significant as deviant is not so much that it is *performed*, as that it is *reacted to* as deviant and the actor accordingly labelled. Lots of people drink heavily, but only some are labelled 'alcoholic' and what would make any individual's drinking significant as deviant in the eyes of others is as and when this reaction (and this label) is elicited. In other words, the interactionist perspective focuses not just on the act itself, but on what is made of the act socially, insisting that this social reaction radically affects the nature, social meaning and implications of the act (Schur 1971: 16). Deviance is, in this sense, the product of social interaction.

The consequences of labelling

If the deviant act becomes socially significant when it receives a social reaction, interactionists are also interested in the further consequences for the actor when he/she receives such a reaction. Of course, negative reactions can vary in degree of seriousness and not all labels are equally damaging, but interactionists note the ways in which labels generally affect the identity of those who receive them, how, for instance, one considered an 'alcoholic' often adopts a new role in society. Tracing what they have called 'deviant careers' and the grouping of those labelled into 'deviant associations', researchers following the interactionist perspective have often exposed the detrimental effects of labelling and the confirmation of deviant identity leading to what has been called 'secondary deviance'. They therefore insist that, far from being a static phenomenon, deviance is actually a complex process, in which the on-going relationship between the actor and the reacting society defines what counts as deviant.

In the limited space of this essay, I can only explore some features of this perspective and will focus solely on the first and foundational notion of deviance as a social product. It is clear, I hope, that this perspective contains a strong strand of relativism. Its interest is as much in the labellers ('Who is judging this activity to be deviant?') as in the activity so labelled. Since those who create and apply the rules vary in their judgements from one society to another, and differ within the same society at different times and in differing circumstances, 'deviance' appears to be, in an important respect, 'in the eye of the beholder'. In social-scientific parlance, it is an ascribed as much as it is an achieved status. When it analyses cases of deviance, delinquency, criminality, apostasy or the like, the interactionist perspective is always asking 'Whose definitions of deviance are operative here?' and (as a supplementary question) 'Whose interests do these definitions serve?' I am convinced that sensitivity to these questions could clarify some of the historical matters which interest us. However, first I should note some of the limitations of this approach and the criticisms which have been levelled against it. These will help us to see more precisely what we can and cannot do in utilizing this perspective in our research.[5]

Limitations of the interactionist perspective

Concerning the limitations of this approach, it is important to say at the outset that it is not intended to explain the origins or the motivations of the deviant act as such. Its focus is, as we have seen, on the reaction to the act (and the effects of that reaction), not on the originating causes of the deviation. This peculiar focus has given the impression that the interactionist perspective views the 'deviant' as merely passive, as one whose actions are simply pounced upon by arbitrary labelling authorities, as indeed 'more sinned against than sinning'. When Becker and others paraded their empathy with the 'deviants' they studied (e.g. Becker 1964: 1–6) in the radical mood of the 1960s, critics suspected them of an anti-establishment bias which sought to blame deviance on the authorities for labelling people and so driving them into crime. In fact, political bias is by no means a necessary consequence of this perspective which properly is concerned neither to excuse nor to blame: it is simply interested in how a society (or an interest group within society) selectively creates its definitions of deviance and how the social significance of an act that deviates from the norms is radically dependent on the sort of reaction which it elicits.[6]

If it does not provide an 'aetiology' of deviant acts, neither does the interactionist perspective in itself explain why societies react as they do to acts they consider 'deviant'. However, it has been allied to various forms of explanation which could shed light on this matter. Becker himself pointed to factors of political and economic power which enable certain individuals or groups to enforce their definitions of deviancy (1963: 17–18). Other sociologists have gone further in exploring the power struggles in which a threatened element in society seeks to identify and label deviants in accordance with its own interests (Lofland 1969: 13–19; Schur 1980).[7] Such analyses tie deviance theory closely to theories of social control, and even if the complexities of modern society make it exceptionally difficult to trace the influence of competing interest groups, the interactionist perspective certainly invites such an investigation of interests and power where it can be pursued.

On a parallel track, Erikson (1966) combined the interactionist perspective with elements of Durkheimian functionalism, in enquiring what functions reactions to deviance serve for society as a whole. He suggested, and sought to illustrate through a study of seventeenth-century New England, that the labelling of deviants can perform an important function in the boundary maintenance of an insecure community.[8] While his thesis (and its functionalist basis) are now considered too simplistic to be applied to modern industrialized societies, Erikson's work may be of value in suggesting avenues of enquiry concerning the simpler forms of community which we can study in early Judaism and early Christianity. In particular, his study could shed light on the situation of a simply structured community encountering serious ambiguities in its definition of norms; such ambiguities could arise in situations of novelty or transition, where norms are inconsistently applied or have become controversial, or where activities appear borderline in relation to previous precedents.[9] Here there is a good case to be made that the identification of 'deviants' can serve to give an insecure community clarity and security in its social identity. As we shall see, this has particular relevance to the social situation of early Christianity, but it may also be applicable to certain aspects of first-century Judaism.

It would be a mistake to regard the interactionist perspective as a theory operating with clear-cut definitions and testable hypotheses. It is better regarded as a 'sensitizing concept' (Schur 1971: 26, 31) which suggests an angle of enquiry, rather than a 'theory' or 'model' generating predictive hypotheses. Some of its notions can only be loosely defined (since negative social reactions can take many different forms) and it is misunderstood if it is taken to predict that labelling deviants always and inevitably sets off a 'deviant career'.[10] In certain respects, therefore, the interactionist perspective can never be established by empirical proof, and its resistance to statistical analysis has caused some frustration among sociologists who regard their subject as a natural science. However, rightly employed this perspective can enable us to ask new questions of the historical material we study: it can suggest some interesting directions in which to look, though not, of course, what we will find when we look there.

JUDAISM AND APOSTASY

It is remarkable how frequently scholars of Judaism appear to regard 'apostasy' as an objectively definable entity, as an inherent quality in certain kinds of behaviour. Discussions of our topic often work on the assumption that we all know what constitutes apostasy: it is only a matter of detecting the cases which crop up here and there in our sources. Yet 'apostasy', like other deviant labels, is essentially a matter of perspective. One may list activities in which Jews were socially assimilated to their gentile environment and thereby abandoned some aspects of their national traditions, but where such assimilation was regarded as 'apostasy' was a matter which different Jews in different locations and times could define in very different ways.[11] A Jew who was assimilated to the extent of attending a Greek school and visiting the Greek theatre might be considered by some Jews as 'apostate' but fully accepted as an observant Jew by others. Given what we know of the diversity of Jewish practice and belief, it is odd how scholars continue to regard the perspective of the Maccabean literature (for instance) as definitive for Judaism as a whole, as if all Jews contrasted 'Judaism' and 'Hellenism' along the lines of 1 and 2 Maccabees, or all regarded the acquisition of Greek citizenship as tantamount to apostasy (as does 3 Maccabees).[12] Where the author of *The Letter of Aristeas* celebrates the social integration of Hellenized Jews in the Ptolemaic court, 3 Maccabees sees only compromise, inevitably entailing idolatry. Given the divergent expressions of Judaism within Palestine before 70 CE and the varieties of Judaism in the Diaspora, we should not be surprised if we find varying definitions of 'deviants' (i.e. 'sinners', 'apostates' etc.) in our Jewish sources.[13] The interactionist perspective suggests that we should regard 'apostate' as a term defined only in relation to the party issuing the label, and what evidence we have from first-century Judaism bears out the truth of this relativistic observation.

I do not mean to suggest that Jewish communities were invariably disunited in their definition of their boundaries or that the definition of 'apostate' was always negotiated anew in each instance. During periods of stability individual Jewish communities could clearly take some definitions for granted and a certain unity of mind is sometimes perceptible both within individual communities and across geographical and temporal bounds. Philo tells us his own opinion on who has 'deserted the ancestral customs', but also indicates the viewpoint of 'the masses' in the Jewish community in Alexandria with which he is largely in accord.[14] We can also discern certain topics (e.g. engagement in 'idolatrous' worship and eating unclean food) on which there appears to have been a fair degree of unanimity across different Jewish communities in our period. Thus we need not suppose that every case of 'deviating' behaviour had to be negotiated from scratch in the community as to its 'deviant' or 'non-deviant' status. Nonetheless, norms do change over time and even where they are generally upheld and applied, exceptions can be allowed in particular circumstances. A homosexual was a 'pervert' only a generation ago, but is less frequently so labelled today, and although most Americans strongly disapprove of adultery, they are prepared to turn a blind eye in certain notable cases. Thus, as the interactionist perspective suggests, when we find a Jew labelled an 'apostate', it is always worth enquiring who is doing the defining and whose interests are involved in this definition.

The case of Tiberius Julius Alexander

Let me take one famous example of an 'apostate' and see what might be suggested by this interactionist perspective. My example is Tiberius Julius Alexander, Philo's nephew, who was born into an exceptionally wealthy Jewish family in Alexandria in c. 15 CE.[15] Alexander features as a sceptic in three philosophical treatises written by Philo, but these do not suggest that he was dissociated from the Jewish community or regarded by Philo as an apostate.[16] In his subsequent career we find Alexander prominent in Roman administration, first as *epistrategos* of the Thebaid (42 CE), then as procurator of Judaea (46–48 CE), as a high-ranking officer in the eastern army (63 CE) and then at the very top of the equestrian ladder as Roman governor of Egypt (66–69 CE). It was during this latter period that he had to suppress a Jewish uprising in Alexandria (Jos. *J. W.* 2.487–498) and in 70 CE he acted as Titus' advisor and second-in-command at the siege of Jerusalem (*J. W.* 5.45–46; 6.237–242). Thereafter he may have become prefect of the praetorian guard in Rome.

It is striking that when recording these aspects of Alexander's life in his *Jewish War* (late 70s CE) Josephus makes no comment on Alexander's Jewish standing. One can imagine what the members of the Jewish community in Alexandria thought of him when he ordered the Roman troops into their quarter, and from the perspective of the Jewish defenders of Jerusalem he was presumably a traitor and renegade, like Josephus himself (*J. W.* 3.438–442; 5.375). In fact the common fate of Alexander and Josephus as advisors of Titus in the Roman camp and their subsequent honours at Rome may have induced Josephus to omit criticism of Alexander's behaviour, though he presumably knew that his duties involved him in officiating at the worship of Egyptian and Roman deities.[17] If we had only Josephus' *War* we would have no explicit evidence that Alexander was ever regarded as an apostate. It is only in his later work, the *Jewish Antiquities*, that Josephus records that Alexander 'did not remain faithful to his ancestral customs' (*J. A.* 20.100). That was published at a date (93 CE) when Alexander was almost certainly dead. The facts of this case prompt two observations.

First, Alexander's prominent position in Roman government brought no advantage to the Jews either in Alexandria or in Judaea. But if events had turned out differently, if (for instance) he had succeeded in averting violence in Alexandria or had saved Jerusalem, would he still have been castigated as an apostate? To what extent were Jewish communities willing to tolerate compromise among their well-placed members so long as their activities worked to the benefit of Jews? One thinks of the tumultuous welcome accorded to Agrippa I in Alexandria after his enthronement as king by Gaius (38 CE), even though he was well known to be a dishonest bankrupt whose close friendship with Gaius must have involved extensive assimilation (Philo, *Flacc.* 25–30; Jos., *J. A.* 18.143–239). Agrippa could play an important role on behalf of the Jews; Alexander, as it turned out, could not.

Secondly, Josephus may have regarded Alexander as an apostate at the time he wrote the *War*, but refrained from saying so either because it would have reflected badly on himself (he was also somewhat compromised in his role during the war) or because he could not afford to alienate a man of such influence in Rome. Perhaps he named Alexander an apostate in the *Antiquities* because it was safe to do so only when Alexander was dead (Turner 1954: 63). This might suggest that charges of apostasy, which could cause offence, were made only when those who levelled them could afford to do so.

These observations on the case of Tiberius Julius Alexander are merely illustrative of the sort of questions which arise when we employ the interactionist perspective on deviance to the phenomenon of apostasy. They suggest that we have to rid ourselves of the notion that everyone knows (and everyone then knew) who was an apostate; we need to watch very carefully who was (or was not) defining and applying the label 'apostate', in what circumstances, from what perspective and in whose interests. Our observations on this particular case also suggest the power factors which could be involved in this process, in which it was easier to label the socially weak than the socially strong.

The case of Christians in the first century

Such considerations could be of benefit in investigating the processes by which Christians were edged out of Jewish communities in the course of the first century CE. As I mentioned at the beginning, Jack Sanders has made interesting use of deviance theory in this connection (1993: 129–151). Sanders' question is: 'Why did the leadership of Roman-period Judaism, normally tolerant of diversity, reject and even persecute the various manifestations of Christianity that it encountered?' (p. 129). He considers that cultural (i.e. theological) factors are insufficient to answer this question (pp. 99, 139) and looks for help from deviance theory, especially that functionalist application developed by Erikson which suggested that the identification of deviants helps to clarify and enforce the boundaries of an insecure community. Taking the early Christians to be a new outcrop of deviants whose status raised difficult questions, Sanders points to the tension-laden years in Judaea both before and after the revolt as the crucial factor in driving the threatened Jewish leadership towards identifying and punishing the Christians as deviants (pp. 136–137).

Several features of this analysis are suggestive, but it requires, I suggest, much closer definition. In the first place, it is not clear whether the 'social identity crisis' which Sanders discovers in Judaea (p. 135) was as severe in the pre-70 period as he suggests, or prevalent to any degree in those parts of the Diaspora where we can trace the growth of the Christian movement.[18] Second, it is extremely hard to discern, and impossible to generalize about, what were the issues on which Christians were considered 'deviant'. It is even difficult to see to what degree such issues were novel or ambiguous; perhaps some Christians were dismissed without much ado as 'apostates' since they had clearly flouted laws long regarded as tests of loyalty to Judaism.[19] Third, if its social identity crisis even before 70 CE caused mainstream Judaism to reject Christianity 'when it had normally accepted similar deviance' (p. 136), why did it not also reject those other 'deviant' forms of Judaism in this period? Sanders cites comparable examples of deviance as including Philo, the Essenes, John the Baptist and the Pharisaic party (pp. 86, 133), none of which was ostracized in the pre-70 era. In fact, if all of these can be regarded as 'similar' in deviance to each other and to Christianity, it appears that the notion of 'deviance' has become far too large a hammer with which to crack this rather delicate nut.

Rather than adopting any such global hypothesis, we should observe that the interactionist perspective suggests that definitions of 'deviance' could vary somewhat between different parties and interest groups in Judaism, and this could help to explain why Christians were in fact so *variously* assessed during the first century. An activity, we recall, is deviant only to the degree to which others react negatively towards it. To some Jews 'Matthean Christians' may have seemed peculiar but not apostate, while other Jews may have considered them to have crossed a crucial boundary out of Judaism. Other Jewish Christians could have evoked different reactions and their gentile Christian adherents may have been variously judged as valuable sympathizers or dangerous diluters of the faith. In fact, given the relativity which is integral to the subject of deviance and the evidence for varying Jewish definitions of sinners and apostates, it may be unhelpful to look for any single issue on which the early Christians made themselves clearly suspect to contemporary Jews. Rather, since deviance is a matter of definition and since the Christians were deviant only as and when they were reacted to as such, we should imagine there to have been a host of variations in local circumstances and a range of reactions to various kinds of Christianity. As we have seen, some of these variations were probably related to power struggles: where the Christians were politically and socially weak it was far easier to 'deviantize' them than where they had a significant power base in numerical or economic terms. Thus, while general social trends in cultural insecurity probably had some part to play in the whole process, we must be ever alert to the innumerable variables of circumstance and personnel through which the earliest Christians sometimes were and sometimes were not rejected by first-century Jews as deviant. It is unfortunate that we can trace very few actual examples of this deviantizing process. Paul is perhaps the best documented and worth considering in some detail.

The case of Paul

From the evidence of his letters it appears that Paul was continually 'endangered' by Jews (2 Cor. 11:26) and felt himself 'persecuted' because of his stance on circumcision (Gal. 5:11). In one passage he mentions being 'banished' and 'prevented from speaking to Gentiles' (1 Thess. 2:15 – its authenticity is questioned by some) and in another revealing comment says he has received the synagogue punishment of the thirty-nine lashes on five occasions (2 Cor. 11:24). It appears that even many Christian Jews strongly opposed him; they considered his eating with gentiles sinful (Gal. 2:11–17) and his teaching an invitation to libertinism (Rom. 3:8). In Acts also the theme of Jewish opposition to Paul is prominent, though perhaps somewhat stereotyped. In that narrative Paul is frequently denounced and expelled from synagogues, and sometimes charged with serious offences. When he arrives in Jerusalem he is met by anxious Jewish Christians who have been told that he teaches 'apostasy' from Moses to the Jews who live among the gentiles, telling them not to circumcise their children or to live in accordance with the Jewish customs (Acts 21:21). Paul's previous fears concerning his reception in Jerusalem (Rom. 15:31) are amply fulfilled in his arrest and subsequent trials.

Such evidence suggests that Paul was frequently denounced as an apostate Jew. Such a reaction was not, however, either automatic or immediate. Some Jewish Christians at least some of the time accepted Paul's stance as compatible with their understanding of Judaism (Peter, Barnabas, Prisca and Aquila, for instance) and there is good reason to believe that Paul was initially accepted as a synagogue member in most locations. The thirty-nine lashes were discipline for a synagogue member, not quite the expulsion and ostracism which an officially designated apostate might receive.[20] There were clearly some ambiguities about Paul which elicited varying reactions, and that is not surprising in relation to a man who said he lived as a Jew among Jews, but without reference to the law among gentiles (1 Cor. 9:20–21), and whom we find in his letters sometimes celebrating and sometimes denigrating his Jewish credentials (2 Cor. 11:22; Rom. 11:1; Gal. 1:13–14; Phil. 3:2–11).

Scholars have recently debated whether Paul was or was not an apostate, but usually without reference to how he was actually perceived in his own day.[21] It should be clear by now that the question requires us to be sensitive to the opinions and judgements of Paul's contemporaries; his deviance, like any other, was in the eye of the beholders. The evidence we have briefly surveyed suggests that many variables could affect their vision of Paul: Jews of different persuasions and in different places reacted differently to this enigmatic figure in their midst. How Paul fared in the Diaspora synagogues perhaps depended on how long he stayed there, what personal animosities he engendered, how his judges at his synagogue trials viewed his defence and what reports (either true or false) they had heard of his behaviour. It is not insignificant that Paul's social position in the Diaspora communities was generally weak: he was a newcomer, of low social status, with no economic or political power base on which to build his defence, and power struggles in the synagogue almost inevitably turned to his disadvantage. Inasmuch as he *was viewed* by his contemporary Jews as an apostate, he *was* (historically speaking) an apostate, and no amount of pleading about the Jewish elements in his theology or the diversity within first-century Judaism can mask or alter that reality.

EARLY CHRISTIANITY AND THE CREATION OF DEVIANTS

I have left myself little space to address that other crucial process of definition which characterizes early Christianity, its internal definition of its own boundaries. We may simply observe here, by way of illustration, a particularly intriguing example of the struggle for the definition of Christian identity in the correspondence of Paul with the church in Corinth. One may read the whole of 1 Corinthians as an attempt by Paul to define the boundaries of the Christian community in Corinth, and an integral part of that effort involves Paul labelling as deviant those he considers should be excluded from the church. Indeed this letter contains a statement which almost precisely summarizes Erikson's thesis on the function of deviance in boundary definition. In 1 Cor. 11:19 Paul introduces his discussion of the Lord's Supper with the stunning comment that 'there must be divisions (*haireseis*) among you in order that those who are genuine (*dokimoi*) among you may be recognized'. That is a proto-sociological statement if ever there was one! Paul recognizes that the creation of distinctions between the 'genuine' (*dokimoi*) and the 'spurious' (*adokimoi*, cf. 1 Cor. 9:27) serves to give the Christian community definition and identity; he even uses a 'functionalist' purpose clause!

Commentators are surprised at this statement, since earlier in the letter Paul deplores party divisions (1 Cor. 1:10–12).[22] But in fact Paul spends a considerable proportion of this letter indicating where he thinks the proper boundaries of Christian practice lie. Though he does not think the Apollos or Cephas party has deviated significantly from Christian norms, he certainly wants the Corinthians to recognize that the man reported to have had sex with his father's wife (1 Cor. 5:1–13) and those who participate in 'idolatry' (1 Cor. 10:1–22) and those who mishandle the Lord's Supper (1 Cor. 11:17–34) are all to be regarded as 'deviants' who have strayed over the boundary out of the community.[23] Here in this clash between Paul and the Corinthians we see very clearly how 'deviance' is defined by social reaction. The Corinthian Christians do not apparently regard the man mentioned in 1 Corinthians 5 as other than a sexually active brother; Paul insists that he is, and must be publicly labelled as, a *pornos* who is only a 'so-called' brother (5:11). It is fascinating to see here how, in a typical deviance process, Paul selects from this individual's many activities the one feature of which he disapproves and makes that the defining character of his identity: this man does not just *indulge in* some *porneia*, he *is* a *pornos* and must be treated as that, whatever else he might also be in character or behaviour.

In fact a fundamental point of dispute between Paul and the Corinthians is the location of their community boundaries. As I have argued elsewhere (Barclay 1992), Paul thinks the Corinthians are far too comfortable in their social integration, and he spends much of the letter erecting barriers where the Corinthians presently see none. Conversely, he does not treat as deviant some whom other Christians might well have considered such: he does not want to see excommunicated those who are married to non-Christians, or those who are uncircumcised or those who cannot speak in tongues. Throughout 1 Corinthians Paul is creating insiders and outsiders on his own terms and he does so with regard to so many different issues that it was almost inevitable that some Corinthians would take exception to his rulings. He identifies deviants in order to establish boundaries and solidify the identity of the Corinthian community, precisely as Erikson suggests. Unfortunately, in this case it was a policy which backfired disastrously, for he lacked the authority to get his understanding of deviance accepted. Turning to 2 Corinthians we find that resistance to Paul takes the form of questioning whether *he* is *dokimos* ('genuine') as a Christian (2 Cor. 13:1–7) and Paul has to respond by questioning the Christian status of this whole congregation and by furious invective against opponents whom he castigates as 'false apostles' (2 Cor. 11:13). It is easy to recognize here what we have seen throughout this discussion, that 'deviant' labels are being applied as part of a power struggle, here a fundamental battle for control of the Christian tradition.

We could of course trace this same process in other early Christian conflicts, where we are nowadays conscious of how perspectival terms like 'heretic' and 'apostate' are. Even so, I suspect there is still a tendency to take the views of the New Testament authors as somehow containing an inevitable and objective 'rightness' in their definition of deviance. The advantage of the interactionist perspective in this regard is that it continually reminds us to ask whose definitions we are hearing and whose interests they serve. It certainly suggests, for instance, a thoroughly suspicious reading of the Pastorals, 2 Peter, Jude and other polemical documents from the late first century which react against (and perhaps even invent) those 'deviants' who threaten the social structures which the authors represent. In the Pastorals we can see how practices recognized and tolerated by Paul (e.g. celibacy) have become 'deviantized' in the interests of a particular construction of church policy. In the highly fluid conditions of early Christianity, there were almost no 'taken-for-granted' norms which commanded universal assent, and it was open to each group and party to designate deviance in its own way. That the future of Christianity was determined by power contests between different groups is something no historian can deny, at least none with any sociological awareness: such is the way with all human society.

As I said at the outset, deviance theory is no magic wand with which to solve the many intricate problems which confront the historian of early Christianity. It can only be used in conjunction with minute historical analysis of the sources and cannot fill in the gaps which they leave. Its chief benefit, however, is to call into question our assumptions concerning the objective status of phenomena like apostasy and to invite us to pay close attention to the individuals or groups responsible for the application of deviant labels. If it helps to highlight a degree of relativism in the Judaism of this period, it also suggests that the process of 'the parting of the ways' cannot simply be traced in relation to certain absolute boundary marks, but was radically dependent on the particularities of location, personnel and social context in which early Christianity took root.[24]

NOTES

1 Saldarini combines deviance theory and sect typology in his analysis of the Matthean community, but at a very high level of generality. His conclusions also seem inconsistent: if societies label 'deviants' in defining their boundaries, it makes little sense to insist that 'deviant groups remain part of the whole' (1991: 47). Despite frequent appeals to Erikson (1966; cited as 'Ericson'), Saldarini's thesis runs quite contrary to Erikson's conclusions. Sanders 1993: 129 151 more accurately reflects the sociological discussion but is inclined to rather sweeping generalizations; see further below (Judaism and Apostasy). Malina and Neyrey have applied deviance theory to the narrative of Matthew (Malina and Neyrey 1988) and Luke (Malina 1991a). But it remains unclear whether their analysis relates to the history of Jesus or to the Gospel narratives;

if the latter, it is hard to see what can be achieved beyond renaming the actors and processes in the story.

2 There are valuable surveys by Pfohl 1985 and Downes and Rock 1988; Davis' survey (1980) is somewhat dense and ideologically biased.

3 Some of the essential elements of the perspective had been outlined by Lemert 1951; but he was somewhat critical of its later expression in the 1960s (Lemert 1972: 14–25).

4 Near contemporaneous definitions of this feature of the interactionist perspective can be found in Kitsuse 1962 and Erikson 1962, both reprinted in Becker 1964.

5 Among the most searching critics of this perspective are Gibbs 1966 and Knutsson 1977; a vulgarized version is sharply rejected by the essayists in Gove 1975, where, however, Kitsuse and Schur defend its central notions as properly understood. There are also critical discussions in Rock 1973: 19–26 and Davis 1980: 197–234.

6 A careful reading of Becker 1963 shows that he is not guilty of suggesting that the deviant act itself is irrelevant to the labelling process, as some have charged: he writes, 'whether a given act is deviant or not depends *in part* on the nature of the act (that is, whether or not it violates some rule) and *in part* on what other people do about it' (1963: 9, my emphasis). This led him to some terminological confusion over the use of the word 'deviant' (e.g. he posits a category of 'secret deviant' which critics observe is logically problematic for an interactionist perspective). But so long as one recognizes the distinction between 'deviant' in the weak sense of 'what deviates from social norms' and 'deviant' in the strong sense of 'what elicits the social reaction that "something should be done about it" ' (see Schur 1971: 24–25), this difficulty is not insuperable.

7 Lofland (1969: 14) writes: 'Deviance is the name of the conflict game in which individuals or loosely organized small groups with little power are strongly feared by a well-organized, sizable minority or majority who have a large amount of power.'

8 'The deviant is a person whose activities have moved outside the margins of the group, and when the community calls him to account for that vagrancy it is making a statement about the nature and placement of its boundaries' (Erikson 1966: 11). Erikson's thesis has been supported and refined by Ben-Yehuda 1985: 23–73.

9 See Schur 1971: 21 and Lemert 1972: 21–22; the latter insists in this connection that 'no one theory or model will suffice to study the societal reaction; models must be appropriate to the area under study, to the values, norms, and structures identifiable in the area, as well as the special qualities of the persons and their acts subject to definition as deviant' (p. 21).

10 Downes and Rock (1988: 183) properly insist that 'interactionism casts deviance as a process which may continue over a lifetime, which has no necessary end, which is anything but inexorable, and which may be built around false starts, diversions and returns'.

11 I have explored this matter in more detail in relation to the Diaspora in Barclay (1994).

12 Kasher 1985 is a particularly clear example of this, but by no means the only one; for an earlier essay based on the spurious notion of 'orthodoxy' in Judaism see Feldman 1960.

13 On the varying definitions of 'sinner' in Palestinian Judaism see Dunn 1990: 71–77; on diversity in the Diaspora see Barclay (forthcoming).

14 For his own opinion see, e.g., *Jos.* 254; *Virt.* 182; *Mos.* 1.31; *Spec. Leg.* 1.54–58; 3.29. For the opinion of the masses, *Migr. Abr.* 89–93.

15 His biography has been fully detailed by Turner 1954 and Burr 1955.

16 *Prov.* 1 and 2 and in *Anim.* Alexander argues against divine providence, but Philo

treats him with warmth and respect and has him retract his doubts at the end of *Prov.* 2. As a caution, note the hesitancy of Hadas-Lebel (1973: 23–46) on the authorship of these treatises and the identity of the Alexander featured in them.

17 We find Alexander in inscriptions honouring Egyptian deities (and their providence!) in *Orientis Graeci Inscriptiones Selectae* 663 and 669; cf. comparable papyri in *Corpus Papyrorum Judaicorum* 418.

18 The external threats to Palestinian Jews in the pre-70 period which Sanders lists (p. 137) are not quite equivalent to the identity-threatening features of Puritan New England which he takes from Erikson as his model. Arguably, the threat of the statue of Gaius (39–41 CE) made Palestinian Jews not less but more certain of their unity and the limits of their tolerance. In the Diaspora, the Jewish communities in Egypt and Cyrene were certainly troubled during this century, but we cannot trace the rise of Christianity there; and in the places where our record for Christianity is strong (Rome, Greece, Asia Minor) there is little evidence of 'crisis' in the synagogue communities (except perhaps in Rome in the 40s CE).

19 Sanders (1993: 136) is aware that old and traditional 'crimes' hardly need a social identity crisis to be identified and punished, and thus has to assert that the Christians ('of course') constituted an ambiguous group, a case of 'soft deviance' which either was not or might not have been punished at other times. But this clearly needs to be established in the first place and the situation may have differed greatly between different expressions of Christianity. Sanders is naturally aware of the diversity in early Christianity on such matters as the admission of gentiles, but seems to assume that any welcome of gentiles, even as proper proselytes, was liable to interpretation as deviance (p. 138); that seems to run against the evidence (e.g. Josephus, *J. W.* 2. 454).

20 See Harvey 1985; Gallas 1990; Horbury 1985.

21 See e.g. Dunn 1990: 183–214; Räisänen 1985: 543–553; Segal 1990.

22 Fee (1987: 538) considers this sentence 'one of the true puzzles in the letter'. Barrett (1971: 262) significantly tones down its meaning and Munck (1959: 136–137) implausibly relegates its reference to the eschatological future.

23 On 1 Corinthians 5 see Forkman 1972: 139–51; on 1 Cor. 11:17–34 see most recently Engberg-Pedersen 1993.

24 I would like to thank my research student Todd Still for his bibliographical assistance and stimulating work on this topic, and the members of the 'Context and Kerygma' conference held in St Andrews in June/July 1994 for their questions and encouragement.

7

THE SOCIAL NATURE OF CONVERSION IN THE EARLY CHRISTIAN WORLD

Nicholas H. Taylor

This essay draws together several strands in recent social-scientific scholarship applicable to the world of early Christianity and the phenomenon of religious conversion. The social aspect of human knowledge and perception has been widely recognized as a consequence largely of the work of Berger and Luckmann (1967). The essentially social nature of human identity in non-Western cultures has been described by Geertz (1976) and Pitt-Rivers (1977), and applied to the ancient Mediterranean context of early Christianity by Malina (1979; 1981; 51–60; Malina and Neyrey 1991b). That religious conversion is a social process as well as an individual transformation has become increasingly apparent in studies of modern religious phenomena (Straus 1979; Long and Hadden 1983; Snow and Machalek 1983). That this applies all the more to early Christianity has not as yet been so widely recognized, and I shall attempt here to explore the issues further, building on the diverse strands of recent scholarship, and attempting to construct a model which will enable further study of conversion in early Christianity.

'Conversion' can function no more precisely than as an umbrella term for a variety of experiences (Lofland and Skonovd 1981; Blasi 1985: 91; Rambo 1993). It varies in form and motif, and in individual and communal significance (Lofland and Skonovd 1981; Kilbourne and Richardson 1988; Rambo 1993: 13–15). A uniform pattern of conversion, and ascription of social significance thereto, cannot therefore be imposed. The distinctions and categories of conversion discussed by Travisano (1981) and McGuire (1992: 72), while raising important questions, tend to concentrate on the cerebral aspects and overlook the social. For the purpose of our present task, a different approach is more appropriate.

That Christianity emerged from within Judaism is of course well known, and there is no recorded gentile recognition of Christians as such before the younger Pliny in 112 CE (*Ep.* 10.96). Writing slightly later, Tacitus (*Ann.* 15.44) and Suetonius (*Nero* 16) relate the persecution of Christians under Nero (c. 64 CE), but in so doing reflect the conditions and attitudes of their own day (cf. Wilken 1984: 48–50). While gentiles in closer social proximity may have been more aware of the distinction between their Christian and other Jewish neighbours, there is no extant record of this. In discussing primitive Christianity, therefore, we are dealing with what was at least initially an essentially Jewish movement in its self-conception, and in the perception of both Jewish and gentile neighbours and observers.

The Jews were a diverse ethnic-religious community scattered throughout the Roman world, and known to attract foreign adherents. It is in this context that conversion to early Christianity is to be understood. The affiliation of gentiles to Judaism and Jewish communities was a diverse and not necessarily religiously motivated occurrence. This has been illustrated most cogently by Cohen in his article 'Crossing the Boundary and Becoming a Jew' (1989). I would suggest that Cohen's paradigm forms a useful framework for understanding the diversity of conversion to early Christianity. Important distinctions between Christianity and other forms of Judaism are nevertheless to be recognized. Irrespective of the extent of proselytizing missionary activity (cf. McKnight 1991; Feldman 1993: 288–341; Goodman 1994), Judaism spread primarily through migration and procreation. Proselytizing mission was, on the other hand, crucial to the spread of Christianity. The early Christians, moreover, did not have a central cultic, economic and political institution comparable to the Temple in Jerusalem, which attracted outsiders. Political stability, if not piety, required respect for the Temple of the Jews. Economic reasons for affiliating to Jewish communities, and thereby gaining access to the economic network which connected them, would not have applied to Christian groups, at least during the earliest period of Christianity. With these limitations in mind, we turn to Cohen's paradigm, and consider its applicability to early Christianity.

Cohen identifies seven categories of increasingly intimate association of gentiles with their neighbouring Jewish communities: (1) admiring some aspect of Judaism; (2) acknowledging the power of the god of the Jews or incorporating him into the pagan pantheon; (3) benefiting the Jews or being conspicuously friendly to Jews; (4) practising some or many of the rituals of the Jews; (5) venerating the god of the Jews and denying or ignoring the pagan gods; (6) joining the Jewish community; (7) converting to Judaism and 'becoming a Jew' (Cohen 1989: 14–15). Conversion to Judaism was therefore a more varied phenomenon than is often appreciated, and the boundaries between Jews and outsiders were perceived differently at different times and in different places, and from different perspectives (Cohen 1989: 26–33). Three independent but overlapping aspects of 'conversion' are discernible: (a) conviction/acknowledgement of divinity, essentially cerebral but potentially involving worship; (b) conformity/observance, involving practice, either negative or positive, of the Law; and (c) socialization, involving affiliation and integration into the community.

The term 'conversion' is one that could probably be applied in any significant way only to Cohen's categories (6) and (7), and possibly also to (5), when the degree of identification with Judaism was such that the person was regarded by self and others as Jewish. Gentiles who adopted Jewish practices (4) or associated closely with Jewish communities (3) could not be regarded as converts, but may have been regarded by their neighbours as deviant, to the extent to which they and the Jews were perceived to have departed from the dominant culture, and thereby to be undermining the fabric of society. This is of course an inherently subjective matter, depending not so much on the behaviour of the Jews and their gentile converts and adherents as on the attitude of the majority in their neighbourhood. John Barclay's essay in the present volume is a valuable study of deviance among first-century Jews which is consonant with this view. Deviancy is therefore an essentially local phenomenon, but is nonetheless important for understanding conversion in the world of early Christianity (Malina and Neyrey 1991b: 103; cf. Lofland and Stark 1965; Parrucci 1968; Matza 1969: 107). However, it raises questions which can most fruitfully be discussed in a treatment of the emergence and growth of Christianity in specific places, rather than within the scope of this study.

We have little, if any, first-century evidence to use in applying Cohen's first category to Christianity. The closest approximation would perhaps be the incidents in Acts where pagans listen with some interest to Paul's preaching, but with clearly no intention of being converted. While Paul's speeches before the Areopagus (Acts 17:16–24) and before Agrippa (Acts 25:23–26:31), and his discussions with Felix (Acts 24:22, 26), are historically extremely dubious, and the attention he received stopped well short of admiration, such incidents were nevertheless conceivable to Luke. The late second-century claim of Tertullian that Christians were known for their love of one another (*Apol.* 39.7), while coming from a Christian source, suggests some degree of admiration. His older contemporary Galen was appreciative, if critical, of some aspects of Christianity as he was of Judaism (*Puls[R].* 2.4; 3.3; *Lib. ord.* 15). We therefore need not doubt that, particularly once Christianity became recognizably distinct from Judaism, it was observed with interest and in some cases respect by its gentile neighbours.

The second category, acknowledging the power of the god of the Christians, is likewise ascertainable for the first century only from Acts. Once again, we cannot be certain of the historicity of particular episodes, but the accounts nevertheless represent what were known types of occurrence in the world of the time. The New Testament contains three allusions to exorcisms in the name of Jesus by outsiders to his community (Matt. 7:21–23; Mark 9:38–41; Acts 19:13–16). The later rabbinic prohibition of exorcism in the name of Jesus (*t. Hullin* 2:22–23; *j. Sabbath* 14:14d; *b. Abodah Zarah* 27b) testifies to the persistence of the practice in non-Christian Judaism. I would suggest that the episode of Simon Magus seeking to appropriate supernatural power through Simon Peter (Acts 8:18–19) belongs to this category, despite the reference to his baptism (Acts 8:13), and represents an attempt to use the power of the name of Jesus for exorcistic and other magical purposes. The claim that Sergius Paulus 'believed' as a consequence of the action of Barnabas and Paul (Acts 13:6–12) reflects no more than an acknowledgement of the power of the god of Barnabas and Paul, and no unequivocal commitment to Christianity. In the Gospel tradition, the incidents of the centurion's servant (Luke 7:1–10) and the Syro-Phoenician woman's daughter (Mark 7:24–30) should likewise be understood as incidental appropriations of the supernatural power perceived in Jesus rather than as conversion to his preaching. The account in the *Augustan History* of the early third-century emperor Alexander Severus including Christ with Abraham, Orpheus and Apollonius of Tyana in a private pantheon (Sev. Alex. 29.2), however historically dubious, reflects a similar, if longer term, co-option of Christ (cf. MacMullen 1981: 92; Frend 1984: 275).

The third category, benefiting the Christians or being conspicuously friendly to them, may have been more widespread than can be recognized when a single rigid divide between Christians and non-Christians is assumed. We know that patronage was a major institution in the ancient world (Garnsey and Saller 1987) and that it impinged upon the life of the church (Meeks 1983a: 74–84; Moxnes 1991; Chow 1992). Voluntary associations and cults, particularly among the lower orders of society, required the protection and beneficence of patrons, drawn from the more elevated orders. Such patrons of Christian groups would not necessarily have been Christians themselves, and their bestowal of protection and support would not necessarily have been motivated by conviction so much as by the patron's need of clients. It is possible that Erastus (Rom. 16:24) and Chloe (1 Cor. 1:12) were non-Christian patrons of Christian groups. At the end of the first century the Roman aristocrat Flavia Domitilla was a benefactor of the Christians, but it is doubtful whether she and her husband Clemens were themselves Christians (Dio, *Hist.* 67.14.2).

Non-Christian benefactors of Christian communities would, in terms of social relationships, often have been closer to the communities than those of the second category who, unlike them, had made some profession of belief (cf. Cohen 1989: 18). This is not to suggest that the second and third categories of adherence were necessarily incompatible, and non-Christian patrons may well on occasion have made some token acknowledgement of the god of the Christians. The two categories nevertheless point to different aspects of association, in the former case an affirmation of divine power, in the latter a social relationship.

Whereas Judaism was defined essentially in terms of ethnicity, Christianity was defined in terms of commitment to Christ. Equivocal commitment would therefore blur the boundaries of the community and undermine its discipline. The fourth category of adherence, practising Christian observances without any particular or exclusive commitment either to the community or to the faith it professed, may underlie much of the strife which beset the Corinthian church. It is clear from 1 Cor. 8:1–13 and 10:14–22 that some who participated in the cultic life of the Corinthian church associated also with pagan cults. It is also clear from 1 Cor. 14:23–24 that non-Christians (*apistoi*) attended Christian worship. Paul clearly seeks an unequivocal commitment on the part of those who participate in Christian worship, as the establishment of a stable community required. It is equally clear, however, that not all his Corinthian addresses made such an exclusive commitment to the church (cf. Hurd 1965; Willis 1985; Chow 1992). The Q version of the dominical saying in Matt. 12:30 and Luke 11:23 may reflect similar concern for clear and unequivocal commitment which was not forthcoming from all adherents.

The fifth category of adherence most closely corresponds to 'godfearers' as they have been understood in the past (cf. Esler 1987: 36–45; Kraabel 1981b). Circumcision and the ritual and dietary laws were an obstacle to full incorporation into non-Christian Judaism, and the essentially ethnic nature of the communities militated against the full incorporation of gentiles. Christianity, on the other hand, required the clear definition of boundaries and the establishment of stable and viable communities. There would therefore have been greater pressure on adherents to be fully initiated and integrated. Exclusive worship of the god of the Christians, but without being initiated into membership of the Christian community, may have been less common than with other forms of Judaism. Nevertheless unbaptized converts may well have been more widespread than is immediately apparent. The *idiotai* in 1 Cor. 14:16 may be uninitiated converts rather than Christians unaccustomed to glossolalia, even if those in 1 Cor. 14:23 are to be identified with the *apistoi* (cf. Conzelmann 1975: 239–243). Clemens and Domitilla, and others accused of atheism at the end of the first century (Dio, *Hist.* 67.14.2) may belong to such a category of Christian allegiance. Clandestine adherence may well have become widespread when Christianity was a proscribed religion in the Roman empire, and is perhaps reflected in the New Testament in the portrayal of Joseph of Arimathea as a secret follower of Jesus (John 19:38). The later occurrence of deferred baptism would also belong to this category, but requires no further discussion at this point.

Cohen identifies three distinct phenomena within his sixth category, involuntary incorporation into the Jewish community as a consequence of social transactions, without having undergone a conversion experience. Incorporation into the Christian community as a consequence of social relationships rather than personal conviction is known to have been widespread in the early church. Household baptisms after the conversion of the *oikodespotes* are reported in Acts (10:24–38; 16:13–15, 29–34) and alluded to by Paul (1 Cor. 1:16). In a world in which it was assumed that the subordinate members of a household conformed to the religion(s) of the head, such occurrences would have been normative (Meeks 1983a: 75–77). Those who subsequently joined the household either through birth or through acquisition as a slave, or even through marriage, may likewise have been initiated. That this was not always the case, however, is clear from the Pauline literature. In 1 Cor. 7:12–14 Paul alludes to marriages which had apparently become mixed upon the conversion of one partner to Christianity. The case of the slave Onesimus is rather more complex. It has generally been assumed that Onesimus, the slave of the Christian Philemon, was not a Christian until Paul 'became his father' (Phlm. 10) subsequent to his flight. As Philemon and (his wife?) Apphia were hosts to the local church (Phlm. 2), it would seem unlikely that we are dealing with a private elite cult from which slaves were excluded. Rather, I would suggest, Onesimus was initiated into the church with the rest of Philemon's household, but without having acquired Christian convictions. His flight from Philemon would have severed his connection with the church as with the household. What changed, presumably through Onesimus' encounter with Paul, was the quality of this Christianity, from involuntary incorporation into a Christian community and conformity therewith, to commitment to the Christian faith. His return to Philemon would combine conviction with socialization and observance, and so complete Onesimus' conversion.

Cohen's final category combines the previous three. Conversion involves observance of the laws, exclusive monotheism and incorporation into the community. It was at this stage that gentile proselytes to Judaism were initiated through circumcision and accompanying rituals (cf. Cohen 1990). For the Christians, however, boundaries were not defined by ethnicity, and therefore needed to be signified clearly through initiatory rituals (cf. Christiansen 1992). These needed to create the community, and therefore to include involuntary adherents within the group. Voluntary converts not exclusively committed and socialized may also have been baptized. The combination of conviction, exclusive commitment and social incorporation was undoubtedly the ideal which the New Testament presupposes. Yet is it equally clear that not all adherents embraced Christianity the same way or to the same degree.

The ideal is reflected by Meeks when he describes conversion to early Christianity as 'an extraordinarily thoroughgoing resocialization, in which the sect [sic] was intended to become virtually the primary group for its members, supplanting all other loyalties' (Meeks 1983a: 78). The social aspect of conversion has for some time been recognized by social scientists (Mead 1934: 219; Berger and Luckmann 1967: 158; Heirich 1977; Straus 1979; Remus 1982; Long and Hadden 1983; Snow and Machalek 1983; McGuire 1992: 70). The social or ecclesial dimension to Christian initiation has also been acknowledged (Cullmann 1950: 23–46; Nissen 1982: 202–204; Christiansen 1992). But the resocialization process consequent upon conversion to early Christianity has hitherto received little social-scientific treatment (cf. Meeks 1983a: 26; Wanamaker 1989).

Philo describes proselytes to Judaism as having become mortal enemies to their own families (*S. Leg.* 4.178; cf. Tacitus, *Hist.* 5.5.2). This may reflect the tension between Jewish and Greek residents of Alexandria during Philo's lifetime as much as the social consequences of conversion to Judaism, but nevertheless the dislocation brought about by proselytism was enormous. This was undoubtedly the case also with converts to Christian Judaism. Paul alludes to tension within households some of whose members are Christian (1 Cor. 7:12–16), and this reflects what was clearly a widespread phenomenon (cf. Mark 13:12; Luke 12:51–53). Not only the household, but the wider network of relationships could potentially be undermined through conversion to Christianity (Blasi 1988: 122–143). This may also account in part for the less complete forms of adherence we have already discussed. But the degree of social dislocation involved in conversion, particularly to a religion with (in principle) absolute claims to exclusive devotion, is not to be underestimated.

The model of conversion as resocialization I propose to follow is that of Snow and Machalek, expounded, *inter alia*, in their article 'The Convert as a Social Type' (1983), which displays clear continuity with the work of Mead (1934) and of Berger and Luckmann (1967). This model has been used previously in studies of Paul (Segal 1990; Taylor 1993), and by Wanamaker in an unpublished study of the Thessalonian church (1989; cf. 1990: 14–15). Snow and Machalek presuppose rather than discuss resocialization as integral to conversion. They identify four aspects of the transformation in the universe of discourse which converts undergo: (1) biographical reconstruction; (2) the assumption of a master attribution scheme; (3) suspension of analogical reasoning; (4) assumption of a master role. It has been observed that of these four characteristics of the religious convert, only the first is unique to converts, while the other three are attested in lifelong practitioners of the same religion (Staples and Mauss 1987). I would question also whether the first, biographical reconstruction, is distinctive to the post-conversion situation, or can apply to other life-transforming experiences (cf. Taylor 1993). Nevertheless, the four indicators identified by Snow and Machalek do relate to aspects of the resocialization process which accompanies and follows conversion.

Biographical reconstruction, or as I prefer to call it autobiographical reconstruction, refers to the process whereby the convert reinterprets his or her past in terms of his or her present, i.e. post-conversion and retrospective, understanding thereof (Snow and Machalek 1983: 66–69; cf. also Beckford 1978; McGuire 1992: 73; Gallagher 1993: 2). While the subjectivity of human recollections is of course well known, it is nevertheless important to acknowledge that this subjectivity of perception is particularly acute when a person is radically reoriented. For those for whom Christianity was a less than absolute commitment, such as Corinthians who continued to participate in pagan cults (1 Cor. 8:1–13; 10:14–22), the reorientation would of course have been less dramatic. But for those who were both intellectually convinced of the truth of Christian professions and fully socialized into Christian communities, the alienation from their previous life and relationships would have been quite fundamental. This is apparent in Paul (Gal. 1:11–2:21; Phil. 3:4–11; cf. Fredriksen 1986; Taylor 1992; 1993), and also in Justin's *Dialogue with Trypho* (2.2–7) and, much later, in Augustine's *Confessions*.

'Master attribution' is closely related to (auto)biographical reconstruction, but concerns the explanation and interpretation of reality beyond as well as pertaining to the self (Snow and Machalek 1983: 169–173). The term is perhaps potentially misleading to non-social scientists, and I would therefore suggest an alternative, 'comprehensive attribution'. This would convey more clearly the sense that causal explanations are found and applied within the framework of the newly acquired belief system. We need to recognize that the degree to which attribution is applied varies according to culture and temperament, and is not limited to the post-conversion situation (cf. Spilka, Shaver and Kirkpatrick 1985). Nevertheless a convert is particularly likely to find explanations for phenomena in terms of the religious system he or she has embraced. In other words, the newly acquired beliefs provide the basis for meaning in the convert's transformed symbolic universe (cf. Berger 1969: 47–51; Heirich 1977: 674–675; McGuire 1992: 58; Hefner 1993). The cosmology and eschatology of early Christianity, and particularly the notion of salvation history (cf. John 3:17–21; Rom. 4:13–14; 9–11; Gal. 3:6–14; Justin, *Trypho* 120.5) reflects such an attribution process, as does Augustine's doctrine of predestination (*Bapt.* 4.34). Adverse circumstances in the present lives of Christians derive from the cosmic-eschatological attribution scheme of early Christianity (Mark 13:9–13; 1 Thess. 3:3–4; cf. Wanamaker 1989: 7–8).

Suspension of analogical reasoning means that the acquired religious system is regarded as unique, and comparable phenomena are regarded as fundamentally and categorically distinct (Snow and Machalek 1983: 273–275). Analogical thinking is of course integral to the functioning of the human mind, and the phenomenon to which Snow and Machalek point could perhaps more usefully be described as the 'assertion of uniqueness' of the acquired belief system. The point is that the religious beliefs and observances assumed by the convert cannot be compared with other human experiences and practices. The uniqueness of Christianity is asserted in several New Testament texts (John 14:6, 9–11; Rom. 3:23–25; 8:1–4; 10:9), and later by Tatian (*Graec.* 29; 35), and less vehemently by Justin (2 *Apol.* 13; *Trypho* 2.3). This notion of the uniqueness of Christianity would of course have corresponded to the degree to which converts were exclusively committed and conforming members of their communities.

By the assumption of a master role, Snow and Machalek refer to the way in which the convert comes to identify totally with the group which he or she has joined, and to seek to represent it to outsiders (Snow and Machalek 1983: 275–278). This clearly involves two distinct aspects: the integration of the convert into the community of believers from and in terms of which he or she derives a new identity (cf. Gallagher 1993), and the convert's determination to realize the way of life and teaching of the community, particularly in self-projection towards outsiders. I would suggest that 'total identification' with the community and assumption of a 'representation role' for the community in dealings with outsiders might describe the phenomenon more clearly than does 'master role'. Identification with the community of course includes conformity to its way of life and discipline, and observance of its moral code (cf. Meeks 1993).

As has been clear from our preceding discussion, the degree to which adherents identified with the primitive Christian communities varied considerably. The identification of the Christian, or at the least the disciple actively engaged in the work of the Gospel, with Christ is reflected in Matt. 25:31–46 and John

13:20. Paul personified this identification with the gospel he preached (Gal. 1:11–2:10) and of himself with his mission to proclaim the gospel (Gal. 1:1; cf. Taylor 1993). Each community would have depended for its survival upon a core group for whom it was their primary socialization, and whose conversion resulted in complete and unequivocal conviction of the truth of Christian doctrines. Paul clearly regarded some of the Corinthian Christians as being less than exemplary in their conduct, and showing themselves in an unfavourable light to outsiders (cf. 1 Cor. 5:1; 6:1; 14:16, 23), and the later Pastoral letters also reflect this concern in the election of leaders (1 Tim. 3:7). Christian missionary work and apologetic writings, such as those of Justin already cited, seek to represent Christianity to the world, and reflect the socialization of their authors as much as the theological truths they proclaim.

Resocialization, therefore, is integral to the conversion process, particularly in societies where human identity is essentially social. Converts become like established members of the community, and adopt the requisite beliefs and practices. In this respect the attributes of the convert described above are not distinctive except insofar as they are acquired rather than inherited, and in that the convert has a previous life which needs to be interpreted in terms of the ideology of the community.

To conclude, three aspects of the conversion process have been identified: the conviction that Christian professions are true, social reorientation into Christian communities and conformity to the discipline of the community. Early Christianity, like the broader ethnic-religious Judaism from which it emerged, attracted adherents who manifested varying degrees of commitment, and who were incorporated to varying degrees into the life of the Christian communities. The abandonment of previous beliefs, practices and social relationships varied accordingly. Further study will need to integrate further the variety and degrees of adherence with patterns of socialization, and with deviancy perceptions in the locality, so far as these can be discerned. This will require treatment of specific communities and their records, rather than the comprehensive and preliminary study presented here.

Part III

FAMILY AND HONOUR IN MATTHEW AND LUKE

8

LOSS OF WEALTH, LOSS OF FAMILY AND LOSS OF HONOUR

The cultural context of the original makarisms in Q

Jerome H. Neyrey

INTRODUCTION: FOCUS AND HYPOTHESIS

This study of 'poor' and 'poverty' brings to the discussion a cultural and social element. Stated most baldly, 'poor' implies not simply scant economic resources, that is, little land or money, but has a decidedly cultural component as well. Most people in antiquity would qualify as 'poor' according to economic standards. But the ancients did not automatically classify the economically deprived as 'poor'. If peasants had what sufficed, Plutarch did not call them 'poor': 'In what suffices, no one is poor' (*On Love of Wealth* 523F). Seneca echoed this:

> Let us return to the law of nature; for then riches are laid up for us. The things which we actually need are free for all, or else cheap; nature craves only bread and water. No one is poor according to this standard; when a man has limited his desires within these bounds, he can challenge the happiness of Jove himself.
>
> (*Ep. Mor.* 25.4)

Peasants or artisans with little of this world's goods have what is deemed 'sufficient', and so are not called 'poor'.[1]

Let us distinguish two Greek terms, *penes* and *ptochos*. Dictionaries translate *penes* as 'the poor man' (e.g. BAGD 642), which misses the root meaning *penomai*, 'to work hard'. *Penes* refers to a person who does manual labour, and so is contrasted with *plousios*, a member of the landed class who does *not* work (Hauck 1968b: 887). At stake is the social status or honour rating of a 'worker'; Gildas Hamel writes of the *penes*:

> He [the worker] was forced to work to live and had to receive some form of wage and to sell; the craftsman was dependent on others' goodwill. In this respect, he was similar to servants and slaves, free but fettered by various customs . . . This lack of time and self-sufficiency, some philosophers argued, made the craftsman unfit to be a citizen, at least an honourable one. One had to be rich to avoid the ties of dependence

> usually associated with work and be able to live like a true Hellene. Work, because it meant subservience and dependence, was seen as an impediment to this ideal and was therefore contemptible. . . . The *penetes* were all those people who needed to work in shops or in the fields and were consequently without the leisure characteristic of the rich gentry, who were free to give their time to politics, education, and war.
>
> (Hamel 1990: 168–169; see Hands 1968: 62)

A *ptochos*, however, is a person reduced to begging, that is, someone who is destitute of all resources (Hauck 1968b: 886–887; Hands 62–63; Esler 1987: 180–181). One gives alms to a *ptochos*. A *penes*, who has little wealth yet has sufficiency, is not called 'poor'. In contrast, the *ptochos*, who lacks sufficiency and most other things, such as social standing, is 'poor' (see Aristophanes, *Plutus* 535–554).

Of the destitute poor person (*ptochos*) Hamel remarks:

> The *ptochos* was someone who had lost many or all of his family and social ties. He often was a wanderer, therefore a foreigner for others, unable to tax for any length of time the resources of a group to which he could contribute very little or nothing at all.
>
> (Hamel 1990: 170)

If 'poor' and 'poverty' are not simply (or primarily) defined in economic terms, let us ask about the cultural and social meaning of these labels in antiquity. My hypothesis about the relationship of a 'poor person' (*ptochos*) to the value of honour/shame may be stated:

1 Honour and shame are closely related to wealth and loss of wealth respectively.
2 In antiquity, wealth and honour were not individual possessions such as we see in the personal fortune of John D. Rockefeller, but the property of the family or kinship group. When a family lost wealth, its status and honour were threatened.
3 Although most people had meagre possessions and low status, there were families or kinship groups who could no longer maintain their inherited status in regard to marriage contracts, dowries, land tenure and the like. Loss of wealth translated into lower status, which meant loss of honour (Hobbs 1989b: 293).

Let us briefly examine the values of honour and shame and explore how wealth is linked with honour, while loss of it could be linked with shame.

WHAT IS HONOUR?

I will presume in what follows a basic understanding of 'honour' in antiquity,[2] so that I might focus on the biblical text. Nevertheless . . .

> Honour is the value of a person in his own eyes, but also in the eyes of his society. It is his estimation of his own worth, his *claim* to pride, but it is also the acknowledgement of that claim, his excellence recognized by society, *his right* to pride.
>
> (Pitt-Rivers 1977:1).

'Honour', then, has to do with one's public standing; as a public phenomenon it entails a public claim to worth and acknowledgement of it. Although one can acquire honour, normally honour is attached to social groups, especially families. All members of a certain clan, tribe or extended family share in its collective honour. In discussing the relevant aspects of honour which constitute the background for the makarisms in the Q tradition, we will focus on three aspects: (1) honour and wealth; (2) honour and the family; and (3) loss of honour and loss of wealth.

Honour and wealth

Honour is not honour unless publicly claimed, displayed and acknowledged. Honour is displayed by the clothing worn in public, which signals status and wealth.[3] Josephus' account of Haman illustrates the importance of public display of wealth, clothing and honour:

> If you wish to cover with glory the man whom you say you love, let him ride on horseback wearing the same dress as yourself, with a necklace of gold, and let one of your close friends precede him and proclaim throughout the whole city that this is the honour shown to him whom the king honours.
>
> (*J. A.* 11.254; see Philo, *Jos.* 120)

Everyone in the city could see the symbols of honour: gold necklace, elegant clothing and proud mount. The renewed honour of the prodigal son is symbolized by the clothing his father allows him to wear: 'Bring the best robe . . . a ring on his finger and shoes on his feet' (Luke 15:22).[4]

Besides clothing, elites claimed honour through the display of their table setting and the manner in which they dined. Plutarch comments on the ostentation of meals among his contemporaries, as well as the need for an adoring public to turn mere possessions into honour:

> With no one to look on, wealth becomes sightless indeed and bereft of radiance. For when the rich man dines with his wife or intimates he lets his tables of citrus-wood and golden beakers rest in peace and uses common furnishings, and his wife attends it without her gold and purple and dressed in plain attire. But when a banquet – that is, *a spectacle and a show* – is got up and the drama of wealth brought on, 'out of the ships he fetches the urns and tripods (*Il.* 23.259),' the repositories of the lamps are given no rest, the cups are changed, the cup-bearers are made to put

> on new attire, nothing is left undisturbed, gold, silver or jewelled plate, the owners thus confessing that their wealth is for others.
>
> (Plutarch, *On Love of Wealth* 528B; see *Table-Talk* 5.7. 679B)

Wedding feasts, for example, were excellent times for families to put on a public display of whatever wealth they had, such as clothing, coverlets, eating utensils, music, food etc. Insufficiency of wine at a wedding feast would bring incalculable shame on a family (John 2:1–11).

Historians of the ancient economy remind our industrial world that 'wealth' in antiquity resided in land. Apropos of this, Carney writes:

> basically land, not capital, was of critical importance in antiquity. The vast bulk of production was agricultural. Technology was simple, and apart from slaves (used mainly in conjunction with land), inexpensive. So power and wealth went with possession of land . . . It was land, not capital, that produced resources in antiquity.
>
> (Carney 1975: 181–182)

Obviously great wealth resided in the hands of aristocrats with vast land holdings, but peasants with small plots of land also enjoyed some 'wealth' because of their land. Thus honour is related to wealth which is displayed; it is based on land holdings, which constitute the basis for wealth in antiquity; yet honour is a family affair, such that all members shared in the collective standing of the kinship group.

Honour and family

In antiquity one is primarily known as the 'son of so-and-so' or the 'daughter of so-and-so'. One's identity and honour derive in large part from membership in a family or clan (Malina and Neyrey 1991b: 74–76). Richard Rohrbaugh brings this out clearly in his essay in this volume. The rules for *encomia* in the *progymnasmata* mandate that when praising or honouring someone, writers begin their praise with mention of the ancestors and family of the honouree.[5] Rules in the *progymnasmata* simply codify the popular appreciation of family honour. A relevant passage from Aristotle summarizes these expectations about birth and family honour:

> Now *good birth* in a race or a state means that its members are indigenous or ancient; that its earliest leaders were distinguished men, and that from them have sprung many who were distinguished for qualities that we admire. The good birth of an individual, which may come either from the male or the female side, implies that both parents are free citizens, and that, as in the case of the state, the founders of the line have been notable for virtue or wealth or something else which is highly prized, and that many distinguished persons belong to the family, men and women, young and old.
>
> (Aristotle, *Rhet.* 1360b31–38)

To know a person, ancient peoples thought it essential to know that person's blood lines (see also Cicero, *De Inventione* 1.24. 34–35; Quintilian, *Inst. Orat.* 3.7. 10–11; 5.10. 24–25; Pelling 1990: 213–244). Hence notice of someone's genealogy, ancestors, clan and parents constituted essential pieces of information about him (Malina 1993a: 28–54; Malina and Neyrey 1991a: 25–65).

Peasants in villages have living memory of the families with whom they live. They know which family has 'wealth' relative to the village (size of land holdings, crop yields, size of flocks etc.). They know the reputations of other families, their noble deeds, their chaste women, or their shameful ancestors. Since arranged marriages, which are family affairs, are contracted with social equals or betters, villagers are very careful to assess the wealth, worth and honour of a family with whom a marriage is contemplated.

Poverty and loss of honour

If honour is symbolized by family and wealth, especially land, loss of honour can be symbolized by loss of family, land and wealth. The ancients distinguished between the deserving poor, whom one should help, and the undeserving poor, who deserve their situation. This is clearest in the distinction made between those who suffer 'misfortune' and those who are poor because of their own fault. Aristotle called it virtuous for a man 'to give to the right people, the right amounts, and at the right time' (*N. E.* 1120a25). The virtuous person will 'refrain from giving to anybody and everybody, that he may have something to give to the right people, at the right time' (*N. E.* 1120b3–4). He does not specify exactly who the 'right' and 'wrong' people are, but indicates that some *should* be poor (1121b6). Cicero offers a similar distinction concerning those whom one should help:

> The case of the man who is overwhelmed by misfortune is different from that of the one who is seeking to better his condition, though he suffers from no actual distress. It will be the duty of charity to incline more to the unfortunate, unless, perchance, they deserve their misfortune.
>
> (Cicero, *De Off.* 2.18.61–62)

Those who experience 'misfortune' suffer undeservedly and so warrant assistance. What then is a legitimate 'misfortune'? In praising generosity, Cicero hints at a class of 'misfortunes' in others, for the alleviation of which a man might prove generous:

> The generous, on the other hand, are those who employ their own means to ransom captives from brigands, or who assume their friends' debts or help in providing dowries for their daughters, or assist them in acquiring property or increasing what they have.
>
> (Cicero, *De Officiis* 2.16.55–56)

Put simply, some people experience misfortune through no fault of their own; they fall below the social level into which they were born, thus provoking sympathy and not contempt.[6] Conversely, the ancients deem others as shamefully 'poor' because the fault is their own. Philo mentions a series of things that wither the spirit, all of which have to do with the family and which have a social as well as an economic component: 'It is true that marriage, and the rearing of children, and provision of necessities, and disrepute following in the wake of poverty (*adoxia te meta achrematias*), and the business of private and public life . . . wither the flower of wisdom before it blooms' (*Gig.* 29). While it is no fault of a wife that her husband died or of a farmer that drought ruined his crops, if a 'fool' loses his wealth, it is shameful (Matthews and Benjamin 1991: 222–226).

Therefore, we have learned, first, that wealth is a component of honour, and both reside primarily in the family; second, if becoming 'poor' (*ptochos*) includes a corresponding loss of status, this could come about through actual loss of wealth (especially loss of land) or of family (especially death of parents or husband); and, thirdly, such losses threaten one's honour rating, as well as one's economic situation. It would, then, be culturally myopic to consider 'poor' and 'poverty' merely in terms of economic levels (Hollenbach 1987: 50–63).

HONOUR AND THE MATTHEAN MAKARISMS

K. C. Hanson recently presented a paper entitled ' "Makarisms" and "Reproaches": A Social Analysis'.[7] He argues that *ʿasre* and *makarios* should be translated as 'esteemed', and *hoy* and *ouai* as 'disreputable' or 'shame on': 'The terminologies of Hebrew *ʿasre* ("esteemed") and *hoy* ("disreputable"), and their Greek counterparts *makarios* and *ouai*, are part of the word field of "honour and shame".' Hanson suggests that when we approach Matthew's 'beatitudes' (5:3–12) from their proper cultural perspective, we should be alert to several things. First, public honour is being accorded to certain people who fit the categories described. *Makarios* should include the cultural note of 'esteemed' or 'honoured'. Second, if 'poor means someone who cannot maintain his or her status and so suffers loss of honour as well as economic hardship, then the makarisms contain an oxymoron: 'How honourable are those who suffer a loss of honour . . .'

LOSS OF FAMILY = LOSS OF WEALTH AND HONOUR: THE ORIGINAL FOUR MAKARISMS

This study of the four original makarisms builds on but challenges certain scholarly opinions. First, we build on the consensus that the original Q source contained only four makarisms and that Luke's version (Luke 6:20–23) seems to be more original than Matthew's (Matt. 5:3–6, 11–12) (Degenhardt 1965: 45–53). We do not, however, direct our attention to the history of the makarisms, whether they originated separately before being gathered together in the Q tradition (see Kloppenborg 1986: 36–44; Mealand 1980: 62; Horsley 1991: 194).

Rather we wish to consider their cultural meaning and to suggest a plausible social and historical situation to explain them. In this we question the assertion that the first three makarisms deal with 'the general human conditions of poverty and suffering' and the fourth makarism 'is oriented toward the specific situation of persecution of the Christian community' (Kloppenborg 1987: 173). Thus, in terms of the Q document, we resist separating the fourth makarism from the other three, whatever their previous independent histories.

The four original makarisms describe someone who has lost both material wealth (poor, hungry), as well as social standing (loss of kin, ostracism). But do they describe four different situations (Kloppenborg's 'general human conditions') or delineate the full extent of the crisis of one person? If they describe the full extent of one crisis (Boring 1985: 24), what likely scenario explains that? Evidently, in posing the question this way, I am advancing a new hypothesis, namely that the original four makarisms describe the composite fate of a disciple who has been ostracized as a 'rebellious son' by his family for loyalty to Jesus. This ostracism entails total loss of all economic support from the family (food, clothing, shelter), as well as total loss of honour and status in the eyes of the village (a good name, marriage prospects, etc.). Such persons would be 'shameful' in the eyes of the family and village, but Jesus proclaims them 'honourable' (*makarioi*).

The fourth makarism

Let us begin our examination with a closer look at the climactic fourth makarism. It enjoys the significant rhetorical position of being last (Daube 1973: 196–201) and it is triple the length of the others. It describes a total loss of honour. Matthew and Luke record different versions of the fourth makarism, but scholars generally credit Luke with the more original wording in this case.

Luke 6:22	*Matt. 5:11*
Honourable are you when people	Honourable are you when people
hate you exclude you revile you cast out your name as evil	revile you drive you out utter all kinds of evil against you falsely
on account of the Son of man	on my account

According to Luke, some person is being shamefully treated; 'persecuted' is infelicitous here because it is too vague and imprecise, nor does it adequately suggest either the source of the opposition or its socio-cultural result. But let us examine more closely the terms Luke uses with an eye to their cultural meanings. This hostility, moreover, is not the formal or informal excommunication from the synagogue:

1 *misesosin*: 'hate', the opposite of love, has to do with group attachment (Pilch and Malina 1993: 110–112); it means formal rejection and denial of loyalty (see Luke 1:71; 16:13; 19:14); sometimes it is considered virtuous to hate what is evil or disobedient (Michel 1967: 688–689).
2 *aphorisosin*: 'separating' regularly takes place between what is holy and what is unclean: unclean lepers were cast out of the camp (Lev. 13:4, Septuagint), as was Miriam for her revolt (Num. 12; 14). 2 Ezra 10:8 suggests the meaning of 'falling under the ban' (Schmidt 1967: 455). In Matthew it means 'separating' so as to judge or punish (13:49; 25:32); it has the sense of 'to outlaw' from a social group (Fitzmyer 1981: 635).
3 *oneidisosin*: reviling and reproaching are acts of shaming another (Matt.11:20; 27:44; Rom. 15:3; 1 Pet. 4:14); the predominant sense is 'disgrace', 'shame', 'scandal', then 'abuse', 'objurgation' (Schneider 1968: 238).
4 *ekbalosin to onoma hymon hos poneron*: although it has been argued that 'the name' here is '*Christianos*' (Fitzmyer 1981: 635), a man's personal name or reputation is at stake; Luke speaks of someone speaking calumny, that is, of attacking the public reputation and honour of another.

The fourth makarism describes the separation of a person from his basic social group, either banning or expulsion; it speaks of his being reviled and reproached; his honour, name and reputation are attacked. He is, thus, completely shamed in the eyes of his neighbours.

The material or economic effects of this are not hard to imagine. The Tosefta describes the plight of someone banned or excommunicated: 'One does not sell to them or receive from them or take from them or give to them. One does not teach their sons a trade, and does not obtain healing from them' (*t. Hullin* 2:20). If the person so treated is an artisan, then public reproach will result in loss of employment and trade; if a peasant farmer, the loss of cooperation in planting and harvesting, a break in marriage contracts, an absence from the reciprocal feasts among villagers at weddings and the like. Such losses entail declining material wealth for a peasant and consequent failure to maintain one's subsistence and previous social standing.

In the case of the fourth makarism, public shame goes hand in hand with severe loss of wealth. The person described there is 'driven out' (*dioxosin*) or 'outlawed' (*aphorisosin*). This implies that he has lost his property: land (if he is a farmer) or market stall (if he is an artisan). Total economic ruin, as well as corresponding collapse of social standing, quickly follow. This person will surely be a *ptochos*, but is he honourably or shamefully destitute? Whence this hostility?

Previous studies of the 'forms of persecution' which befell the early disciples of Jesus focused on formal judicial acts (Hare 1967, Forkman 1972). They describe 'persecution' as a form of exclusion from the synagogue, not, however, the formal *niddui*, but rather 'an informal ban employed by every community . . . toward individuals it despises' (Hare 1967: 53). Although the New Testament speaks of disciples 'cast out of the synagogue' (John 9:22; 12:42; 16:2) or simply 'expelled' (John 9:34; Hauck 1968a: 527–528), there is another possibility for banning or exclusion, namely family sanctions against rebellious sons. I suggest that a likely scenario for the fourth makarism is the situation of a son being disinherited by his father and shunned by his family.

And while 'itinerancy' may be the role of certain Cynic-like disciples (Theissen 1973; Mack 1993: 114–121), fresh discussions are emerging from Q scholars about stable communities (Theissen 1977: 17–23; Horsley 1989: 197). Not every person ostracized by family necessarily became an itinerant, much less assumed that formal missionary role.

The other three makarisms

The other three beatitudes in their Lukan and probably more original form are:

> Honourable are you beggars, because yours is the Kingdom of God.
> Honourable are you who are hungry now, because you will be filled.
> Honourable are you who mourn now, because you will laugh.
>
> (Luke 6:20–21)

Let us examine these makarisms in the light of the fourth one, for they can be understood as specifying more exactly the economic or material loss that follows the loss of honour and social standing (see Robbins 1985: 39–44 and 51–54). My strategy is to imagine them as literally and realistically as possible in the economic and cultural world of peasants and artisans.

As regards the first makarism, most peasants and artisans in antiquity possessed little material wealth; and, as we said, they were not thereby called 'poor' (*ptochos*) if they had what was sufficient (i.e. subsistence). Ulrich Luz describes a 'poor' person as one who is not simply lacking in wealth:

> 'Poor,' according to Semitic usage, means indeed not only those who are lacking in money, but, more comprehensively, the oppressed, miserable, dependent, humiliated . . . the translation by the Greek word *ptochos*, the strongest available Greek word for social poverty, speaks in favor of this interpretation. The basic rule is: The *penes* has to work, the *ptochos* has to beg.
>
> (Luz 1989: 231)

In the first makarism, those addressed are called *ptochoi*, which we take to refer to destitute beggars, not *penes* or the general peasant audience of have-nots (see Esler 1987: 180–181). I favour, moreover, understanding this reference to *ptochos* as a general statement concerning persons who have suffered a recent and severe loss of means (Guelich 1976a: 426); more specificity is given in the subsequent makarisms.

The literal and simple meaning of 'hunger' as lacking food seems warranted. Drought and famine may cause hunger in the land (Josephus, *J. A.* 15.299–316; 20.51–53; Acts 11:28; Garnsey 1988: 219–223), as well as excessive taxation (Kloppenborg 1991: 86–88). While landed peasants have resources and relationships to alleviate starvation, not so landless peasants. They have scant money with which to purchase food; even if they had, the money could hardly last for long. These 'hungry' folk are promised that they will 'eat their fill', but at present they are *ptochoi* in regard to their daily bread (Hamel 1990: 8–52; Oakman 1986: 22–28).

Finally, those who 'mourn' might be said to be engaged in mourning for the dead (see Gen. 50:3; 1 Esdr. 1:32; 1 Macc. 12:52; 13:26); they are not lamenting sins or awaiting the eschatological day: they will be 'consoled'.[8] Since we find the combination of 'mourning' for the dead and 'comfort' in ancient literature, the mourning envisioned here most probably involves the loss of family and kin. The text gives no reason for supposing that the 'mourners' are the ubiquitous widows and orphans of antiquity (on life expectancy in antiquity, see Carney 1975: 88). Nevertheless, someone lacks parents, family and kin, with all the economic and social loss attendant upon this.

The relationship of the fourth and the other makarisms

The final makarism offers a plausible scenario for understanding the other three. If a son were banned or disinherited by his father, he would be 'hated' by the family and 'outlawed' from the family house and land. He would then truly be 'poor' (*ptochos*), that is, suffering a severe loss of all resources, material as well as social. He could truly be said to be 'mourning' the loss of kin and experiencing the loss of status that comes with being without family. Finally, if a son were driven away from the family land, he would immediately experience the loss of access to the grain, vegetables, fruits etc. which were the daily food of peasants; no doubt he would literally be 'hungry and thirsty'. The ostracism described in the last makarism, therefore, describes a situation where sufficiency and subsistence fail. Furthermore, each of the four makarisms, either individually or taken together, genuinely describe a *ptochos*, someone who has suffered a loss of subsistence and so cannot maintain the social position and status into which he was born.

Moreover, this peasant would suffer a true and total loss of honour and status. His name would be reviled, his reputation held up to rebuke and his character calumniated. Business deals and marriage arrangements with such an outcast would be unthinkable. With loss of wealth, he would hardly be in a position to maintain his social obligations and social status. This loss of honour, I suggest, would deprive him of all standing in the village or town. He would be looked on by his neighbours as a person reaping a harvest of shame. This possible scenario is by no means the only one. What would make it probable?

LOSS OF FAMILY IN THE Q SOURCE

Several passages in the Q source support the probability of the scenario described above. Two describe family crises (Luke 12:51–53//Matt. 10:34–36 and Luke 14:25–26//Matt. 10:37–39) and two deal with loss of wealth (Luke 12:22–32//Matt. 6:25–32 and Luke 12:33–34//Matt. 6:19–21). Three of these passages are found in one continuous discourse in Luke 12; and if the general presumption of the originality of the Lukan sequence prevails here, then the materials on family crisis were originally linked with those about loss of wealth. The loss of family could be the probable context for loss of wealth and thus of honour.

Crisis in the family

One passage records Jesus attacking the social debt of obedience owed by sons to their fathers and family (Luke 12:51–53//Matt. 10:34–36).

Luke 12:51–53	*Matt. 10:34–36*
Do you think that I have come to give peace on earth? No, I tell you, but rather division;	Do not think that I have come to bring peace on earth; I have not come to bring peace, but a sword.
henceforth in one house there shall be five divided, three against two and two against three;	
they will be divided, father against son, and son against father, mother against daughter and daughter against her mother, mother-in-law against daughter-in-law and daughter-in-law against her mother-in-law.	I have come to set a man against his father, and a daughter against her mother, and a daughter-in-law against her mother-in-law
	and a man's foes will be those of his own household.

Despite other sayings of Jesus in support of family (Mark 7:9–12; see Pilch 1988: 32–59), he is attacking here the basic solidarity and loyalty family members owe to each other. This passage implies that the division of the family occurs precisely because of Jesus ('I have come to . . .'); it envisions some members loyal to family traditions but others joining the circle of Jesus and espousing his teachings.

Linked with this is a second passage (Luke 14:25–27//Matt. 10:37–39) which also has to do with family loyalty. It presents a totally divided household:

Luke 14:26–27	*Matt. 10:37–38*
He who loves father or mother more than me is not worthy of me; and who loves son or daughter more than me	If anyone comes to me and does not hate his own father and mother and wife and children and brothers and sisters, yes, and even his own life,
is not worthy of me	he cannot be my disciple
And he who does not take up his cross and follow me	Whoever does not bear his own cross and come after me
is not worthy of me.	cannot be my disciple.

Matthew's version emphasizes 'love X more than me'; this connotes a posture of respect for or acceptance of the approval of another, which is the essence of honour. Who 'loves X more than me' is 'not worthy' of me, another term of honour. Luke's account stresses 'hating' parents and family members, which translates into disregard for filial obligations of obedience and respect (see Luke 9:59–60//Matt. 8:21–22). This son would hardly be 'honouring father and mother'. Who does not hate the family group (with its social standing, land and wealth) cannot find affiliation, status and respect in Jesus' group. Again the issue focuses on the source of honour, either from family or Jesus. Loyalty either to family or to Jesus occasions the choice.

Both versions contain an exhortation to 'take up one's cross' and become a member of Jesus' fictive kinship group. The 'cross' must surely be a metaphor for negative experiences, possibly physical sufferings (begging, hunger) and/or social ones (loss of family, shame). These sufferings are not the result of taxation, drought or some other 'misfortune', but precisely the results of becoming Jesus' disciple. There would be, then, shame from the family, but honour from Jesus.

It takes little imagination to see how 'hatred' of one's family would lead to a 'cross'. Disobedience to one's parents, a paramount vice condemned by custom and law, can easily lead to social and economic ruin. A rebellious son should be banned by the family (Deut. 21:18–20). If banned, he will surely take up a 'cross' to be Jesus' disciple, namely, suffering as physical (hunger) as it is social (mourning, begging, being an outcast). The crux of the crisis lies in honour and loyalty, either traditional loyalty to parents and family with its concomitant honour, wealth and status or affiliation with Jesus. Loss and gain: loyalty to Jesus entails *loss of honour* in the family and kinship network, because the honour code between father and son is violated, but also a *gain of honour*, because Jesus honours those loyal to him (*makarioi*) and acclaims them 'worthy'.

Although these passages do not say that the father eventually bans the rebellious son and disinherits him or that the son quits his father's house, yet they offer an immediate and plausible scenario for the ostracism described in the fourth makarism. If any form of banning or disinheriting results from a son's loyalty to Jesus, then he will truly be 'poor', as well as hungry and mourning.

Other remarks on loss of wealth

Two other passages need to be examined (Luke 12:22–32//Matt. 5:24–34 and Luke 12:33–34//Matt. 6:19–21), the correct social interpretation of which can shed light on the economic and cultural effects of families being divided over loyalty to Jesus. In the Lukan and Matthean versions, both passages are linked together, an editorial clue which we respect.

Luke 12:22–32//Matt. 6:25–34 explicitly treats loss of wealth and its relationship to honour. The passage begins with a topic statement:

Do not be concerned about:
what to eat
what to wear

(Luke 12:22//Matt. 6:25)

The scenario envisioned here reflects the gender division of society common in antiquity: a male world (public tasks in public places) and a female world (private or household tasks in the household). The person 'concerned about what to eat' is a male, whom I call the husband. When he looks at the birds of the air, he 'sees' fields, which in the gender-divided world of antiquity were the male places where males did the male task of farming. Birds, however, do not perform the tasks typically done by males, i.e. 'sowing, reaping, gathering into barns or storehouses' (Luke 12:24//Matt. 6:26). Yet God gives them subsistence food. The issue is food production, the proper concern of a male peasant.

Alternately a female scenario is imagined. The female in the family is concerned about 'what to wear', i.e. 'clothing', which was produced by females in the household.[9] This female is presumably the wife of the male addressed above, so that the basic male and female tasks (farming/clothing) are in view, which are the primary tasks of a peasant household. A basic family unit is envisioned which is typically divided into the characteristic gender-specific tasks – males: food production, and females: clothing production. When this female looks at the fields with a gender-specific eye, she sees stuff for weaving. The lilies 'neither spin, nor toil', yet they are more gorgeous than the royal robes woven by Solomon's harem.

Beyond this gender-specific reading, the exhortation treats the loss of wealth, that is, insufficiency of food and clothing; peasant subsistence in these two basic areas is failing. The text does not say why, but the options are limited. Drought, which produces famine for humans and lack of fodder for wool-bearing sheep. Or excessive taxation, which leads to peasant indebtedness, which when foreclosed results in lost of land. Or family conflict, such that a son (and his wife) were disinherited, 'driven away' from the family farm, and set adrift without land or animals. Which option seems appropriate? Since the exhortation is addressed to disciples (*mathetas*, Luke 12:22), loss of wealth is formally related to issues of group loyalty, and not to 'general human conditions'.

The passage, moreover, links wealth with honour and status. At the very beginning, the topic is announced with an imperative (*me merimnate*). As part of the topic, a value statement is made that the 'soul' is more valuable (*pleion*) than food, and the 'body' more important than clothing. The comparative term *pleion* relates to the world of worth: whether it has a quantitative or qualitative note, *pleion* ranks one thing above another, thus giving respect and honour to it. After the male is told to look at the birds, he is asked (Matthew) or told (Luke) that he is 'of more value' than they, another term connoting honourable status. Rhetorically this repeats the earlier value question, and explicitly bestows honour to the man who lacks food (and land). A male is worth more than mere birds. Likewise with the female; after she looks at the lilies of the field, she is told that a paternal figure values her more than them, and so is promised honour and respect.[10] What may we say about this passage? The husband and wife are peasants who are falling below the subsistence level in regard to food and clothing. Nothing in the passage explicitly states that loss of land, especially family land, is at stake. But something is missing from the horizon: there is no family, no household and no kinship network to catch them as they fall. In fact, the addressees are told to turn to a heavenly paternal figure, rather than to the obvious kinship network (Luke 12:30; Matt. 6:26, 32). Of course, the family may have all died out; but then the son should have inherited his father's land.

Nevertheless, the loss of wealth by this husband and wife entails a concomitant loss of honour and social standing, for a major element in the exhortation has to do with 'worth' and 'value', i.e. honour. Therefore, this husband and wife are truly becoming 'poor' in the eyes of the rest of the peasants, thus losing familial honour but gaining worthiness and respect in Jesus' and God's eyes.

Family banning or disinheritance of a rebellious son would account for the loss of subsistence envisioned here, as well as the loss of honour attendant on such an economic catastrophe. This option becomes plausible and probable when we recall that this passage in Luke 12 is linked directly with other remarks about family conflict. We presume that Luke retains the correct sequence of the original Q source:

> 'do not be anxious about your life' (12:22–32)
> 'treasure in heaven' (12:33–34)
> 'a house divided' (12:51–53).

This Lukan collection concerns itself with disinheritance (12:13) and covetousness (12:15), the former directly dealing with family conflict. The original source, then, saw a connection between loss of wealth, family conflict and discipleship. It envisions a scenario which would make a person needy of food and clothing as described in 12:22–32, namely loss of family through disinheritance or banning.

In an adjoining passage (Luke 12:33–34//Matt. 6:19–21) disciples are instructed about 'treasure'. Like the previous passage, it begins with a command from Jesus: 'Sell your possessions and give alms' (Luke 12:33) or 'Do not lay up treasure on earth' (Matt. 6:19). Since Luke regularly exhorts disciples to give alms (Luke 11:41; Acts 3:2–6; 9:36; 10:2, 4, 31), Matthew contains the more original wording here. The imperative in Matt. 6:19 ('do not lay up treasure') is formally parallel in structure to that in Matt. 6:25 and Luke 12:22 ('do not be anxious').

Jesus' remarks about 'treasure' are clearly hyperbolic, for subsistence peasants simply do not have 'treasure', especially in this period of ruinous taxation. Peasants could have an ox (for ploughing), some sheep (for wool/clothing), some goats (for milk) and some fruit trees and vines (for food). But this is hardly 'treasure'. The moth threatens the few blankets and garments the peasant has (on the cost and scarcity of clothing, see Hamel 1990: 64–67) and corruption (*brosis*) rots wood (house or wooden plough) and corrodes metal (an iron plough?). Thieves (*kleptai*) abound in Galilee in this period, whose prime targets would be villages unprotected by walls (on widespread banditry, see Horsley and Hanson 1985: 48–87).

However meagre his wealth, it is a peasant's 'treasure' and the key indicator of his status and honour in the village. Jesus' remark, moreover, tells the peasant not to value what all his family and neighbours value, but rather to value something else superior to 'treasure on earth'. At a minimum, Jesus attacks peasant covetousness (Luke 12:15 and Delling 1968: 266–270) and the honour attached to wealth. Nothing explicit is said about loss of wealth here, except that moths, corruption and thieves cause loss. But we remember that wealth and honour reside in the family, not the individual. Hence a family's collective honour is in view.

From the discussion in this section, one clear theme emerges. The Q document contains a number of statements which attack family unity and loyalty. These statements, moreover, are often linked with remarks on loss of wealth and honour. Thus crisis within the family emerges as a probable cause of the disinheritance, banning or excommunication envisioned in the fourth makarism. Such a radical action by a family against a disobedient or rebellious son would surely entail immediate, severe economic and social loss.

SUMMARY, CONCLUSION AND FURTHER CONVERSATION

Summary

To the extent that the early part of this study was successful, we have shown that being 'poor' (i.e. *ptochos*) contains a social and cultural component as well as an economic one. Clearly 'wealth' is a component of 'honour'; and the loss of wealth entails a corresponding threat of loss of honour. When a man moves from being *penes* to *ptochos*, he loses the resources to maintain his social status or honour rating. This loss of honour is more serious to ancient peasants than the mere loss of wealth.

The scenario or *Sitz im Leben* envisioned by the makarisms in Q has to do with both loss of honour (*makarios* = 'honourable') as well as loss of wealth. But the question remains: why did a person suffer loss of wealth according to the makarisms? My hypothesis has been that a son and his wife are envisioned as banned or disinherited by a father and family, and so they suffer both loss of wealth and honour. I will now summarize the results of this investigation.

The four makarisms are addressed to disciples, not the crowds. As such they do not speak of 'the general human conditions of poverty and suffering' applicable to the crowds, or the generic 'anxiety about the basic necessities' (Horsley 1991:194), but of specific consequences of discipleship.

The four makarisms, whatever their tradition history, are joined by the time of the Q document, and should be taken as a unit, as a comprehensive statement about the economic and social situation of certain persons. Daube's arguments (1973) persuade us that the fourth makarism constitutes the appropriate climax of the series, and so should not be separated from the other three.

The makarisms contrast the way of Jesus with other 'ways' of living (Guelich 1976a: 416–419). Hence, the general *Sitz im Leben* envisioned is one of discipleship and loyalty shown to Jesus. Disciples 'take up their cross' and follow him; they are willing to lose all to gain his favour and approval (Matt. 19:29). Thus they are active players who make choices which have consequences. They are not mere passive victims, who suffer 'misfortune' independent of their actions. Dennis Duling distinguishes 'involuntary marginals' from 'voluntary' ones (1993: 644–648). 'Involuntary marginals' cannot participate in the normative social life of a group because of race, ethnicity, gender and the like; 'voluntary marginals', however, consciously and by choice live outside the normative social patterns. The beatitudes address 'voluntary marginals' who by choosing to follow Jesus are excluded from their normative social statuses, roles, offices and the like (Duling 1993: 653).

But discipleship with a deviant like Jesus is costly. Thus, the four original makarisms should be seen as Jesus' 'honouring' of disciples who have paid a price and been shamed by their kinship network. They are not just typical peasants in the audience, all of whom are *penes*; rather they are *ptochoi*, that is, people who have suffered a recent loss of wealth and status, which directly results from discipleship or loyalty to Jesus.

But what type of loss? If a village turned on someone, he would presumably still have family to fall back on, either his father's house and land or his own house and land. He would still have kin in the area, whose first loyalty would be to him. He would not necessarily be hungry or mourning. But a disciple who suffered disinheritance by his father or banning from the family land would become a *ptochos*, and immediately suffer lack of subsistence, kinship and honour.

The Hebrew scriptures are quite concerned with the proper obedience of sons to their fathers; obedience to and respect for parents are cornerstones of the Hebrew scriptures,[11] although less emphasis is found in early Christian writings on this theme (Mark 7:9–13//Matt. 15:3–6; Eph. 6:2–3). One finds the motif of 'the rebellious son' in scripture (Deut. 21:18–20) and rabbinic literature (Malina 1993c: 2–4). Ancient childrearing practices consisted of disciplining children who were perceived to be naturally rebellious (Pilch 1993b: 102–107; Blidstein 1975: 37–53). The right relationship of sons and fathers, therefore, was a recurring, common problem thoughout the life cycle (see Mark 7:10–12; Matt. 21:28–29; Luke 15:11–13). Issues of family loyalty and parental authority, not religious excommunication from the synagogue, emerge as an important locus of crisis in the lives of ordinary peasants. We attended to passages in the Q source where Jesus boldly claims to have caused division in families. These divisions would not be worth mentioning if they did not result in social consequences. Luke 12:51–53//Matt. 10:34–36 and Luke 14:26–27//Matt. 10:37–38 envision disciples of Jesus experiencing hostility from their kinship groups, which I argue results in some form of disinheritance or banning (i.e. the fourth makarism), and so loss of wealth and honour.

The Q document contains a number of explicit remarks about the troubled relationships within families caused by discipleship with Jesus:

Luke 9:59–60//Matt. 8:21–22
Luke 12:51–53//Matt. 10:34–36
Luke 14:26–27//Matt. 10:37–39

In addition to these, there are other passages which seem to have family members in view, who suffer a crisis in the kinship network (see 1 Cor. 7:12–16). One passage envisions the plight of a family (husband and wife) who has neither food nor clothing (Luke 12:22–32//Matt. 6:25–33). Although one can imagine many reasons for this social tragedy, the persons addressed are clearly disciples to whom Jesus issues commands. The question returns, then, as to why a disciple is in such dire straits. Alternative answers such as debt foreclosure or drought do not satisfy the criterion that such a tragedy is befalling a disciple. A probable scenario seems to be the same one envisioned above in Luke 12: 51–53//Matt. 10:34–39, namely some form of kinship crisis which results in a loss of land, wealth, food and clothing. Seen in combination with Luke 12:51–53//Matt. 10:34–36, Luke 12:22–32//Matt. 6:25–33 probably reflects the same situation: discipleship has caused family division and resulted in disinheritance or banning from the basic kinship network. Thus the family is seen in the Q tradition as a primary source of 'persecution'.

Our investigation of a focus in the original Q document on family crisis does not contradict the data in Matthew's Gospel which treats of the polemic between the disciples of Jesus and 'your synagogue'. The relationship of Matthew and the *birkat ha-minim* is a valid explanation for various passages dealing with a social crisis. But these later clues about social dislocation do not adequately explain the earlier crises of disciples described in the Q document.

Conclusion

What, then, is the cultural meaning of Jesus' four makarisms? The mere loss of wealth would make those described *ptochoi*, but what of their honour rating and its relationship to their loss of wealth? My scenario envisions those disinherited or banned as suffering a frightful social stigma in the village as disobedient and rebellious sons. They clearly lose honour and so become shameful, at least in the eyes of their neighbours. According to the materials we read earlier, they would not be the objects of compassion or sympathy. They got what they deserved, because they did not suffer 'misfortune'. They experience shame from family and kin for their rebellion against family tradition. But these people are disciples of Jesus. In his perspective 'last is first', 'least is greatest' and 'shame is honour'. Hence a disciple who has suffered shame in the eyes of his neighbours precisely for honouring Jesus is honoured by him in turn. 'How honourable are those who . . .' They indeed are 'worthy' to be his disciples. Thus Jesus' remarks admit economic loss and the consequent loss of honour. But he honours the dishonoured.

Further conversation

This study engages the current conversation on Q in several ways. Concern over the social context of Q is receiving much attention.[12] The tendency to downplay the crises faced by disciples from religious to economic factors is welcome; this study suggests that the family factor be emphasized more, as many passages in Q indicate. Second, although passing mention is made of crises within families by Q scholars (Kloppenborg 1987: 241; Mack 1988b: 634), the materials in Q which we have examined suggest that division of families and banning of rebellious sons should be taken more seriously as part of the historical and cultural background for many aspects of the Q tradition. Third, the importance of 'itinerancy' as a hallmark of 'missionaries' in Q still enjoys support (Catchpole 1991), especially with recent interest in Cynic parallels. But not all disciples were itinerant; some who were ostracized by their families did not necessarily become itinerants. It is often claimed that disciples in the Q tradition are called to a 'life of protest' against society (i.e. prophets). But 'voluntary marginals' whose allegiance to Jesus caused them banishment from their families need not be classified as espousing a life of protest (Horsley 1991: 184), but considered rather as requiring support in a crisis of kinship authority created by discipleship. Finally, more serious consideration needs to be given to the basic social institution of antiquity, namely the family and the role of the *paterfamilias* (Hennessey 1993). Further studies in Q would do well to investigate the role of families in socializing new members and exercising social control. Issues of family and (fictive) kinship remain underdeveloped in scholarship.

NOTES

1 'Sufficiency' (*autarcheia*) was a value regularly praised among the ancients; for a peasant to live by this principle is probably making a virtue of necessity. 'Sufficiency' applies even to wealth: 'Do you ask what is the proper limit to wealth? It is, first, to have what is necessary, and, second, to have what is enough' (Seneca, *Ep. Mor.* 2.6).

2 See Malina 1993a, Neyrey 1991a: 25 65 and Esler 1994a: 19 36.

3 In Isa. 3:18 24 we are given a description of the wealth of certain elite females in the Jerusalem of the prophet's day; noteworthy is the sense of 'conspicuous display' of the wealth of these elite persons. Conspicuous consumption and display are said to be consistent features of the eastern Mediterranean. See the praise of Solomon's sumptuous palace by the Queen of Sheba (1 Kgs 10:4 5); it gained him further wealth (10:10) and public honour (10:6 8).

4 Luke's Jesus says that peasants can notice the 'fine linen and purple' of a rich man (Luke 16:19) and that those who wear soft raiment and are gorgeously apparelled live in kings' courts (Luke 7:25). Cotton from Egypt (Isa. 19:9) and silk from the orient (Ezek. 16:10, 13; Rev. 18:12) were available for the rich. And the clothing of the elite would be dyed in blue, scarlet and purple (Exod. 28:5 6; Jer. 10:9; 1 Macc. 4:23; Rev. 18:12). We can imagine Herod's splendour when 'he put on his royal robe' to take his seat on his throne (Acts 12:21).

5 Ancient rhetorical handbooks and the instructions on writing *encomia* in the *progymnasmata* all instruct the orator or writer to attend carefully to the ancestors and family of the person under discussion, for 'honour resides in the blood.' See Isocrates, *Panegyricus* 23 25; Quintilian, *Inst. Orat.* 5.5.23 25; Josephus, *Life* 1 6. The ancient concern with genealogy belongs here.

6 This idea of 'honourable misfortune' might be compared with three 'misfortunes' mentioned in Lev. 25, which render a person truly 'poor': (1) 'if your brother becomes poor and sells part of his property' (v. 25); (2) 'if your brother becomes poor and cannot maintain himself with you' (v. 35); (3) 'if your brother becomes poor beside you, and sells himself to you' (vs. 39). Thus, loss of land, loss of means to meet basic social obligations, and debt that drives a family into slavery are examples of 'misfortune' for which there should be 'redemption' in the Jubilee year. Thus families may suffer misfortune by (1) loss of family land, which is as much a status as an economic indicator; (2) debt bondage; and (3) loss of resources to maintain one's status. To these could be added others: a widow in a village might be called 'poor' because she has no male to defend her interests and safeguard her reputation. This is not simply an economic issue (i.e. loss of her house; see Mark 12:40; Luke 20:47).

7 Forthcoming in *Semeia.*

8 One thinks of 'consolation' literature in the Graeco-Roman world, which gave advice to those who were grieving and mourning the death of kin; see Plutarch, *Consol. ad Apoll.* 112A-B or 1 Thess. 4:13 17; Malherbe 1989: 64 65.

9 Xenophon describes the respective places of males and females in a household: 'Human beings live not in the open air, like beasts, but obviously need shelter. Nevertheless, those who mean to win store to fill the covered place, have need for someone to work at the open-air occupations; since plowing, sowing, planting and grazing are all such open-air employments; and these supply the needful food. Then again, as soon as this is stored in the covered place, then there is need for someone to keep it and to work at the things that must be done under cover. Cover is needed for the nursing of the infants; cover is needed for the making of corn into

bread, and likewise for the manufacture of clothing from the wool. And since both the indoor and the outdoor tasks demand labour and attention, God from the first adapted the woman's nature, I think, to the indoor and man's to the outdoor tasks and cares' (*Oecomenicus* 7.19 22).

10 On the relationship of clothing to honour, see Neyrey 1993a: 20–22; 1993b: 120–122.

11 See Exod. 20:12; 21:17; Lev. 20:9; 5:16; Tobit 4:3 4; 14:12–13; Prov. 1:8; 6:20; Sir. 3:1 16.

12 See Mack 1988b: 620 632; Horsley 1989: 195 200; Kloppenborg 1989: 211–212; 1991: 85 88, 96 99.

9

THE MATTHEAN BROTHERHOOD AND MARGINAL SCRIBAL LEADERSHIP

Dennis C. Duling

The cult-association is primarily a family. Its head is called 'pater' . . . The members of these sodalities are brothers . . .

A. D. Nock, 1924

INTRODUCTION

Research on the Gospel of Matthew in the last half-century is rich with studies about the Matthean 'church' (Stanton 1985; Meier 1992: 625). Within the last few years social-historical and social-scientific critics have also begun to analyze the Matthean group. Studies include the Matthean 'honour code' (White 1986), insider and outsider labelling (Malina and Neyrey 1988), economics and household themes (Crosby 1988; Love 1993), the Matthean community as a form of sectarian Judaism (Overman 1990; Saldarini 1994), intragroup conflicts and the geographical location of the community (Viviano 1990; Balch 1991; Theissen 1991; Saldarini 1992a), gender issues (Anderson 1983; Corley 1993b; Love 1993; 1994), marginality (Duling 1993), and a variety of other social concerns (Stanton 1992a; 1992b; Duling 1992).

In this study I take up voluntary associations in ancient Mediterranean antiquity and then look at the brotherhood and scribe texts in Matthew in relation to them. The ancient voluntary associations do not explain every aspect of the Matthean group; nonetheless, as brotherhood associations they explain some of its features. My view is that the Matthean group is in the process of formation beyond the stage of a Jewish faction recruited by Jesus of Nazareth; indeed, it has factions within it. Further, while retaining certain features of a sect, it is beginning to move to a level of assimilation, formal organization, development of norms and style of leadership which suggest that it might be called an 'incipient corporation'. This hypothesis will have to be eventually tested with other variables in the Gospel. Here I focus on three features: 'brotherhood' language, related internal disciplinary processes and scribal leadership. The level of analysis is primarily microsocial and, while conflict between the Matthean group and other groups plays its role, my focus is on the Matthean group itself.

In the present volume the essays by Malina, utilizing small group theory, and Elliott, reworking notions of sectarianism, represent distinct ways of explaining the broad social nature of early Christianity. There are tensions between these two broad approaches which arise both because of the different provinces of social-scientific research they each draw upon and because of the complexity of the larger Graeco-Roman social system within which discrete groups developed.

One way to deal with the issues is to look at the Graeco-Roman macrosociety as a 'middle range' society, one that has evolved beyond the simple society into a complex social system (Goody 1968: 4). Such societies have social arrangements that are remnants of 'primitive' societies, especially in rural, peasant contexts, but have also developed more complex social arrangements, including the possibility of discrete microsocial groups, especially in urban contexts. Such a perception of Graeco-Roman macrosociety is consistent with the views of John Kautsky who argues that there are three broad phases of history, though they are not necessarily or mechanically sequential: the 'primitive', the 'traditional aristocratic' and the 'modern' (Kautsky 1982: 21–27). Kautsky's view can be diagramatically represented as follows:

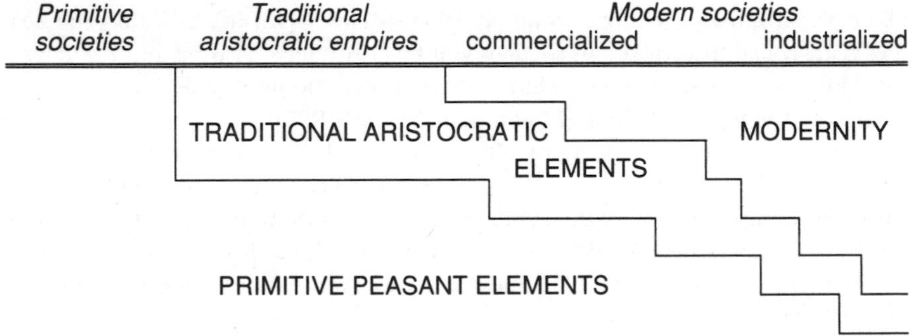

Figure 5 Societies representing the three phases of history (adapted from Kautsky 1982: 27)

Kautsky's key categories are 'aristocracy' and 'aristocratic empire':

> An aristocracy . . . is a ruling class in an agrarian economy that does not engage in productive labor but lives wholly or primarily off the labor of peasants. Hence aristocratic empires must contain not only aristocrats but also peasants who, in turn, live in agrarian primitive societies. Because . . . it takes many peasants to support one aristocrat, this also implies that aristocratic empires are necessarily a good deal larger than primitive societies.
>
> (Kautsky 1982: 24)

Kautsky's typical 'traditional aristocratic empires' are found among ancient Egyptian, Mesopotamian and early medieval civilizations. While Kautsky will allow for a certain amount of trade in his traditional aristocratic empire, he excludes from this type empires in which aristocrats have yielded some of their power to merchants or have become merchants themselves. Such societies have now become influenced by 'commercialization', that is, a developed class of merchants, financiers and tax collectors. He places such commercialized societies in the early phase of the modern society. From this perspective, the Roman empire is not a classic aristocratic empire, but has one foot, or at least a toe, in modern society (Kautsky 1982: 38). Yet it still contains some 'primitive peasant elements', as do modern societies.

In this study I take a similar position insofar as I accept Gerhard Lenski's and Jonathan Turner's view that the Roman empire is an advanced agrarian society in which small fictive kin groups emerge as surrogate groups when real family groups are in decline.[1] These voluntary associations are substitute primary groups, or surrogate kinship groups. Such a view is not totally inconsistent with Elliott's attempt to maintain the 'sect' category, and it corresponds to other scholars who analyze Judaism and early Christianity in terms of a 'sect' (Saldarini 1994), some of whom use the parent/child analogy indebted to Weber and Troeltsch.[2] However, my view is that the Matthean group has moved not only beyond the 'Jesus faction' as Malina describes it, but is also beginning to move beyond the 'sect' as Elliott describes it, though it preserves certain forms of 'sectarian' ideology and practice. One might say that as the Roman empire has moved slightly in the direction of the modern world because of its commercialism, the Matthean group has moved slightly towards the emergent bureaucratic institution because of its growing assimilation, formal organization, development of norms, and style of leadership. Thus, while the Matthean group has recently been described as a Christian-Jewish 'sect', I suggest that it might be described as an 'incipient corporation' with many sect-type remnants (Duling 1993). While this judgement is a matter of degree of formation based on a broader typological continuum than ideal types, and may contain a 'Western' organizational criterion rejected by Bryan Wilson (1973: 11–16), I shall attempt to undergird that view by looking at a lower level of abstraction, the Matthew group in relation to small groups in Mediterranean society, as well as emergent leadership roles within the Matthean group, specifically 'the scribe'.

VOLUNTARY ASSOCIATIONS IN MEDITERRANEAN ANTIQUITY

Following in part the views of Gerhard Lenski, Jonathan Turner holds that in advanced agrarian societies increasing vertical stratification is accompanied by some weakening of the extended family and the multiplication of small groups (Turner 1984: 63–64; also Saldarini 1988: 60). Turner states:

> Kinship, while still important, becomes less dominant as the organization axis of the society as alternate structures proliferate and expand. . . . Voluntary associations increase as a highly differentiated population seeks friends and contacts in a variety of economic, political, religious, and social associations.
>
> (Turner 1984: 86–87)

The point should not be overstated: actual families and households are still one of the indispensable social units for understanding Mediterranean society.[3] Yet the tendency is nonetheless present. Anthropologists have often observed that voluntary associations help rural people who migrate to urban areas to preserve their ethnic heritage and cultural traditions and to adapt to a new, rapidly changing cultural context. Such associations are sometimes called 'fictive kinship groups'.[4]

Lenski's primary example of an advanced agrarian society is the Roman empire (Lenski and Lenski 1987: 176–91). Thus, it is not surprising that scholars of Graeco-Roman antiquity have analyzed groups corresponding to Lenski's and Turner's small groups in agrarian societies.[5] Typical are the so-called 'voluntary associations'. These associations are, of course, not voluntary associations as they appear in modern, free societies (Robertson 1966). Nonetheless, such groups existed in antiquity. Evidence for *koinoniai* (Latin *collegia*) comes primarily from inscriptions and documentary papyri.[6] Most are small, often about twenty to thirty members, and mainly local. Some are coalitions of the 'action-set' or 'faction' type, and some factions become, or are perceived by the Romans as 'social movements', that is, 'revolutionary' or 'reforming' sects. However, they can also become more permanent 'corporations' with governing rules and a hierarchy of offices. I shall briefly say more about such groups.

There were different sub-types of associations: ethnic groups originally modelled on the *polis* (*koina*; *politeiai*); older boys' and young men's 'athletic clubs' (*ephebeia*; *neoi*) linked to the *gymnasium*; numerous 'industrial' guilds and associations of traders (listed in Broughton 1938: 841–844); a great number of trade guilds; professional associations; theatre guilds of actors, dancers and artists; burial societies; and philosophical schools. Normally they were supported by patrons, some of whom endowed shrines to preserve their memories in annual birthday rites. Though association members could come from various social strata there was also the natural tendency to preserve the larger society's ranking system.

The aim of most associations was broadly 'social'. In them members could sometimes achieve some semblance of social status otherwise denied. Freedmen, for example,

> saw in the association the only means to escape their isolation and weakness, to acquire some little consideration and even a little influence, finally to create for themselves in the society, in the city, an honourable place.
>
> (Jean Waltzing [1895] quoted in Wilken 1971: 281)

The associations offered people 'a sense of identity and comradeship, a social unit larger than the family and smaller than the state where they could meet together with friends, eat and drink, worship, play, and share common experiences' (Wilken 1971: 281; see Dill 1905: 267). When they disturbed public order or were suspected of being politically motivated social movements, however, these *sodalitates* were labelled by the Roman authorities *hetaeriae* and, from time to time, the Romans clearly sought to dissolve them,[7] or control them by forbidding new groups to form, requiring official membership registration, and limiting frequency of meetings. Yet, in most cases associations were legally tolerated and even sanctioned.

In varying degrees the associations were 'religious'. However, some were specifically 'cult associations' (*thiasoi*), formed to venerate some deity. Rostovtzeff states that native cult associations had long been known in the East and that these groups were progenitors of the Greek *thiasoi* known from inscriptions at Palmyra and Dura. In this part of the Mediterranean world Greeks often joined the native professional and religious associations found in the cities, and thus the associations become Hellenized and contained persons from different ethnic backgrounds, though they were of similar social strata in their respective collectivities (Rostovtzeff 1957: 2.1064–1065). Again, they were 'fictive kinship groups'. A. D. Nock put it this way:

> The cult-association is primarily a family. Its head is called 'pater'. . . . The members of these sodalities are brothers. . . . The cult-association, then, is a family and feels itself such. Its great importance in history is that it provided an opportunity for the evolution of new religious ideas.
>
> (Nock 1924: 105)

This description could describe many early Christian groups, and certainly does describe the Matthean group.

Before returning to Matthew, a comment must be made about Jewish associations. Jewish professional guilds were common in Palestine and elsewhere.[8] In the Diaspora, Jews formed ethnic associations;[9] some evolved out of Jewish military settlements (*katoikia*). The name for the 'coming together' of Jewish cult associations in the Diaspora was *synagoge* (Danker 1982: 81; Kraabel 1987), or *proseuche*, 'house of prayer', though the latter term was sometimes reserved for a place of worship (Leon 1960: 139; Gutman 1981: 3). Evidence from four of the six major Diaspora synagogues – Priene (Asia Minor), Delos (Aegean islands), Dura (Syria) and probably Stobi (Macedonia) – shows that Jewish associations met first in converted houses, and were thus 'house-synagogues' (Hebrew *bet keneset*, 'meeting-house'); only subsequently was money raised to convert them into buildings for community use (Kraabel 1981a: 81). The Dura example is especially important, for it demonstrates the conversion of a house into a house-synagogue in Syria at the end of the first century CE, the time of Matthew (Thompson 1992: 242). It corresponds to recent views that 'house-synagogues' were only beginning to be transformed into actual community buildings in late first- and early second-century Palestine.[10]

In Alexandria there was an officially recognized *politeuma*, or political body of foreigners, in effect an umbrella corporation of smaller associations headed by a central council of elders and priests (*gerousia*) and an ethnarch (Applebaum 1974: 475); in Rome the smaller associations seem to have been more independent (Leon 1960: 170, 181). As with most ancient voluntary associations, Jewish associations held regular meetings, passed resolutions, honoured members and non-members, sent delegations to authorities, collected state taxes, worshipped and studied (Applebaum 1974: 488).

Finally, some of the Palestinian Jewish groups were associations. Based on Josephus rather than the later rabbinic literature, Anthony Saldarini claims that

> the Pharisees . . . were a literate, corporate, voluntary association which constantly sought influence with the governing class. As such they belonged to the retainer class, a group of people above the peasants and other lower classes but dependent on the governing class and ruler for their place in society. . . . The Pharisees' association probably functioned as a social movement organization seeking to change society.
>
> (Saldarini 1988: 281; 1992b: 301–302)

Most would view the Essenes as another 'literary, corporate, voluntary association', though not a 'reformist sect', like the Pharisees, but an 'introversionist sect', at least the group for whom 1QS was written (Esler 1994a: 79–84). In addition, a variety of social-movement groups might be considered voluntary associations.[11] Having looked at some actual groups in the ancient Mediterranean world, I now move to an even lower level of abstraction, the Matthean group.

THE MATTHEAN BROTHERHOOD

Among the Gospel writers Matthew alone uses the term *ekklesia*, usually translated 'church' (16:18; 18:17, twice); thus, it has become the usual term to designate the Matthean 'community'. Given the Septuagint rendering of Hebrew 'assembly' (*qahal*) as both *synagoge* and *ekklesia* and the relation of these two terms to the 'house-synagogue' and 'house-church', it is naturally the central option for the Matthean group. Nonetheless, for this study I focus on the term 'brotherhood' (*adelphotes*) for three reasons. First, the *ekklesia* translated by English 'church' has become overloaded with Christian content. Second, while *ekklesia* can be correlated with Matthew's extensive household and family/kinship language (Crosby 1988: 49–75; Love 1993; 1994), 'brotherhood' is a fictive kinship term that comes closer to capturing the overtones of surrogate family language in Graeco-Roman associations (von Soden 1964: 144; Nock 1924), including Jewish associations such as the Essenes[12] and, if they existed this early, the Pharisaic *Haburoth.*[13] Third, though the term 'brotherhood' is not found in Matthew (it is attested in 1 Pet. 2:17 in a 'household code' context [2:11–3:12; cf. 5:9]), 'brother' occurs frequently, about twice as much as in Mark and Luke (Mark 20 times; Luke 24 times; Matthew 39 times; see Luz 1989: 54). Sometimes it refers to actual kin or is 'plurisignificant' (Duling 1992: 109), but, in contrast to only one passage in Mark (Mark 3:31–35 = Matt. 12:46–50 = Luke 8:19–21), it refers to 'fictive kinship' in seven Matthean passages (5:21–26; 7:1–5; 12:46–50; 18:15–22, 35; 23:8–10; 25:40; 28:10). This usage points to a 'fictive kinship association'.[14] These passages suggest that the group in and for which the author of the first Gospel writes considers itself a 'brotherhood'.[15] Thus, one description of Matthew's *ekklesia* is an *adelphotes*. I shall now discuss these seven passages in relation to groups in Mediterranean antiquity.

Matthew 12:46–50: Jesus' true kin

Outside the canonical texts, there are various versions of this anecdote (*Gos. Thom.* 99; *Gos. Eb.* 5 [Epiphanius *Against Heresies* 30.14.5], dependent on Matthew) and its climactic conclusion (2 Clem. 9:11). The Matthean author follows his Markan source so closely that he creates and reproduces anachronisms: he says that Jesus is standing 'outside' (12:46b: *exo*) though he omits Mark's setting in 'a house' (Mark 3:19b); his context demands only 'mother' and 'brothers' (Mark 3:31, 32 [S, B etc.]), but he follows Mark in adding 'sister' (12:50 [Mark 3:35]; contrast 2 Clem 9:11: 'my brothers'), as he also does in the Nazareth scene (13:55–56 [Mark 6:3]); *Gos. Eb.* 5). Thus, he makes only minor changes: Jesus speaks to the people (12:46a; cf. 12:15, 23), the anonymous individual reports to Jesus (12:47a) and Jesus says 'my father in heaven' (12:50; see 6:9 and Luke 11:2).

Despite his close adherence to Mark, the Matthean writer places this passage in a strategic location, and thus it has strategic importance. In Matthew 11–12 the people increasingly lack understanding and the Pharisees increasingly oppose Jesus. Q material about 'an evil and adulterous generation' is inserted just before the true kinship passage (12:39). Immediately after the passage, Jesus explains with parables and allegories (Matt. 13). Then, Matthew 14–17, increasingly diverging from sources, portrays Jesus as turning more and more to his core group. Thus, this passage in chapter 12 is pivotal: Jesus' true kin are those who, in contrast to Pharisaic-led 'Israel', do the will of 'my Father'.

Matthew 23:8–10: ranking forbidden: 'You are all brothers'

In a passage that occurs only in this Gospel, the author forbids three titles for teachers, 'Rabbi', 'Father' and 'Tutor' (23:8–10). Four added phrases break the flow of the passage (Viviano 1990: 8; Duling 1993: 660). These 'run-ons' are: 'on earth', 'the heavenly', 'the Christ' and 'you are all brothers'. The first three 'run-ons' are clearly Matthean (heaven/earth contrasts: see Syreeni 1990;

Christos: Mark 7 times; Luke 12 times; Matthew 16 times, plus 7 redactional [Luz 1989: 70]). It is therefore highly likely that the statement 'you are all brothers' is also Matthean, as other 'brother' passages will confirm. The point of the passage is that the group should not use titles of honour for teachers because God in heaven is the only Father, Christ is the only Rabbi and Christ is the only Tutor: '*you are all brothers*'. When such strong prohibitions occur, it is probable that the group desires to practise what is forbidden, or even is carrying out such practices.

It is now commonly held that this passage rejects synagogue titles of honour/status and corresponding 'offices' emerging at Pharisee-led Jamnia in the late first century.[16] While this is undoubtedly correct, the titles need to be seen in the light of a broader range of Jewish cult associations. Diaspora synagogues were often formally organized as corporations and had a variety of officers with titles: *archisynagogos, archon, prostatis* and *presbyteros*.[17] Cohen suggests that the local *archisynagogos* might be translated 'head of the association' (Cohen 1987: 116). 'Father of the Synagogue' and 'Mother of the Synagogue' seem to have been titles for honoured members of the associations at Rome (Leon 1960: 188–189). Thus, 'Father' occurs as an honorary title on synagogue inscriptions[18] and for authoritative teachers in the wisdom literature (Lemaire 1992: 311), early rabbinic sources, including Hillel and Shammai, and Saul ben Batnith (c. 80–120 CE) (Kohler 1901; Urbach 1987: 186, 906 n. 38). It was said that King Johoshaphat addressed the scholar-disciple as 'Father, Father', 'Rabbi, Rabbi', 'Lord, Lord'.[19] 'That pupils are related to their teachers as sons to fathers is a simile or parallel quite familiar in the Semitic (indeed the Asian) world' (Derrett 1981: 373). 'Father' is reserved by Matthew, of course, primarily for the heavenly father, as in this passage (Syreeni 1990).

'Rabbi' is found on Jerusalem ossuaries before 100 CE (Frey 1936: 2.249, 275–277, 277–279), on later Palestinian cemetery inscriptions (Cohen 1981; Lapin 1992: 601) and in the Talmud for Pharisaic/rabbinic teachers before 125 CE (Lapin 1992: 601; Garland 1979: 58 n. 23). Matthew elsewhere demotes this title by attributing its use to the traitor Judas (Matt. 26:25, 49).

Finally, the unusual Greek term *kathegetes*, or 'private tutor' (Winter 1991), could be 'used of founders and heads of philosophical schools' (Saldarini 1992a: 670). Speculation exists that it might also represent Hebrew *moreh*, 'teacher', as in *moreh hazzedek*, the 'Teacher of Righteousness' (4QpPs[a] 37 [= 4Q171] 3:15–16; 1QpHab 2:8; CD 1:9–11), the founder of the Essenes, who, again, use 'brothers' for their association (Josephus, *J. W.* 2.8.3; 1QS 6:1; CD 9:2; Gnilka 1963).

In summary, Matthew disparages honorary titles that were in use among associations, especially at Jamnia, but also elsewhere; again, it is possible that some Christians in the Matthean group preferred such titles, or were using them. For Matthew they should not be used, 'for you are all brothers'. Yet, there is evidence that authoritative teachers did exist in the Matthean group (Duling 1993). Below I shall say more about this apparent contradiction.

Matthew 18:15–22, 35: Guidelines for conflict resolution in the brotherhood

Matthew 18, the fourth of Matthew's five great discourses, is a tapestry of brotherhood rules. They are woven together from Mark, Q, Special M and Matthew's own additions.[20] The chapter can be divided into six units:

1 18:1–5 (Mark 9:33–37; 10:15)
2 18:6–9 (Mark 9:42–49; Q 17:1–2)
3 18:10–14 (Q 15:3–7)
4 18:15–20 (Q 17:3)
5 18:21–22 (Q 17:4)
6 18:23–35 (probably Special M plus Matthew).

While the whole chapter is important for my theme, I discuss here only the last three units, held together by the catchword 'brother'.

The fourth unit contains a sub-unit (vss. 15–17) that reflects a legal process for conflict resolution within the Matthean group.

vs. 15a: if your brother	sins against you	convince him of his fault
vs. 15: if he	listens to you	you have gained your brother
vs. 16: if he does not	listen [to you]	take two or three witnesses
vs. 17a: if he refuses to	listen to them	tell it to the *ekklesia*
vs. 17b: if he refuses to	listen to the *ekklesia*	shun him ('tax collector/ gentile')

In this connection, one should not forget that by-laws for a Dionysiac association at Athens, the *Iobakchoi*, include penalties for quarrelling or fighting and speechmaking without permission of the presiding priest (Danker 1982: 156–166; Kroll 1916); similar by-laws survive from a cult to Diana in the town of Lanuvium, Italy (Wilken 1971: 280–281). More specifically, Matt. 18:15 follows Q 17:3, but *his* version (*kerdaino*: Matthew 6 times; Mark once; Luke once; *paralambano*: Matthew 16 times; Mark 6 times; Luke 7 times [Luz 1989: 65]) more clearly echoes Lev. 19:15–18 (Bornkamm 1963: 40), especially verse 17: 'You shall not hate your brother in your heart; you shall surely reproach your neighbour, and you shall bear no sin because of him' (see also 18:21; cf. 5:22). Lev. 19:15–18 contains not only the famous second commandment, 'Love your neighbour as yourself' (19:18). It emphasizes that hatred should not simmer inside ('in your heart') for, otherwise, lying and deceit result. Thus, one should argue one's case with the brother/neighbour. This theme was a major wisdom theme (Prov. 26:24–25; 10:18; 25:9–10) and became central for regulating behaviour in Jewish groups.[21] Thus, Ben Sira stresses, 'reproach a friend before getting angry' (19:13–17). *Testament of Gad* stresses that hatred, unlike love, does not correct a stumbling brother who has committed the slightest sin, but spreads the tale around so he may be punished (*T. Gad* 4:1–3). The Essene brotherhood bases its judicial discipline on this Torah passage: 'Let no man accuse his companion (brother) before the Congregation without having first admonished him in the presence of witnesses'.[22] The *Sifra* on Leviticus picks up the theme, as well (see below).

In Matthew these group norms and judicial processes are combined. Matthew adds verses 16–17: should private reconciliation fail, taking along one or two others gives a total of 'two or three witnesses'. This rule echoes the Torah regulation to protect against perjury (Deut 19:15; cf. vss. 19–20); a parallel occurs in the Talmud (*j. Yoma* 45c). Again, the regulations also sound similar to the rules of the *Iobakchoi* (Douglas 1992: 13–15). Matthew's final step, to report to the *ekklesia*, does not explicitly mention a council of elders or other leaders, such as bishops. In responding to Beare's view that none is present, Davies and Allison write: 'This is an argument from silence. . . . Could one not just as easily assert that the presence of leaders is taken for granted?' (Davies and Allison 1991: 786; cf. Brown and Meier 1983: 68–70). Perhaps Matthew is attempting to view the process in accord with the 'egalitarian' ideology in 23:8–10; in any case there are leaders in the Matthean group (Duling 1993). Finally, Matthew says that if the final step fails, the person is to be treated 'as a Gentile and a tax collector' (Matt. 5:46–47; 15:26; contrast 11:19 and 8:10 [Q]), that is, 'shunned'.[23]

The 'binding and loosing' saying, previously applied to Peter in Matthew 16:19, has been introduced in verse 18 by Matthew ('Truly I say to you . . .'; Thompson 1970: 193–194). In this context, the most convincing interpretation of *deo* ('bind') and *luo* ('loose'), used here in the plural (contrast chapter 16) is the rabbinic sense of the excommunication from, perhaps because of sin (John 20:23), and readmittance to, the group.[24] The human decision 'on earth' will be honoured by God 'in heaven'. The issue is discipline in the brotherhood. With regard to the above question about leaders within the assembled *ekklesia*, Bornkamm comments that in Judaism the terms *deo* and *luo* 'describe the office which is conferred on the scribes' (Bornkamm 1970: 40).

Another sub-unit (vss. 19–20) inserted by Matthew (vs. 19: 'Again, I say to you') nails down the point in Matthean language, perhaps prayer language ('ask': 7:7–11; 'in my name': 7:22; 10:22; 'Father in heaven': Mark once; Luke nil; Matthew 12 times [Luz 1989: 65]); yet 'two or three' could be witnesses/judges, that is, judicial (Harrington 1991: 269), and analogous to scholars who gather to study Torah with the *shekinah* (Dwelling Presence of God, or Spirit) in their midst (*m., Abot* 3:2).

The fifth unit (18:21–22) stresses unending reconciliation with one's 'brother' (seven times seventy or seventy-seven) taken from Q 17:4 (Gen. 4:24). As noted above, the *Sifra* on Lev. 19:17 has the reproaching one's brother theme, and stresses it by doubling its 'even four or five times', a rabbinic technique that means 'it is to be repeated as often as necessary' (Kugel 1987: 56). For

Matthew, the theme is further illustrated by the sixth unit, the parable of the unforgiving servant (18:23–35) and Matthew's conclusion of the necessity of forgiving 'your brother' 'from your heart' (18:35; *T. Gad* 6:7). Thus, one is again reminded of the Jewish sayings prohibiting anger, as well as the next passage to be considered, Matt. 5:21–26.

In short, Matthew 18 incorporates a legal process for conflict resolution, a brotherhood discipline very reminiscent of other groups in Mediterranean antiquity, especially Jewish cult associations such as the Essenes.

Matthew 5:21–26: Do not be angry with your brother

This text segment, the first of the six 'antitheses' in the Sermon on the Mount, is similar to the just-discussed conflict resolution passage in Matt. 18:15–17, but without the developed three-step legal process. Here the Torah command against murder (Exod. 20:13; Deut. 5:17) is heightened by condemning anger against one's 'brother' (Bultmann 1968: 133–135; Guelich 1982: 445).

The last two verses (vss. 25–26) from Q (Q 12:57–59; Kloppenborg 1987: 146) may go back to Jesus (Funk *et al.* 1993: 141–142), and there may be other Jesus traditions behind the anti-anger statements (esp. vs. 22a; Brooks 1987: 30–33). However, verses 21–24 in their *present* form have been formulated by Matthew. First, verse 21b restates the Torah prohibition against murder by summarizing Mosaic legislation about capital offenses (vs. 21b: Exod. 20:13; Deut. 5:17; Exod. 21:12 = Lev. 24:17; Num. 35:12; Deut. 17:8–13), and in so doing it becomes formally like the verses that follow. Second, the initial thesis/antithesis (vss. 21–22a) is a Matthean form repeated in 5:33–34, modified in the other four antitheses and analogous to rabbinic teaching forms.[25] Third, verses 23–24 are packed with Matthean vocabulary (Luz 1989: 281 n. 9: vs. 23: *krisis, oun, prosphero, ekei, mimneskomai*; vs. 24: *aphes* [aorist imperative], *ekei, emprosthen, hypago* [imperative?] *tote, elthon* + verb). Fourth, verse 22, formally like verse 21b, appears to contain expansions based on the Matthean tendency to form triads, and contains parallel insults in Aramaic (*raka*) and Greek (*more*) (cf. 5:18; Davies and Allison 1988: 491). Fifth, verse 24 is close to Matt. 6:2, 5, 16, but it has echoes in Mark 11:25 and *Didache* 14:2, each of which refers to 'any one'; thus, it is likely that Matthew changed 'any one' to 'brother' (cf. Matt. 23:18–19). In short, Matthew has created the first antithesis 'on murder' from at least one Jesus tradition (vs. 25–27), probably more (vss. 22a, 24b), against anger. He stresses reconciliation with one's brother.

What does 'brother' mean in these verses? Some commentators have argued that pre-Matthean traditions here require 'fellow Israelite'. They say that the altar (*thysiasterion*, vss. 23, 24) is the Jerusalem altar and that *synhedrion* (vs. 22) refers to the pre-70 Jerusalem Sanhedrin, thus giving progressively intensive forms of punishment (village tribunal–Jerusalem Sanhedrin–Gehenna fire). However, the argument that Matthew formulated the passage offers an alternative. Matthew's love of triads and millennial themes can have led to the anachronistic *thysiasterion*; an analogy is that Mishnaic pronouncements about the Temple continued to be made in the post-Temple period (Harrington 1991: 87). Correspondingly, the Matthean *synhedrion* can refer to a local court, as it does in Matthew 10:17, thus suggesting the process for conflict resolution just discussed (Mark 13:9).[26]

In any case, the passage presents four communal rules for the brotherhood (vss. 22–26). I lay out the verses as follows:

whoever	murders	shall be liable to the judgement
1 every one who	is angry to *his brother*	shall be liable to the judgement
2 whoever	says *raka* to *his brother*	shall be liable to the Sanhedrin
3 whoever	says,'You fool!'	shall be liable to the Gehenna fire
4 If you	remember your *brother*	leave . . . go . . . be reconciled with your *brother*

Formally, these rules look like the much-discussed *lex talionis*-type 'sentences of holy law' (Käsemann 1969: 67), examples of which are in Matthew (e.g. Matt. 5:19; 6:14–15). From the perspective of content, the first rule opposes anger towards a brother (vs. 22a); it echoes the influential legal text for Jewish groups noted in connection with 18:15–17, Lev. 19:17 ('You shall not hate your brother in your heart . . .'). Again, parallels are found in Leviticus 'reproach' traditions of Jewish associations, especially the Dead Sea Scrolls. 1QS 5:25 builds on this Leviticus text when it states: 'Let no man address his [brother] with anger, or ill-temper, or obduracy or with envy prompted by the spirit of wickedness.'[27] Matthew's second and third rules (vss. 22b, 22c) oppose insulting one's brother. The fourth rule (vss. 23–24) stresses reconciliation towards one's brother before sacrifice. Then comes the Q saying that one should make friends with one's accuser (vss. 25–26). In this context, this rule can also be applied to one's brother.

In short, 'brother' language occurs in a Matthean context where it is transparent for a brotherhood and its rules to help resolve conflicts. The rules themselves are similar to by-laws in Graeco-Roman associations and to rules of behaviour in Jewish associations, notably the Essenes.

Matthew 7:1–5: Do not judge your brother hypocritically

This passage has two parts: a communal rule against judging and its elaboration (vss. 1–2), and the 'speck and log' parable (vss. 3–5). The first part is a 'Mark-Q overlap'[28] that contains another 'sentence of holy law';[29] its lesson derives from ancient and familiar market-place weighing practices: 'By the measure you measure it will be measured to you.' Matthew may have deleted some sayings from Q (Q 7:37b–38; Crossan 1983: 182), but he has intercalated his own 'sentence of holy law' in 7:2a as a balance.

The *lex talionis*-type communal rule, again reminiscent of the 'sentences of holy law', is illustrated in the second part by the 'speck and log' aphorism (Q 6:41–42; Matt. 7:3–5) also found in the Talmud (*b. ʿArak.* 16b) and the *Gospel of Thomas* 26. However, the Q version contains the hypocrisy charge, also a favourite of Matthew.[30] As in chapter 18, 'brothers' (vss. 3, 5) must engage in *merciful* judging; otherwise, they judge *hypocritically* like outsiders (Duling 1992), and might as well be Pharisees. The irony, of course, is that Matthew's Jesus and the Matthean author are constantly making judgements. Again, these are group norms of the 'higher righteousness' honour code, the true meaning of the Law and the prophets (7:12; 5:17; White 1986).

Matthew 25:40: The least of these my brothers

John R. Donahue calls the 'parable' of the sheep and the goats (Matt. 25:31–46) the hermeneutical key to the Matthean Gospel (Donahue 1986: 3; 1988: 125). Interpretations of the key verse 'least of my brothers' have been varied (Gray 1989). Three possibilities can be suggested: (1) it refers to charity towards *anyone* who is hungry, thirsty, strangers, poor, sick or imprisoned; (2) it refers to charity towards *Matthean brothers* of the same description; (3) it refers to hospitality towards *emissaries from among the brothers*, that is apostles, prophets, sages, righteous ones or scribes (10:40–42; 23:34) of the same description. Given the discipleship context (25:1–30) and Matthew's view of brothers, the first interpretation is unlikely. Of the alternatives, there is a tendency in recent study to accept the third (Cope 1969), but without totally excluding its social implications for the poor and needy, or the first (Donahue 1986; 1988: 120–125).

Matthew 28:10: 'My brothers' as the 'eleven disciples'

Psalm 22 is one of the most important psalms for the passion story, and Matt. 28:10 may allude to verse 22, 'I will tell of your name to *my brothers*, in the midst of the *congregation* (Septuagint: *ekklesia*) I will praise you', cited elsewhere in early Christianity in reference to the vindication of the resurrected Jesus.[31] In any case, the resurrected Jesus' words to the women witnesses parallel the angel's earlier commands to them:

Matt. 28:5, 7 + 8 *(angel speaks to women)*	*Matt. 28:10 + 16* *(Jesus speaks to women)*
'Do not be afraid . . . go . . . tell his *disciples* . . . going to Galilee there you will see him.' ran to tell his disciples	'Do not be afraid: go and and tell my *brothers* to go to Galilee, there you will see me.' . . . eleven disciples

These passages reinforce the Matthean view that 'brothers' are disciples. In this case the reference is narrowed to the eleven representative disciples who receive Jesus' commission to baptize and teach his commandments.

In conclusion, six of the above seven text segments stress group norms for the 'brotherhood': Jesus' true brothers (12:46–50); ranking forbidden because 'you are all brothers' (23:8–10); the legal process for settling disputes in the group (18:15–22); warnings against anger among the brothers (5:21–26); warnings against hypocritical judging of brothers (7:1–5); and the necessity for hospitality towards emissaries of the brotherhood (25:40). The seventh passage refers to the eleven representative disciples as 'my brothers'. Since the sixth, emissary passage includes scribes, I would like to specify them further.

SCRIBES IN THE GOSPEL OF MATTHEW

According to the best textual evidence, the Gospel of Matthew contains twenty-two references to 'scribe(s)', ten from Mark, twelve in Matthew alone. The special Matthean uses show that the writer has a serious interest in scribes, but what sort of interest? One common opinion is that the Matthean view of the scribes is at best unclear (e.g. Walker 1967; Van Tilborg 1972), at worst confused (e.g. Cook 1978: 58–67). In ten polemical contexts, only one from Mark (15:1 [Mark 7:1]), Matthew links scribes with opponent Pharisees (5:20; 12:38; 23:2, 13, 15, 23, 25, 27, 29) whom he in turn elsewhere links with Sadducees (3:7; 16:1, 6, 11, 12; Meier 1992: 19), a historically unlikely combination. Thus, goes the argument, Matthew blurs the historical distinctions between these three groups to portray the opponents of Jesus as a 'united front'.

With regard to scribes this conclusion has often been challenged, recently by Saldarini (1988), Orton (1989) and Overman (1990). For these three scholars, the Matthean contexts are determinative. Both Saldarini and Orton argue that deletions or replacements of 'scribes' with 'chief priests and elders' in Jerusalem settings (21:23 [Mark 11:27]; 26:3 [Mark 14:1]; 26:47 [Mark 14:43]; 27:1 [Mark 15:1]) and replacing scribes with Pharisees in conflict stories about purity (9:11 [Mark 2:16]; 15:12, cf. 15:1 [Mark 7:1]) are quite plausible historically (Saldarini 1988: 160–161; Orton 1989: 26). Orton adds that the linking of scribes with other opponent groups than the Pharisees, mostly from Mark – 'high priests' (20:18 [Mark 10:33]; 21:15 [cf. Mark 11:18]; 'elders' (26:57 [Mark 14:53 (+ high priests)]); both 'elders' and 'high priests' (16:21 [Mark 8:31]); 27:41 [Mark 15:31]; exception Matt 2:4) – means that '*the scribes* per se *never stand alone as opponents of Jesus*. They are tainted by the company they keep. This looks like a tempering of the criticism of the scribes in Mark' (Orton 1989: 28).[32] For Orton, it is the *Pharisaic* scribes whom Matthew opposes (1989: 27). To be sure, a positive view of scribes is not always present: in three cases Matthew follows Mark in stressing Jesus' teaching authority in *contrast* to scribes.[33] Yet in one of these cases Matthew replaces 'the scribes' (Mark 1:22) with '*their* scribes' (Matt. 7:29; Overman 1990: 115), referring to outsiders controlled by the Pharisees.[34] On the other side, Matthew allows that 'the scribes and Pharisees sit on Moses' seat' and one should 'practise and observe whatever they tell you . . .' (23:2–3a).[35] Also, the scribes' view that Elijah must come first is accepted (17:10 [Mark 9:11]). On the basis of 'their scribes' (7:28) versus 'sent' scribes (23:34), as well as scribal activity in the Gospel itself and the scribe 'discipled' for the kingdom (13:52), Overman concludes that 'the office and function of the scribe were developing in Matthew's setting. There were good scribes and bad' (Overman 1990: 117).

Finally, three references confirm the argument that some scribes in Matthew are viewed positively: 8:19, 13:52 and 23:34.

Matthew 8:19

In 8:19–23 Matthew has made insertions into Q as follows:

Matthew 8:18–23 *(Geographical setting: Galilee)*	*Luke 9:57–61* *(Geographical setting: Samaria)*
19 And *a (heis) scribe* came up and said to him, 'Teacher, I will follow you wherever you go.'	57 *someone* said to him, 'I will follow you wherever you go.'
21 *Another (heteros) of his disciples* said, 'Lord, let me first go and bury my father.'	59 To *another* he said, 'Follow me.' But he said, 'Lord, let me first go and bury my father.'
23 And when he got into the boat, *his disciples* followed him . . . [Stilling of the storm, vss. 23–27]	61 Yet *another* said, 'I will *follow* you Lord; but first let me say farewell to those at my home.'

A debated question is this: do the Matthean insertions, 'a scribe' (8:19) and its parallel expression 'another of his disciples' (8:21) imply that the author considers 'a scribe' to be a disciple? While a number of recent scholars have answered 'no',[36] many have answered 'yes' (cf. Kingsbury 1978: 59 n. 20). Saldarini, Orton and Gundry have now joined their ranks. Saldarini stresses that the scribe's wish looks sincere (Saldarini 1988: 159). Orton emphasizes that Matthew's changes from Q's indefinite 'someone' (Q 9:57: *tis*) to definite 'a (literally, *one*) scribe' (Matt 8:19: *heis grammateus*) and from Q's 'another' (Q 9:59) to 'another *of the disciples*' (Matt 8:21) clearly show that the scribe is a disciple (Orton 1989: 36–37). Robert Gundry's fine-tuned analysis (1994) suggests that the sequence implies two scribes, the *first* good, the *second* bad. Building on four minor arguments of Kiilunen against Kingsbury (Kiilunen 1991), Gundry adds seven more: (1) Matthew *always* uses 'another' (*heteros*) to compare *two of the same kind*

(9 times); (2) 'one' (*heis*) in Matthew is always emphatic (11 times), and thus 'one' (vs. 19) contrasts with 'another' (vs. 21); (3) in Matthew 'one' can depend on its substantive (8 times), which here must mean not 'one, a scribe', but 'one scribe'; (4) 'another of his disciples' points to the previously mentioned scribe because when Matthew adds a possessive genitive to a noun already mentioned, he does not reclassify the noun; (5) there are other Matthean contexts where one who is already a disciple 'follows' Jesus (5 times); (6) Matthew's sequence 'one scribe' (vs. 19), 'another of his disciples' (vs. 21) and 'his disciples' (vs. 23) shows that the scribe is among the disciples. Gundry's final argument (7) is that Matthew has probably omitted a Q saying (= Luke 9:61; cf. Kloppenborg 1986: 64) and thus creates a pair in which the first scribe/disciple is true, not the second scribe/disciple.[37] In short, this passage does not portray a scribe negatively, quite the reverse: it supports the view that there are 'good scribes' among Jesus' followers/disciples.

Matthew 23:34

In this verse Matthew has taken over 'prophets' (*prophetai*) from Q 11:49 but has replaced 'apostles' (only once, Matt 10:2) with 'sages' and 'scribes'. How are these groups perceived? Matthew is elsewhere very positive towards prophets,[38] though he has warnings about *false* prophets.[39] 'Sages' (*sophoi*) occurs negatively in 11:25 (= Q 10:21), but there they are sages *of the world*, probably Pharisaic sages (12:2, 14, 24, 38) (Suggs 1970: 84–87). In contrast, the above prophets, sages and scribes are 'sent out' (*apostello*: 17 times; *pempo*: twice), that is, apparently they are itinerant emissaries.[40] Again, scribes are viewed positively.

Matthew 13:52

Most critics agree that Matthew has composed 13:51–53 as a conclusion to the third of his five major discourses (Davies and Allison 1991: 444). Verse 51 is Matthew's editorial transition; in contrast to obtuse disciples in Mark, in Matthew disciples 'understand' (13:13 [Isa. 6:9], 19, 23, 51), specifically all 'these things', or Jesus' just-told 'parables of the Kingdom' (13:34; cf. 13:56; Davies and Allison 1991: 399 n. 100). Word statistics overwhelmingly support Matthean composition of verse 52 (listed in Orton 1989: 230–231). Orton's suggestion is very plausible (Orton 1989: 171–174): Matthew created verse 52 from Q sayings about the teacher/disciple relationship (Q 6:40) and the good man who produces good fruit out of the treasure of his heart (Q 6:45) as follows:

Everyone	fully trained	will be like	his teacher
Every scribe	discipled	is like	a householder

Finally, verse 53 is commonly recognized as one of Matthew's five discourse-ending formulae (7:28; 11:1; 13:53; 19:1; 26:1; Bacon 1918; 1930).

How does the scribe fare in this passage? The scribe is 'discipled', a transitive passive meaning 'instructed as a disciple'.[41] He is discipled for the 'Kingdom of heaven', Jesus' most central teaching in Matthew,[42] which ultimately disciples also will teach (28:19; cf. 27:57 [replacing 'looking for the kingdom of God', Mark 15:43]). The 'householder' or 'house-steward' brings forth all of the household imagery in Matthew (Crosby 1988; Love 1993). Bringing out of his storehouse what is new and what is old is Matthew's view of Jesus' interpretation of the law.

Insofar as Jesus' followers are 'transparent' for followers in Matthew's day (Luz 1983), the positive instances of scribes points to scribes in the Matthean brotherhood. Matthew 13:52 determines the certain existence of scribes/disciples in the Matthean group.[43] Indeed, it is now commonly held that the verse may refer to the creative scribal activity of the Gospel's author himself. Thus, a 'scribe discipled for the Kingdom' is both a 'self portrait of the evangelist' (Harrington 1991: 208) and a portrait of the scribes who were leaders in the Matthean brotherhood.

THE SOCIAL STATUS OF SCRIBES IN JEWISH ANTIQUITY

Advanced education in antiquity was the privilege of urban elites. Despite the absence of statistics, and problems such as degrees of literacy, the distinction between reading and writing literacy, the difference between full literacy and 'craftsman's literacy' and the variety of conditions from place to place, 'the likely overall [full] illiteracy level of the Roman Empire under the principate is almost certain to have been above 90 per cent' (Harris 1989: 22).

The goal of advanced Greek education was *paideia*, or 'culture', that quality of highest value; *paideia* was the 'religion of culture' (Moreau 1956: 137–146; Nock 1933: 167). One of the places one could learn *paideia* was in the philosophical schools. Philosophical schools were not exactly voluntary associations. Yet voluntary associations often supported the *ephebeia*, and, indeed, they shared many features in common with cult associations (Culpepper 1975: 259). After pointing to some common features and common terminology (*secta*, *synodos*, *thiasos*) between the associations and philosophical schools, Robert Wilken concludes:

> My point is not that philosophical schools and associations were the same, nor even that one could have been mistaken for the other. My contention is that there were some similarities and that these similarities help us to understand, on the one hand, the social dimensions of philosophy at this time, and, on the other hand, the religious and ethical dimensions of associations.
>
> (Wilken 1971: 280)

The question about the status of Jewish scribes is in part a question about the importance of education and schools. Most modern scholars say that in an agrarian society the literacy level of Jews mirrored the low literacy level of the population in general, that is, not more than 10 per cent.[44] Thus, despite rabbinic traditions to the contrary, it is unlikely that universal compulsory education for children existed in Judaism (so Cohen 1987: 120).

Jewish schools for the upper social strata is another matter.[45] Scribal schools for kings and priests probably existed in Jerusalem in the pre-exilic period, as recently argued with vigour by Heaton (1994), but the term 'school' is explicitly mentioned first in Ben Sira 51:23 (c. 180 BCE): 'Draw near to me, you who are uneducated, and lodge in the "house of instruction" [Hebrew: *bet-midrash*; Greek *oikia paideias*].' The reference is probably to a scribal school in Ben Sira's house. Though representative of Jewish nationalism, Ben Sira's writings betray an important shift for advanced education, namely the influence of Hellenistic *paideia* on Jewish wisdom (Hengel 1974: 79, 132). A few short years later, in 175 BCE, Jason's 'Hellenistic reform', supported by the Jerusalem priestly aristocracy, included a gymnasium and *ephebeion* (2 Macc. 4:9; Tcherikover 1970: 161). Yet Ben Sira also portrays a growing independence from the priestly aristocracy. 1 Macc. 7:12 mentions a *synagoge grammateion*, probably an 'association of lay scribes'. There also developed chains of tradition associated with great teachers and demands that teachers should teach without payment. Hengel writes that in this regard

> the comparison between the Jewish sects and the Greek philosophical schools in Josephus is not completely unjustified. Even the master–pupil relationship in the Rabbinate, bound up with the principle of tradition, has its model less in the Old Testament . . . than in Greece. The *didaskalos* [teacher] corresponded to the *rab* [teacher] and the *talmid* [scholar–disciple] to the *mathetes* [disciple].
>
> (Hengel 1974: 81)

There were also, no doubt, more conservative scribal 'schools', and they may well have been in the majority. One thinks also of certain Jewish associations as schools, for example the Essenes.

What then of the social status of these scribes? Shaye Cohen observes that modern scholars have used two different, contrasting grids of ranking for Palestine, one 'economic', the other 'religious' (Cohen 1986: 48–49), and he ranks the scribes in the religious grid. However, Saldarini, using the Lenski model mentioned above, thinks of most scribes as agents or 'retainers' of the Jerusalem aristocracy (Saldarini 1988: 274). Certainly both religious and socio-economic dimensions are crucial. As educated and literate, scribes tended to come from the elite classes (Bar-Ilan 1988: 21–22) and thus to serve the political establishment. The 'retainer' ranking fits. Yet scribes in Judaism had a special prestige or honour captured in their specifically 'religious' functions over long periods of Jewish history (Lemaire 1990).

Both social and religious status can be found in the texts themselves. As noted above, Ben Sira seems to have had a scribal school in his house. He was of priestly stock, but was essentially a lay scribe (Gammie 1990: 364–368). He sums up the ideal scribe (38:24: *grammateus*) in two consecutive poems, 38:24–34 and 39:1–11, the latter building on the former which appears to be dependent on the Egyptian 'Satire on the Trades'.[46] In these poems, the scribes study Torah, the law of covenants and the wisdom of the ancients; they penetrate prophecies, the subtleties of parables and the hidden meanings of proverbs; they offer thanksgiving to God and pray for forgiveness of their sins; and they pour forth their own wisdom, showing learning. They meditate on the Lord's mysteries and are filled with the spirit of understanding. This is the religious dimension. However, the religious dimension is an 'ideal of life which is determined by social role' (Nickelsburg and Stone 1983: 94). The poems can be summarized from the perspective of the contrast between scribes and other social groups as follows:

Scribes

- have leisure = opportunity for Wisdom
- are found among and appear before *rulers*
- serve among *the great*
- travel in foreign lands (learn good and evil)
- preserve sayings of the famous
- sit in judge's seat
- understand and make court decisions
- expound discipline and judgement
- are sought out for the people's council
- are eminent in the public assembly
- have names praised by community and nations

Peasants and Artisans

- work night and day
- *Peasants*: plow furrows, goad oxen, talk about cattle, careful about heifers' fodder
- *Artisans/Master Artisans*: labour with their hands into the night to finish their work well. Examples:
  - signet engraver making exact images
  - the smith at the anvil: quality work
  - the potter: quantity and quality work

The italicized references can be ranked socially:

'the great'
rulers
scribes
master artisans
artisans
peasants

This social ranking matches perfectly the stratification model of Lenski (1984) and Fiensy (1991) for an agrarian society, and it is interlocked with the religious dimension. The scribes are in the 'middle strata'; again, they would be 'retainers' of the elite classes.

Here I can stress only two further points. First, Ben Sira's scribal ideal sums up what has gone before and is determinative for what comes after, including scribalism in the Dead Sea Scrolls. After carefully examining the scribal ideal in intertestamental literature, David Orton concludes:

> Typically in [the intertestamental] literature the concept of the scribe involves: (1) social eminence and religious authority of the scribe – as in *Ben Sira* and the OT; (2) occupation with hidden meanings, of scripture, visions, prophecies and 'parables' – as in *Ben Sira*; (3) a concomitant emphasis on 'understanding', especially divinely inspired insight, and on 'interpretation' – as in *Ben Sira* and the levitical scribalism of the OT; (4) function as a mediator of revealed insights, a writing teacher of contemporary and future generations, whose concern is to cause others to understand – like *Ben Sira*; (5) a 'prophetic' or quasi-prophetic charisma and vocation – like some of the OT scribes (and their representation in the targums) and once again *Ben Sira*.
>
> (Orton 1989: 120, my emphasis)

Orton adds: 'We shall find this general concept of the scribe to be very significant for a full understanding of Matthew's own concept of the scribe, as also of his Gospel' (1989: 120).

Not only does Ben Sira indicate the social ranking and give the religious ideology of the scribe for Jewish society in general; it is likely that Matthew and some in his group know and have studied Ben Sira. Of Matt. 27:43 and 11:29 related to the Hebrew of Jer. 6:16, Krister Stendahl writes of the section where Ben Sira's 'house of instruction' is mentioned:

> Now the context in Matthew is strongly influenced by Eccles. 51:23ff., where Wisdom (as an hypostasis) is speaking and where the true teaching of the school [of St. Matthew] will give the disciples the *anapausis* ('rest'). *This type of literature seems to have been studied in the school of Matthew and related to Jesus, equating Him with Wisdom.*
>
> (Stendahl 1968: 142, my emphasis; see Suggs 1970: 100)

MARGINAL SCRIBAL LEADERSHIP IN THE MATTHEAN BROTHERHOOD

The Matthean *ekklesia* can be described as a fictive kinship group or fictive brotherhood association. Its ideology is that God is the only 'father', Christ is the only 'teacher'/'tutor' and all others are brothers. This is household imagery. It overlaps another household image, namely the servants/slaves who serve their master. In Matthew, the master/slave relationship overlaps both the Christ/brothers relationship and the teacher/disciple relationship (10:24). It is possible to infer that among 'brothers'/'disciples'/'slaves', all titles of honour are discouraged (23:8–10).

Yet despite this 'egalitarian' ideology typical of some coalitions and sects, the Matthean brotherhood has moved beyond a 'coalition' of the 'faction' type. I think that it is also moving beyond the 'sect', especially if one thinks of a 'reformist sect' (Wilson 1973). One reason – there are others – is that it has several specific leadership roles. Thus, in Matt. 23:34 we find 'prophets', 'sages' and 'scribes' linked. In 10:40–42 'prophet' is listed with 'righteous one' and 'little ones'. If apostle is added to the list (10:2) – only the verb *apostello* is common in Matthew – there are at least six terms for functional leaders within the Matthean brotherhood (Duling 1993; see Krentz 1987):

1 'prophet' (*prophetes* 37 times, 20 times redactional [Luz 1989: 67])
2 'scribe' (*grammateus* 22 times, c. 16 times redactional [Luz 1989: 56])
3 'righteous (one)' (*dikaios* 17 times, 7 times redactional [Luz 1989: 57])
4 'teacher' (*didaskalos* 12 times, 4 times redactional [Luz 1989: 57])
5 'sage' (*sophos* twice)
6 'apostle' (*apostolos* once [10:2], but *apostello* 17 times; *pempo* twice).

In this list, 'scribe' is the second most common Matthean leadership designation. In the Matthean brotherhood good scribes are honoured, and indeed the author of the Gospel is most likely a scribe (13:52). He is educated, literate and sees the secrets of scripture in a sophisticated fashion. He is steeped in apocalyptic/millennial themes typical of scribes.[17] He is probably located where most scribes are normally located, namely in an urban setting (Kingsbury 1978; 1991: 264). He embodies the ideal of the 'understanding scribe' found especially in Ben Sira (Orton 1989).

Can one say more about the scribes of Matthew's group? Antoinette Wire has tried to illumine 'scribal communities' in agrarian societies by developing a model based on anthropological studies of Chinese scribal clans in the Qing Dynasty (1644–1911) and then noting how the Essenes, Pharisees and Matthean Christians are comparable (Wire 1991: 87–121). She claims of such scribes that

> (1) they reinterpret in writing a revered literary tradition (2) in such a way as to teach concrete ritual and ethical behaviour (3) which can assure the proper fulfillment of set roles within a community of identification (4) sanctioned by adequate rewards and punishments (5) in order to reassert right order in a situation where it is perceived to be under some threat.
> (Wire 1991: 91)

Her respondent, Pheme Perkins, is probably correct to suggest that for Matthew the model does not fit at one important point: scribal literacy in China was used to gain access to imperial power (Perkins 1991: 123). Also, as Wire seems to be aware, her model struggles a little in relation to point three, assuring the proper fulfilment of 'set roles' in what she calls a 'hierarchically ordered world' (Wire 1991: 92). Certainly, Matthew's *ideology* discourages 'set roles' and the 'roles' mentioned are not clearly defined. Nonetheless, I think that Wire is on the right track in her judgement that Matthew and his reading audience represent a classically educated, self-sufficient scribal group that dominates a mixed community (Wire 1991: 114, 118). I would like to take her judgement a little further.

I suggest that Matthew's scribes are 'marginal scribes' (Duling 1993). This statement needs clarification because in many analyses the term 'marginal' has become identified almost exclusively with the poor and dispossessed, or in antiquity with peasants, the degraded, the expendable, in certain contexts the 'unclean' and occasionally women. This view of marginality correctly stresses those at or near the bottom of the (macro)social hierarchy. Yet I would like to emphasize that the classic analyses of marginality – those that gave it its sociological currency – had a broader view of marginality. Both Park (1928; 1931) and Stonequist (1937), who is indebted to Park, stressed a subtle dimension related to ethnicity and culture that should not be forgotten. Here is Stonequist's view:

> the marginal personality is most clearly portrayed in those individuals who are unwittingly initiated into *two or more historic traditions, languages, political loyalties, moral codes, or religions.*
>
> (Stonequist 1937: 3, my emphasis)

More recently, Gino Germani's theoretical work on marginality makes a similar point. While 'marginals' can be and often are equated with the lower strata of any normative scheme of social ranking, one may also consider marginals at *each level* of the social hierarchy:

> we may define marginality as the lack of participation of individuals and groups in those spheres in which, according to determined criteria, *they might be expected to participate.*
>
> (Germani 1980: 49, my emphasis)

Such persons are unable to conform to expected social roles with respect to sex, age, civil life, occupation and social life, at *whatever level of the social strata they may be.* Such lack of participation may occur because of some new and competing 'normative scheme', so that, again, a person may be on the margin *between two (or more) competing normative schemes.*

From this perspective, a classically educated, self-sufficient scribal group that dominates a mixed community that itself is perceived as 'marginal' by the larger society, but especially the rival Pharisees within Judaism, is and experiences itself to be, despite implied claims to the contrary, 'marginal'. This conclusion would help to explain the Matthean writer's ideological apologetic stance vis-à-vis the Pharisees, their scribes and their titles of honour, while at the same time accounting for the praise of the scribal role and its authority within the brotherhood. From this larger perspective on marginality, the Matthean brotherhood is led by scribes who, though having a measure of status in general, are 'marginal'. They understand, bring out of their treasure what is new and what is old (13:52), and teach others (5:19; 28:20).

NOTES

1 See Lenski 1984; Lenski and Lenski 1987: 164–208; Turner 1984.

2 For example, Blenkinsopp 1981: 1–4; Overman 1990: 8–9; Stanton 1992b: 85–107; Kampen 1994.

3 So Banks 1980; White 1987; Crosby 1988; Elliott 1990b; Malina 1993a: 117–148.

4 So Little 1957: 594; also see Kerri 1976; Eisenstadt 1956; Geertz 1962; Kerr 1978; Caulkins 1995.

5 As in Dill 1905: 255; Forbes 1993: 2–3; Heichelheim 1938: 208; Rostovtzeff 1957: 2.1048–1051, 1057–1066; MacMullen 1974: 17–20, 71–85; Judge 1960b; Wilken 1971: 280; Meeks 1983a: 31, 77, 205 n. 139; Kraabel 1987: 52–53.

6 See Waltzing 1895; Ziebarth 1896; Kornemann 1900; Broughton 1938: 841–46; Rostovtzeff 1957: 2.1057–1066; Danker 1992: 501.

7 Johnson *et al.* 1961: 82; see esp. Suetonius *Julius Caesar* 42.3; *Augustus* 32.1.

8 Applebaum 1974: 464–466; Cohen 1987: 119–120; Jeremias 1969: 18–21.

9 Leon 1960; Applebaum 1974; Kraabel 1981a; 1987; Cohen 1987.

10 See Meyers and Strange 1981: 140–141; Kee 1990; Cohen 1987: 114.

11 Theissen 1978; Horsley and Hanson 1985.

12 Josephus *J. W.* 2.8.3; 1QS 6:1; CD 9:2; Gnilka 1963.

13 Neusner 1960; Urbach 1987: 584–585; Douglas 1992; Wilkins 1992: 783.

14 Jeremias 1963: 109, n. 82; Davies and Allison 1988: 512–513; see Pitt-Rivers 1968.

15 Gnilka 1963: 51; Trilling 1964: 212; Overman 1990: 95; Davies and Allison 1988: 512–513.

16 Significant discussions include Schürer *et al.* 1979: 325–327; Derrett 1981: 378–384; Viviano 1990: 10; Saldarini 1992a: 670–671.

17 See Ziebarth 1896; Setzer 1992: 841; Leon 1960: 186–88; Meeks 1983: 31.

18 For the evidence, see Nock 1924: 105; Leon 1960: 188–189; Frey 1936: 1.494, 509, 511; Townsend 1961; Hengel 1966; Hachlili 1992: 260; Viviano 1990: 20 n. 32.

19 See *b. Mak* 24a; *m. 'Abot* 6.3; Garland 1979: 58 n. 92; cf. Matt 7:21: 'Lord, Lord'.

20 This issue is discussed by Bornkamm 1970: 37–40; Brooks 1987: 99–107; Davies and Allison 1991: 750–753.

21 Kugel 1987; Schiffman 1983: 89–109; Davies and Allison 1991: 786–787.

22 1QS 6:1; Vermes 1987: 69; see also CD 9:2–9; Gnilka 1963: 51, 57; Davies 1964: 221–224; Douglas 1992: 12.

23 Harrington 1991: 269 cites 1 Cor. 5:1–5; 2 Thess. 3:6–15; 2 John 10.

24 *Moed Qat* 16a; Dalman 1930: 174–178; Billerbeck 1926: 738–739; Duling 1987: 9.

25 Smith 1951: 27–50; Daube 1973: 55–60; Suggs 1970: 111–115; Duling 1990: 99–100.

26 Luz 1989: 282 n. 17; Davies and Allison 1988: 511; see 18:15–20; cf. Mantel 1976: 784.

27 Vermes 1987: 68; cf. CD 9:6–8; Kugel 1987: 52–54.

28 Vss. 1, 2b = Q 6:37a, 38c–42; cf. Jas 4:12; vs. 2b also = Mark 4:24b; see 1 Clem. 13:2; Pol *Phil* 2:3b.

29 See Davies and Allison 1988: 670 for many Jewish parallels; Luke 6:38.

30 Luz 1989: 70: Mark once; Luke 3 times; Matthew 14 times, c. 9 redactional.

31 So John 20:17; Heb. 2:12; Justin *Dial* 106; *Barn.* 6:16; Lindars 1961: 93; Schweizer 1975: 523.

32 Indeed, Matthew's six deletions of Mark's 'scribe(s)' (21:23 [Mark 11:27]; 26:47 [Mark 14:43]; 27:1 [Mark 15:1]; 15:1 [Mark 7:5; cf. 7:1 = Matt. 15:1]; 17:14 [Mark 9:14]; 22:40 [Mark 12:32]) and his five replacements of scribes with Pharisees (9:11 [Mark 2:16 'scribes of the Pharisees']; 9:34 and 12:24 [Mark 3:22]; Matt. 22:41 [Mark 12:35]; 22:34 [Mark 12:28]) are clarifications related to Matthew's anti-Pharisaic polemic (Matt. 9:11, 34; 12:24, 38; 15:12; 21:45; 16:11; 22:15, 34–35; 27:62). For example, Matthew omits Mark's praise of the scribe 'not far from the Kingdom

of God' (Mark 12:32 34) because he has just transformed him into a lawyer of the Pharisees (Matt. 22:34 [Mark 12:28]).

33 They are 7:29 [Mark 1:22]; 9:3 [Mark 2:6]; 17:10 [Mark 9:11]); Saldarini 1988: 159.

34 Cf. '*their* synagogues', 4:23; 9:35; 10:17; 12:9; 13:54; '*your* synagogues', 23:34; '*their* cities', 11:1; cf. 12:38; Kilpatrick 1950: 286; Stanton 1992b: 119 120, 128.

35 See the discussion at Hummel 1963: 31 and Garland 1979: 20 22, 46 55.

36 For example Kingsbury 1978: 59 60; 1988; Luz 1990: 23; Davies and Allison 1991: 41, 53 54; Kiilunen 1991; Stanton 1992a: 383; 1992b: 127.

37 Gundry offers four grounds for this argument: those who request a *delay* to 'follow' Jesus in Matthew are false disciples (9 times); family obligations in Matthew are secondary to 'following' Jesus (4:22; 10:35, 37; 19:29); Matthew pairs good/bad frequently; and false disciples in Matthew can also address Jesus as 'Lord'.

38 See Luz 1989: 67: 37 times, 20 perhaps redactional.

39 See 7:15 23; cf. 24:11 12, 24; Bornkamm 1963: 39 n. 1; Schweizer 1970; Hill 1976; Overman 1990: 118.

40 Cf. 10:40 42; Hill 1965; Schweizer 1970; 1974a; cf. Stanton 1977; Duling 1983.

41 So Kingsbury 1975: 126 127; Gundry 1982: 291; Luz 1983: 109; Orton 1989: 231 n. 9.

42 Luz 1989: 56: Mark nil; Luke nil; Matt 32 times; Duling 1992: 57 58.

43 The scholarly discussion includes Hoh 1926; Bacon 1930: ch. 10; Kilpatrick 1950: 111; Stendahl 1968: 30, 34 n. 4; Hummel 1963: 17 18, 26 28; Trilling 1964: 146; Strecker 1966: 30, 37, 192; Kingsbury 1975: 166, n. 149; Overman 1990: 116; Orton 1989.

44 Cf. Ackroyd and Evans 1970: 37; Bar-Ilan 1988: 22; contrast Millard 1985 and responses.

45 Hengel 1974: 1.58 106, esp. 78 83; Townsend 1971: 139 163; 1992: 312 317; Cohen 1987: 120 123; Fishbane 1985; 1989; Elder 1991: 138 149; Lemaire 1990; 1992.

46 So Orton 1989: 66 67; Skehan and DiLella 1987: 445 453; Gammie 1990.

47 See Smith 1976; Davies 1989; Crossan 1991: 158.

10

LEGITIMATING SONSHIP – A TEST OF HONOUR

A social-scientific study of Luke 4:1–30

Richard L. Rohrbaugh

In Luke 4:1–30 we are presented with two remarkable scenes in which the birthright of Jesus is seriously challenged: first at the cosmic level, where no secrets of the heart can ever be concealed, and then at the most uncompromising level of all, where unwarranted honour claims would quickly be cut to ribbons, in Jesus' own home town. The tension in Luke 4 rises sharply as claims and counter-claims, challenges and counter-challenges are played out in a drama where the honour of both Jesus and Luke is on the line. In order to understand the nature of these challenges and their import for Luke's story, however, it is necessary to see them (as far as we are able) through the eyes of the honour–shame society to which the story was originally addressed.

HONOUR AND SHAME

The working assumption in what follows is that Luke 4, like every other text in the New Testament, emerged from a Mediterranean society in which honour was the core social value. Since the basic concepts of honour and shame in ancient Mediterranean societies are increasingly well known among New Testament scholars, however, there is no need to repeat all the details here.[1] It will suffice to remind the reader of a few salient features of honour/shame societies that play a key role in the texts we are examining.

Essential is the fact that concern for honour permeates every aspect of public life in the Mediterranean world. Honour is the fundamental value. It is the core, the heart, the soul. Philo speaks of 'wealth, fame, official posts, honours and everything of that sort with which the majority of mankind are busy' (*Det.* 122). He complains that 'fame and honour are a most precarious possession, tossed about on the reckless tempers and flighty words of careless men' (*Abr.* 264). Fundamental, then, is the notion that concern for honour pervades *all* social interaction in the world of Luke. We should not be surprised to find it as an overriding concern in his Gospel as well (Malina and Neyrey 1991a: 26).

Simply stated, honour is public reputation. It is name or place. It is one's status or standing in the village *together with the public recognition of it.* Public recognition is all-important: 'Honour is the value of a person in his own eyes, but also in the eyes of his society' (Pitt-Rivers 1977: 21). To claim honour that is not publicly recognized is to play the fool. To grasp more honour than the public will allow is to be a greedy thief. To hang on to what honour one has is essential to life itself.

It is likewise a relative matter in which one claims to excel over others, to be superior (Pitt-Rivers 1977: 21). It thus implies a claim to *rights* on the basis of social precedence (Pitt-Rivers 1977: 23). As a result, honour and shame are forms of social evaluation in which both men and women are constantly compelled to assess 'their own conduct and that of their fellows' in relation to each other (Peristiany 1966: 9). The vocabulary of praise (*kalos*) and blame (*aischros*) can therefore function as a social sanction on moral behaviour (Kee 1974). It is perpetuated by a network of evaluation, the gossip network, which creates an informal but effective mechanism of social control.

Honour is also a limited good – related to control of scarce resources including land, crops, livestock, political clout and female sexuality (Brandes 1987: 121–122). Being limited, honour gained is always honour taken from another. Legitimate honour that is publicly recognized opens doors to patrons; honour withheld cuts off access to the resources patrons can bestow. In a very pervasive way, then, honour determines dress, mannerisms, gestures, vocation, posture, who can eat with whom, who sits at what places at a meal, who can open a conversation, who has the right to speak and who is accorded an audience. It serves as the prime indicator of social place (precedence) and provides the essential map for persons to interact with superiors, inferiors and equals in socially prescribed or appropriate ways.

As Paul Friedrich points out in his study of the *Iliad*, honour is at the centre of a wide network of related values: 'power, wealth, magnanimity, personal loyalty, "precedence", sense of shame, fame or "reputation," courage, and excellence' (Friedrich 1977: 290). We are not surprised, therefore, to find that the vocabulary of honour/shame is pervasive in the literature of antiquity. Josephus speaks of honours bestowed by Caesar, Vespasian, David, Saul, Jonathan, Augustus, Claudius and the city of Athens.[2] He tells of the honour that belongs to consuls, governors, priests, village judges and prophets.[3] Philo speaks often of honour, glory, fame, high reputations, being adorned with honours and public offices, noble birth, the desire for glory, honour in the present and a good name for the future.[4]

In the same way, the Old Testament speaks often of honour: *hadar* (Ps. 8:5; Dan. 4:37), *kavod* (Job 14:21, Nah. 3:10), *hod* (1 Sam. 9:6; Isa. 23:9), *adar* (Isa. 42:21), *yaqar* (Ps. 49:12; Dan. 2:6). It speaks of being 'lifted up of face': *nasa fanim* (2 Kgs 5:1; Isa. 3:3; 9:15).[5] Obviously equivalent terms are common in the New Testament as well: *time* (John 4:44; Rom. 2:7; 2:10; 9:21; 12:10; 1 Cor. 12:23; 1 Thess. 4:4; 1 Tim.1:17; 5:17; 6:1; 2 Tim. 2:20; Heb. 2:7; 3:3; 1 Pet. 1:7; 2 Pet. 1:17; Rev. 4:9; 4:11; 5:12; 19:1; 21:26), *timao* (Matt. 15:8; John 5:23; Acts 28:10), *entimos* (Luke 14:8), *doxa* (John 5:41; 2 Cor. 6:8; Rev. 19:7), *doxazo* (John 8:54; 1 Cor. 12:26), *endoxos* (1 Cor. 4:10), *timios* (Heb. 13:4); and for dishonour: *atimos* (Matt. 13:57; 1 Cor. 12:23).[6]

It is important here to recall how honour is obtained. The overwhelming way is via birth. An honour status is *ascribed* the day one is born and is derived from the standing one's family has – and has always had – in the village (honour as status or precedence). Because it is derived from birth, all members of the family, both male and female, have the same general honour rating, though significant differences could also occur within families (birth-order is an obvious example). As Herod (according to Josephus) reminds the people of Jerusalem, they must take care how they honour his three sons:

> Do not pay undue or equal respects to them, but to every one according to the prerogative of their births; for he that pays such respects unduly, will thereby not make him that is honoured beyond what his age requires so joyful, as he will make him that is dishonoured sorrowful.
>
> (Josephus, *J. W.* 1.459)

Obviously honour could also be gained or lost. Thus *acquired* honour (honour as virtue) might be bestowed as the result of favours done for a beneficent patron. It could be won in the pursuit of virtue, or granted to those with skill in the pattern of social interaction known as 'challenge and response'. Significant gain might result from great exploits of one family member and all would benefit. Major loss could occur from some public shame and every member of the family would suffer grief.

But most of the gains and losses of honour in ancient village life were small and came on a daily basis. They were the result of the never-ending game of challenge–response that goes on among Mediterranean males in every waking, public moment. In virtually every public interaction of whatever kind, honour is subject to challenge. It can be challenged positively by means of a gift or compliment, sometimes so subtly it is hard for non-Mediterraneans to catch the drift. Or it can be challenged negatively with some small slander or insult, with some gift not given in an appropriate way or time, or even with a question.

In every case the challenge must be met, and that too can be done in a variety of ways. An equal gift or compliment can be returned and a relationship has returned to equilibrium. Or a comparable insult can be offered and the playing field is level once again. Sometimes a challenge is met by a greater challenge, a slightly more expensive gift or deeper insult, and a game of one-up-manship ensues. Challenges may be answered, brushed aside with the scorn allowed a superior, or responded to in kind, but they are never, ever, under any circumstances, run from or ignored. To ignore a challenge is to have no shame. To run from one is a coward's disgrace.

At its best, the game of challenge–response is primarily a game of wits. Sometimes things could go too far, however, and result in excessive public damage to the honour of another. Because uncontrolled challenge–response could result in violence (feuding) that would disrupt the stability of the village, a family or group would normally 'restrain its own obstreperous members in order to keep them from getting into a feud unnecessarily' (Boehm 1984: 97). In a sense, then, the over-quick resort to violence was frequently an unintended public admission of failure in the game of wits.

As in all honour–shame societies, of course, this means that family loyalty – doing whatever is necessary to uphold the honour of the family in public – is the quintessential Mediterranean virtue. Family honour determines everything. It determines who can marry whom, who will do business with whom, who will eat with whom, even who can initiate a conversation. For this reason aspersions cast on lineage, that is on family honour, are the most serious insults the Middle East has to offer. They are considered vulgar in the extreme. Thus it is possible to understand how in Luke 3:7 when John (also Jesus in Matt. 12:34; 23:33) calls the crowd the 'offspring of female snakes', literally snake-bastards, we have the Mediterranean equivalent of a dirty mouth.

Of key importance in all this is that honour status determined who talked and who listened. Inferiors did not initiate conversations nor were they accorded a public audience. They had no 'authority' to speak. 'Tell us, by what authority are you doing these things?' (Luke 20:2) Jesus is asked. The question is a serious challenge. Moreover, assuming that Jesus had no *ascribed* honour justifying the public initiative he was taking, his interrogators pressed the proper question: 'Who is it who *gave* you this authority?' Since the birth status of Jesus warranted nothing like the behaviour he exhibited, the challengers naturally assumed the honour must have been *acquired*, i.e. bestowed by someone with the right to confer it.

This is exactly the problem with which Luke's drama confronts the reader. In antiquity persons were expected to act in accord with birth status and anyone who did not represented a troublesome social anomaly. Satisfactory explanation was required in order to avoid a dysfunctional social compass. Moreover, in providing such explanations, several alternatives were available for a writer or speaker.

A claim could be made that the case was one of mistaken identity. Perhaps the person was someone other than he appeared to be. As the Babylonian proverb has it, 'A servant in a strange town may be taken for a high officer' (Harper 1901: 448). Alternatively, it could be a case of outside sources working through the person: either the controller of demons ('He casts out demons by Beelzebul, the ruler of demons'; Luke 11:15) or God ('but if it is by the finger of God. . . .'; Luke 11:20). But the best explanation for anomalous positive behaviour was simply that legitimating status had been bestowed by someone with the authority to give it (see examples cited by Josephus above). If that were the case, however, some public record of the grant of honour would be necessary if the claim were to be widely acknowledged.

LUKE'S RHETORICAL STRATEGY

These basic characteristics of honour–shame social interaction are sufficient context for us now to assert a thesis regarding the rhetorical strategy Luke uses to persuade his readers.[7] Luke intends to tell the story of Jesus to an audience that is sceptical of his authority to speak and act. They know (or assume they do) that his ascribed honour status is one of no account. It neither justifies nor legitimates the initiative Jesus takes and thus makes Luke's appeal to an audience for him problematic. Jesus is the kind of person who should be listening, not speaking. Early in his story, therefore, Luke must resort to one or more of the available strategies for explaining Jesus-the-social-anomaly if he wants his story taken seriously.[8] Moreover, if he expects his explanation of the anomaly to hold up under fire, he must subject it to harsh scrutiny in front of his reading public. It is our thesis in what follows that this scrutiny is exactly what Luke displays for his readers in chapter 4.

The honour claim

First, of course, we must be clear that an honour claim is being made. It is therefore striking to note that Luke offers the genealogy of Jesus immediately before we get to the tests of Luke 4.[9] A number of commentators have seen Luke's genealogy as awkwardly placed or even argued that it has only minimal relation to what follows (Fitzmyer 1981: 98). Yet when one considers the social function of genealogies in antiquity that judgement must be revised.

Anthropological studies indicate a wide variety of social purposes for genealogies which in turn affect their form and character. They are used to preserve tribal homogeneity or cohesion, interrelate diverse traditions, acknowledge marriage contracts between extended families, legitimate fictive kinship, maintain ethnic identity and so on. But above all else, *genealogies are honour claims.* They seek to establish social status (ascribed honour) and thereby provide the all-important map for proper social interaction (K. C. Hanson 1989: 75–84).

In a neglected but excellent study of genealogies in antiquity, Rodney Hood points out that lineage was not only a source of pride, but also a device for self-aggrandizement.[10] It was a claim to authority, to place, to political or civil rights, to various social roles, or to the right to speak (Hood 1961: 3–8). The best known case is that of Josephus who begins his autobiography with a lengthy and somewhat convoluted (probably concocted) claim to come from Jerusalem's finest royal and priestly stock (*Life* 1.1–6). As Hood notes, 'With this dazzling pedigree, which he gives in detail to the fifth generation, he (Josephus) feels that his would-be slanderers are effectively silenced' (Hood 1961: 4).

In providing his genealogy Josephus conforms to social convention: he offers the reader the justifying evidence for his right to speak (Hood 1961: 6–8; Mason 1992: 37).[11] To further solidify the claim, he asserts that his father was not only born a man of honour (ascribed honour, honour as precedence), but was also a man of righteous reputation (acquired honour, honour as virtue) in Jerusalem (*Life* 1.7).[12] Thus being who he, Josephus, claims to be, he asserts a right to the attention and sympathy of the reader. We note with some amusement, of course, how he defensively insists that the Jerusalem archives provide the necessary public record confirming his status claims. Naturally he knows all too well that his Roman readers would have no access to these archives to confirm his story (Mason 1992: 38).

Since genealogies justified privilege (office, inheritance, civil, political and economic roles), they were also subject to considerable manipulation. Plutarch tells of a group of writers ingratiating themselves with noble Roman families by producing fictitious genealogies for the families showing descent from Numa Pompilius (*Numa* 21.2). To have a written pedigree, and especially a long one, was a mark of honour. However, most ancient people did not have written genealogies because they could not read them. Peasant genealogies usually consisted only of the three generations in living memory, sometimes attached to a short list of eponymous ancestors (Abraham, Isaac and Jacob).[13]

In publicly acknowledging a boy to be his son, that is a member of his genealogical tree, a father not only accepted responsibility for him and made him his heir, he determined his status (honour) in the community as well. Genealogies thus documented what rituals of naming and circumcision acknowledged. It is significant, therefore, that the genealogy in Luke follows immediately on the baptism scene in which God acknowledges both paternity ('my beloved son' – *ascribed* honour, honour as precedence), and pleasure ('in whom I am well pleased' – *acquired* honour, honour as virtue) in regard to Jesus.

Equally important is the form of the Lukan genealogy which gives special stress to the notion 'son of' (*tou*. . .). It suggests one of the important social functions of genealogies, what Hood terms 'characterization' (Hood 1961: 5–6). He cites the example of Theophrastus who claims that backbiters tell you about the character of a person 'the way a genealogist does' (Hood 1961: 5). What he means is that ancestry both signifies *and determines* character.[14] Thus in the New Testament we are told: 'Cretans are always liars, vicious brutes, lazy gluttons' (Tit. 1:12); 'Judeans have no dealings with Samaritans' (John 4:9); nothing good can 'come out of Nazareth' (John 1:46). Such stereotyping worked because antiquity believed the dictum: Like father like son. 'Son of' thus tells us not only *who* the genealogical subject is, but *what kind of person* we should expect him to be. In this way honour as precedence is connected with honour as virtue.

In sum, the genealogy of Jesus is a stunning claim to honour all out of keeping with the actual circumstances of Jesus' birth.[15] It declares him to be no less than the son of Adam, son of God.

A claim challenged, a heart revealed: Luke 4:1–13

A claim this outlandish, however, must be challenged. After all, the claim is being made that one born in the lowliest of peasant circumstances has been raised to Son of God. Virtually the entire social spectrum has been traversed. Luke's Jesus is thus a classic social anomaly who acts entirely out of keeping with his birth status and social authority. Hence Luke must explain himself quickly or risk losing his reading audience.

In so doing, he avails himself of several of the strategies cited above. He claims that the customary conclusions drawn from genealogy are wrong (3:23; see n. 15). He tells a birth story designed to show that the power of God has been active from the beginning in such a way as to alter the apparent genealogy of Jesus (2:1–38). He narrates the obligatory (in Hellenistic biography) single childhood event portraying the character of the man (2:41–52; Malina 1990: 54–64). He describes how, in an act of bestowing honour, God, who has the power to do so, has claimed paternity, named the child and publicly ritualized his fictive status (3:21–22; Gordon 1977: 101). Finally, he gives us a very long genealogy (in fact the longest possible!) in which he seeks to confirm what he has been claiming all along: Jesus' honour status is not what it appears to be. In the genealogy he thus provides the necessary public record an ancient audience would expect for the honour claims he has made.[16]

But if that claim is going to justify why Jesus should speak and the reader should listen, it must be verified. In fact, it must be tested by an adversary no ordinary village carpenter (if indeed that is what Jesus really was) could be expected to match.[17] Luke therefore goes immediately from the honour claim (genealogy) to the first of the honour tests (4:1–13).

In looking at 4:1–13 it is important at the outset to be clear on the term *peirazo* (4:2, 13). Note that it is a part of the semantic field of honour–shame we explored earlier. Its focus is testing, not seduction. It is used in the Septuagint of both God testing humans (Gen. 22:1–19; Exod 16:4; 20:20; Deut. 8:2; 13:2ff.) and humans testing God (Exod. 17:2) (Gerhardsson 1966: 25–35). There it primarily addresses the issue of covenant loyalty. Birger Gerhardsson has shown how it refers to the 'testing of the partner in the covenant to see whether he is keeping his side of the agreement' (Gerhardsson 1966: 26, 31). As Deut. 8:2 says, 'Remember the long way that YHWH your God has led you these forty years in the wilderness, in order to humble you, testing you (Septuagint: *hopos an kakose se kai ekpeirase se*) to know what was in your heart.' What is offered here, then, is a test of Jesus' true heart.

We come now to the crux of the matter: a challenge-response drama occurs in which the very foundation of Luke's honour claim for Jesus is put to the test. It occurs at the cosmic level where false hearts are inexorably exposed and no secrets can be hidden. Note carefully how the Devil frames the challenge. '*If* you are the son of God . . .' Precisely that has been the claim and precisely that is what is being tested.

It is common among commentators, of course, to suggest that what is being tested here is Jesus' misuse of his miraculous powers or the character of his messianic mission. But Gerhardsson has correctly noted that such comment reads into the text what is not there (Gerhardsson 1966: 19–24). He sees this first and foremost as a test of kinship and points out that 'the term *Son of God* is *the key term* in the narrative' (Gerhardsson 1966: 19, emphasis in the original; Fitzmyer 1981: 512). We would agree that it is. However, what neither Gerhardsson nor any other commentator to date has noticed is that in the series of challenges which the Devil puts to Jesus the issues of kinship are very cleverly intertwined with those of patronage. The result is subtlety that is truly astonishing. We shall see this as we look at the text in more detail. But in anticipating it we must not lose sight of the overall point. Whatever this story may have meant in Q or elsewhere, Luke uses it to test a claim of status. He signals that clearly by placing it immediately following the genealogy.

So note how carefully Jesus answers when his lineage is questioned. He does *not* answer in his own words, as if his honour derives from what he is in himself. To do that would be to grasp honour above that of his own Father and turn honour into dishonour. So he answers like a loyal Middle Eastern son would always answer – with something from his family tradition. He offers the words of his true Father in Deuteronomy and by such laudable behaviour he gains honour as virtue. Jesus wins that round hands down.

The second challenge asks Jesus to worship – the term should be translated honour – the Devil rather than God. Here terms from the semantic field of honour–shame abound: authority (*exousia*), glory (*doxa*), worship (*proskuneo*). The term *proskuneo* is especially important. It is widely used in antiquity to describe the gesture of falling down before a person and kissing his feet, the hem of his garment or the ground on which he walked.[18] It is thus clear that this time kinship is not the issue, patronage is. The Devil makes the audacious claim to be God's broker, saying that both the kingdoms of the world and the right to dispose of their resources in whatever manner he wishes have been given to him (*emoi paradedotai kai ho ean thelo didomi auten*). He thereby introduces a brazen counter-claim to that which Luke makes for Jesus.

Equally interesting are both the Devil's offer and the request he makes of Jesus. He asks Jesus to give two of the most important responses a client owes a patron: worship (praise, honour) and the proper gesture to indicate inferiority (falling down before a superior – *enopion*). In return he offers to make Jesus a client-broker in the patronage chain running from God to the Devil to Jesus to whatever clients Jesus may subsequently garner (*soi doso ten exousian tauten hapasan*). He even throws in the honour status that goes with the client-broker role (*ten doxan auton*).

Here Jesus' client-loyalty to his patron (God), the inviolable basis of the Mediterranean patronage system, is being fundamentally challenged. Since the test involves a counter-claim in which the Devil asserts his own priority over Jesus in the patronage chain, if Jesus acquiesces in the Devil's request, Luke's claim that Jesus acts by the power of God's Spirit (4:1) would be effectively refuted. But a true and honourable client would never switch patrons in this way or try to serve two masters at the same time (Luke 16:13).[19] So the loyalty challenge is thrust aside once again with the words of God, the true Patron of all. (In this regard the rejected reading in some Byzantine and Caesarean texts *hupage opiso mou, Satana* – almost certainly imported from Matthew – is somewhat amusing. In it Jesus rather forcefully commands the Devil to move down the patronage chain one notch and take a place behind him!)

Finally, in the third test – the best challenge stories must have three tests (cf. Wis. 2:17–18) – the Adversary again presses the matter of lineage. '*If* you are the son of God . . .' A challenge over the roles of patron, broker and client did not work, so kinship again becomes the issue. But the challenge here takes a subtle new form not seen in the first test.

The Devil quotes Scripture himself (Ps. 91:11–12). Implied is a subtle counter-claim Western commentators have either missed or misconstrued. Who has the right to speak the words of the Father? Only a son. By thus adopting the strategy that Jesus-the-honourable-son had used in the first test, the Devil here poses the possibility that he, rather than Jesus, is the true son of the Father. Lineage-claim and counter lineage-claim are being juxtaposed.

The particular quotation the Devil uses is carefully chosen, demonstrating that he too is adept at calling upon the tradition of the Father. What the content of that quotation offers is the kind of protection a patron offers a client. 'He will command his angels concerning you, to protect you' and 'on their hands they will bear you up, lest you strike your foot against a stone' (4:10–11). This is protection indeed; stubbing one's toe against a stone is not a very serious injury.

As Luke's readers might well know, the quotation from Psalm 91 continues: 'Because he loves me I will deliver him,' says the Lord, 'I will protect him for he knows my name. He will call upon me, and I will answer him; I will be with him in trouble, I will deliver him and honour him' (Ps. 91:14).[20] The difficulty here is to know whether this is the language of kinship or the language of patronage.

This could be the language of kinship, of a father protecting a son. This is the assumption of most critics who cite the abundant evidence from the Old Testament in which God as Father is said to protect his son Israel (Gerhardsson 1966: 54–56). In that case the phrase, 'for he knows my name' could refer to a son who owns up to his lineage in public, a son who is loyal. If that is the case, the scenario here is somewhat complicated. One son (the Devil, the one assuming the right to use the Father's words) would be reassuring another son (younger?) of the Father's protection. However, while this kinship alternative is certainly possible, it seems open to question in light of the military imagery of Psalm 91.

Alternatively, then, it could be the vocabulary of patronage.[21] The language of Psalm 91 suggests a king protecting his subjects, or perhaps a suzerain protecting his vassal (e.g. an emperor protecting a vassal-king, or a king protecting a local chieftain).[22] Military imagery abounds. The use of the phrase 'for he knows my name' would then suggest a client willing to honour the reputation of his protecting patron in public. If patronage is what Luke has in mind, the implication is that the Devil adopts the role of son, the one who knows and uses the Father's words, and proposes that Jesus adopt instead the role of protected client who 'knows the name' of his patron.[23]

Nonetheless, whether the language of kinship or of patronage is intended, Jesus once again passes a test of loyalty and shows himself to be worthy of the outrageous honour claim. In a classic Middle Eastern game of challenge–response he has bested an adversary that would frighten any mortal man. His honour has been vindicated in a frightening contest of wits.[24] Thus with a final note of satisfaction and relief, Luke tells us (4:13) that the Devil slinks off to await an opportune moment to strike again.

A public notice: Luke 4:14–15

By now any Middle Eastern reader would be awestruck Jesus has demolished a challenge of superhuman proportions. But a challenge on the cosmic level alone is not sufficient because only the story's readers can be the confirming public such a victory requires. A more solid test, one down-to-earth and plausible enough for even the most suspicious peasant to appreciate, would simply be to check with the people who know Jesus best: his home town folks. They know his origin, they know his family, they know his proper honour level and hence outrageous honour claims can be refuted there if anywhere. So being a good Mediterranean type, Luke takes us next to Jesus' home town.

Before he does so, however, Luke prepares his readers for the fact that another honour challenge will follow (4:14–15). Lest the reader misunderstand, he once again makes clear that what Jesus will do in Galilee is possible because the power of the Spirit has been given to him (4:14). Though readers would have been a bit awestruck by the performance of Jesus so far, they would also have been a bit nervous. Jesus might be reaching for too much honour and thus violating the notion of limited good. Thus Luke wants the reader to understand that God (Spirit) is still at work.

He also provides a public notice. This short text in 4:14–15 is almost universally labelled a 'summary' (Fitzmyer 1981, Marshall 1978, Tannehill 1986 *et al.*), but the label is not a good one. It is actually in the form of a public notice which provides the necessary rationale for what will follow (4:16–30). It reports two pieces of critical infomation.

One is that the gossip network has been functioning properly (Malina and Rohrbaugh 1992: 44–46). Among non-literate people communication is basically by word-of-mouth. Where reputation (honour status) is concerned, gossip informed the community about (and validated) on-going gains and losses and thereby provided an updated guide to proper social interaction. Its effects could be both positive (confirm honour, spread reputation, shape and guide public interaction) and negative (undermine others), though overall it tended to maintain the status quo in the village by highlighting deviance or improper behaviour.

The other item Luke reports is that the gossip network is in the process of validating a new honour status for Jesus (*doxamenos upo panton*) throughout Galilee. This is especially important information because it tells the reader to assume (1) that the news would have spread to Jesus' home town; and (2) that people there would thus be in a position to test what the notice indicates is going on.

Honour challenged, honour vindicated: Luke 4:16–30

The story of the ruckus at Nazareth is well known.[25] Jesus reads from the book of Isaiah and all are amazed. That is what the notice in 4:15 said he had been doing elsewhere, so that is what needs to be tested here. Perhaps the new honour status being validated in the gossip network is true. It is possible that there is more to this Jesus than meets the eye.

Luke begins by carefully reminding his readers that Nazareth is where Jesus grew up. Some have seen this as unnecessary, given the preceding chapters, but it is very much to the point. It clarifies the fact that this second test of Jesus' honorific status is going to take place where the most knowledgeable and critical audience possible is located. Luke wants us to know that harsh scrutiny is being given to the claim being made.

At first the crowd in Nazareth appears ready to grant the honour that Jesus' way with words and with the tradition might properly warrant. But then notice what someone asks. 'Is this not Joseph's son?' (4:22). Is this not the son of the menial family we all know so well? That is the way you get to someone in the Middle East. That is how you deflate overblown egos. That is how you cut down to size those who make claims all out of keeping with their proper place in the honour system. You remind them of where they were born.

In coming to vs. 22 we pause to note the astonishing volume of ink poured out in the attempt to explain what Western interpreters see as a break here in the chain of logic (Bultmann 1963; O'Fearghail 1985; Fitzmyer 1981, 1985; Hill 1971; Kilgallen 1989; Marshall 1978; Tannehill 1986 and many others). As John Kilgallen puts it, the sentiments in vs. 22 'do not justify Jesus's words in vs. 23'.[26] It appears to Westerners that the positive and appreciative reaction to Jesus in vs. 22 is illogically followed by an angry outburst of Jesus in vss. 23–27. Moreover, the angry congregation in vs. 28 appears to have switched its opinion rather quickly and sharply. Especially puzzling has been Jesus' negative reaction when the crowd seems to have responded to him in such a positive manner.

We cannot take the time here to review all of the proposed solutions to this problem. They are diverse. They range from assuming that Luke has clumsily collated sources (Fitzmyer 1981, 1985; Bultmann 1963), to badly contrived attempts at finding negative connotations in the terms *martureo* and *thaumazo* (Jeremias 1963), to imagining that Luke was a somewhat preoccupied (and therefore clumsy) narrator (Kilgallen 1989), to supposing that the home town audience felt slighted by comparison with Capernaum (Tannehill 1986), to assuming that trouble arose because of the implication that gentiles would be included in Jesus' mission (Siker 1992).

Among the various ways of construing the troublesome narrative logic, O'Fearghail has perhaps come closest to recognizing that Jesus' identity is the issue, though he sees it primarily as a theological matter. He suggests that a failure on the part of the audience to recognize the salvific import of Jesus triggers the impatient reaction from Jesus in vs. 23 (O'Fearghail 1985: 70). He recognizes the importance of Luke's notice that Nazareth was where Jesus grew up, and suggests that because the audience there knew Jesus so well they could not quite handle what the theological implications of his words implied for his personal identity (O'Fearghail 1985: 70).

O'Fearghail is on the right track. Identity is indeed the issue. But it is social identity first of all.[27] The social implications of the question put to Jesus are crystal clear: in asking if Jesus is Joseph's son, the synagogue participants are pondering Jesus-the-social-anomaly. They want to know how such honourable teaching could come from one born to a lowly village artisan. And as always, the question is a challenge which anyone sensitive to his own precarious honour status must pick up. Thus Jesus knows immediately that he has been insulted and that a failure to respond will belie every claim he might later try to make. He is on the spot. As Luke points out, 'the eyes of all in the synagogue were fixed on him' (4:21).

It has shocked most Western interpreters that Luke's Jesus responds by grossly insulting the entire audience. His attitude does not seem to accord with the (apparently) positive reaction of the crowd. What has been completely missed, however, is the magnitude of the insult in the question asked about Jesus' lineage. Obviously some in the crowd react positively. O'Fearghail is correct that no other connotation is really possible (Jeremias' contrived attempts to claim otherwise notwithstanding) for the term *martureo* or the words *hoi logoi tes charitos* (4:22). But the person in the crowd who asked the insulting question about Jesus' lineage does not respond positively at all. We must recall that aspersions cast on lineage are the most extreme insults Mediterranean cultures have to offer.

Corroborating evidence has been there all along, even if Western commentators have not understood what to do with it. Long ago Cyril of Alexandria (fourth to fifth centuries CE) recognized the question as a serious insult. He comments that the ones who first marvelled at the gracious words coming from the mouth of Jesus later 'wished to disparage him (*kateutelizein*), for they were asserting: Is this not Joseph's son?' (*Explanatio in Lucae Evangelium*, PG 72, 541 D). The Byzantine exegete Theophylactus (fl. 1070 CE) writes similarly: 'Hearing the things being said by Christ, the crowds were marvelling at his gracious words. But at the same time, they were ridiculing him (*diekomodoun*), saying, 'Is this not the son of the carpenter?' (*Enarratio in Evangelium Lucae*, PG 123, 752 BC). To both writers it is clear that the question is an attempt to belittle Jesus' birth status. Theophylactus pointedly notes that it is Joseph's vocation (low-status village artisan) that is the cause of the ridicule.

Of course once the insulting character of the question is understood, Jesus' negative reaction is perfectly clear. There is no 'break' in the chain of logic at all. Moreover, Jesus anticipates that once raised, the question of honour (4:23) will not go away. So he offers a riposte (4:24) which he illustrates from scripture (4:25–27). He implies with two examples that God's favour extends far beyond the native sons of Israel (4:23–24, 25–27), and that Israelite genealogy has been overrated. Now Israelite honour has been insulted and the game turns deadly serious.

The crowd knows immediately and unmistakably that it has been insulted. In fact the ante has just gone up significantly. Someone in the crowd challenged Jesus by raising the question of his ascribed honour status. But he turns the tables and questions whether the very lineage of which those in the audience are so proud has the exclusive value they imagine it to have. Note that he does not question their lineage as Israelites, he simply questions its value.

It is important to recognize that an insult like the one that Jesus offers in response to the crowd is directly confrontational. Even the proverb he quotes (4:25) is especially insulting since it implies that the crowd in Nazareth has no shame (the ability to understand what is honourable and what is not). Obviously a negative challenge of this magnitude could not go unanswered. So the outraged crowd takes Jesus to the edge of town to throw him off a cliff.

But ironically at that very moment they lose the exchange. The death of a challenger is sometimes a worthy response to public dishonour, though as we noted earlier, in the Middle East an over-quick resort to violence is an inadvertent admission that one has lost control of the challenge situation. Wits have failed and bully tactics have taken over. As the crowd gives in to violence, therefore, Jesus wins the exchange. Thus the Lukan reader once again sees Jesus upholding the outrageous honour claim of the genealogy in front of the most critical audience Luke could conjure up.

Conclusions

Had we time to follow this narrative strategy of the Lukan author all the way to its conclusion we would discover that he plays out the nuances of claim and counter-claim, challenge and counter-challenge all the way to the end. Indeed his defence of the name of Jesus sets the stage for Peter in Acts 4 to reply boldly to the authorities who question him about the name in which the apostles act. They do so in the name of 'Jesus Christ of Nazareth' (4:10). But already here in Luke 4 Mediterranean readers know that this Jesus is capable of far more than his birth status would suggest. Is he the Son of God? Perhaps it is too early to acknowledge that. But there is clearly more to him than meets the eye; of that we are already convinced. Luke has drawn us into a Mediterranean melodrama that would have had every Middle Eastern reader clinging to the edge of the seat.

NOTES

1 For a more complete review of the concept in the New Testament see: Malina 1993a; Malina and Neyrey 1991a.

2 *J. W.* 1.194; 1.199; 1.358; 1.396; 1.607; 3.408; *Life* 423; *J. A.* 7.117; 6.168; 6.251; 13.102; 14.152; 19.292.

3 *J. W.* 4.149; 7.82; *J. A.* 4.215; 10.92; 11.309; 15.217.

4 *Migr.* 172; *Leg. All.* 3.87; *Det.* 33; 157; *Post.* 112; *Abr.* 185; 263.

5 Cf. the Arabic *Wajh*, meaning to have a flushed face, i.e. to be shamed.

6 Plutarch makes a modest attempt at exploring the semantic field of honour by commenting on Greek equivalents for the Latin term *honor*. He suggests *doxa* and *time* as appropriate substitutes for his Greek readers (*Moralia* 4. 266). For a much more substantial semantic field see Malina and Neyrey (1991a: 46). We shall have occasion to review some of these terms in more detail as our study of Luke 4 proceeds.

7 In using the term 'rhetorical strategy' we are pointing to one of the central concerns of sociological exegesis. By it we mean the social impact a text is designed to have upon its readers. As John Elliott (1990b: 10–11) has put it, 'I prefer the term "strategy" rather than "purpose" or "intention" because, as in the strategy of a game plan or the tactics of military warfare, strategy implies not simply the communication of ideas but the deliberate design of a document calculated to have a specific social effect on its intended hearers or readers. Sociological exegesis thus seeks to discover the manner in which a given document has been designed as a response to a given situation, and how it has been composed to elicit a social response on the part of its audience.'

8 For an excellent discussion of the trouble caused by social anomalies and the strategies for dealing with them, see Malina 1993a: 154–159.

9 We shall leave aside the many critical questions relating to the origin of the genealogy, including its historicity, its relation to Matthew and its purported numerology. These questions have been studied often and are reviewed by Fitzmyer 1981, Hood 1961 *et al.*

10 Much of the following discussion is taken from Hood 1961, including a number of the primary sources which he cites. He describes six important functions of genealogical lists in antiquity.

11 Note that Josephus does the same thing in *J. W.* 1.3 and *Apion.* 1.54.

12 Tobit provides a similar example. He first gives his ascribed honour status (genealogy) and then claims to have acquired additional honour by walking in the ways of truth and righteousness and performing numerous acts of charity to family and countrymen (1:1–4).

13 As Rodney Hood points out, an incipient genealogy (Joshua, Son of Nun, Simon; Son of Jonah) could function as a personal name (1961: 3).

14 For the importance of character in those held up as models to emulate (modal personality), see Malina and Neyrey 1991b.

15 A fact which may provide sufficient explanation for the curious phrase *hos enomizeto* (3:23). The usual explanation is that Luke edited in the comment at the time the infancy narratives were added in order to harmonize the genealogy with his story of the virgin birth (so Danker 1972: 53; Marshall 1978: 162). But the verb *nomizo* can refer to something habitual or customary, hence Hood (1961: 12) speculates that it might be translated 'as his genealogy was ordinarily reckoned'. If that is appropriate, and if the clause modifies only 'the son of Joseph', as has been argued (Fitzmyer 1981: 499), it could be understood as a reference to the stereotyping of Jesus commonly prevailing among those who knew his father.

16 It should now be clear that the connection between 3:21–38 and 4:1–13 is both direct and crucial to Luke's rhetorical strategy.

17 As we look at 4:1–13 it should be clear that in a short article on Luke's use of social

dynamics we cannot address the many important critical questions regarding this text. Many of the questions, particularly those regarding the origin, authenticity, composition, place in the life of Jesus and use in the earliest Christian communities relate to Q rather than Luke. Many others, however, relate specifically to Luke. Many questions have been raised about the sequence of the units, about a variety of nuances in the use of scripture, the wilderness motif, the testing of Israel by God and God by Israel and the differences between the four accounts (Mark, Q, Matthew and Luke) that are beyond the scope of our study. For a detailed discussion of these and other important questions regarding this pericope see Gerhardsson 1966.

18 BAGD (716–717) collects the evidence from the tragedians, Philo, Herodotus, Josephus *et al.*

19 For a discussion of competition for clients among patrons in the provinces and the revulsion against such perfidy among elite Romans, see Malina and Rohrbaugh 1992: 326–329.

20 In Jewish exegesis citations such as this implied the context surrounding them (Stegner 1990: 36).

21 On the patronage implications of kinship language in the Gospels, see Malina 1988a.

22 Similar examples are cited by Kalluveettil 1982. From a treaty between emperor Suppiluliumash of Hatti and his vassal Tette, king of Nukash: 'Yea, vassal of the king of the Hatti land I am, so save me' (96). Note also the very explicit association of kinship and patronage language in 2 Kgs 16:5–7: 'Then Rezin king of Syria and Pekah the son of Remaliah, king of Israel, came up to wage war on Jerusalem, and they besieged Ahaz but could not conquer him. At that time the king of Edom recovered Elath for Edom . . . So Ahaz sent messengers to Tiglath-Pileser king of Assyria, saying: "I am your servant and your son. Come up, and rescue me from the hand of the king of Syria and from the hand of the king of Israel, who are attacking me."' Here too you have master/servant language combined with kinship language as metaphors for clientage in a text describing a patron providing military protection. For the best discussion of how the dominant motifs of Psalm 91 are royal, see Eaton 1976: 57–58, 143, 158–159.

23 A further interesting note on Psalm 91: 'The ancient rabbinical interpretation of the psalm as "A song for evil encounters" [Bab. Talmud, *Sheboth* 15b; Hugger, *Jahwe meine Zufluct*, 331–333], i.e., one to be used to avert the attacks of demons (who were thought to be responsible for illnesses and various kinds of pestilences)' (Tate 1990: 451).

24 Marshall (1978: 166) complains that reducing the story 'to the level of a *Streitgespräch*' wrongly places the emphasis on Jesus' 'dialectical skill'. Admittedly there is more to this story than winning a debate. Nonetheless debating skill was much prized in the agonistic world of the first century and would have been properly appreciated by Luke's Graeco-Roman readers

25 One more time we must make the disclaimer: there are many important interpretive and critical issues regarding this pericope which lie outside the scope of this essay. Our work here is not meant to substitute for the many fine studies addressing those issues. It is intended only to add an analysis of the social dynamics in the text.

26 Kilgallen 1989: 514. For an excellent review of the many positions taken to explain the apparent break in logic, see O'Fearghail 1985.

27 On Mediterranean social identity see Malina 1992: 66–87.

11

WOMEN AND MEN AT HELLENISTIC SYMPOSIA MEALS IN LUKE

Stuart L. Love

INTRODUCTION

Two related topics in the Gospel of Luke are gender (women and men) and food (hospitality, meals, table fellowship). Concerning food, David P. Moessner states, '*At table* Jesus reveals himself as the Lord-Host of the Heavenly Banquet which is now dynamically being fulfilled in his *journeying* to Jerusalem' (1989: 174).[1] So strategic is this topic that one might be led to believe, as Robert J. Karris points out, 'Jesus is either going to a meal, at a meal, or coming from a meal' (1985: 47). Jesus seems to eat with nearly everyone – toll collectors, sinners, disciples, crowds, Pharisees and women.

Food and meals are the social context in which a number of Lukan concerns are expressed. At table, Luke depicts how God fellowships Jews and gentiles (Esler 1987: 71–109) and outcasts,[2] and in so doing is concerned for justice in the treatment of the poor, maimed, lame and blind (Luke 14:13, 21).[3] By eating with outcasts Jesus provides an 'acted parable' of the Kingdom (Karris 1985: 58). As Norman Perrin observes, 'Scribe, tax collector, fisherman and Zealot' come together around the table at which they celebrate 'the joy of the present experience' and anticipate 'its consummation in the future' (1967: 102–108).

The topic of gender also underscores Luke's view of the Kingdom and God's concern for outcasts. For example, the treatment of particular women such as Elizabeth (ch. 1), Mary (chs 1–2), Anna (2:36–38), the widow of Nain (7:11–17), the women who followed Jesus out of Galilee (8:2–3; 23:55; 24:10; Acts 1:12–14), the woman healed in the synagogue on the Sabbath (13:16) and the poor widow who gave up all (20:45–21:4) helps bind the narrative together by highlighting the humble position of women, their socio-religious marginality, their crucial place in the story of God's salvation and their inclusion (pairing) alongside men in the Lukan redaction.[4] A direct linkage between women and meals is found in the stories of Simon's banquet (7:36–50) and Martha's hospitality to Jesus (10:38–42).

In the treatment of women, however, Luke appears to take deliberate care in exercising social restraint illustrated by the barrenness of Elizabeth, the silent submission of Mary and the deferential posture and silence of Mary, the sister of Martha, as she listens to the words of Jesus (10:38–42). Mary Rose D'Angelo observes, 'Women speak in the Gospel only to be corrected by Jesus' (1990: 452).[5]

HYPOTHESIS

I will further link the topics of meals and gender through a cross-cultural social analysis of four symposia banquets in Luke which follow in modified form the Hellenistic symposium genus. The meals take place at the houses of Levi (5:29–39), Simon the Pharisee (7:36–50), a Pharisee (11:37–52) and a ruler of the Pharisees (14:1–26). A cross-cultural analysis is justified due to apparent similarities between gender-specific practices in Roman and Jewish public meal settings and the Lukan banquets. My hypothesis is threefold:

1 Following traditional Graeco-Roman practices, meal settings in the houses of Pharisees are male-centered and dominated, with the significant exception of the woman at Simon's house (7:36–50). Even though this anomaly includes elements of social restraint it serves as a gender-specific example of a Lukan reversal, the inclusion of outcasts.
2 Gender is not an issue at the banquet hosted by the outcast Levi; however, if women are present they probably are not many, distinguished, or heard.
3 Although additional evidence is needed, Luke's treatment of the woman pariah at Simon's banquet (7:36–50) and the reception of outcasts at Levi's banquet (5:29–39) indicates the inclusion of a number of marginalized persons including outcast women at Christian fellowship meals among Luke's churches.

I will establish my hypothesis as follows: first, by surveying gender-specific expectations of public meals in the larger society of the period to establish a possible *Sitz im Leben* for the Lukan meals in question; second, by demonstrating Luke's use of the Hellenistic symposium genus as a justifiable parallel to the Graeco-Roman evidence; and third, by validating the hypothesis through a gender-specific analysis of those present at the Lukan meals.

WOMEN AT PUBLIC MEALS IN GRAECO-ROMAN SOCIETY

Traditional practices

According to established Greek traditions, a respectable woman usually ate in the private space known as 'the women's quarters' and did not accompany her husband to banquets or attend banquets alone where 'public' women, courtesans, entertained men.[6] Proper behaviour required a wife to be silent, 'a sign' of her submission to her husband and her lack of participation in the public sphere of men.[7] Kathleen E. Corley states, 'A properly trained woman, then, was also one who had been trained to keep her mouth shut' (1989: 502; 1993a: 43–44). In contrast, courtesans entertained men at banquets by talking and displaying their education and knowledge (Corley 1989: 501–502; 1993a: 34–41).

Traditional practices challenged

However, during the late republic and early empire, involvement of some elite Roman women in public spheres including public meals became more prevalent.[8] This 'progress', especially in the legal and economic realms and to a lesser extent in the political sphere, began during the Hellenistic period and possibly reached its pinnacle just before and during the first century CE.[9] Specifically, there was an increased attendance of Roman women with their husbands at public banquets and religious meal settings.[10] However, the majority of women attending banquets belonged to Graeco-Roman *collegia* and other associations both secular and religious,[11] or were courtesans, and freedwomen (who were often former prostitutes) (Corley 1993a: 38–52).

Apparently, a parallel 'progress' took place among Jewish women which impacted everyday experience as well as some aspects of the institutional life of Judaism.[12] Specifically, it included the presence of women and children at Passover meals,[13] some married women at banquets (Sirach 9:9; 31:12–32:9) and the fellowship of certain wealthy Jewish women at the communal meals of the Therapeutic society in Egypt.[14]

Collision of the old and the new

These changes, however, clashed with the earlier traditional conventions.[15] Peter Brown refers to the 'emancipation' of women during the early empire as a 'freedom born of contempt' (1987: 247–248), permitted as long as it did not have political impact and restricted when it was harmful to the male political order. Eva Cantarella (1987: 142–143) sees the liberation as relative, certainly not the widespread 'emancipation' often described. Perhaps, following the Greeks of an earlier period, Roman men began again to restrict women's freedoms and put them back 'under their thumbs'. As Corley puts it, 'The new independence of women was therefore only tolerated as long as it did not interfere with the real world of male politics' (1989: 506).

Evidence for the 'real world' points to at least four phenomena. First, there was a renewed concern for the respectability of wives, their reputation and behaviour at public meals.[16] Matrons who attended banquets were expected to avoid social criticism by leaving after the meal before the symposium began (Corley 1989: 490; 1993a: 30). If a wife attended the symposium, ordinarily she remained silent and nameless (Corley 1989: 501–502; 1993a; 42–44). Care was also given to the spatial location of wives and the posture they assumed while eating. Although some Roman matrons reclined at meals,[17] men and women customarily reclined separately,[18] since women who reclined with men often were identified as prostitutes (Lucian, *Dial. Meret.* 1, 3, 11, 12, 15). Second, the number of wives attending public meals was probably quite small. MacMullen notes that when women were invited 'largesses might be given out in the ratio 30:20:3 to town senators, Augustales and women' (1980: 212–213). Third, 'progressive' Roman ways apparently did not prevail everywhere since there is evidence that Hellenistic peoples under Roman control remained constant to the customs of their Greek heritage (Cicero, *Contra Verrem* II.1.26.65–27.68). And finally, although Jewish women attended Passover meals with their husbands they did not involve themselves in the Seder liturgy (Stein 1957: 32–34; Wegner 1988: 156–159).

Accordingly, what might we anticipate in the Lukan banquet scenes? If banquet decorum corresponds to traditional expectations, respectable women probably would not be present. If present, they would either recline separately with other matrons, recline quietly with their husbands or sit submissively and silently with their husbands and leave after the meal proper. If present for the symposium, they would not entertain or converse with the male guests. Those in attendance most likely would be women invited to recline with the male guests and entertain them with their wit, knowledge and sexual sport.

LUKAN BANQUETS AND THE HELLENISTIC SYMPOSIUM GENUS

But are the Lukan meal scenes sufficiently similar to the public meals just described? I believe they are since the Lukan redaction of the four meals under consideration follows a modified form of the Hellenistic symposium genus.[19] The requirements of the genus include a host, a guest of honour, other guests, an invitation, an unfolding of the host's identity and of the other guests and a *fait divers* or action that prompts the speech of the chief guest.

Fulfilled requirements in the story of Levi's banquet (5:29–39; Sterling 1992: 370–371; Steele 1984: 390–392) are a host, Levi (5:29), a guest of honour, Jesus, ('And Levi made him a great feast in his house', 5:29), other guests (5:29, 30), an implied invitation, a *fait divers* or action that prompts the speech of the chief guest (5:30–32) and a further statement (5:33) followed by Jesus' response (5:34–35, 36–39). Levi's banquet differs from Pharisee-hosted meals in that Levi, the host, does not criticize Jesus or ally himself with those responsible for the *fait divers*.[20] Instead, the triggering issue originates with the Pharisees and their scribes, a peripheral adversarial group who see and hear the proceedings but probably do not recline at the meal since they do not fraternize with 'sinners'.[21] The observation by Charles Talbert (1986: 86) that at such meals 'the door of the dining room was left open so the uninvited could pass in and out during the festivities' and that they would 'take seats by the wall' and listen 'to the conversation between the host and guests' is a possible explanation for the separated presence of Jesus' critics.

Fulfilled requirements in the meal scene at the house of Simon the Pharisee (7:36–50; Steele 1984: 379) include a host, Simon (7:36), a guest of honour, Jesus (7:36), other guests (7:49), an invitation (7:36), a gradual unfolding of the host's identity (7:40) and of the other guests (7:49). Jesus' association with a woman looked upon as a sinner (7:37–38) precipitates a controversy and prompts the host's reaction: 'If this man were a prophet, he would have known who and what sort of woman this is who is touching him, for she is a sinner' (7:39; Jeremias 1966: 20–21; Steele 1984: 379–380). The ensuing conversation involves a speech and 'Socratic' type interrogation by Jesus of the host (7:39–44) which leads to a question by those at table (7:49) and Jesus' final response (7:50).

At the third banquet (11:37–52; Steele 1984: 379–394) the host is identified simply as a Pharisee (11:37). Jesus, the chief guest, is named, specifically invited (11:37, 38) and addressed as 'Teacher' (11:45). Two (possibly three) groups of guests are gradually revealed: Pharisees (11:39, 42, 43, 53), lawyers and scribes (11:45, 46, 52, 53). The host's unspoken astonishment that Jesus did not wash his hands serves as the *fait divers*, the event or 'news item' which triggers Jesus' pronouncement of woes against the Pharisees (11:39–44). It is followed by a lawyer's statement (11:45) and Jesus' final response (11:46–52). Jesus' lack of courtesy towards his host demonstrates that Jesus 'bests his opponents and is wiser than Solomon' (Steele 1984: 389).

At the final meal, a Sabbath banquet with a ruler of the Pharisees (14:1–26), the role of the host is muted (14:1–2). Jesus, the chief guest (14:1), demonstrates his ability to overcome his opponents in argument (14:1–6). Instead of stressing a 'Socratic interrogation', the incident features the significance of the seating arrangement (Plato, *Symposium* 90–91, 98–99; Plutarch, *Quaest. Conviv.* 1.2: 615–619), two contrasting guests' lists (14:12–13) and Jesus' story of the great banquet (14:16–24). Those who clash with Jesus are the 'lawyers' and 'Pharisees' (14:2–6).

The four Lukan meals correspond sufficiently with the Hellenistic symposium genus to establish their *Sitz im Leben* within the social context of the larger society. In so doing, they provide a commensurate social analogy. Modifications to the genus may play into Luke's special concerns. The ensuing gender analysis explores whether the third Gospel conforms to traditional public social conventions, parallels the 'progressive' behaviour of a minority of elite Roman and Jewish women or pursues an independent path. In other words, I am interested in commensurate and deviant social data, what the meal scenes emphasize and imply, weighing carefully anomalous or exceptional behaviour.

A GENDER-SPECIFIC SOCIAL ANALYSIS OF THE LUKAN BANQUETS

First, I will examine the two banquets hosted by Pharisees at which women are not explicitly mentioned (11:37–52; 14:1–26), followed by the Pharisee meal where a woman is present (7:36–50) and, finally, Levi's banquet (5:29–39).

A banquet with a Pharisee (11:37–52)

Those known to be in attendance are male – the host (11:37), Jesus (11:37, 38), Pharisees (11:39, 42, 43, 53) and lawyers and scribes (11:45, 46, 52, 53). This is supported as well by the topics and issues raised. The charges made to the Pharisees – extortion (11:39) and love for 'the best seat in the synagogues and salutations in market places' (11:43), as well as the religious practices of almsgiving (11:39, 41) and tithing (11:42), correspond to the religious social world of men. The charges made to the lawyers, that they 'load men with burdens hard to bear' (11:46), build tombs of the prophets (11:47), witness and consent to 'the deeds of your fathers' (11:48), kill and persecute prophets and apostles sent by God (11:49), shed blood and take away the 'key of knowledge' (11:52), are male-centered. The public meal is attended by cultivated males of high religious and social standing. If women are present they are not seen or heard.

A Sabbath banquet with a ruler of the Pharisees (14:1–26)

Those attending the meal are males – the host (14:1–2), Jesus (14:1), lawyers and Pharisees (14:2–6). It is unlikely that the man with dropsy (14:2–6), a possible male counterpart to the woman at Simon's banquet, is an invited guest since he is the basis of the *fait divers* and an example of those Jesus would invite to the Great Supper (van Staden 1991: 220–221). The hypothetical guest list (14:12) is a distillation of traditional practices of dinner invitations in the larger society. The four invited groups, friends (*tous philous*), brothers (*tous adelphous*), kinsmen (*tous suggeneis*) and rich neighbours (*geitonas plousious*), are male and constitute patronage ties to the host (Moxnes 1991: 242–250; van Staden 1991: 204). Further, those who make excuses not to attend the Great Supper are male (14:18–21). The first buys a field, the second purchases five yoke of oxen and the third has just married a wife (14:18–21). Karris finds in the first two, a field and five oxen, excuses which 'involve the pursuit of mammon' (Karris 1990: 706). A wife, however, might also be perceived as property, making all three excuses property issues for wealthy males. Accordingly, the final statement, 'none of those men who were invited shall taste my banquet' (14:24), should also be viewed as a gender-specific reference.

But what about Luke's reversal, those who eat bread in the Kingdom of God, the poor, maimed, blind, and lame, and those found in 'the streets and lanes of the city' and along 'the highways and hedges' (14:21–23)? Richard Rohrbaugh has identified the social location of persons from 'the streets and lanes of the city' as well as along the 'highways and hedges' (1991: 144; Sanders 1974). The former live in walled-off areas within the city, separated from the central areas occupied by the elite. They are invited 'to come into a part of the city in which they do not belong'. Rohrbaugh identifies those found along the roads and hedges as people who live just outside the city walls including ethnic groups, tanners, traders, beggars and prostitutes, people not allowed to live in the city but who eked out a living within its walls (1991: 144–145). Thus, Luke refers not only to socially forbidden groups but also to long-standing segregated spaces which served as barriers to social contact. People from these locations would need to be 'compelled' (14:23) to attend such a banquet.

Further, there is nothing gender-specific about those who eat at table in the Kingdom. As Karris states, 'Jesus reveals a God who "eats with", shares life with society's handicapped and declares a person righteous who does the same' (1985: 61). Accordingly, although not specified, women might be among the poor, maimed, blind and lame as well as those found along the highways and hedges. Luke includes women among the socially marginalized. Elizabeth, Mary, Anna (chs 1–2) and the widow who gave all (20:45–21:4) are examples of the poor. The itinerant women who ministered to Jesus and his disciples (8:1–3) had been cured either of evil spirits or infirmities. The woman with a continuous haemorrhage (8:43–48) and the crippled woman in the synagogue (13:10–17) are examples of unclean and/or outcast women. The very nature of the Lukan reversal makes possible the inclusion of women even though the pericope makes no mention of women. The more fundamental issue for both men and women is whether wealthy Christians are willing to share their abundance as well as accept outcasts at Christian meals (Esler 1987: 197–200). Table fellowship in the Kingdom concerns the use of wealth and justice for the poor.[22] Thus, the banquet story seems to critique traditional Graeco-Roman gender practices which preserved prevailing religious, economic and social structural lines of stratification.[23] In addition, the Lukan reversal sets forth a contrasting social model which cuts across existing lines of social stratification (van Staden 1991: 225–229). Simon and Jesus hold two different visions of 'the coming Kingdom', two different 'eatings and drinkings' and the two 'are at loggerheads' (Moessner 1989: 199, 209). Accordingly, criteria for inclusion at table in the Kingdom are not based on economic patronage, physical wholeness, spatial location or gender (Esler 1987: 71–109, 197–200; van Staden 1991: 225–229).

A banquet at Simon the Pharisee's house (7:36–50)

Except for the presence of an unnamed woman 'of the city' (7:37) identified as a 'sinner' (7:39) by Simon, the gender of those in attendance at Simon's meal are comparable to the previous Pharisee-hosted banquets. But what is the social identity of the woman? Four matters aid us in attempting to answer this question.

A forgiven 'sinner'

Since the woman is labelled a 'sinner' who has been forgiven much, some have identified her social deviancy as prostitution (Corley 1993a: 124 n. 89). Fitzmyer, however, has identified the social makeup of the character group 'sinners' as having two elements, neither of which necessarily centres on women or women as prostitutes. Sinners are '(a) Jews who fell short of Mosaic obligations (without restricting these to the Pharisaic interpretation), but who could repent and be reconciled to God; and (b) Gentiles, who were *a-nomoi* (Law-less) and *a-theoi* (Godless), often considered hopeless in Jewish apocalyptic literature' (Fitzmyer 1981: 1.591; see Jeremias 1931: 293–300; 1957–1965: 6, cols 1927–1928). Fitzmyer hesitates to identify the woman as a prostitute (1981: 1.689). Yet, following a different approach, Luke labels the woman and Zacchaeus as sinners (7:37; 19:2, 7). Dio Chrysostom depicts toll collecting and brothel keeping as two base and unseemly legal occupations (*Oration* 14:14; MacMullen 1974: 140; Karris 1985: 74). Most women at Graeco-Roman banquets were prostitutes (Corley 1993a). Accordingly, one might view the woman as a prostitute, but the connection is not direct.

The same may be said of the woman's forgiveness. Her experience of being forgiven much may identify her as a prostitute, but Luke also links forgiveness with Jesus' healing activity (5:17–26; cf. Mark 2:1–12; Matt. 9:1–9) as well as Jesus' prophetic role as God's servant whose mission is to set free the oppressed. For example, in the programmatic scene at Nazareth (4:16–30) Jesus announces that his ministry brings 'release (*aphesin*) to the captives' and 'liberty' (*aphesei*) to 'those who are oppressed' (4:18). Further, the woman in the synagogue (13:10–17) had been 'bound (*edesen*)' by Satan for eighteen years. When Jesus heals her he declares, 'you are freed (*apolelusai*) from your infirmity' (13:12), and she is identified as 'a daughter of Abraham' (13:16; see Zacchaeus, 19:9). Finally, the women who follow Jesus out of Galilee were persons cured of diseases or evil spirits (Luke 8:2). The declaration of the woman's great forgiveness does not demand or exclude the woman's identity as a prostitute.

A 'woman of the city'

But does the expression a 'woman of the city' (7:37) contain a clue to the woman's social identity? The phrase may simply refer to the woman's social location at the time, 'a woman in the city' (NRSV). Fitzmyer renders a literal translation of the expression as one 'who was in the town a sinner' (1981: 1.688). However, the phrase seems to connote more. Following Rohrbaugh, the woman's 'home' may have been 'the streets and lanes of the city' (14:21), that is her social location may have been among those who lived and worked within walled off and/or sequestered areas which included an assortment of outcasts including prostitutes (Rohrbaugh 1991: 144). If so, the phrase possibly connotes a morally negative notion such as 'a public woman' ('woman of the city/public woman'). Corley has identified two Greek epigrams (*Anth. Graec.* 5.175; 7.403) which describe a 'public woman' as one who is 'common to all' (1993a: 38–39). Admittedly, Luke's phrase (*gune . . . en te polei*) and the expression of the epigrams (*gunai pagkoine*) are different, yet two possible correspondences to the Lukan story can be detected in one of the epigrams:

> I know thy oath is void, for they betray thy wantonness, these locks still moist with scented essences. They betray thee, thy eyes all heavy for want of sleep, and the garland's track all round thy head. Thy ringlets are in unchaste disorder all freshly tousled, and all thy limbs are tottering with the wine. Away from me, public woman; they are calling thee, the lyre that loves the revel and the clatter of the castanets rattled by the fingers.
>
> (*Anth. Graec.* 5.175)

The locks of the 'public woman' are 'still moist with scented essences'. The woman at Simon's house has an 'alabaster flask of ointment' (7:37). The ringlets of the 'public woman' are 'in unchaste disorder all freshly tousled'. The forgiven woman uses her hair to wipe Jesus' feet (7:38). If the analogy holds, the woman is outcast because she is a prostitute.

Uninvited

I believe the woman is uninvited. First, she is not a matron (Corley 1989: 488–490; 1993a: 28–31), that is, a wife of an invited male. Second, her silence probably indicates she is not a courtesan, a prostitute having a wealthy or upper-class clientele who would be invited to carry on conversation as well engage in 'sexual sport' (Corley 1989: 488–490; 1993a: 38–48). Third, Simon as a respected Pharisee would not invite a courtesan to entertain at a banquet given in honour of an alleged prophet (contrast the banquet of Herod Antipas in Mark 6:17–29), or have as a guest 'a person of the land'. Finally, the pericope indicates the woman was uninvited. She situates herself at the feet of Jesus because she learns that Jesus 'was at table in the Pharisee's house' (7:37). The woman 'crashed' the banquet. Perhaps she was from among the crowds (8:43–48; 11:27), one of the uninvited who passed in and out during the festivities because the door of the dining room was left open (Talbert 1986: 86). Her uninvited status reinforces her outcast station.

Violation of social boundaries

The woman violates space and time boundary markers related to Simon's house and meal.[24] Stephen Barton, drawing on Mary Douglas, describes such boundaries as 'foci of human world-constructions' and sources of anxiety, and states that 'They separate order from chaos, dirt from non-dirt, friend from enemy (or stranger), beginning from end, life from death, male from female, unmarried from married, body from soul, heaven from hell, and so on. . . . Pollution occurs when the boundaries are disregarded or infringed' (Barton 1986: 225–226). The woman has trespassed upon the Pharisee's ordered, undefiled, dirt-free place and time (Douglas 1966). Simon's boundaries, however, are not the basis of table fellowship for Jesus whose boundary of space is the Kingdom of God and boundary of time is the Christian fellowship meal. Hospitality of the Kingdom is based on criteria such as repentance, love and faith. The woman qualifies. So, by allowing the woman to touch him, Jesus receives and reciprocates the woman's hospitality (see 15:2; 19:6), and simultaneously challenges Simon's worldview (Malina 1986a: 182). The *fait divers*, then, is a religiously driven social crisis: a polluted public woman has trespassed upon a male-centred meal in a Pharisee's unpolluted house. Her social identify is twofold: for Simon she is a social deviant, an outcast, probably a prostitute; but for Jesus she is a model disciple (7:38, 44, 47, 50).[25]

If my analysis is correct, the Lukan reversal probably indicates both a breaking up of conventional Graeco-Roman gender expectations at public meal settings and the future inclusion of women at early Christian meals.[26] The issue is not whether the woman actually eats with Jesus. After all this is Simon's meal in Simon's house, both of which will be vacated by the salvation of the Kingdom (Moessner 1989: 157). The critical issue is the giving and receiving of hospitality, something Simon has not done. The woman's posture at the feet of Jesus does not underscore 'her servile' position, as Corley claims (1993a: 130). After all, Peter, too, when confronted by what Jesus had done for him and his partners, fell down at Jesus' knees (5:8). Like Mary the woman 'rejoices in God my Saviour' for the Lord has done 'great things' for her. The woman knows first-hand that the Lord exalts 'those of low degree' and scatters 'the proud in the imagination of their hearts' (1:47–53). Luke does treat the woman with social restraint. She remains nameless and silent. There is an element of 'control' because Luke is concerned for 'what is acceptable to the convention of the imperial world' (D'Angelo 1990: 442). However, at minimum, the incident stretches traditional social boundaries to their limit and validates the statement, 'The Son of man has come eating and drinking; and you say, "Behold, a glutton and a drunkard, a friend of tax collectors and sinners!"' (7:34; cf. 5:30; 15:1–2; 19:1–10).

Jesus at Levi's banquet (5:29–39)

Levi's banquet is a reversal of the three Pharisee-hosted banquets. Besides Levi and Jesus, four groups are present: toll collectors (5:29), sinners (5:30), disciples (5:30) and Pharisees and their scribes (5:30). Of the four groups, two definitely are male (toll collectors and Pharisees and their scribes) and two are without specific gender identification (sinners and disciples). Our concern is with the latter two groups.

As already noted of the woman at Simon's meal, the group designated 'sinners' may include women. However, if women 'sinners' are present, I believe their numbers are probably small, given the ratio of women to men at symposia meals of the time. The term 'disciple' encompasses both women and men in Luke–Acts. It has gender-specific meaning in reference to the Twelve (6:13–16), but the Twelve are chosen from a larger group of disciples (6:13). Women follow Jesus and alongside the Twelve are 'guarantors of the facts of the Christ event' (8:1–3;

23:49, 55; 24:10; Acts 1:14; 13:31) (Talbert 1986: 90). But women are probably not among the disciples at Levi's banquet, for three reasons. First, up to chapter 5 Luke mentions only the calling of male disciples, Simon Peter and his partners (5:11) and Levi (5:27–28). Emphasis upon women as disciples in Jesus' ministry does not take centre stage until the story of the woman at Simon's meal, followed by the introduction of the women in chapter 8. Second, given the scrupulous character of Jesus' critics, it is doubtful they would converse with a gender-mixed group, especially over a religious matter. Last, when women are present in Luke–Acts the author tends to emphasize the fact (Acts 5:14; see Acts 1:14; 8:3, 12; 9:2 etc.). The feast may be an all-male event attended and criticized by men. Women may be present among those labelled as 'sinners' and 'disciples', but it is not until the banquet at Simon's house that a woman outcast becomes a socio-religious issue.

Finally, Levi's meal should not be viewed in isolation. First, it is related to Zacchaeus' meal. The two meals form a pair as they open and conclude (bracket) the sequence of food and meal scenes in the Galilean (4:14–9:50) and Journey (9:51; 19:28) sections. In each a mission statement is found (5:32; 19:10), Jesus' personal concern for outcasts is manifest (5:31; 19:9) and the 'murmuring' of critics is underscored (5:30; 19:7). Second, both toll collector meals are coupled to the issue of table fellowship in Luke 15. Four features are common to all three settings: first, those who receive and render hospitality include Jesus, toll collectors and sinners (5:29; 15:1; 19:7); second, the religious elite are unable to accept and to celebrate the inclusion of sinners at the meal (5:30; 15:23–28; 19:6–7); third, the theme of murmuring is underscored (5:30; 15:2, 27–30; 19:7); and fourth, the toll collector meals share with Simon's meal Luke's concern for outcasts. The woman is parallel to Levi and Zacchaeus in that she renders hospitality to Jesus, not by hosting, preparing or eating a meal but by washing his feet and anointing his head (7:44–46). All three outcasts and Jesus are censored by Jesus' critics (5:30; 7:39; 19:7). But, ironically, all three are hosts to Jesus who is 'the Lord-Host of the Heavenly Banquet'.

CONCLUSION

Our analysis is incomplete. The data of other meals such as at Martha's house (10:38–42), the Last Supper (22:7–38), the home (?) of the Emmaus disciples (24:28–35) and various references in Acts require further study. To this point, however, the inter-related topics of meals and gender demonstrate Luke's concern for a variety of outcasts. It is clear that meals hosted by Pharisees follow traditional Graeco-Roman practices. They are male-centered and dominated. At these meals there is no indication of the presence of matrons or courtesans. However, the case of the woman at Simon's meal underscores the importance of women outcasts as being worthy to receive and give hospitality in the Kingdom. In other words, Luke's treatment of the woman at Simon's banquet is intentional. But we still do not know what gender-specific decorum was practised at early Christian fellowship meals. Did women disciples recline with their husbands, recline only with women, or sit? How were widows or celibate women treated? The evidence indicates they were included and treated with dignity. The woman's silence attests that Luke honoured some conventional gender-specific expectations. If that is the case, we should be cautious not to present Luke as an advocate of post-Enlightenment egalitarianism. Even so, the writing forges an independent path as it challenges conventional gender-specific public meal conventions and to that degree what happened 'was not done in a corner' (Acts 26:26).

NOTES

1 See Boesen 1980; Karris 1985; Steele 1981; Jeremias 1966; Davis 1967; Elliott 1989: 2; Esler 1987: 71–109; Flender 1967; Hofius 1967; Navone 1979; Neyrey 1985: 8–11; 1986; 1996; Mussner 1975; Ernst 1978; Dillon 1978; Thibeaux 1990; van Staden 1991: 216–230.

2 See Esler 1987: 197–200; Moxnes 1988: 163–165; Jeremias 1971: 115–116; Karris 1985: 58–59.

3 See Esler 1987: 197–200; van Staden 1991: 216–33; Sanders 1974: 247–271; Karris 1985: 61.

4 So Talbert 1974; 1986: 90; D'Angelo 1990: 444–445.

5 See Anderson 1987; Tetlow 1980; Fiorenza 1983, 1986; Corley 1993a; *contra*, see Kopas 1986; Ryan 1985; Witherington III 1979, 1984, 1988; Parvey 1974.

6 Demosthenes, *In Neaer.* 24; Isaeus, Pyr. 13–14; Becker 1889: 490; Corley 1989: 489–490; 1993a: 25–28.

7 Plutarch, *Lyc. and Num.* 3.5; Corley 1987: 18–20; Hock 1982: 11.

8 Smith 1980: 34–36, 209–210; Klosinski 1988: 67–69.

9 Balsdon 1962; Hallett 1984; Lefkowitz 1981; Lefkowitz and Fant 1982; Pomeroy 1975; MacMullen 1974, 1989; Baskin 1985; Rosaldo and Lamphere 1974; Wegner 1988; Corley 1993a: 53–66.

10 Aune 1978: 51–105; Smith 1980: 34–48; Klosinski: 1988: 67–73; Corley 1989: 487–521; 1993a: 28–31; Mack 1988a: 80–83; McMahan 1987.

11 Corley 1993a: 31; Horsley 1982: 75; MacMullen 1980: 212; Smith 1980: 109ff.

12 Cohen 1980: 232–239; Brooten 1982; Kraemer 1986a, 1986b: 183–200; Neusner 1978; 1979a; 1979b; Swidler 1976; Archer 1983: 272–287; Wegner 1988; Corley 1993a: 66–75.

13 Horsley 1982: 75; Stein 1957: 13–44; Bahr 1970: 181; Smith 1980: 178; Corley 1989: 515; 1993a: 69–70.

14 Kraemer 1989; Philo, *Vit. Cont.* 69, 73; Smith 1980: 616; Corley 1989: 513–514; 1993a: 70–71; Brooten 1986: 22–30.

15 Arthur 1977: 84–86; Cantarella 1987: 142–144; Rouselle 1988: 85–87; Brown 1987: 247–248; Csillag 1976; Richlin 1981: 379–404; Pomeroy 1975: 159–161; Balsdon 1962: 217; Corley 1989: 505–507; 1993a: 28–66.

16 Juvenal, *Sat.* 6; Tacitus, *Annals* 13:45; Sallust, *Cat.* 24.3–25.5; Cicero, *Cael.* 20.44–49; Livy, 1:57–60; Arthur 1977: 84–85; Cantarella 1987: 131–133; Lefkowitz 1981: 32.

17 Plutarch, *De Gen.* 594D–F; Dio Chysostom, *Or.* 7.67–68; Plutarch, *Quaest. Conviviales* 5.7.712.

18 Ovid, *Met.* 12. 210–220; Lucian, *Symp.* 8–9; Petronius, *Satyr.* 67–69; Smith 1980: 35.

19 Steele 1981; 1984: 379–394; Delobel 1966; Martin 1931; de Meeus 1961: 847–870; Aune 1987: 122; Sterling 1992: 370–371.

20 Steele 1984: 381; Plato, *Symposium* 98 99; Xenophon, *Symposium*, 382 383, 402 403.
21 Ferguson 1987: 409; Jeremias 1969: 267; Bultmann 1921: 8; *m. Dem.* ii.3; *b. Ber.* 43b.
22 Davies 1991: 187 188; Pilgrim 1981: 87 102; Johnson 1981; Esler 1987: 197 199.
23 Esler 1987: 197 198; van Staden 1991: 222 233; Moxnes 1988: 165.
24 Berger and Luckmann 1967; Leach 1974; 1976; Douglas 1966; Neyrey 1991b; Barton 1986.
25 D'Angelo 1990: 452; Moessner 1989: 191 192, 98 110.
26 Corley 1993a: 121 130 takes a contrary view; but see the review of Corley 1993a in Esler 1995.

Part IV

PAUL, KINSHIP AND IDEOLOGY

12

MANAGING THE HOUSEHOLD

Paul as *paterfamilias* of the Christian household group in Corinth

Stephan J. Joubert

'COMMON-SENSE KNOWLEDGE' IN THE FIRST-CENTURY MEDITERRANEAN WORLD

To speak at a fairly high level of abstraction, the first-century Mediterranean world, with its pivotal values of honour and shame (Plevnik 1993: 95–99), was demarcated in terms of power, gender and social status. Kinship and its set of interlocking rules formed the central social institution (von Lips 1979: 126). Politics was the other major institution, with religion embedded in both of these. First-century people were thus socialized into a world where these values and institutions were part and parcel of their 'taken-for-granted' reality.

Clientela or patronage also dominated the Mediterranean world, from the Latin West to the Greek East (Wallace-Hadrill 1989; Malina and Rohrbaugh 1992: 235; Meeks 1993: 40). In this world with its strict social stratifications, patronal relationships entailed a reciprocal exchange of goods and services, a personal relation of some duration and an asymmetrical relationship where the parties of unequal status offered each other different goods and services in exchange (Saller 1990: 49). The role of brokers, the intermediaries between patron and client, was often crucial to maintaining the relationship (Wallace-Hadrill 1989: 81–84). The broker 'functions as a mediator who gives a client access to the resources of a more powerful patron' (Moxnes 1991: 248). According to Lacey (1987: 140) patronage, both as an ideology and as a social relation, was founded on the ideas inherent in the Roman *patria potestas* (discussed below) and thus originated from the social sphere of the family.[1] An assumption underlying first-century institutions was that the Roman empire was one big family with the emperor as the *paterfamilias* of its inhabitants (Elliott 1993a: 85). The emperor had the same power (*potestas*) over the Roman world that a father had over his children. A so-called 'patriarchal religion' also took shape in the empire ever since Augustus (who officially acquired the title *pater patriae* in 2 BCE) became *pontifex maximus* in 12 BCE and associated his family gods with those of the state. Imperial rule now became an image of the divine rule since Jupiter was also regarded as the paternal guardian of the empire. His rule as father of the gods and mankind thus provided the analogy for the 'patriarchal' reign of the emperors.

The core values of the Mediterranean world ('honour–shame') were not only embedded in general 'meaning-structures' such as a common language, central myths ('Jupiter as father of the empire'), the social differentiation of roles ('males as heads of households; gender division of labour'), rituals ('religious sacrifices'), basic perceptions ('limited good') and the like, but were also communicated and institutionalized through these meaning-structures. These values and meaning-structures thus comprised the 'social stock of knowledge' (Schutz and Luckmann 1974: 251), or the 'common-sense knowledge' of the Mediterranean world. Due to the fact that a relatively limited portion of this knowledge consisted of 'special knowledge' for which the expertise of particular individuals (such as priests and magicians) was needed, the first-century social world was relatively unproblematic. People generally knew what their respective social roles were and how to behave accordingly.

The *paterfamilias* in the Roman world

Moving to a lower level of abstraction, we find specific nuances with regard to the statuses, functions and roles of family members in first-century Roman culture which were regulated by specific Roman laws and customs. The Corinthian Christians also lived in a Roman city. Corinth, the capital of the Roman province Achaia, was destroyed in the year 146 BCE. It lay desolate until Julius Caesar refounded it and started rebuilding it in 44 BCE. By the time Paul visited the city, it was an important centre of commerce because of its location close to the ports of Cenchreae and Lechaeum (Murphy-O'Connor 1983: 53). Although the city was bilingual with many Greek-speaking inhabitants, the constitution and official language of Corinth was Latin (Theissen 1990: 79; Klauck 1992: 18). The Corinthian community was thus socialized in the Roman way of life with its own peculiar customs, laws and beliefs, so that Paul had to link up with their common-sense knowledge, as well as with their basic cultural perceptions of the family.[2]

In the period of the Roman republic and during the imperial period the formal head of the *familia* was called the *paterfamilias* (see Bradley 1991; Dixon 1992; Schultz 1992). The Roman concept *familia* had various meanings. Apart from referring to the slaves and freed slaves attached to a married couple, it was also used with reference to the kin as well as to the property or family estate (Gardner and Wiedemann 1991: 3–4). The *familia* thus included more than just the nuclear family, which was commonly referred to as the *domus*. Although the Roman *familia* consisted of husband, wife, children, slaves, freedmen and foster-children, it was definitely not an extended or joint family which included the more remote relatives or even several generations of the stem family (Rawson 1987: 7).

Members of the Roman *familia* were subjected to the lifelong authority (*potestas*) of the *paterfamilias*, the oldest surviving male ascendant. His *potestas* over his ascendants and slaves was legally recognized and protected. Children had no power to own property in their own right and could not make valid wills, since the *paterfamilias* retained full power over all property in possession of the family. Roman fathers' power over their children was thus not a sort of guardianship which ceased to exist when the children grew up and got married, unless, of course, the children were released by a legal act (Dixon 1992: 40).

The status of a child in the power of his/her father was not much better than that of a slave. It was the *paterfamilias'* task to decide whether a new-born child would be reared or exposed to die. A father could also legally sell, imprison or even kill his children, although some paternal rights were limited as Roman society became more humane from the days of the empire onwards. This was, however, a protracted process. The right of fathers to kill their children in the course of their management of domestic affairs was only abolished by Valentinian in 374 CE.

In order to get married any son or daughter needed the consent of his or her father, who in many cases also arranged these matches beforehand. Fathers could also dissolve their children's marriages by imposing a divorce. In the case of daughters, many so-called free marriages were entered into, which meant that they either stayed under the *potestas* of their biological fathers, or remained independent (*sui iuris*) if their fathers had already passed away. Only when a father transferred his daughter to the *manus* (subordination) of her husband did she lose her right to equal inheritance from his will together with her brothers. By the first century BCE most women preferred to stay in the family of their birth, although the children born of the marriage took the father's name and were legally held under his power.

The *paterfamilias*' lifelong power over his slaves, adopted children and biological children formed the backbone of Roman society; it was a palladium of Romanism (Schulz 1992: 142). However, in spite of the theoretically extreme powers vested in the role of the *patresfamiliarum*, their behaviour was moderated in practice by social pressures such as the values of their families, the morality of the day and the role of the gods in their lives. Especially in the late Roman republic and during the reign of the emperors a so-called 'sentimental idea of the family' flourished which not only emphasized the ideal of harmony (*concordia*) between husbands and wives, but also stressed the extension of affection to the children of the family (Dixon 1991: 99–113). *Pietas*, affection, was now articulated more and more as the basis of *patria potestas*. Although children were still expected to obey and respect their fathers, the personal element of fatherly love was frequently stressed. Writers such as Cicero, Seneca and Plutarch encouraged fathers to love all their children even more than their own honour and wealth, to be proud of them, to take an interest in their studies, to be concerned about their future marriages, to cherish high ambitions for them and to be worried about their physical and moral well being (Eyben 1991: 118–119). At the same time fathers had to accept responsibility for the teaching of their children.

STEPHAN J. JOUBERT

PAUL AS *PATERFAMILIAS* OF THE CORINTHIANS

Paul as broker for the heavenly patrons

As a typical first-century Mediterranean personality, Paul shared the common-sense knowledge available to most people at this time. But he was also acquainted with the meaning-structures peculiar to the Jews and the Romans and applied many of these in his communication of a new symbolic universe to the Corinthians (who themselves came from Jewish and non-Jewish circles). Although Paul was born in Tarsus, a city renowned as a centre of Graeco-Roman culture, his own religious socialization took place in a Jewish context. As a devout Pharisee he learnt to organize and classify the world in terms of Jewish views on purity and order (see Neyrey 1990; Craffert 1993). Even after his conversion he did not abandon all the 'taken-for-granted' aspects of his Jewish past. He still called upon Israel's symbols, traditions and holy books (that is, the Septuagint in preference to the Hebrew Bible) to legitimize his new perceptions of the cosmos. At the same time, however, he also made use of typical Roman concepts in his letters. For example, in 2 Cor. 5:20 he describes his role as mediator of the 'Christ-event' in terms of a Roman *legatus*, a diplomat of the state, who had to help keep the peace between Rome and its provinces.

Paul, in his role as apostle, presented himself as broker on behalf of God, Jesus and the Holy Spirit (the heavenly patrons) to the Corinthians (the clients). He claimed to have direct access to the invisible world of his heavenly patrons who controlled all 'first order resources' in the cosmos, such as the power over life and death, health, nature, funds and land (Malina 1988a: 12; 1993b). Not only could Paul claim that he had seen the face of Jesus Christ in a revelation (2 Cor. 4:6), but he also claimed that God had appointed him as his apostle (1 Cor. 1:1; 15:1–2). He was thus ascribed with supernatural authority. While all other leadership roles within the Corinthian community were of a local nature, his apostolic authority derived from outside the community. Paul could therefore claim the highest rank for himself within the *ekklesia* (Neyrey 1990: 38–39); he was subordinate to nobody else.

As broker of God's patronage Paul also considered himself to be in possession of special knowledge which was not routinely transmitted to people in Corinth. Only he had access to the 'mysteries of God' (1 Cor. 2:1, 7; 4:1), and only he could communicate its contents to others. His words (of proclamation – kerygma) were different from those spoken by other 'specialists' in the Mediterranean world, such as the philosophers, since he uttered them under the guidance of the Holy Spirit (1 Cor. 2:1–4). At the same time Paul also performed miracles (2 Cor. 12:12) and undertook heavenly journeys (2 Cor. 12:1–5), which substantiated his apostolic claim and which illustrated that he had the power to control at least some of the resources in possession of his heavenly patrons.

Paul described the invisible world of God in terms of the first-century Mediterranean institutions of kinship and politics. According to him God was at the head of the cosmos as the heavenly *paterfamilias* (1 Cor. 8:4). Not only was he the father of Jesus (1 Cor. 1:9; 2 Cor. 11:31) who had put all things in the cosmos in subjection under his son (1 Cor. 15:27–28), but he was also the father of the new family of believers (1 Cor. 8:6; 2 Cor. 1:3).[3]

Apart from Paul's use of kinship terminology to describe the Corinthians and Jesus' relationship to God, he also referred to Jesus by means of a term borrowed from the political sphere, namely 'Kyrios' (1 Cor. 8:6; 12:3). Oriental-Hellenistic deities such as Serapis, Isis and Osiris were also addressed as Kyrios/Kyria, as well as the Roman emperors (Cullmann 1980: 195–198). To Paul this term primarily explained the present lordship of Christ over the new community of believers (as a protest against the emperor as master of the empire?).[4] However, in Paul's opinion Christ as the heavenly Lord, who exercised control over all his earthly subjects, was the firstborn son of God (the heavenly *paterfamilias*) who, through his act of reconciliation (2 Cor. 5:16–21), changed God's enemies into his children. In turn God adopted them into his new family of believers (2 Cor. 5:17; cf. also Gal. 4:4–7). The kinship system thus provided the basic structure of Paul's symbolic universe, with the images from the political sphere referring to but one aspect thereof, namely the present reign of Christ over the community of believers.

Paul and the household of believers in Corinth

Paul's views on, and his structuring of, the different social roles within the Christian household group in Corinth were determined by his perceptions of the cosmos. In this regard the different roles he played served to symbolize and institutionalize his superordinate position as official emissary of the heavenly *paterfamilias*. This includes even those roles which expressed his humbleness and his obedience to Christ, such as 'ambassador' (2 Cor 5:20), 'servant' (1 Cor. 4:1) and 'builder' (1 Cor. 1:11). They were all metaphors which masked his apostolic superiority. Furthermore, Paul's use of egalitarian images such as 'brothers' when addressing the Corinthians, or that of 'partners and fellow workers' (2 Cor. 8:23) when referring to his helpers, also masked a relationship other than the one they implied, since these persons were in fact not his equals. They were socially inferior to him, because he had the authority to command their obedience.

Paul also made explicit use of family images in his letters to the Corinthians (1 Cor. 3:1–3a; 4:14–21; 2 Cor. 6:11–13; 12:14–15). Not only did he explain the invisible world of his heavenly patrons in kinship terminology as we have already seen, but he also presented himself as earthly *paterfamilias* of the new community of believers. Even when Paul did not make explicit use of familial concepts, he acted out typical role expectations associated with that of a *paterfamilias* and at the same time also conferred the role of 'children' upon the

Corinthians (as dealt with below). Of course, at this level of voluntary association, Paul's definition of the roles of the new converts in terms of well-known, institutionalized roles from the environment, had the effect that his social world took on the character of a preconstituted system ('the household') where individuals' roles and identities have already been predetermined ('head of the household' and 'children of the household').

In the process of communicating a new version of the cosmos to the Corinthians, Paul made use not only of the language of primary socialization, but also of the corresponding social structures. As a fictive kinship group the Corinthians thus became part of the new household of God and also held their meetings in the houses of individual members of the *ekklesia* (1 Cor. 6:19; Rom. 16:5). Although the household setting was constitutive of the organizational form and character of this new community, intimate connections with existing households were retained by him. In this regard he could state that he baptized the household (*oikos*) of Stephanas (1 Cor. 1:16). The book of Acts confirms this picture of Paul working within the social setting of existing households. Acts 18:8, for example, refers to Crispus and his *oikos* who became Christians as a result of his preaching (cf. also 16:15, 31–34; 17:6–7; 18:1–8).[5]

Paul provides us with some information about the household community in Corinth from which we can construe the following broad picture of their social situation:

1 Members of the Corinthian church came from different cultural groups. Priscilla and Acquilla (1 Cor. 16:19) and Crispus, the ruler of the synagogue (1 Cor. 1:14), were Jews, while (most?) other members, such as Titius Justus, Tertius and Quartus, were non-Jews.
2 Members came from different social strata. Although in 1 Cor. 1:26–29 Paul refers to the fact that not many members of the Corinthian community were learned, powerful and of noble birth, Theissen (1990: 94–95), in his investigation of the social stratification of the Corinthians, identifies at least nine members who belonged to the upper classes. This includes Crispus the synagogue ruler and Erastus the city treasurer.
3 Men as well as women were allowed as members of the Corinthian community. Apart from references to the *patresfamiliarum* of certain Christian households, such as Gaius and Crispus (1 Cor. 1:14), Paul also refers to women of high standing within this community, such as Phoebe who was not only a *diakonos* of the *ekklesia* in Cenchreae, but also a *prostatis*, a leader (Rom. 16:1–2).

According to the available information in Paul's letters, the Corinthian community was characterized by a new network of social relations. Wealthy and influential members, such as Gaius, Priscilla and Acquilla, Sosthenes and Phoebe, probably acted as patrons by rendering services to the rest of the community, such as donating money and providing their houses as meeting places. In response, they were accorded leadership roles. Existing Mediterranean patterns of social, ethnic and sexual classification were also moderated and qualified within this group, since all new members, be it Jews or Greeks, slave or free, were now baptized into the one body of Christ (1 Cor. 12:13) and associated freely with each another. Through the ritual of baptism people who joined this household group thus received the salvation and the new life promised to all God's children by Paul. They were now considered brothers and sisters of one another and children of God.

Behaviour within the household

Apart from reflecting his views of the cosmos, Paul's use of kinship terminology was also related to his efforts to control the Corinthians' behaviour. In 1 Cor. 4:14–15 he, for example, referred to them as his 'beloved children' and to himself as their father since he had begotten them by the transmission of the gospel of Christ. Therefore he could claim the right to demand respect as well as obedience from them (1 Cor. 4:16; 2 Cor. 2:9; 10:6). As *paterfamilias* he also frequently stressed his affection for the Corinthians (Holmberg 1980: 78–79; Best 1988: 29–58). For example, in 2 Cor. 12:14–15, after explaining his unwillingness to accept any financial support from them, he stated that he was prepared to spend himself on them because of his love for them. In this regard Paul referred to the well-known first-century practice of parents saving up an inheritance for their children as motivation for his conduct.

Paul also accepted responsibility for the 'religious education' of the Corinthians. He frequently exhorted them, in view of their ignorance with regard to the correct moral conduct, to imitate his own behaviour (see 1 Cor. 4:16; 10:33; 11:1). As the person who gave them access to the benefactions of God, Paul considered himself to be the perfect role-model. He was living proof of the presence of Christ among the Corinthians, since he in turn imitated him as his own Lord and Master (1 Cor. 4:17; 11:1). He thus not only symbolized the social honour of the new household group as their *paterfamilias*, but also symbolized their ethical honour because he exemplified the contents of his own message.

Apart from holding himself up as an example, Paul also instructed the Corinthians on a wide range of issues regarding their 'bodily behaviour'. Since for Paul their physical bodies were also symbols of the 'social body', the *ekklesia*, his concern for the purity of their bodies reflected his correspondingly strong concern for the purity of the community as a whole (Neyrey 1990: 102–146). Therefore he used his patriarchal authority to create a structured social world where the Corinthians would understand their respective roles and duties. In his management of domestic affairs within this household, Paul, for example, exercised control over their sexual behaviour by stipulating with whom they could have sexual relations and with whom it was forbidden. Incest (5:1–5) and fornification were forbidden (6:12–20), while sex was allowed within the confines of marriage. He also regulated the frequency of intercourse within marriage (1 Cor. 7:2–5); the choice of marriage partners in the case of unmarried members

(1 Cor. 7:39; 2 Cor. 6:14–7:1) and the correct conduct in the case of mixed marriages between community members and unbelievers (1 Cor. 7:10–16). At the same time Paul laid down rules for the proper ('honourable') conduct for women within the public domain of the community, that is, at their religious meetings (1 Cor. 11:3–16; 14:33–35); the eating habits of members at their communal meals (1 Cor. 11:17–34) and the organization of a collection for the poverty-stricken members of the Christian community in Jerusalem (16:1–4).

Conflict in the household

Although Paul claimed a superordinate position for himself in his relationship with the Corinthians, some members of the community rejected his moral teaching (1 Cor. 5:1–13), doubted his authority (1 Cor. 4) and even formed factions around other influential figures, such as Apollos and Peter (1 Cor. 1:10–17; 3:1–9). Therefore Paul had to spend a lot of energy to secure his position as head of the Corinthian household group.

In 1 Corinthians Paul reacted to the Corinthians' disloyalty to him in a rather authoritarian fashion by presenting himself as the symbol of their honour and as the arbiter of right and wrong (as already discussed). In this regard, for example, he used his patriarchal authority to 'punish' the shameless members who rejected the rules of interaction and the social boundaries within their new household, by ordering their excommunication (5:1–5). Paul also demarcated the Corinthian community's role, by stipulating how they should conduct themselves towards him as their *paterfamilias*. In this respect he made it clear that, since they were 'children' who were not only inferior to him, but also still immature, they could not judge or criticize any of his actions (3:1–3; 4:1–4). As a matter of fact, Paul stated that they were like small children who were not yet ready for food for adults, since they quarrelled about 'irrelevant issues' such as his importance or that of Apollos, above other leaders (3:1–8). Although he pointed out that he and Apollos were only servants of God (3:5–8), Paul shifted the focus to his patriarchal role in 4:15, thus explicitly claiming the superordinate position for himself within the community. As *paterfamilias* Paul was above criticism. The only legitimate options available to the Corinthians within this relationship were to trust him, to be proud of him, to imitate him and to obey him (4:21; 9:1–23; 10:31–11:1).

1 Corinthians was, however, not favourably received by the Corinthian community. In fact, relations between Paul and them deteriorated to such an extent after this letter that he had to change his itinerary in order to visit them (2 Cor. 1:15–21). During the visit he apparently clashed with one of the members whereafter he left deeply grieved and wrote them the so-called 'Letter of Tears' (the present 2 Cor 10–13).[6] In this letter Paul decidedly defended his own position as official broker of the heavenly patrons. He also sarcastically addressed the 'foolish' behaviour of the Corinthians, such as confusing his fatherly affection

for them with weakness (10:1, 10–11; 13:2, 10), doubting his own *bona fides* (11:7–9) and allowing certain 'apostles' into their midst, who falsely claimed that they were brokers of God's patronage (10:12–17; 11:12–15). At the same time Paul explained the motives for his actions to the Corinthians, by stating that his only concern was their spiritual maturity (12:19; 13:9–11). He did not seek any material gain from this relationship (12:16–18). As a matter of fact, due to his unselfish love for them, he was even prepared to spend himself for them (11:11; 12:14–15).

Paul did not leave the Corinthians any other choice than to identify with the role he conferred upon them in the 'Letter of Tears', namely that of obedient children. Should they refuse to behave accordingly, Paul stated that he himself would be humbled by God (12:19–21). His claim to worthiness in God's eyes was thus dependent on the correct identity and moral behaviour of the Corinthians. Although Paul did not perceive their disrespect for his person as a challenge to his own honour, since he did not consider them as his equals in social terms, he knew that God (and other people who had contact with the Corinthians) could ridicule him because of his lack of control over his 'household'.

Paul sent Titus, one of his helpers, with this intermediate letter to the Corinthians (2 Cor. 7:13–15). When he met up with Titus in Macedonia, after he had completed this task (2 Cor. 2:13; 7:5), Paul was relieved to hear that the Corinthians were deeply moved to remorse because of their disobedience to their 'father' (2 Cor. 2:9; 7:8–13). In response he quickly sent Titus back with a conciliatory letter, the present 2 Corinthians 1–9.

The favourable results of the 'Letter of Tears', which caused the Corinthians to submit themselves and repent of their insubordinate behaviour, filled Paul with joy since order within the household was restored once again (2 Cor. 7:4–13). More importantly, this public demonstration of respect for his patriarchal authority facilitated the realization of his own honour in God's eyes and in the eyes of others who had contact with the Corinthian household.

Paul adopted a very mild patriarchal role throughout 2 Corinthians 1–9. Especially in chs 8–9, which refer to the collection project for the believers in Judaea (see Joubert 1992), he emphasized the intimate bond between the Corinthians and himself. This project was of course very important to Paul since he had already earlier given his 'word of honour' to Peter (Gal. 2:10) that he would help the impoverished members of the Jerusalem community to maintain their honour. However, due to the disturbed relations between Paul and the Corinthian community after the writing of 1 Corinthians, the collection came to an abrupt halt. In order to involve them in this project yet again, he now brought much pressure to bear on them (see 2 Cor. 8–9). But instead of issuing direct commands as he did in 1 Cor. 16:1–4, by supplying autocratic instructions and commands with regard to the organization of the collection (16:1–2), he now opted for a milder approach. After the successful intermediate letter which caused the change of heart in the Corinthians, Paul viewed them as mature, responsible 'children' who did not need not be ordered and directed as before (8:7–8). Only their positive attributes were now of importance (2 Cor. 8:7; 9:2). At the same time he could also stress his abundant love for them (8:10), offer his advice to them in their own interest (8:10) and boast to others about their exemplary conduct (9:2–3). However, within this intimate situation the implicit pressure on the Corinthians to complete the collection was just as great, if not greater than within an explicit authoritative situation, since now their integrity would be implicated if they did not commit themselves to this task.

Paul's use of paternal images of affection and care in 2 Corinthians 8–9, and elsewhere in the Corinthian correspondence, does not imply, as Petersen maintains (1985: 158–170), that his fatherhood was a transparent mask for his apostolic role, through which he (in anti-structural fashion) tried to break the strict hierarchical system that existed between himself and the Corinthians. They were two distinct roles. While Paul's apostolic role reflected his position as mediator of the heavenly patrons, his patriarchal role was again related to his status in the household communities under his care. In this regard typical first-century expectations associated with the role of the *paterfamilias*, such as a father's lifelong authority over and affection for his children, elucidated the relation between Paul and the Corinthians. Although Paul oscillated between hierarchical and intimate aspects of his patriarchal role, depending on his perception of the nature of the relationship between him and them, he still, at all times, claimed the superordinate position for himself.

CONCLUSION

As broker of the heavenly patrons Paul considered himself the social and ethical embodiment of the honour of the Corinthian household group. His authority as their *paterfamilias* was beyond dispute. Members who threatened the cohesion of the new family of believers were therefore disciplined in order to instil subordination and obedience to himself and restore harmony within the household. In this regard Paul demanded that some members be excommunicated, while he threatened others with punishment by God, revealed their 'shameless behaviour' and even used their own lack of 'religious maturity and integrity' as a leverage to put pressure on them to comply with his requests. Since Paul accepted responsibility for the maintenance of the Corinthians' honour or social standing, he also used different strategies, ranging from the adoption of a more authoritarian to a milder patriarchal role, to bring their behaviour in line with the religious values and truths he taught them.

Paul's interaction with the Corinthians was to a large extent focused on their recognition and acceptance of his patriarchal authority. Clearly, he was of the opinion that his effective management of the Corinthian household, which entailed total obedience to his instructions and teaching, could facilitate the realization of his own honour in the eyes of his heavenly patrons.

NOTES

1 *Patria potestas* was, however, not unique to Roman life. It was also known elsewhere in the Hellenistic world (Schulz 1992: 150–151).

2 Although Paul had to link up with the Corinthians' basic cultural asssumptions with regard to the family, we can nevertheless agree with von Lips (1979: 126) and Cohen (1993: 2) that, in spite of specific 'modifications' to roles within the family in Jewish, Roman and Greek circles, the structure and dynamics of families seem to have been very similar all over the Mediterranean world (see also Jacobs-Malina 1993: 1–6).

3 Sociologically, this image of God's fatherhood helped to shape the Pauline household group's corporate identity. It also served to distinguish them from those who adhered to the 'patriarchal' politics and religion of the emperors.

4 This, amongst others, pertained to their baptism in the name of the Kyrios (1 Cor. 6:11; 12:12–13); the ritual confession of his lordship (1 Cor. 12:3); the 'Lord's Supper' (1 Cor. 10:21; 11:21) and the like (see Petersen 1985: 240–257).

5 A typical Corinthian *oikos* consisted of the *paterfamilias* (in Greek: *oikodespotes*), all immediate relatives, slaves and freedmen.

6 It is my contention that Paul wrote 2 Cor. 10–13 prior to 2 Corinthians, after a painful visit to the Corinthians (see Joubert 1992).

13

THE DEVELOPMENT OF THEOLOGICAL IDEOLOGY IN PAULINE CHRISTIANITY

A structuration theory perspective[1]

David G. Horrell

INTRODUCTION

The purpose of this essay is to offer a brief sketch of just one of the ways in which Anthony Giddens' 'structuration theory' might provide a framework for a fruitful and significant social-scientific approach to the New Testament. It is not an approach that has nothing in common with previous studies, both sociological and historical, but, I suggest, it draws their insights into a more adequate and critical framework.[2]

Giddens is one of the most prominent contemporary figures in the field of social theory. Structuration theory, as critical social theory, is, in Giddens' view, relevant to 'the whole range of the social sciences' (Giddens 1982: 5). It is not, however, a theory which offers detailed models or explanations which could be tested against the New Testament evidence. It seeks to offer conceptual resources, or an 'ontological framework' (Giddens 1991: 201), with which to approach the study of social life. It offers resources for a theoretical framework, yet encourages the researcher also to remain open to the contextually and historically specific nature of the arena of investigation.

ELEMENTS OF STRUCTURATION THEORY

The formulation of structuration theory is profoundly influenced by perhaps the most 'fundamental problem [which] stalks through the history of sociological theory' (Archer 1990: 73): the dualism between action and structure, or between subject and object. Opposing schools of sociology have emphasized one at the expense of the other (see Giddens 1982: 28–30). Central to Giddens' attempt to overcome this problem is the assertion that this dualism 'must cede place to recognition of a *duality* which is implicated in all social reproduction, the *duality of structure*. By the "duality of structure" I refer to the essentially recursive character of social life: the structural properties of social systems are both medium and outcome of the practices that constitute those systems' (Giddens 1982: 36–37).

The duality of structure is illustrated by the case of language: anyone who produces a sentence draws upon the structural features, the 'rules and resources', of a language in order to do so, yet by so doing they simultaneously contribute to the reproduction of that language (cf. Giddens 1982: 37). The structure of the language is both the medium which permits meaningful communication and the outcome of that communication. Thus, 'in the theory of structuration, "structure" refers to rules and resources instantiated in social systems, but having only a "virtual" existence' (Giddens 1982: 9). Giddens divides structures into three types: signification, domination and legitimation, while stressing that these are separable only analytically and are always linked in social institutions (see Giddens 1984: 28–34).

The concept of the duality of structure, as the linguistic analogy shows, brings reproduction into central focus. Indeed, Cohen considers that this is perhaps the major achievement of structuration theory (I. J. Cohen 1987: 306). Each time I speak I contribute to the reproduction of the English language. Thus the central notion of 'structuration' refers essentially to a process, to 'the structuring of social relations across time and space, in virtue of the duality of structure' (Giddens 1984: 376). Moreover, reproduction, it is clear, is inextricably linked with transformation. Again, the linguistic analogy makes this clear; language is transformed as it is used (cf. Giddens 1976: 128). Thus Giddens insists that 'with a conception of structuration, the possibility of change is recognized as inherent in every circumstance of social reproduction' (Giddens 1979: 210). As the rules and resources which structure social life are reproduced, they may be transformed, and this transformation is one of the things that a structuration theory perspective will seek to illuminate.

Discussion of the reproduction and transformation of structured social life immediately raises the issue of power. Power, Giddens suggests, may be defined, in its broadest sense, as 'the *transformative capacity* of human action' (Giddens 1976: 110). Differentials of power mean different levels of influence over the reproduction and transformation of the rules and resources which structure social life. The powerful, therefore, are potentially in a position to shape social life in a way which serves and legitimates their own sectional interests. This, for Giddens, is essentially what ideology is. As he conceptualizes it, 'ideology refers to the *ideological*, this being understood in terms of the capability of dominant groups or classes to make their own sectional interests appear to others as universal ones' (Giddens 1979: 6). Giddens' notion of ideology, then, is a 'critical' one, using the distinction between 'neutral' and 'critical' made by Thompson in his discussion of the ways in which the term ideology is employed (Thompson 1984: 3–4). Ideology, used in this critical sense, is not a term to be applied to any system of thought or belief, but refers specifically to 'the ways in which meaning (or signification) serves to sustain relations of domination' (Thompson 1984: 4).[3] Giddens suggests that there are three principal ideological forms: the representation of sectional interests as universal ones, the denial or transmutation of contradictions and the naturalization of the present (reification) (Giddens 1979: 193–196; cf. Thompson 1984: 131). It is perhaps in this third form that religion is most likely to feature, for it has a particular opportunity to legitimate and sustain forms of social organization, elevating such forms above the status of merely human products and reifying or naturalizing them by rooting them in the divine will.

Although Giddens stresses throughout his work the capability and knowledgeability of human actors – and relative capability links in a clear way to differentials of power – it must also be affirmed that he emphasizes the fact that human agents do not always, or even generally, understand fully the conditions upon which their action is based; nor do they intend, or foresee, all of its consequences. In other words, human action takes place in the context of a set of conditions, some of which are unacknowledged, and it produces a range of consequences, some of which are unintended (see Giddens 1984: 5, 8, 27). To link this with the ideological question is to state that the legitimation of relations of domination, or of sectional interests, may not be the intended consequence of a particular action, though it may be a consequence nonetheless. Texts, in particular, Giddens suggests, may 'escape' the intentions of their authors and take on new meanings in new contexts. He suggests that:

> One of the main tasks of the study of the text, or indeed cultural products of any kind, must be precisely to examine the divergencies which can become instituted between the circumstances of their production, and the meanings sustained by their subsequent escape from the horizon of their creator or creators.
>
> (Giddens 1979: 44)

A STRUCTURATION THEORY PERSPECTIVE ON PAULINE CHRISTIANITY

How might all of this form a framework for a sociological interpretation of the Pauline letters? Structuration theory, it seems to me, offers two fundamentals: firstly, a theoretical framework with which to analyze the on-going reproduction and transformation of Pauline Christianity; within which, secondly, the critical ideological questions may be asked.

Pauline Christianity, in structuration theory terms, may best be viewed as a symbolic order, an institution in which structures especially of signification, but also of domination and legitimation, are instantiated (cf. Giddens 1984: 31, 33). That is to say, it is a coagulation of symbols (embodied in rituals), a linguistic framework, a collection of rules and resources, which shapes the life of particular communities. This is notably similar to Berger and Luckmann's conception of a symbolic universe, a theoretical perspective which has already proved fruitful for New Testament study (see Esler 1987: 16–23; 1994a: 4–12). The most important differences, however, relate to Giddens' more adequate theorization of the relation between action and structure, and to his critical perspectives on issues of power, interests and ideology, issues neglected by Berger and Luckmann (see Horrell 1993: 85–93). It is attention to precisely these issues that is implied by the label *critical* social theory.

Drawing upon the notion of the duality of structure, we may suggest that the symbolic order – the symbols, rules and resources – of Pauline Christianity is both medium and outcome of the community's life. It is the 'medium' which shapes the belief, behaviour and interaction of the members, but is at the same time reshaped and reproduced by them; the 'outcome' of their life together. This is where the issue of power becomes crucial. Differentials of power mean differentials of influence over the reproduction and transformation of the symbolic order. 'What passes for social reality,' Giddens insists, 'stands in immediate relation to the distribution of power' (Giddens 1976: 113). Who were the people who possessed the power to reformulate the faith and thus to shape the community's life? Clearly Paul, of course, during his lifetime; though the role of other leaders and teachers should not be overlooked. After Paul's removal from the scene, this position of power falls to others, and the sociological ramifications of this change should not be ignored.

To raise the critical questions concerning ideology in this connection is to investigate the extent to which the symbolic order of Pauline Christianity reflects the interests of dominant social groups. When and in what ways might the Christian symbolic order be said to offer a religious ideology, theologically legitimating the dominant social order, in relation, say, to the institution of slavery, or to the power and position of the *paterfamilias* as head of his household? 'Symbolic orders and associated modes of discourse', Giddens maintains, 'are a major institutional locus of ideology' (Giddens 1984: 33). To investigate the ideological dimensions of Pauline teaching is not necessarily to assume that such teaching is intended to be ideological. Indeed, the development of theological ideology in Pauline Christianity may in part be a product of the unintended consequences which flow from contextual human action, particularly when this 'action' is the writing of a text which not only 'escapes from the horizon of its creator', but also acquires the status of normative and (eventually) canonical teaching.

AN EXEGETICAL TRAJECTORY

It is clearly beyond the scope of this essay to attempt a comprehensive investigation of Pauline Christianity in terms of the framework outlined above. What follows is a limited example, which forges an exploratory and selective trajectory through the Pauline corpus, focusing only upon some of the obvious places where we might discern the development of theological ideology.[4] Nevertheless, I hope to give some flavour of the interpretive shape which a structuration theory perspective might place upon our texts, and of the questions and issues which thereby emerge. In this selective trajectory, the Pauline texts will be approached in a way similar to that adopted by MacDonald (1988), where Colossians and

Ephesians, and then the Pastorals, are taken to reflect successive stages of institutionalization, after the death of the apostle Paul. However, it will become clear that the questions raised by a structuration theory perspective add a 'critical' dimension through their concern with issues of power, interests and ideology.

1 Corinthians 7:17–24

I begin with 1 Corinthians, and, specifically, with chapters 7 and 11. In 1 Corinthians 7, Paul is explicitly responding to the Corinthians' questions concerning marriage and sexual relations (7:1, 25); part of a series of responses he makes to a range of issues, including those raised in their letter to him.[5] As such questions and problems arise, so Paul is engaged in the process of reformulating, reshaping and expanding the Christian symbolic order, in response to the situation now faced; a situation which may in part be an unintended consequence of Paul's earlier teaching. Much of Paul's instruction here, as has often been pointed out, is formulated in a remarkably parallel and reciprocal way, apparently ascribing to both male and female equal value and responsibility.[6] Male domination is not here ideologically legitimated.

Paul's advice, at its most general, is 'do not seek a change in status' (Fee 1987: 268); on the whole, those who are married should remain married, and those who are single should remain single. It is in this context that Paul illustrates his point by referring to circumcision and slavery (7:17–24), illustrations which are associated with male–female issues due to the pattern of Gal. 3:28 (Bartchy 1973: 162–165).[7] The primary focus of the instruction to 'remain as you are' is upon sexual relationships. However, as is the case with sexual relationships, Paul shows that racial and social status do not have to be changed when a person is called by God. The sign of circumcision should be neither removed nor sought (vss. 18f.). Slaves, similarly, do not need to change their status, though here Paul makes a point of stating a clear exception: 'But if indeed you are able to become free, by all means make use of the opportunity.'[8]

Paul's contextual concern in this chapter of 1 Corinthians is to answer the Corinthians' questions regarding marriage and sexual relations. His comments on circumcision and slavery are primarily illustrative. However, these illustrative formulations contained within the text thus become a part of the rules and resources which determine the nature of the Christian symbolic order, and may shape the community's self-understanding in an on-going way, a way which may diverge or escape from the intentions and circumstances of their production. Are there elements here which might be said, if unintentionally, to contribute to the development of a theological ideology?

One such element may be found in the repeated advice in verses 17, 20 and 24: 'let each one remain in the calling in which they were called' (vs. 20). Even if the primary reference of the term *klesis* is to the believer's calling by God to live in Christ (so Bartchy 1973: 132–159), and even though Paul does not quite take the step of equating a person's *klesis* with their social position (Fee 1987: 309), the text is certainly open to the interpretation that each person's social position is a 'calling' given to them by God, and in which, therefore, they are called to remain. Such a theology may indeed be called a theological ideology, for it naturalizes, reifies, the present social order (Giddens' third ideological form) so as to portray social position as something ordained by God, and thus to imply that the Christian's duty is to remain in that position.

A second ideological element within this short passage may perhaps be discerned in Paul's mention of slave and free. Paul does not, in my view, urge slaves to refuse the chance of manumission (see endnote 8) – that would certainly add an ideological dimension to this passage – though he does implicitly sanction the continuance of master–slave relationships (even within the Christian community?). He insists, however, from the Christian point of view, that the slave is *apeleutheros kyriou* and that the free person is *doulos Christou* (vs. 22). In some ways this insistence may be viewed as subversive: the Christian symbolic order reverses the conventional social valuations placed upon slave and free. However, its ideological potential should not be ignored. It is possible to see here religion in the role Marx identified: as offering (illusory) comfort and consolation to the underclass, thereby encouraging them to tolerate and accept, rather than protest against and resist, the inequalities of life (Marx and Engels 1957: 41–42, 82–83). Telling slaves that they are 'free in the Lord' is perhaps unintentionally a means by which discontent is dissolved and the status quo maintained.[9]

1 Corinthians 11:2–16

1 Cor. 11:2–16 is another passage which addresses a particular and contextual issue: appropriate head-attire for women who pray and prophesy *en ekklesia*. Once again Paul must reformulate and develop the content of the symbolic order in response to a situation which owes at least something to his previous teaching (vs. 2), but which now requires correction.

Paul happily accepts the situation in which both men and women are free to pray and prophesy (vs. 5; cf. vs. 2); his practical aim, whether he is talking about veils or hairstyles (a point of debate), is to ensure that men and particularly women are properly attired in worship. The created differences between them should not be dissolved.[10]

The main theological points upon which Paul builds his argument are presented in verse 3 and verses 7–9. (His arguments in verses 13–16 are more varied: propriety, nature and general church practice.) In verse 3 he outlines a hierarchy: God – Christ – man – woman. There has been much debate over the precise meaning of *kephale* in this verse, but even if it means 'source', as the advocates of a less patriarchal reading of this passage argue,[11] the hierarchical nature of the theology can hardly be denied: man is closer to God and to Christ than woman. Indeed, man's priority is underlined still further in the use Paul makes of the creation narratives in verses 7–9. It is man, *aner*, who is the image and glory of God (*eikon kai doxa theou*); woman is *doxa andros*, precisely because man came first and woman was created from man.

Paul's specific and contextual concerns clearly motivate the whole passage: he uses the word *kephale* precisely because his concern is with the way in which the *kephale* must be attired in worship. He follows the assertion of woman's secondary place in the order of creation (vs. 8f.) not with a command for her to be subordinate, but with an insistence that her correct attire is a sign of her *exousia* to pray and prophesy. Paul's purpose seems to be the establishment of 'proper' distinction between men and women rather than with male superiority or authority. The practical issue of attire is uppermost in his mind. This appears to be confirmed by the note of qualification or correction expressed in vss. 11–12, where Paul seems to oppose a subordinationist interpretation of what he has said. Verse 11 stresses the interdependence, even, according to Kürzinger (1978), the equality, of men and women; and verse 12 seems clearly to 'correct', or at least to counterbalance, the perspective of verse 8, stating that 'just as woman came from man, so man comes through woman, and all things are from God'. Paul's somewhat desperate arguments in the remainder of the passage (vss. 13–16) are clearly intended to underpin his main point; that a woman should not pray or prophesy *akatakalupton*.

Once again, however much the text reflects the specific circumstances of its production, we must consider the extent to which its formulations have ideological potential. It is quite clear that, even if Paul did not intend it to convey these implications, the theology presented in vss. 3–9 draws on the Genesis narratives in a particular way and builds into the Christian symbolic order the notion that woman has a secondary place, below man, in the created order (cf. Watson 1992: 91–99). Although this theology is presented in a passage which relates to the context of worship, it may easily be taken to have wider implications: a social relationship of domination may be legitimized, 'reified', by rooting it in the fundamental and God-given pattern of creation. 1 Corinthians 11 provides the earliest written Christian contribution to the formulation of a profoundly influential theological ideology which supports a hierarchical relationship between the sexes.

The *Haustafeln* of Colossians and Ephesians

If we now turn to Colossians and Ephesians, as letters reflecting the work of a Pauline school perhaps a decade or two after Paul's death, then the so-called *Haustafeln*, or domestic codes, within these letters form an obvious focus of interest. Colossians and Ephesians represent the earliest written evidence of a domestic code in a Christian context. Here, as in 1 Corinthians 7 and 11, women and slaves are a focus (though not an exclusive focus) of attention. Unlike in 1 Corinthians, however, where the mention of slaves appeared almost incidentally, as an illustration of the substantial point, and where the concern in relation to women was with their attire in worship, here the roles and responsibilities of these and other social groups are quite deliberately addressed, in their household context. The particular sections in the two epistles are remarkably similar, with many precise verbal parallels. They address, in the same order, wives and husbands, children and fathers, slaves and masters. With one notable exception – the section in Ephesians addressed to husbands – the proportion of space they devote to each of these groups is basically similar, though the code in Ephesians is generally more extended. It is unnecessary for my argument to rehearse the various theories which have been advanced as to the relationship between the two letters.

From a structuration theory perspective, the *Haustafeln* of Colossians and Ephesians, as indeed the epistles as a whole, will be viewed as evidence of the developments and transformations which occurred as the Christian symbolic order was reproduced over time, as its rules and resources were restated and developed, by those in a position of power, or those attempting to use power – as Paul did – to shape the Christian symbolic order and thereby its social embodiment. New forms of presenting and expressing what it means to be Christian develop.

The codes begin with an instruction to wives to submit to their husbands; this is what their Christian discipleship demands. The theological legitimation for this, which Eph. 5:23–24 provides, picks up Paul's presentation of the *kephale* hierarchy in 1 Cor. 11:3, though the context now is not worship but the household. Here in Ephesians, however, it is a parallelism which is developed: the husband is 'head' of the wife, as Christ is 'head' of the church. The rules and resources of the symbolic order are picked up, reproduced but also transformed. Christ as *kephale* of the church is a major theological development in Colossians and Ephesians (Col. 1:18; Eph. 4:15f. etc.). The conclusion which follows with regard to a wife's behaviour is clear and explicit: 'as the church submits to Christ, so also wives to husbands *in everything*' (Eph. 5:24). The parallelism in Ephesians also provides the basis for an expansion of the simple command in Col. 3:19: 'Husbands, love your wives.' In Ephesians this is explicitly developed as a role which imitates Christ. Those who seek to read these domestic codes as positively as possible stress here how the model for the husband is one of self-giving, sacrificial love.[12] Certainly this is the case; though one must equally recognize that Christ (in Colossians and Ephesians) is also the exalted Lord in whom all the fullness of God dwells (Col. 2:9f.; Eph. 1:22f. etc.). Moreover, the form of the parallelism excludes the possibility that a wife's discipleship might consist in a call to be like Christ (cf. Lincoln 1990: 392). Not unlike 1 Cor. 11:7–9, it is the man who is the image, the representation of Christ. The summarizing conclusion is clear: the husband's duty is to love his wife as himself, the wife's response is to fear her husband (Eph. 5:33).

The fact that children are also addressed in these codes demonstrates, as Schrage notes, that the formulation of these instructions can hardly be explained solely as a defensive response to emancipatory movements among women and slaves (Schrage 1974–1975: 5–6). They are also 'ein offensives Moment' (Schrage 1974–1975: 5), a positive attempt to ensure that a certain set of social relations is sustained and legitimated by the Christian faith itself. Notably it is the fathers who are addressed with regard to the discipline and care of children.

Slaves are urged to fulfil their duties completely and wholeheartedly. Colossians and Ephesians introduce the idea of a service which does not merely attend to what human masters can see and notice, but which is willing and eager at all times. The theological motivation for this is stressed: they are to work as for the Lord (Col. 3:23–24), as slaves of Christ (Eph. 6:6); and good work, it is promised, will ultimately be rewarded (Col. 3:24; Eph. 6:8). In Ephesians particularly the parallel between serving earthly masters and serving the Lord is closely drawn (Eph. 6:5–6). The interests of slave owners are clearly sustained by this particular formulation of the Christian symbolic order: the *Christian* duty of a slave is to be a good slave, to work wholeheartedly and to serve willingly, as if such service were done for Christ.

However, the ideology of these codes is balanced to a degree by their reciprocality. The *Haustafeln* do not only sustain the interests of the dominant social group. The subordination required is ameliorated by the demands placed upon those in authority: to be loving husbands, caring and non-provocative fathers, and just and fair masters. Masters are reminded that they too are under the heavenly Lord (Col. 4:1; Eph. 6:9). This is indeed '*love*-patriarchalism' and not merely 'patriarchalism' (MacDonald 1988: 102–122; Theissen 1982: 107). The power and position of the *paterfamilias* are sustained and legitimated; yet his use of this power and position is regulated and subject to obligations. Moreover, each group, including even the children, is addressed as comprising active, responsible subjects to whom moral appeal can be made (contrast 1 Clem. 21:6–8).

Commentators sometimes speak positively of the fact that the subordination demanded of the woman (using the middle imperative *hupotassesthe*; Col. 3:18; cf. Eph. 5:21–24) is a voluntary, self-willed act.[13] Yoder sees the voluntary subordination for which the *Haustafeln* call as 'revolutionary' (Yoder 1972: 163–192). Similarly, the new motivation given to the slave – serving Christ – is seen as a positive and noble elevation of the work of the slave, and as a relativizing of the position of the human master.[14]

However, a critical sociological approach will interpret such texts very differently. The appeal of the domestic codes for voluntary subordination must be interpreted critically. Relations of domination and exploitation are not always, or even generally, sustained by brute force alone; though brute force was not infrequently used in the Roman empire (e.g. Tacitus *Annals* 14.42–45). This is precisely the impact of ideology: it presents 'reality' in such a way as to convince the dominated, the subordinate, that it is right and proper, or inevitable, or in everyone's best interests, for them to remain willingly and voluntarily in their place and to fulfil their duties. The point, of course, is that 'everyone's best interests' may actually mean 'in the ruling class' interests'. Giddens' fundamental description of ideology, we recall, was in terms of 'the capability of dominant groups or classes to make their own sectional interests appear to others as universal ones' (Giddens 1979: 6). The particular impact of religious, or theological, ideology is to legitimate particular social relations by granting them divine sanction. Wives should submit to husbands as if to Christ; slaves should serve their masters as if serving Christ. It should be noted, however, that the *Haustafeln* of Colossians and Ephesians do not present the social order as itself of divine origin; the social positions of masters and slaves, for example, are not rooted in a theology of the created order. We do not find this form of theological ideology here (cf. Schweitzer 1982: 216–217).

With time, the symbolic order of Pauline Christianity is reproduced and transformed, like a language which is continually spoken and written. Colossians and Ephesians represent, like every such statement including those of Paul, an attempt to use power to make others 'see it this way too'. In the *Haustafeln* of Colossians and Ephesians, the hierarchical order of the Graeco-Roman household is sustained and legitimated in a thoroughly Christian way. The form of conduct expected is unexceptional in its social setting; what is distinctive is the Christian basis with which the instruction is motivated.[15] Some commentators see this as the key to the positive evaluation of these *Haustafeln* (e.g. Bruce 1984: 162); but from the particular perspective of an investigation into the development of theological ideology in Pauline Christianity our judgement must be somewhat different. It is precisely in these domestic codes that the Christian symbolic order is first used to legitimate the hierarchical relations of the household; to ensure that subordinate groups remain in that position, appropriately obedient to their master. This, they are told, is what serving Christ demands. Colossians and Ephesians provide an *ideology for the household*; though, it must be stressed, an ideology which is ameliorated through an explicit concern for love and justice.

The Pastoral Epistles[16]

Elements of domestic code teaching are taken up – reproduced and transformed – in the Pastoral Epistles, though in a less compact and formalized way. The most compact set of instructions is found in the most compact letter: Titus (Tit. 2:2–10). Here the appeal is not directly to the groups concerned, rather, the responsibility to 'teach what is consistent with sound doctrine' (2:1) is enjoined upon Titus, formally at least, the letter's addressee (1:4). The older women are responsible for ensuring that the younger women conform to the ideal of the submissive, domestic wife, who loves her husband and children (2:4–5). Notably here both love and submission are required from the wife without any explicit and reciprocal instructions for husbands (contrast Ephesians). The Christian legitimation for this is 'that the word of God may not be slandered' (2:5). Slaves too are urged to be submissive to their masters 'in everything', pleasing their owners by showing themselves to be good, honest and faithful (2:9–10). Again a Christian motivation is offered: their behaviour is 'to adorn the teaching of God our saviour' (2:10). No instruction is given to masters.

These reformulations of Christian teaching seem to be increasingly ideological, in that they declare that it is good Christian witness and practice for these subordinate groups to be dutifully subordinate, without enjoining any reciprocal responsibilities upon the socially dominant. It is, in effect, sectional social interests which are being sustained and legitimated. Both older and younger men are indeed urged to be decent and respectable, 'sound in faith, love and endurance' (2:2); but specific responsibilities of love and justice in connection with any subordinates in their charge are not mentioned.

Similar instructions are found in 1 Timothy, where again it is the addressee, 'Timothy', who is urged to 'teach and exhort these things' (6:2). Slaves are to be good slaves in order, as in Titus, 'that the name of God and the teaching may not be slandered' (6:1). There is apparently no consideration of the fact that harsh or unjust treatment on the part of a slave-owner might also bring slander upon the name of God or 'the teaching'. There clearly are Christian masters within the church, as the next verse shows, but the author's concern in this connection is to ensure that these people are served even better by their slaves. Christian teaching is clearly supporting and sustaining the interests of the socially dominant.

The theological resources deployed by Paul in 1 Corinthians 11 are used by the author of 1 Timothy to exclude women from roles of teaching and authority in the church (1 Tim. 2:9–15). As in 1 Cor. 11:8–9, the fundamental reason is that man (here 'Adam') was formed first, then woman (here 'Eve') (2:13). Furthermore, the author presents Eve and not Adam as the first transgressor, the one who was subject to deception (2:14). Woman can be saved, it seems, by fulfilling her rightful place in the created order and bearing children; a polemic perhaps against those who would follow Paul's recommendation to remain single (2:15).

The Pastorals do in a sense exhibit considerable concern over the behaviour of the socially dominant group – male heads of households – but the concern is with these people in their roles as *episkopoi* and *diakonoi* (and, in Titus, *presbyteroi*). Their social position seems to be assumed as the qualification for leadership ('husband of one wife, governing his household well'; 1 Tim. 3:4). There are hints, moreover, that their households may have included slaves: 1 Tim. 3:12 requires that deacons be 'husbands of one wife, governing their children *and their households* well'.

A significant transformation has taken place. In Colossians and Ephesians there emerged an ideology for the household, a formulation of Christian teaching which legitimates and sustains the established social hierarchy within the household. In the Pastoral Epistles this ideology has, in a sense, become an ideology for the church; with the social hierarchy of the household being transferred into the church as a whole, now seen as the *oikos theou* (1 Tim. 3:15; cf. Eph. 2:19). Alongside this change, it is clear that the male heads of household whose social position in the household was sustained in the *Haustafeln* of Colossians and Ephesians have become the leaders of the Christian community in the Pastorals. Not that this change is uncontroversially established. On the contrary, the author of the Pastoral Epistles is clearly engaged in strenuous polemic against those whose conduct and teaching is different.

MacDonald is surely correct to point out that: 'The Colossian and Ephesian *Haustafeln* represent a placing of power more firmly in the hands of the rulers of the households (husbands, fathers, masters), ensuring that leadership positions fall to members of this group' (1988: 121–122). The consequence of this, whether intended or unintended, becomes clear in the Pastoral Epistles, where we find that such people are indeed acquiring the positions of leadership – though not without continuing struggle and contention – and that the teaching of these epistles serves to reinforce their position of social and ecclesiastical dominance.

CONCLUSION

There is, of course, much more that could be said, and a great deal more material which could be supplied. I hope, however, that this essay has offered some hints of the ways in which structuration theory might inform a sociologically orientated study of Pauline Christianity. As *critical* social theory it requires us to examine the issues of ideology, power and interests: How is power used and in whose interests? When and how are the resources of Pauline Christianity used to sustain and legitimate (whether intentionally or not) established forms of social domination? A search for the origins of theological ideology in Pauline Christianity would certainly have to begin with Paul himself, where the seeds of later development are sown. But a structuration theory perspective encourages us to consider the ways in which the Pauline Christian communities are shaped by an on-going process of structuration: formulations of Christian teaching arise from, and in reaction to, particular contexts, and they have an impact, a range of consequences, both intended and unintended, within that context and beyond it. These consequences form part of the context within which further reformulations of the symbolic order take place. On our brief and exploratory trajectory we have seen how each expression of Christian teaching is both an expression of power and a bestower of power. Paul's own energies are at times devoted to protecting or defending his own position as apostle and leader, while the formalized *Haustafeln* of Colossians and Ephesians begin to focus power in the male heads of households resident in the Christian communities. In the Pastoral Epistles the power of leadership in the church has become more or less exclusively focused upon such people, and the teaching itself sustains and legitimates their social interests.

There have been many attempts to explain the emergence through the Pauline corpus of increasingly socially conservative teaching: the delay of the parousia, missionary apologetic, fear of persecution, reaction against emancipatory movements, community-protecting institutionalization. The theoretical framework adopted here might suggest a complementary (not alternative) hypothesis: that as power is increasingly concentrated in the hands of a certain social group – male heads of households – so at the same time Christian teaching increasingly serves the social interests of this group. The church becomes 'the household of God' – a household over which these men, as representatives of God, are, of course, *episkopoi*. Viewed from a structuration theory perspective, the theological ideology which develops within Pauline Christianity is both producer *and* product of this transformation.

NOTES

1 I am most grateful to Professor Stephan Joubert for his response to my original paper, and to the other conference participants who made comments and raised questions. The shortcomings of the essay which remain are, of course, my own responsibility.

2 The methodology is outlined in more detail in Horrell 1994, chs 1–2. The works in which structuration theory is developed most fully are Giddens 1979 and Giddens 1984. For a concise overview see Giddens 1982: 28–39.

3 Eagleton (1991: 5) states that: 'This is probably the single most widely accepted definition of ideology.'

4 For a wider assessment of the Corinthian correspondence (including 1 Clement), see Horrell 1994.

5 Cf. Hurd 1965: 65–74; but note now the caution of Mitchell 1989, who shows that *peri de* need not introduce topics from the Corinthians' letter, as Hurd argued.

6 See esp. vss. 2–4, 8, 10f., 12f., 14–16, 28, 32–34; Scroggs 1972: 294–295; Meeks 1974: 199.

7 On the verses as illustrations of Paul's main point, see Dawes 1990: 684–689.

8 1 Cor. 7:21b. This phrase is notoriously ambiguous in the Greek, but I believe the translation above represents the most plausible interpretation; see further Horrell 1994: 114–118; Bartchy 1973; Trummer 1975; Dawes 1990.

9 Cf. Ste Croix 1975: 19–20 and further 1981: 416–441.

10 Cf. Meeks 1974: 201–203; Murphy-O'Connor 1980: 491–500; MacDonald 1987: 102–111; Theissen 1987: 167–175.

11 E.g. Bedale 1954; Scroggs 1972: 298–299; Fee 1987: 502–504; for the opposing viewpoint see esp. Grudem 1985; 1990; Fitzmyer 1989; 1993.

12 E.g. Barth 1974: 700–708; Wright 1986: 147–148; O'Brien 1982: 223.

13 Barth 1974: 710–715; O'Brien 1982: 220–222.

14 O'Brien 1982: 228; Bruce 1984: 168–169, 400–401.

15 Cf. Wedderburn 1993: 56–57; Lincoln 1990: 365, 390–391.

16 Cf. further Horrell 1993: 93–102, with fuller documentation there.

Part V

OPPRESSION, WAR AND PEACE

14

GOD'S HONOUR AND ROME'S TRIUMPH

Responses to the fall of Jerusalem in 70 CE in three Jewish apocalypses

Philip F. Esler

ROME, WAR AND IDEOLOGY

Von Clausewitz, the great military tactician, considered that war was politics conducted by other means. Michel Foucault inverted this to assert that politics is war conducted by other means (Rabinow 1986: 64–65). This inversion was in accord with Foucault's abiding view that 'The history which bears and determines us has the form of war rather than that of a language: relations of power not relations of meaning.'[1] Foucault's perspective, that conflict lies at the heart of the matter, emerges in the following statement from his 1971 essay 'Nietzsche, Genealogy, History':

> Humanity does not gradually progress from combat to combat until it arrives at universal reciprocity, where the rule of law finally replaces warfare; humanity installs each of its violences in a system of rules and thus proceeds from domination to domination.
>
> (Rabinow 1986: 85)

In this essay I wish to deal with one particular domination – that of ancient Rome – and the responses to one particular Roman victory, that over the Jews in the revolt of 66–73 CE. War came naturally to the Romans. Throughout much of the republican period, Rome sent its legions out to war with neighbouring states nearly every spring. C. Nicolet has accurately remarked that there was almost a biological necessity to this annual event (cited in Harris 1979: 19). War was also a game the Romans played with more determination and ferocity than other peoples of their time, as their Greek contemporaries observed (Harris 1979: 51–53). There was something of a pathological dimension to the extreme violence practised by Rome upon its defeated enemies which seemed extreme even to the Greeks. Thus, Polybius, in the course of writing about the First Punic War, but speaking in the present tense, says that it is characteristic of the Romans to use violent force, *bia*, for all purposes (Harris 1979: 50–53). That Roman proclivities in this regard persisted into the imperial period can be seen by the enormity of the horrors wreaked on Jerusalem by the legions of Titus in 70 CE, as described by Josephus in Book 7 of his *Jewish War*.

Although there is a vast literature on ideology and a distressing failure to define what one means by the term, one perspective on ideology is to regard it as the pattern of meaning imposed by a dominant power (see David Horrell's essay in this volume for a similar perspective). Foucault argued persuasively that such domination frequently expressed itself in the discourse (understood very widely) employed by a ruling group. For Foucault there was an ineluctable connection between discourse and power.[2] He once said in an interview:

> What makes power hold good, what makes it accepted, is simply the fact that it does not only weigh on us as a force that says no, but that it traverses and produces things, it induces pleasure, forms knowledge, *produces discourse.*
>
> (cited in Rabinow: 61; my emphasis)

This type of ideology or power/discourse can be seen in the outlook of the Romans. Accompanying their vast imperial subjugation was an imperial ideology. It is expressed unashamedly by the Augustan poet Virgil in the *Aeneid* in a passage which describes one aspect of it as *parcere subiectis et debellare superbos* (6.853). I paraphrase: 'Grovel and live; resist and die.'

Yet there *was* resistance and one of the most dramatic instances of it came with the revolt of the Jews in Judaea in 66 CE which the Romans took some six years finally to put down. To set such resistance in a larger frame let me go back to Foucault. Immediately after the passage quoted above, to the effect that there is a set of rules into which humans install their various violences, he goes on to say:

> The nature of these rules allows violence to be inflicted on violence and the resurgence of new forces that are sufficiently strong to dominate those in power. Rules are empty in themselves, violent and unfinalized; they are impersonal and can be bent to any purpose. The successes of history belong to those who are capable of seizing these rules, to replace those who had used them, to disguise themselves so as to pervert them, invert their meaning, and redirect them against those who had initially imposed them; controlling this complex mechanism, they will make it function so as to overcome the rulers through their own rules.
>
> (Rabinow 1986: 85–86)

One pervasive type of subversion is through the development by the subjugated of a discourse to counter that of the subjugators.

THE POST-70 CE JEWISH APOCALYPSES

My interest in this essay lies in three Jewish apocalyptic works which respond to the Jewish disaster in 70 and were probably written about 30 years later:

4 Ezra, 2 Baruch and the Apocalypse of Abraham.[3] All of these texts are apocalypses; they relate direct visions of God at a time when the main Jewish mode of access to the divine will, the Temple, lay in ruins. They all point forward to a period when the Jewish people will be reconstituted, have their identity re-established, around the Law. Moreover, all of these works are pseudepigraphic, that is they all purport to have been written by some great figure from Israel's past and the first two have as their dramatic subject the sack of Jerusalem and Solomon's Temple by the Babylonians 650 years previously, in 587 BCE, and this topic also figures in the Apocalypse of Abraham (ch. 27). Under the guise of describing the horrors of the distant past, they summon before their audiences their own recent experience. Here we see a case where literary strategies may be said to lessen the visibility of conflict, yet this process may well have a profound political significance if its aim or result is to provide a form of disguise for subverting the rules of those holding the reins of power.

My thesis is that each of the three apocalypses under discussion seeks in its own way to seize the rules by which Israel had been dominated, by disguising and subverting them, with the most audacious enterprise of this type to be found in 2 Baruch.

THE FLAVIAN TRIUMPH AND ITS AFTERMATH

Defeat, dishonour and the Temple vessels

To explore this question we need to consider the circumstances of the Roman victory and its aftermath, in particular, as we will see, the lengths to which the Romans went to shame the defeated Jews. The historical context is significant. When the province of Judaea had risen against Roman rule in 66 CE, Nero had sent T. Flavius Vespasianus, an experienced general of Italian stock, to bring the Jewish revolt to an end. Vespasian arrived in Judaea with his son Titus in 67 CE and began his appointed task. Upon the death of Nero in 68 CE, however, the empire was riven with civil war as a succession of generals, Galba, Otho and Vitellius, claimed the Principate. In July 69 Vespasian threw his own hat into the ring and set out on what would be a six-month journey to Rome, leaving Titus in command of the Roman legions besieging Jerusalem. By December 69 CE Vespasian had reached Rome and been acknowledged emperor there. Almost immediately he had to face trouble on the Rhine and the Danube. In these difficult times, the capture of Jerusalem by Titus on 7–8 September 70 CE, the news of which must have been the happiest Vespasian ever received, went far both practically and symbolically to lay the foundation for the Flavian dynasty.

The sack of Jerusalem and the events which followed are described, in much of their horror, by Josephus in Book 7 of the *Jewish War*. We also get the flavour of the context from one of these three apocalyptic texts, 4 Ezra, as it recounts the events of 70 CE:

For you see that
our sanctuary has been laid waste,
our altar thrown down,
our temple destroyed;
our harp has been laid low,
our song has been silenced,
and our rejoicing has been ended;
the light of our lampstand has been put out,
the ark of our covenant has been plundered,
our holy things have been polluted,
and the name by which we are
called has been profaned;
our free men have suffered abuse,
our priests have been burned to death,
our Levites have gone into captivity;
our virgins have been defiled,
and our wives have been ravished;
our righteous men have been carried off,
our little ones have been cast out,
our young men have been enslaved,
and our strong men made powerless.
(10.21–22; Stone 1990: 316–317)

We know from Josephus that the Romans did obtain some of the most important vessels from the Temple, including the golden table of shew-bread, the golden seven-branched lampstand (*menorah*) and a copy of the Jewish Law (*J. W.* 7.148–150). In June 71 CE Titus returned to Rome and at the end of that month he and Vespasian celebrated a joint triumph, described in detail by Josephus. The Temple vessels were actually paraded through Rome in triumph. A triumphal arch erected in honour of Titus at the top of the Roman forum in 81 CE depicts the *menorah*, as well as the table (to judge from the somewhat eroded relief) and trumpets (which Josephus does not mention) being carried along in the triumphal procession by a crowd of soldiers.[4] It seems that statues were also used to commemorate the victory over the Jews, because from as far afield as Sabratha in North Africa a torso of a statue, probably of Vespasian, has been discovered which has a cuirass bearing a relief of Victory writing on a shield affixed to a palm tree, to the right of which stands a captive Jew and beneath which sprawls a Jewess depicting conquered Judaea (Hart 1952: 172 and plate). The imagery of the cuirass is similar to that on the coins discussed below.

I have developed elsewhere the proposal that a Roman triumph functioned socially as a tightly linked pair of rituals: a status elevation ritual for the successful Roman general and for Rome and its gods generally and a status degradation ritual for the vanquished, who were led along in the procession, and their gods.[5] The centrality of the honour/shame script and the importance of the pattern of social interaction known as challenge-and-response which anthropologists have identified as key aspects of Mediterranean culture,[6] induces us to investigate any military confrontation involving Rome and other powers as an opportunity for the leaders and the rank and file of each army to enhance their honour, and the honour of their gods and fellow citizens, at the expense of their enemies. In fact, we would expect this to be one of the most significant aspects of any campaign. A war represents the game of challenge and response played out on the largest scale. The historical sources confirm that these hunches turn out to be close to the mark.

A Roman general who sought a triumph had to have succeeded in a contest *par excellence*, by achieving a very significant military victory over a powerful enemy.[7] Underlying these requirements is clearly the fundamental feature of Mediterranean culture that the game of challenge-and-response be played out between social equals, otherwise no honour can be won from it. To earn a triumph, one had to have conquered a worthy enemy and in honourable circumstances, that is, where he put up a hard fight. Aulus Gellius tells us this explicitly when describing the victories of lesser significance which could merit an *ovatio*:

> The occasion for awarding an ovation, and not a triumph, is that wars have not been declared in due form (*rite indicta*) and so have not been waged with a legitimate enemy, or that the adversaries' character is low or unworthy (*hostium nomen humile et non idoneum est*), as in the case of slaves or pirates, or that because of a quick surrender, a victory was won which was 'dustless' (*inpulveres*) as the saying is, and bloodless.
>
> (*Attic Nights* 5.6.21, trans. Rolfe 1927: 395–397)

This aspect no doubt explains why Titus brought home from his successful Jewish campaign in 70 CE 700 prisoners remarkable for their stature and beauty to produce at his triumph (Josephus, *J. W.* 7.118), since to demonstrate natural attributes of the enemy enhances one's honour in having overcome him. The onerous conditions attaching to the grant of a triumph therefore meant that an *imperator* became entitled to a triumph only upon the successful conclusion of an *agon* which was more significant in its human impact and consequences than any other which could be imagined in this context. The model suggests that a victory on this scale would result in the victor becoming entitled to a grant of immense honour from the Roman state. This expectation raised by the model is satisfied by the ancient evidence.

A large number of ancient testimonia, in Livy in particular, suggest that the acquisition of honour constituted the primary reason for a successful Roman general to seek a triumph.[8] The two primary emic expressions for 'honour' in this context are *gloria* and *honos*. Thus on one occasion, in 480 BCE, a consul who had richly earned a triumph over the Etruscans turned it down for the reason that since his own brother and his fellow consul had died in the fighting, the current state of private and national mourning made a triumph inappropriate. Livy comments:

> No triumph ever celebrated was more famous than was his refusal to accept a triumph (*Omni acto triumpho depositus triumphus clarior fuit*), so true is it that a seasonable rejection of glory sometimes but increases it (*adeo spreta in tempore gloria interdum cumulatior rediit*).
>
> (Livy, *History of Rome* 2.47.11, trans. Foster 1939)

In 191 BCE another Roman consul, Publius Cornelius, during the course of argument in the senate as to whether the triumph which he sought for having conquered a Gallic tribe should be postponed until he had subdued their neighbours, concluded his address on the following note:

> So far as he was personally concerned, he had won sufficient glory (*gloria*) for his whole life on that day when the senate had judged him the best man (*vir optimus*) and sent him to receive the Idaean Mother. From that one inscription, even if no consulship or triumph were added, the *imago* of Publius Scipio Nasica (his ancestor) would have enough of honour and regard (*satis honesta honorataque*).
>
> (Livy, *History of Rome* 36.40.9, trans. Sage 1935)

When speaking of the decision of Aemilius Lepidus to attack the Vaccaei, a Spanish tribe, without proper authorization, Appian notes that some men took on military campaigns not to advantage the city but for other motives, including the honour of a triumph (*thriambou philotimia*) (*History of Rome* 6.13).

It is clear that the soldiers under the successful general, and even the Roman people in general, also shared in the honour, which is a point expressly made during a speech by a former consul in 167 BCE (Livy, 45.38.3–6). In relation to a victory of 461 BCE, Livy reports that:

> then the general and his army received their honour (*tum imperatori exercituique honos suus redditus*); Lucretius triumphed over the Volsci and the Aequi (*triumphavit de Volscis Aequisque*), and his own legions followed him as he triumphed (*triumphantem secutae suae legiones*).
>
> (Livy, *History of Rome* 3.9.4, my trans.)

In similar vein, we find references to the honour which accrues to the gods as a result of a triumph. Livy describes one general saying during a speech in 167 BCE that 'for it is to the gods too, not only to men, that a triumph is owed (*dis quoque enim, non solum hominibus, debetur triumphus*)' (45.39.10, my trans.).

The Mediterranean pattern of challenge-and-response mentioned above emphasizes that a grant of honour to the victor in a conflict is balanced by the shaming of the loser. There is abundant data from literary and even numismatic sources that the shameful public exposure of the people who had been vanquished played an essential part in every triumph. The three central elements in this aspect of the phenomenon were the visual representation of features of the campaign at an early stage in the event, the inclusion of captured representatives of the enemy, especially their leader, in the procession before the general and, very often, the torture and execution of the captured king or general when the *triumphator* reached the Capitol. That the whole point of these features was to heap shame upon the heads of the defeated enemy is starkly revealed in an incident in Plutarch's *Life of Aemilius Paulus*. Prior to the triumph of Aemilius to celebrate his victory over the Macedonians, Perseus, the Macedonian leader, sent a message to him begging to be left out of the procession. Aemilius rejected his request for the reason that it lay within his own power to choose death (presumably by suicide) in preference to disgrace (*aischyne*). Plutarch tells us that Perseus was not brave enough for this and that he formed part of the procession (*Aem. Paul.* 34).

A particularly valuable source in this connection is the description by Josephus of the joint triumph of Vespasian and Titus in June 71 CE to celebrate the capture of Jerusalem (*J. W.* 7.121–157). During the course of the triumph various scenes of Roman victories were depicted on movable stages, the vessels from the Temple were carried along with the booty and hundreds of Jewish prisoners were paraded before the *triumphatores*. The public display of the Temple vessels involved the dishonour of the god who had been unable to protect them. When the triumphal procession came to its climax at the Temple of Jupiter, where the *triumphator* would offer sacrifice, the leaders of the defeated enemy were often publicly humiliated, tortured and executed. This was the fate of the Jewish leader Simon bar Gioras in 71 (Josephus, *J. W.* 7.154).

There is a further aspect of the humiliation of the Jews in 70 CE which bears upon the question of the Temple vessels. The early Byzantine historian Malalas tells us that Vespasian erected the winged cherubim from the Temple over the main gates of Antioch in Syria, which were thereafter called the Gates of the Cherubim:

> Titus celebrated a triumph for his victory and went off to Rome. Out of the spoils from Judaea Vespasian built in Antioch the Great, outside the city gate, what are known as the Cherubim, for he fixed there the bronze Cherubim, which Titus his son had found fixed to the temple, of Solomon. When he destroyed the temple, he removed them from there and brought them to Antioch with the Seraphim, celebrating a triumph for the victory over the Jews that had taken place during his reign.
>
> (Malalas, 260–261)[9]

Moreover, whereas the Jews had previously paid a tax to the Temple in Jerusalem, Vespasian made this payable to the Temple of Jupiter Capitolinus in Rome, which was a very transparent statement of the superiority of the Roman high god over the Jewish one (Smallwood 1976: 344–345). He extended its incidence, moreover, by making it payable by Jews of both sexes, child or adult, whereas previously it had been paid only by adult Jewish males.

The Flavian *Iudaea capta* coins from the West

But it is in the *Iudaea capta* coinage minted by the Flavians that their efforts to exult over the humiliation of Judaea reach their peak. Vespasian had been acknowledged emperor almost exactly one hundred years after Octavian's defeat of Antony at Actium, and the capture of Jerusalem gave the Flavians a victory the significance of which paralleled that of Octavian, at least in the way in which it solidified and legitimated their rule. It is possible to observe a developing iconography in the coinage (although without proffering a strict chronological sequence), which functions to honour Rome and the Flavians and to shame Israel and the Israelite god. Although I will cover most of the main types,[10] there is considerable variation in the series.[11] We should see these coins as a primary means whereby the Flavians developed a discourse to communicate an imperial ideology in connection with their defeat of the Jews and the establishment of their line. Although, as Ian Carradice has pointed out, we must doubt the practical usefulness of coins for this purpose, seeing that the inhabitants of the empire would have been carrying around collections of coins of various ages and may not have noticed the latest legends appearing on the new ones, there can be no doubting the nature of the intention on the part of the Flavians or their administrators which led to their being minted (Carradice 1993: 173).

The first coin, a gold aureus minted at Lugdunum in 72 CE (Illustration 1), consists of a trophy in the middle of the reverse side (consisting of helmet with cheek-pieces, cuirass, spear and two oblong shields on arm left, spear and round shield on two oblong shields on arm right, greaves and round and oval shields on the ground) with the words DE IUDAEIS around the sides.

In the second coin, a gold aureus minted at Rome in 69 70 CE (Illustration 2), the trophy is on the left, while a Jewess draped and veiled appears with her back to the trophy, sitting slumped with head on hand and knees drawn up, in the middle of the coin. The word IUDAEA is engraved underneath her. In this image we begin to see a personification of the disgrace of Israel which will typify many coins in this series.

In the third coin, an as minted at Rome in 77 78 CE (Illustration 3), a large palm tree replaces the trophy in the centre left, while a Jewess sits slumped head on hand in the middle of the coin with her back to the tree. The words IUDEA (sic) CAPTA are featured around the sides and S C on the base. In a variation on this type (Illustration 4), bearing the inscription IUDAEA and minted at Rome in 69 70 CE, the hands of the Jewess are bound behind her back to the palm tree, deepening the degradation.

In the fifth coin depicted (Illustration 5), an undated denarius from Lugdunum, there is a large palm tree on the right, with a Jewess standing with hands bound in front of her, with the words IUDAEA DEVICTA.

The sixth coin (Illustration 6), a denarius of Vespasian minted in 78 CE, shows an image which was to undergo sustained development. It has a trophy in the middle, one captive sitting slumped on either side, and the letters TR P IX IMP on the left side. This motif was developed, as in the seventh coin, a sestertius from Rome in 71 CE (Illustration 7), by the substitution of the trophy for a large palm tree, a Jewess sitting slumped on the right facing right with head in hand, and a bound Jewish male captive standing on the left with feet apart and also facing right, with the words IUDAEA CAPTA around the side and S C on the base. Once again, a very strong sense of dishonour is conveyed by the imagery.

In a variation of this type the standing Jew was replaced by a standing emperor, as in Illustration 8, a drawing of a sestertius minted in Rome in 72 CE, which has a large palm tree in the centre, a Jewess sitting slumped on the right facing right with head in hand, while on the left stands a large Roman prince (Titus, since he appears on the obverse) in military dress, holding spear and with left foot on a helmet. The words IUDAEA CAPTA appear around the sides and S C on the base. This is a significant coin since it depicts the exaltation of Rome and the humiliation of Judaea in the one image.

The next coin, a sestertius from Rome in 72–73 CE (Illustration 9), has Titus standing on the right, with his foot on the prow of a boat, holding a spear (and possibly Victory), while there is a Jew kneeling at his feet and a Jew or Jewess running up to ask for mercy, with a palm tree in the background. The letters S C appear on the base. This coin well illustrates the Virgilian caption *parcere subiectis*, which I suggested above could be interpreted 'grovel and live'.

A number of coins deal with the joint triumph of 71 CE. Thus, in Illustration 10, a sestertius minted in Rome in 71 CE, Vespasian is portrayed in his triumphal *quadriga*, holding a branch in his right hand and an eagle-tipped sceptre in his left, while the front of the car is ornamented with Victory and a palm. The letters S C appear at the base.

An aureus minted at Lugdunum (of uncertain date) (Illustration 11) is a truly remarkable coin. It depicts Vespasian in triumphal *quadriga* (possibly with Victory behind him and crowning him), holding a branch and eagle-tipped sceptre, while in front of the four horses is a Jewish captive with bound hands escorted by a Roman soldier, as a man stands in the background blowing a trumpet, with the legend TRIUMP AUG. In the one image we see both aspects of the ritual of the triumph, the status elevation of the emperor and the status degradation of the vanquished. The captive may well be Simon.

Another gold aureus from Rome and dated 77–78 CE (Illustration 12) has Vespasian standing left and facing left, in military dress, resting on a spear in his right hand and holding a parazonium in his left, while behind him stands Victory holding a wreath in her right hand above his head and a palm in her left. In the next coin, a sestertius from Rome in 71 CE (Illustration 13) we have Winged Victory affixing a shield to a palm tree, with the words VICTORIA AUGUSTI, while on the shield are the letters OB CIVES SER (VANDOS).

The Flavian *Iudaea capta* coins minted in Palestine after the Roman victory

A significant aspect of Roman coinage policy in Palestine further brings out the extent to which the Flavians went to emphasize how much Israel and her god had been dishonoured by their defeat. Ian Carradice has demonstrated that whereas before the revolt of 66 CE Roman procurators in Judaea had minted coins which were sensitive to Jewish aniconic beliefs by not containing any images, of emperors or otherwise, typically in the form of the small Hasmonean-style bronzes, after 70 they dropped this type and minted coins which did contain imperial portraits, similar to that of Rome or of the Greek cities of the East (Carradice 1982–1983: 17). At the same time, moreover, a number of coins of the *Iudaea capta* series were minted in Palestine early in the Flavian period, although sometimes with Greek rather than Latin legends. Thus, we find a coin of Titus showing Winged Victory affixing a shield to a palm tree with the words IOUDAIAS EALOKUIAS (= 'Judaea captured') (Illustration 14).

RESPONSES TO THE CATASTROPHE OF 70 CE IN 4 EZRA AND THE APOCALYPSE OF ABRAHAM

My detailed views on the meaning and social function of 4 Ezra are set out elsewhere (Esler 1994a: 110–130 = 1994b). It is a work of towering moral integrity and imaginative power. Suffice it to say for present purposes that the text recognizes, as appears in the passage cited earlier, that in addition to the sheer physical realities of slaughter and enslavement, upon which falls the primary emphasis, the Temple vessels had been plundered and Israel and the name of God had been dishonoured.

The first part of the Apocalypse of Abraham is a narrative (chs 1–8) describing Abraham's conversion from idolatry, and the second (chs 9–32) is an apocalypse depicting his dealing with an angel and his ascent to heaven where he is granted a vision of the enthroned deity and revelations concerning the cosmos and the future. Ch. 27 describes the destruction of the Temple in terms which no doubt reflect the actions of the Roman legions in 70. The text relates that the heathens captured men, women and children, slaughtering some and keeping others, and that they destroyed the Temple with fire and plundered the beautiful and holy things which were in it. This could well reflect what happened in 70, including the fact that the Temple vessels fell in to the hands of Titus. No reference is made to the honour of God being besmirched by these events; instead, the author is interested in locating their cause in God's being provoked by Jewish idolatry, which reflects the work's major theme of right and wrong cultic activity.

Illustration 1 Aureus minted at Lugdunum in 72 CE (pl. 14.2 in Mattingly 1930)

Illustration 2 Aureus minted at Rome in 69–70 CE (pl. 1.11 in Mattingly 1930)

Illustration 3 As minted at Rome in 77–78 CE (pl. 30.4 in Mattingly 1930)

Illustration 4 Denarius minted at Rome in 69–70 CE (pl. 1.13 in Mattingly 1930)

Illustration 5 Denarius minted at Lugdunum (pl. 13.9 in Mattingly 1930)

Illustration 6 Denarius (hybrid type) (pl. 10.12 in Mattingly 1930)

Illustration 7 Sestertius minted at Rome in 71 CE
(pl. 20.5 in Mattingly 1930)

Illustration 8 Sestertius minted at Rome in 72 CE
(pl. 25.1 in Mattingly 1930)

Illustration 9 Sestertius minted at Rome in 72 73 CE
(pl. 26.2 in Mattingly 1930)

Illustration 10 Sestertius minted at Rome in 71 CE
(pl. 22.6 in Mattingly 1930)

Illustration 11 Aureus minted at Lugdunum
(pl. 13.16 in Mattingly 1930)

Illustration 12 Aureus minted at Rome in 77 78 CE
(pl. 6.7 in Mattingly 1930)

Illustration 13 Sestertius minted at Rome in 71 CE
(pl. 22.12 in Mattingly 1930)

Illustration 14 Bronze coin minted in Palestine in early Flavian era
(pl. XXXI.3 in Hill 1914)

THE RESPONSE IN 2 BARUCH

The name of Yahweh and of Israel

When one begins to read 2 Baruch one of its most puzzling features is that the sense of the tragedy in human terms of the events of 70, the violent brutality of it all, hardly figures. For the author of this text the problem of the sack of Jerusalem is the damage it has or may have done to the name of Israel and, more importantly, to the name of Israel's God. The foundation for an appreciation of the sensitivity to the name of Israel and of Israel's God in 2 Baruch rests upon the understanding developed recently by anthropologists such as Pitt-Rivers, Peristiany and Campbell of the centrality of honour as the pivotal value in Mediterranean culture. In being defeated by the Romans so totally in 70, the honour of Israel and of Yahweh had been dealt a swingeing blow.

2 Baruch opens with the word of the Lord coming to Baruch at a time which is meant to be just prior to the Babylonian conquest of Jerusalem, to warn him of this event (1–2; Klijn 1983: 621). Baruch's reply to God's address raises issues of critical importance for understanding the first twelve chapters and for the work as a whole. His initial response is not unexpected: he disclaims any desire to see the destruction of 'his mother' (Jerusalem) and expresses a wish to die first. Yet then he continues by asking:

> Now, what will happen after these things? For if you destroy your city and deliver up your country to those who hate us, how will the name of Israel be remembered again? Or how shall we speak again of your glorious deeds? Or to whom will that which is in your Law be explained? Or will the universe return to its nature and the world go back to its original silence?
>
> (3.5–7; Klijn 1983: 621)

What makes this passage so remarkable is that in speaking of the potentially painful consequences of the sack of Jerusalem Baruch does not mention the death and exile and suffering which this would cause but cites the damage which would be occasioned to the 'name' of Israel and to God by his loss of a people to speak of his 'glorious deeds' and to explain his law.

The same emphasis emerges in the dialogue which follows. God tells Baruch that, for a time, the city will be delivered and the people will be chastened and the world will not be forgotten. In addition, the heavenly Jerusalem, prepared from the moment he decided to create Paradise and which was seen by Adam, Abraham and Moses, is the one to be revealed, not this one. To this Baruch answers:

> So then I shall be guilty in Zion,
> that your haters will come to this place and pollute your sanctuary,
> and carry off your heritage into captivity,

> and rule over them whom you love.
> And then they will go away again to the land of their idols,
> and boast before them.
> And what have you done to your great name?
> (5.1; Klijn 1983: 622)

Although there is sorrow here for the fact that God's heritage will be carried off into captivity and ruled over by people who hate God, the text shows little of the interest in the details of human tragedy this involved and the climax of the passage falls on the final question. The real issue at stake is not human suffering but injury to the 'name' of God, which parallels the earlier reference to the 'name' of Israel. It is this last point which God takes up as he seeks to reassure Baruch:

> My name and my glory shall last unto eternity.
> My judgement, however, shall assert its rights in its own time.
> And you shall see with your eyes that the
> enemy shall not destroy Zion and burn Jerusalem,
> but that they shall serve the Judge for a time.
> (5.2–4; Klijn 1983: 622)

In this regard 2 Baruch stands in stark contrast to 4 Ezra, where, in addition to the theme of the loss of the 'glory' of Zion, the horrors of the events of 70 CE (under the guise of 587 BCE) are powerfully conveyed, as evident in the passage quoted above.

The entry of the Babylonians and the lost Temple vessels

The interest in the name of Yahweh is related to two other features of 2 Baruch. First there is the curious circumstance that God's angels actually break down the walls so as to facilitate the entry of the Babylonians. We are expressly told that this happens so that: 'the enemies do not boast and say, "We have overthrown the wall of Zion and we have burnt down the place of the mighty God" ' (7.1; Klijn 1983: 623). Second, we have the fact that the Temple vessels are not captured by the Babylonians, but are hidden in the earth:

> until the last times,
> so that you may restore them when you are ordered,
> so that the strangers may not get possession of them.
> For the time has arrived when Jerusalem will also be
> delivered up for a time,
> until the time when Jerusalem will be restored for ever.
> (6.8–9; Klijn 1983: 623)

The question which arises from this passage is why an assertion that the vessels from the first Temple did not fall into enemy hands should figure so prominently in a text written in response to the sack of the second Temple by the Romans. To return to the perspectives from Foucault with which we began this essay, how may such a feature be seen as a subversion of the rules of violence, or a counter-ideological strategy?

COUNTER-IDEOLOGY IN 2 BARUCH

The theme of the hidden Temple vessels makes admirable sense in this context. Faced with a situation in which not only had Israel and Israel's God been grievously shamed by the Romans, but the Temple vessels had been central in that process, the text takes the reader back to an earlier occasion when Jerusalem had been captured and yet Yahweh had preserved his honour both by letting the enemy in and preserving the Temple vessels for the future. Implied in this process is the notion that these older vessels are the ones that really matter.

The author was assisted in this development by the fact that the Old Testament picture of what happened to the original objects which Solomon deposited in his Temple is very clouded indeed. This uncertainty as to their fate, which still attracts popular speculation and Hollywood blockbusters such as *The Raiders of the Lost Ark*, had generated a variety of traditions by the time 2 Baruch was composed, and the particular theme of the vessels being hidden in the earth seems to derive from 2 Maccabees 2, which describes Jeremiah hiding them in a cave.[12]

Yet it was not only with respect to the past that the author sought to subvert the reality of Roman domination by a counter-ideological mythopoiesis. For the text also looks to the future and in one of its powerful visions of the coming end of this world it picks up the old theme of the four kingdoms, one succeeding the other, a schema originally developed by other peoples of the eastern Mediterranean in response to Greek oppression, and applies it to Rome. Having described how the Fourth Kingdom, 'whose power is harsher and more evil than those which were before it' will rise and fall with the coming of the Messiah, the text continues as follows:

> The last ruler who is left alive at that time will be bound, whereas the entire host will be destroyed. And they will carry him on Mount Zion, and my Anointed One will convict him of all his wicked deeds and will assemble and set before him all the works of his hosts. And after these things he will kill him and protect the rest of my people who will be found in the place that I have chosen.
>
> (40.1–3; Klijn 1983: 633)

This scene plainly constitutes a parody of the Roman triumph. What the Romans dealt out to the Jews will be paid back to them with interest. In Foucault's terms, we have here an inversion of the Roman processes of violence and their re-direction against those who had originally imposed them. The rulers will be overcome by their own rules. The Messiah will visit the Roman ideology of *debellare superbos* upon Rome itself. Rome's triumph will become God's. At the heart of the artistic achievement of 2 Baruch, therefore, lies an on-going conflict, a progression from combat to combat installed in a mythological framework spanning the remote past and the distant future.

NOTES

1 The statement comes from an interview with Alessandro Fontana and Pasquale Pasquino, cited in Rabinow 1986: 56; excerpted from Gordon 1981.

2 See the various essays on power and knowledge in Gordon 1981.

3 For my broad approach to apocalypses dealing with political oppression, see Esler 1993a and 1994a: 92–146. For a different approach to Jewish reactions to the destruction of the Temple in 70 CE, see Stone 1981.

4 For reproductions of the reliefs on the Arch of Titus, see Seltman 1939: 78. The relief on the other side is of Titus in his triumphal chariot.

5 Paper entitled ' "Io Triumphe": The Social Function of a Roman Ritual', delivered to the Classics Seminar in the University of St Andrews on 29 October 1993.

6 Some of the primary research may be found in Campbell 1964, Peristiany 1966, Pitt-Rivers 1977 and Peristiany and Pitt-Rivers 1992. Malina 1993a represents a brilliant formulation and application of this material to the New Testament.

7 Victories of less significance could be marked by an ovation given to the general on his return.

8 For a very detailed discussion of this subject by a Roman historian, see Harris 1979: 17–41.

9 Translation from Jeffreys *et al.* 1986: 138. I am indebted to Dr John Barclay of the University of Glasgow for drawing this passage from Malalas to my attention.

10 The illustrations of the coins have been drawn by Miss Tessa Rickards from the originals in the British Museum for the School of Divinity, University of St Andrews. Copyright is reserved by the University.

11 For another treatment of these coins, see Hart 1952.

12 It is impossible for me within the limited confines of this essay to explore the data bearing on the fate of the vessels from Solomon's Temple; but see Collins 1972 and Murphy 1987.

15

THE LANGUAGE OF WARFARE IN THE NEW TESTAMENT

Raymond Hobbs

INTRODUCTION

This essay is a continuation of my interests in warfare in the Bronze Age and Iron Age and the literature related to it (Hobbs 1989a; Hobbs and Jackson 1991). In this present form it is more an invitation to discourse than a finished product, and will form the basis of further research. In my book on warfare in ancient Israel (1989a) I wrote much in the concluding chapter about the 'transformation' of the language of warfare in the New Testament. I must confess now that the nature of that transformation was not quite as I had imagined it.

The design of this essay will be, first, to note some of the phenomena of the language of warfare in the New Testament and, second, to employ social science models appropriate to the traditional Mediterranean society which offer some explanation of the use of such language. Important in the study will be the work of Daniel Bar Tal on what he calls the 'Masada syndrome' (Bar Tal 1984).[1] One additional word of explanation is offered. Because of the size of the task, and because I believe it deserves a separate treatment, I will not comment on the war language in the Apocalypse.[2] My comments on that topic in the last chapter of my 1989 book are now, I believe, in need of drastic revision.

OBSERVATIONS ON THE LANGUAGE OF WARFARE IN THE NEW TESTAMENT

The language of warfare is by no means the dominant mode of discourse throughout the New Testament. In the Gospels, the domestic domain is more often the implied metaphor.[3] Belying its lack of prominence, military language seems to have tweaked the imagination of many Christian writers from the earliest days. In spite of the tendency to see the heart of the Gospel in terms of pacifism (Gliddon 1971), the reality of Christianity has portrayed the opposite. Throughout Christian history there seems to be a ready adoption of the language of warfare in both central and more eccentric forms of theology (Harnack 1981: 30–32; Holmes 1976; Kent 1986).[4]

First, some manageable breakdowns of the language in the New Testament. At the surface level the language is used in three simple descriptive ways. It describes activities in warfare, personnel and weaponry. Below is a synopsis of the lexical distribution in the New Testament pertaining to the language of warfare. It is a selection culled from Robert Morgenthaler's valuable tables in *Statistik des neutestamentliches Wortschatzes* (Morgenthaler 1958).

	Gospels	Acts	Paul	Pseudo-Paul	Other	Apoc.	(Total)
agon			3	2	1		6
polemos	6		1		1	9	17
polemein					1		1
strateuomai	1		1	2	2		6
stratiotes	12	13		1			26
sustratiotes			1	1			2
nike					1		1
nikao	2		3		6	17	28
agonizesthai	2		3	3			8
pale				1			1
hopla	1		5				6
panoplian	1			2			3
machaira	17	2	2	1	3	4	29
thoraka			1	2		2	5
belos			1				1
rhomphaia	1					6	7
Total	43	15	21	15	15	38	147

To be noted is that the language is fairly evenly distributed with some anomalies, such as the absence of many of the words from the book of Acts. I have omitted other disputed words and phrases, which I believe to be of a military nature. Important examples are the phrases 'be manly!' 'be strong!' (*andrizesthai*, *krataiousthe*, *endunamousthe*). The three exhortations of this type occur in passages in which the military metaphor is most prominent (1 Cor. 16:13; Eph. 6:10; 2 Tim. 2:1). In the light of this and its Old Testament (e.g. Josh. 1:7, 9, 18) and Qumran usage (1QM 15:6–8), this is not a mere word of encouragement to strengthen the 'inner spirit' as Barth argues (1974: 760) but an exhortation for 'valour', a quality of the soldier (Lincoln 1990: 441).[5]

I want to make three further refinements on the distribution and use of this language. First, the bulk of the language is *referential*. That is, it is simply descriptive of soldiering, soldiers, war and war-waging and the weapons used. For example, the word *polemos*, although quite common in the Gospels (6 out of 17) is used most often of war or conflict as signs of the end in Matthew 24 and Mark 13. The same can be said of the occurrences of the word *machaira* (19 out of 29 in Gospels and Acts) and the word *stratiotes* (25 out of 26 found in the Gospels and Acts). These referential occurrences are nuanced by different perspectives and are never objective descriptions. A rhetorical/actantial analysis might wish to note that in the Gospels, with few exceptions, soldiers appear as agents of alien power, such as Herod (Luke 23:11). It is soldiers who arrest and guard Jesus (Matt. 27:27; Luke 7:8). It is soldiers who mock Jesus (Luke 23:36). It is soldiers who are bribed to put the lie to the story of the resurrection (Matt. 28:12) and in the fourth Gospel they are almost always opponents and agents of death (John 19:2, 23 (bis), 32, 34). In the Acts of the Apostles soldiers appear as much more benign. They can be devout (Acts 10:7); they protect disciples from the mob (12:4, 6, 8; 23:31; 27:42; 28:16); and they are even cast in the role of rescuers (21:32, 35; 27:31, 32, 42).

Secondly, beyond this the language of warfare is used in an *illustrative* way. For example, and continuing with the word *polemos*, in Luke 14:31 it is deployed as an illustration of counting the costs of discipleship. In 1 Cor. 14:8 it is part of an exhortation for good Christian service and witness, and in Heb. 11.34 it appears in the Haggadah on former exemplary saints.

But there is a third and most important element of the use of such language in the New Testament, and that is the *metaphorical*. War language as metaphor is relatively uncommon when compared to other metaphors, but, as stated earlier, the language as metaphor has a particular appeal to certain forms of Christianity, and it emerges with often destructive effect from time to time. I would suggest that the reason for this is that the language of metaphor is the language of self-definition.[6] The language in this mode is used to striking effect in many of the letters of the New Testament. In 2 Cor. 10:1–5 Paul couches the Christian life clearly in terms of warfare:[7]

> I myself, Paul, appeal to you by the meekness and gentleness of Christ – I who am humble when face to face with you, but bold toward you when I am away! – I ask that when I am present I need not show boldness by daring to oppose those who think we are acting according to human standards. Indeed, we live as human beings, but we do not wage war according to human standards; for the weapons of our warfare are not merely human, but they have divine power to destroy strongholds. We destroy arguments and every proud obstacle raised up against the knowledge of God, and we take every thought captive to obey Christ.
>
> (2 Cor. 10:1–5)

Without implying anything about authorship I note that this has clear links with the understanding of Christian leadership expounded in 1 Tim. 1:18: 'I am giving you these instructions, Timothy, my child, in accordance with the prophecies made earlier about you, so that by following them you may fight the good fight' and 2 Tim. 2:3–4: 'Share in suffering like a good soldier of Christ Jesus. No one serving in the army gets entangled in everyday affairs; the soldier's aim is to please the enlisting officer'. Here, not only is the Christian life a life of warfare, but the dedication of the soldier is the pattern for the Christian (vs. 4). Further, in Phil. 2:25 and Phlm 2 Epaphroditus and Archippus are called 'fellow soldiers' (*sustratiotes*) of Paul: 'Still, I think it necessary to send to you Epaphroditus – my brother and co-worker and fellow soldier, your messenger and minister to my need' (Phil. 2:25); 'to Apphia our sister, to Archippus our fellow soldier, and to the church in your house . . .' (Phlm 2). As if to push this military metaphor home, suffering in the cause of Christ, according to the writer of 2 Timothy, now becomes the scars of warfare caused by wounds on the battlefield (2 Tim. 2:3).

The *locus classicus* of this metaphorical use of the language of warfare is Eph. 6:11–18:

> Put on the whole armour of God, so that you may be able to stand against the wiles of the devil. For our struggle is not against enemies of blood and flesh, but against the rulers, against the authorities, against the cosmic powers of this present darkness, against the spiritual forces of evil in the heavenly places. Therefore take up the whole armour of God, so that you may be able to withstand on that evil day, and having done everything, to stand to firm. Stand therefore,[8] and fasten the belt of truth around your waist, and put on the breastplate of righteousness. As shoes for your feet put on whatever will make you ready to proclaim the Gospel of peace. With all of these, take the shield of faith, with which you will be able to quench all the flaming arrows of the evil one. Take the helmet of salvation, and the sword of the Spirit, which is the word of God. Pray in the Spirit at all times in every prayer and supplication. To that end keep alert and always persevere in supplication for all the saints.

POSSIBLE 'BACKGROUNDS'

The war language in Ephesians just cited and elsewhere in the New Testament has been the subject of wide and thorough treatment by traditional commentators. Most, however, have concentrated on the 'background' of this language in typical fashion either by looking at the possible literary antecedents or by seeking a literary genre of the style.

Literary antecedents

Within the literature of Judaism there are several specific passages which figure in this search. They are:

> He put on righteousness like a breastplate, and a helmet of salvation on his head; he put on garments of vengeance for clothing, and wrapped himself in fury like a mantle.
>
> (Isa. 59:17)

> He extended the glory of his people. Like a giant he put on his breastplate; he bound on his armour of war and waged battles, protecting the camp with his sword.
>
> (1 Macc. 3:3)

> The Lord will take his zeal as his whole armour, and will arm all creation to repel his enemies; he will put on righteousness as a breastplate, and wear impartial justice as a helmet; he will take holiness as an invincible shield, and sharpen stern wrath for a sword, and creation will join with him to fight against his frenzied foes. Shafts of lightning will fly with true aim, and will leap from the clouds to the target, as from a well-drawn bow, and hailstones full of wrath will be hurled as from a catapult; the water of the sea will rage against them, and rivers will relentlessly overwhelm them; a mighty wind will rise against them, and like a tempest it will winnow them away. Lawlessness will lay waste the whole earth, and evildoing will overturn the thrones of rulers.
>
> (Wisd. 5:17–23)

To this list one can also add the War Scroll of the Dead Sea collection. The implication of this kind of search for literary antecedents is that the New Testament writers who came later were concerned only with literary allusions, in much the same way as a Western novelist or essayist. Such domestication of the language does not take into consideration the nature of ancient Mediterranean society as an honour–shame society, nor does it take into consideration the way metaphor functions within such a high-context society, which tends to produce texts that take for granted large amounts of information.[9] In passing, one can note that the sight of a soldier donning his armour in the sequence given in all of these passages would have been common in antiquity and beyond, and is found in works from the *Iliad*[10] to the films of Ingmar Bergman[11] and beyond. Interpretation needs to move beyond this simple recognition.

Formal antecedents

Commentators on Ephesians are indebted to an article by T. C. Burgess entitled 'Epideictic Literature' (Burgess 1902). Burgess draws together several literary examples of military rhetoric, or troop rallying speeches by commanders before engagement. They include Phormio in Thucydides, *Peloponnesian War* 2.89; Cyrus in Xenophon, *Cyrop.* 1.4; Hannibal and Scipio in Polybius, 3.63; Postumius in Dionysius of Halicarnassus, 18.15; Alexander in Arrian, 2.83; Caesar and Antony in Dio Cassius, 38.36–46; 50.16–30; and Severus in Herodian *History*, 3.6. To this one could also add the speech of Eleazar to the doomed occupants of Masada in Josephus, *Jewish War* 7.323–336, and the numerous speeches in the *Iliad* of frustrated generals to their war-weary troops. It is an extremely common stylistic strategy, and beyond the literature cited above one could also mention, among hundreds of others, Henry before Agincourt in Shakespeare's *Henry V*, Nelson before Trafalgar and Churchill before D-Day (Eisenhower 1948: 245).

Assessment

In commentaries on the other passages where war/military language appears, the metaphor is also underplayed. In 2 Corinthians 10 Paul clearly defends his apostleship using the language of the military leader, but even in the latest commentary on the passage, the language is treated simply as rhetoric without context or meaning. Martin states only that Paul's 'apostolic career is illustrated by the use of military language' (Martin 1986: 305). But the language of self-defence in 2 Corinthians 10 is littered with demands for obedience (vss. 5–6) and claims for authority (v. 8) in the context of warfare.

Similarly, Lohse, in treating Paul's reference to Archippus in Phlm 2 states: 'If Paul calls him a comrade-in-arms, he is using the term in a figurative sense to refer to the fact that he is a fellow-worker' (Lohse 1971: 190). Likewise O'Brien's more recent work on the same text suggests that the term 'fellow-soldier' is reserved for Paul and his co-workers, and is simply a way of referring to his faithful allies in his missionary work (O'Brien 1982: 273).

In Dylan Thomas' *A Child's Christmas in Wales*, the child of the piece received a Christmas gift, 'a book about the wasp that told me everything except why'. The difficulty with such 'background studies' as indicated above is that they tell everything and yet nothing. The bulk of the studies on, for example, Ephesians 6, concentrate upon the notion of the heavenly places, the 'spiritual' aspects of the passage and other such topics (Lincoln 1990: 429) as though they were immediately applicable to the life of the twentieth-century Western Christian. In passing, I suggest that they should be seen against the background of what John Pilch has already referred to as 'the pervasive Mediterranean belief in a densely populated spirit world and the regular and ready interference of those spirits in human life' (p. 55 above).[12] Since Harnack (Harnack 1981) the basic metaphor, that of warfare and its language, is taken for granted. In other words, it is never really explained. As mentioned earlier, the role of metaphor in high-context societies is important. Further, this specific metaphor, with its emphasis upon outward symbols of honour (armour), aggressive weapons, obedience to one's commander and suffering for a noble cause, has special significance in a society like the traditional Mediterranean which was populated by persons bound by concepts of honour and shame, and which was structured according to patterns of patronage.[13]

In effect, traditional commentaries which ignore the socio-cultural context of words imply that language means nothing, and that lexical choices betray nothing about the writer. Words exist without context, and combinations of words become mere poetic or rhetorical adornment. One needs to do two things to probe further into the significance of the use of this language. The first is to investigate the importance of the use of metaphor as a mode of speech, and the second is to look at a comparison with other metaphors.

METAPHOR

The subject of metaphor is one of considerable complexity.[14] I will present two quotations on the topic to make a simple point. The first is from Paul Brooks Duff's essay on the triumphal procession imagery used in 2 Corinthians by Paul: 'Metaphors are particularly appropriate tools because they function as a concealed invitation to look at things differently' (Duff 1992: 163). The second is a lengthier quotation from Karl Plank's study of irony in Paul:

> Through the use of symbolic speech a writer taps the potential of language to estrange ordinary images and notions from their expected contexts thereby jolting readers out of their familiar continuities. Arrested by the novelty of symbolic speech, its readers are diverted from their well-defended patterns of thinking and may find their perception of new insights now block any retreat into the familiar system of values.
>
> (Plank 1988: 77)

Leaving aside the obvious fuzziness of some of the terms used here (e.g. 'values'), and the attachment to the aesthetic approach, it is worth noting that both quotations push the notion of deliberateness and intentionality in the use of metaphor. Taking this we shall now move on to a different path, that of socio-cultural contextualization of the use of metaphor. In other words, pursue the questions as to why people use metaphors, and why this one.

Uses of metaphor

In this pursuit I shall take as a tool for the journey the article by B. Bernstein entitled 'Social Class, Language and Socialization' (1972). Bernstein's ideas were the acknowledged inspiration for Mary Douglas' work *Natural Symbols* (1970). Bernstein made clear his belief in the strong connection between language and social context, or, as he put it, 'The concept of socio-linguistic code points to the social structure of meaning *and* to their diverse but *related* contextual linguistic realizations' (1972: 158). He writes also of the hidden rules 'which regulate the options we take up in various contexts in which we find ourselves' (p. 161). In fact, 'the speech form is a quality of the social structure' (p. 161). Further, and highly significant, is his comment that 'Because the speech form is initially a function of a given social arrangement . . . *I am suggesting a relationship between forms of boundary maintenance at the cultural level and forms of speech*' (p. 162, my emphasis).

Bernstein then develops the contrast between elaborated codes, which are universalistic and allow the possibility of change, and restricted codes which are high-context and particularistic. In the language with which most of us are now familiar, elaborated codes are at home in Weak Group/High Grid contexts, and restricted codes in Strong Group/High Grid contexts. This is a characterization of traditional Mediterranean society (Malina 1986c: 68–97). Bernstein continues, 'I shall . . . suggest that restricted codes have their basis in condensed symbols . . . *That restricted codes draw upon metaphor whereas elaborated codes draw upon rationality*' (p. 164, my emphasis), and it is these variants which 'can be considered as the contextual constraints upon grammatical-lexical choices' (p. 165). He concludes: 'the deep structure of the communication is a restricted code having its basis in communalized roles, realizing context-bound meanings, i.e. particularistic meaning orders. Clearly the specific grammatical and lexical choices will vary from one context to another' (p. 171).

Bernstein serves as a serious challenge to the types of interpretation I have sketched above. First, his study cements the relationship between language and social and cultural context; and, second, it forces us to look more closely at the social context and its social systems. Lexical choice, like any other group decision, is not done in a vacuum beyond the realm of social and cultural values. Metaphors have to be taken seriously as indicators of the social values of the group. They are a means of self-definition, and one needs hardly mention that the social and cultural values one is dealing with when reading the New Testament are the social and cultural values of traditional Mediterranean society. This is a society alien to most Western interpreters of the Bible.

Comparison of metaphors

It helps to sharpen the edges of the military metaphor by comparing it with another dominant one in the New Testament. That is the metaphor of household. This metaphor has been finely expounded in Elliott's seminal work on 1 Peter, *A Home for the Homeless* (1981; 1990b). It has recently received treatment from a different perspective in Jacobs-Malina's book *Beyond Patriarchy* (1993; see also Dubisch 1986). Without going into too much detail, I offer a simple comparison of household and military in familiar terms, which is set out on p. 267.[15]

The scope of the military metaphor cannot be under-estimated. In comparison with the domestic metaphor, which is dominant in but not exclusive to the Gospels, the military metaphor presents a decisive shift in the self-understanding of at least a substantial part of the primitive Christian community. I believe that not only in the references to specific military items, like soldiers and weapons, but in the wider literary context the language of warfare dominates. I will point out a few examples, which I believe are worthy of much more detailed study.

There is an emphasis on the outer, visible aspects of a person's behaviour and demeanour. I assume here that the writers are speaking almost exclusively to males. This is most clear in the description of armour in Ephesians 6. Armour is not only a protective coat for the body, but a public display of rank and status. Within the moral world of the traditional Mediterranean proper public dress, as well as proper public behaviour, was appropriate to the honourable male (Bremmer

Household	*Military*
Private	Public
Inner	Outer
Outsiders as potential members	Outsiders (and deviants within) as enemies lacking faith and disobedient
Shame	Honour
Quality of inner life	Public display
	Uniform
	Wounds
Boundary consciousness	Boundary consciousness
In the Gospels, porous	Fixed
War as illustration	War as reality
War as others' activity	War as our activity
Female characteristics	Male characteristics
Submissiveness	Heroism
	Stoicism
	Comradeship
Suffering	Suffering
Natural	Badge of office

1991; Graf 1991). Correct armour betrays a sense of belonging and a sense of order. Herodotus (*Histories* 4.180) makes reference to the wild Anseans whose *women* do the fighting, but inappropriately in mixed armour (Greek helmets and Egyptian shields) and whose mating habits are wild and undisciplined. By way of contrast, the well-dressed and well-equipped soldier is a disciplined one.[16]

There is a strong emphasis on boundary control. This coincides with Bernstein's observation on the use of restricted symbols and metaphor (Bernstein 1972), and is offered in more detail in Douglas (Douglas 1970). Not only are lines of demarcation drawn between those on the inside and those on the outside – the enemy – but there is a clear attempt at controlling what is on the inside. Scattered throughout these passages are words and concepts like 'obedience', 'faithfulness', 'dedication' etc. Paul refers to the fight against 'arguments' (2 Cor. 10:5), presumably heresy, which is equated with 'every proud obstacle to the knowledge of God'. This suggests an attempt at internal control. The passage in Eph. 6:10–17 is preceded by two passages about the household (Eph. 6:1–4 and 5–9), but this is not the household of the Gospels. It is a rigidly controlled household in which levels of authority and obedience are clearly marked.

There is an emphasis on heroic suffering. This is clear in the passage to Timothy (2 Tim. 2:3). Here, as I indicated earlier, the wounds of the disciple are not the wounds of the slave who 'takes up his cross' to follow his servant-lord to death, but the wounds of the brave and faithful soldier. They are symbols of experience in battle and become badges of honour, badges to which perhaps Paul himself appealed as a sign of his authority in Gal. 6.17.

The discipline and bearing of the soldier reflected in these passages has its inspiration not in a Western, domesticated view of the role of soldiers in society – something like the National Guard, the Territorials or the Militia, whose members are civilians in different clothing – but in the ancient Mediterranean context. In this context one of the most rigid forms of client-patronage is to be found in the military culture. It is most clearly exemplified in the oath of loyalty (*sacramentum*) which every imperial soldier had to offer, and which formed a radical transition between civilian and military life. The *sacramentum* was a rite of passage. The kind of commitment demanded of the soldier and the Christian warrior is the same. An article in a recent issue of the art history journal *Representations*, which came to my attention after I had drawn this conclusion,[17] but which I have been unable to locate, makes the telling point that early Christians (i.e. second century and beyond) 'appropriated and trumped the Roman military *sacramentum* and that of the gladiator – the readiness to be burned, bound, beaten and slain in demonstrating *fides*' (Barton 1994).

Jacobs-Malina suggests that the call and response of the first disciples (Mark 1:1–20) is 'the behavior . . . of the bride who leaves her family', and further, 'The degree to which the ideal wife was expected to demonstrate commitment to her husband is the degree to which both male and female believers are expected to commit themselves to God, as witnessed in their words and actions' (Jacobs-Malina 1993: 12). If this is so, then the military metaphor, employed by Paul and other writers of the New Testament letters, is the male, public, honour-bound counterpart. If it can be argued, and I believe it can, that the ethos of this metaphor is the soldier's commitment by means of the *sacramentum*, then we have a decisive shift in the self-consciousness of the primitive Christian community.[18]

THE 'WHY' QUESTION

The underlying question in all of this is that of the contextualization of this metaphor, i.e. the mutual relationship between group values, concepts and indeed perceptions and the use of language. One implication of Bernstein's analysis of the use of language in its social context is that with metaphor-restricted codes we are dealing with group values and beliefs. The assumptions behind the language are widely shared. It is here that I return to the model I mentioned at the beginning, Daniel Bar Tal's 'Masada syndrome'.

The model he draws is one from the field of social psychology. The name of the syndrome is drawn from the familiar story by Josephus of the last days of the fortress at Masada. Bar Tal prefers the term 'syndrome' to 'complex' because the latter implies a pathological state, whereas the former a recognizable set of symptoms which can be flexible. The subtitle of his essay is 'A Case of Central Belief'. Conditions needed for the central nature are that a sufficient number of central figures support the belief. The belief is a psychologically subjective state, the content of which is described as follows: 'The Masada syndrome is a state in which members of a group hold a central belief that the rest of the world has highly negative behavioural intentions toward that group' (Bar Tal 1984: 34). The belief is usually accompanied by others, such as a sense of being alone in the world, that there is a threat to their existence and that they can expect no human help (Bar Tal 1984: 35). After providing some fascinating historical examples of this belief, all of which are drawn from Strong Group/High Grid societies like the Soviet Union at its paranoid height, white South Africa in the 1960s and early 1970s and Israel during the 1950s and 1960s, Bar Tal moves to a discussion of its possible origins. He is writing in broad theoretical terms.

One first cause of the belief is the past history of the group. The group's history may indeed be one of conflict and may give good ground for believing in a hostile world. But past history is the stuff of socialization, and the belief that causes the Masada syndrome may be perpetuated in this way. The view of the world is skewed so that evidence of validation of the belief is sought and found in the actions of others.

Another cause may be the perceived intentions of others. Threats, hostile declarations or attacks by others, for whatever reason, may be sufficient cause for the belief. Attention of outsiders on the group, whether benign or not, is often perceived as a threat.

A third cause may be group needs. Bar Tal states:

> the belief that other groups have negative intentions may not be based on past experience or a present perceived threat, but may originate within the group, independently of information coming from others. . . . In this case channels of information within the group may provide information indicating that other groups have negative intentions.
>
> (Bar Tal 1984: 43)

There is a strong element of control from within the group. The advantage of this for the group is that it can see the environment in relatively simple terms, as 'us' and 'them' with clearly defined boundaries. Another advantage is that it allows the group to prepare for the worst. And a third, and probably most interesting, is that the perception of outside hostile intentions allows the members of the group to act freely, or according to their own rules. There is an overt rejection of the standards of others.[19]

Parallel to these causes of the syndrome are the consequences, which Bar Tal lists as four. They are, first, the perpetuation of negative attitudes through socialization of the members; second, the development of a sensitivity to signs and cues from supposed enemies; and, third, there is internal pressure to conformity. Bar Tal states:

> At times when members of the group believe that the other groups have negative intentions toward them, they prepare themselves for the worst possible coming actions. At these times cohesiveness and uniformity are important conditions to withstand a possible threat.
>
> (Bar Tal 1984: 48)

Citing other commentators, Bar Tal posits that 'Groups engaged in struggle with the outside tend to be intolerant within. They are unlikely to tolerate more than a limited departure from the group unity' (Bar Tal 1984: 48).

The fourth element is self-defence in which speakers for the group will defend the group's actions. In the cause of self-defence the members are imposed upon to conform, to give up individual rights. In summary Bar Tal states:

> From the group perspective, Coser . . . describes the functionality of an intergroup conflict. He suggests two principal functions: (1) outside conflict heightens morale within the group, and (2) conflict with other groups 'leads to mobilization of the energies of the group members and hence to increased cohesion of the group'. . . . It is thus not surprising that various elements within the group may use the belief to increase unity, personal sacrifice, or cohesiveness, or to facilitate achievement of desired objectives.
>
> (Bar Tal 1984: 45)

CONCLUSIONS

This model/template has a particularly appropriate fit in the agonistic world of the traditional Mediterranean which is assumed by the writers and readers/listeners of the New Testament.[20] 'Honour' states Campbell (1964: 193), 'represents the moral solidarity of the group, an ideal circle that must be defended from outsiders'. This, of course is a male duty within this society. Such protection is found in everyday life in the creation and maintenance of protective factions and cliques, or by cultivation of patronage.

But now in the use of this metaphor of warfare and military service the nature of the moral community is reshaped. Campbell's observation on the perception of the Sarakatsani shepherds that 'ill-faith, doubt and suspicion characterize the relations of men who are not kinsmen' (1964: 104) is now taken a step further by what amounts to a formalization of the attitudes pertaining to this male role. This formalization consists of enforced behaviour within, proper protection from dangers from without and an aggressive stance to the enemy, however perceived. The use of the military metaphor is not accidental and it enables this to happen with relative ease. Its use reflects a community which sees itself as a community under threat from human and superhuman powers.

I have offered here only a sketch of the issues of this essay, something like a constellation of data on the topic. I have tried to see patterns which I believe can be supported by the use of the models I have employed. I would also suggest that the socio-cultural context of the use of the language of warfare opens up ways of understanding the literature which have been either ignored or only partially explored.

It would be tempting to try to draw historical conclusions from this data. I would suggest that the shift in metaphors corresponds to the shift between Gospels and Letters. The nature of the relationships between these bodies of literature is difficult to say with certainty, and I am no expert in the *Literaturgeschichte* of the New Testament. If one takes the material in the Gospels as primary, then the use of the military metaphor in the Letters represents a development beyond that of the new household expounded in the Gospels (Jacobs-Malina 1993). This is the opinion of Harnack (Harnack 1981: 27), who adopted a rigid developmental view of religion. If, on the other hand, one adopts a strict chronology and views the Letters as prior to the Gospels, then the Gospels represent a corrective to the metaphor in the Letters.

Perhaps the truth lies somewhere in between and one does not have to draw strict diachronic lines of development. Rather, one can see these metaphors as, if not competing, then certainly alternative understandings of the life of the Christian. Harnack suggested that there were elements of the ethos of warfare and the military that no self-respecting religion ('higher religion') could afford to ignore. These are 'inalienable virtues which find their highest expression at least symbolically in the warrior's calling: obedience and courage, loyalty unto death, self-abnegation and *virtus*' (Harnack 1981: 27–28). Whether the adoption of these characteristics is deliberate or accidental, we do note that they soon become part and parcel of the advice to the Christian in Clement's *Miscellanies* (Books II and IV), and become a fundamental metaphor in the letter of 1 Clement. They are also, however, standards of behaviour embedded in traditional Mediterranean culture (Brandes 1980; Gilmore and Gilmore 1979; Gilmore and Uhl 1987; Gilmore 1991). They are the patterns expected of the honour-conscious male in this society, and, as such, an exclusive set of patterns.

In J. Glenn Gray's superb book *The Warriors: Reflections of Men in Battle* he wrote of *homo furens*, the fighter:

> Man as warrior is only partly a man, yet, fatefully enough this aspect of him is capable of transforming the whole. When given free play, it is able to subordinate other aspects of the personality, repress civilian habits of mind, and make the soldier as fighter a different kind of creature from the former worker, farmer or clerk.
>
> (Gray 1959: 27–28)

This is certainly acceptable, and indeed encouraged in the military ethos. In the light of the use of the language of warfare in the New Testament, I have doubts that it is one of the costs of discipleship one should be prepared to bear today.

NOTES

1 For a study of the nature and ideology of imperial Roman warfare as experienced by the Jews in 70 CE see Philip Esler's essay 'God's Honour and Rome's Triumph: Responses to the fall of Jerusalem in 70 CE in three Jewish apocalypses' in the present volume.

2 Although there is an excellent survey on the topic by Bauckham (1993), I do not think I would tackle the topic from the point of *Traditionsgeschichte* as he does. As in this essay, I believe the subject needs to be dealt with from the perspective of war as a social institution in the first- and second-century Mediterranean world.

3 See Jacobs-Malina 1993 and the recent discussion in the *BTB* by Batten 1994, Love 1994, LaHurd 1994, Neyrey 1994 and the essay by Joubert in the present volume.

4 See also the relative extremes of a Mennonite, pacifist interpretation such as Barrett 1987 and the philosophical approach of Simmons 1986. The former 'spiritualizes' the historical horrors of war in the Bible, whereas the latter makes a spiritual virtue out of winning wars, ancient or modern.

5 Note also the comments on the extended military vocabulary in the letters of the New Testament in Harnack (1981); the military character of the phrases is well captured in the *Iliad* in Agamemnon's speech to the Danaans, 'My friends, *be men*, have a stout heart, and in the field fear nothing but dishonour in each other's eyes' (5.529–530; trans. Rieu 1950: 106).

6 With what follows compare the discussion on metaphor in the Bible in Pfisterer Darr (1994). Much of what Pfisterer Darr states is important. If there is one criticism to be levelled it is that the cultural element of the use of metaphor is absent from the discussion. It is no accident that when this cultural variable is missing theories of 'substitution', that is, that metaphors are mere embellishments for other accessible words, can take root. In what follows close attention is paid to the cultural context of the use of metaphor.

7 All biblical quotations that follow are from the New Revised Standard Version.

8 The need to 'stand fast' was paramount in armies of antiquity. When a line of infantry broke and fled, panic ensued and the killing times began. A fleeing army, unable to defend itself and lacking in cohesion, was easy prey for the pursuers. Estimates of casualties among the defeated force were as high as 80 per cent. See V. D. Hanson (1989: 135–209); R. Gabriel and K. Metz (1991: 81–110). The poet of Ps. 18 knows this experience of killing a fleeing enemy (see vss. 7–15).

9 For a discussion of high and low context societies, see Malina 1991a: 19–20.

10 In the *Iliad* Athene (5.733–747; Rieu 1950: 112), Agamemnon (11.15–46; Rieu 1950: 197–198), Patroclus (16.130–144; Rieu 1950: 295–296) and Achilles (19.364–390; Rieu 1950: 363–364) all are portrayed as donning their armour with deliberation before conflict.

11 The stunning scene in which the vengeful father dresses in his armour before searching out his daughter's killers is the highlight of Bergman's *Virgin Spring*. The device has been copied, with lessening effect, in many inferior films.

12 I would suggest that 'natural' and 'supernatural' in modern jargon are a post-Enlightenment construct and have little to do with what Paul refers to as the 'fleshly' (*sarkikos*) and the 'spiritual' (*psychikos*). Both Testaments of the Christian Bible and much other narrative literature of the ancient Mediterranean world (e.g. the *Iliad*) take for granted the interaction between humans and the gods at a level of reality lost to Western thinkers. For a deeper analysis see Pilch 1993a and his essay in the present volume.

13 See the articles by Plevnik and Malina in Pilch and Malina 1993: 95–103; 133–136.

14 For a good discussion of the use of metaphor in religious language see Soskice 1985. The use of metaphor in connection with apocalyptic literature is raised by Esler 1994a: 107.

15 This sketch of the domestic metaphor as used in the Gospels owes much to the exposition in Jacobs-Malina 1993.

16 It is worth noting the advice on lack of care for clothing found in the Sermon on the Mount (Matt. 6:25–34), and the story of David's early disdain for the royal armour of Saul (1 Sam. 17:38–40).

17 I am grateful to D. Tomkins for providing me with an abstract.

18 The soldier's oath of office was a common feature of the Roman army from the republic through to the empire. It ostensibly bound the soldier to his general–patron for life. Without taking the oath the soldier could not fight. It marked a transition between civilian and military life. The history of the oath was chequered. Tiberius imposed the oath on all of Rome in his paranoia. Under Claudius the legions that remained faithful to him during a revolt were given the honour *Pia fidelis*. Domitian linked the renewal of the oath to a rise in pay, a pragmatic move that was repeated by Caracalla. During a potential revolt by his soldiers in Britain Caracalla appealed to the soldiers' sense of honour, backed by a sizeable monetary compensation. Thus he played their patron, as his speech betrays. On the surface the speech has a remarkably Pauline ring to it, but it is an expression of the classic male, public, honour-bound view the soldier had of himself. 'On entering the camp he exclaimed, "Rejoice fellow soldiers (note Paul's use of the same expression), for now I am in a position to do you a favour!" . . . "I am one of you," he said, "and it is because of you alone that I care to live, in order that I may confer on you many favours; for all the treasures are yours." And he further said, "I pray to live with, if possible, but if not, at any rate to die with you. For I do not fear death in any form, and it is my desire to end my days in warfare, there should a man die, and nowhere else!" ' (Dio LXXVII 3.1ff., Loeb edition pp. 282ff.).

19 These sketches of a group developing the 'Masada syndrome' should be compared with the essay 'The Jewish Messianic Movement: From faction to sect' by J. H. Elliott in the current volume.

20 On the notion of the 'agonistic' world of the Mediterranean see Banfield 1958.

16

SOCIAL-SCIENTIFIC CRITICISM AND LITERARY STUDIES

Prospects for cooperation in biblical interpretation

Vernon K. Robbins

During the last two decades both literary and social-scientific approaches to biblical texts have developed at an increasing pace, significantly changing the appearance and the substance of biblical interpretation. For some interpreters, these two approaches represent opposite interests: any marriage of the two produces either bastard or stillborn children. For other interpreters, some kind of merger is desirable or even essential.

DISCIPLINARY, INTERDISCIPLINARY AND ECLECTIC METHODS OF INTERPRETATION

The dominant mode of twentieth-century biblical criticism prior to the 1970s was disciplinary, and this was the mode in which literary and social-scientific approaches began their work. Disciplines of study emerged vigorously during the nineteenth century and began to represent the 'true nature of things' during the twentieth century. A discipline emerges when a group of people acquires authoritative status to guide research, analysis and interpretation. The major means for establishing a discipline is to identify certain phenomena for investigation and certain strategies for investigating the phenomena. Anyone who investigates the same data with different strategies is 'out of the bounds' of the discipline, as well as anyone who investigates different data with the same or similar strategies.

A disciplinary approach, therefore, is a power structure, and its inherent nature is hierarchical. An overarching model or method provides a framework for negotiating the use of subdisciplines and practices. During the first seventy years of the twentieth century, the disciplines of history and theology sparred with one another for ascendancy in biblical interpretation. Sparring between disciplines, of course, establishes an essentially hidden polarity that excludes a wide range of approaches from the realm of 'serious exegesis' of the Bible. Prior to 1970, data in the Bible was either 'historical' or 'theological', it could represent either historical theology or theological history but not something else.

The battles, victories and defeats – drawn in historical versus theological lines – kept other disciplines from entering the battlefield, or playing field if you prefer, with any kind of status. Theologians decided what kind of philosophy they would use as a subdiscipline, if they used any; historians decided on the terms on which they would incorporate insights from anthropology, sociology or literary analysis into their practices and results, if they incorporated any.

The boundaries of a discipline not only create a power structure; they evoke a purity system for interpreters whereby any 'mixing' of approaches, practices or methods creates 'impurities'. The primary way to keep impurities out is to establish an overarching method or model for filtering the impurities when practices or methods are incorporated from other disciplines. In other words, a disciplinary approach only uses the methods of another discipline on the terms of the 'home' discipline that uses another discipline. The home discipline 'incorporates' methods from other disciplines in a subordinate position – as subdisciplines. I vividly recall a discussion with Martin Hengel at Emory University where he agreed that literary analysis could be informative if it were 'kept in control' by theology and history working together as co-partners.

For the most part, a disciplinary mood guided the emergence both of literary and social-scientific approaches during the last two decades. For most literary critics, the discipline of literary criticism – with its primary location either in New Criticism, Russian Formalism or some combination of the two – stood in a polar relation to historical criticism. Literary critics, they said, were interested in issues 'intrinsic to texts'; historical critics in issues 'extrinsic to texts'. Social-scientific critics, on the other hand, appear to be somewhat more divided on their relation to historical criticism. Bruce Malina appears to perceive social-scientific criticism as a discipline on its own terms. For him, social science rather than the discipline of history or literary study offers an overarching model for negotiating a comprehensive range of methods, strategies and subdisciplines (Malina 1993a). John H. Elliott, on the other hand, has persistently described social-scientific criticism as a subdiscipline of historical criticism. For him, it appears that social-scientific criticism is the subdiscipline that brings historical criticism to its fullest expression. For this reason, Elliott first called his method 'sociological exegesis' (Elliott 1981; 1990b) and incorporated the full range of practices of historical criticism in his work. Through the influence of Malina, he has changed the name of his activity to 'social-scientific criticism' (Elliott 1986c, 1990b, 1993a), but he still emphasizes that his method is an expansion – a completion, if you will – of historical criticism.

Whether social-scientific critics have considered their activity to be disciplinary on its own terms or part of the discipline of history, until recently most have emphasized the distinct difference between their discipline and the kind of approach that distinguishes between authors, implied authors, narrators, narratees, implied readers and real readers – i.e. literary criticism. Most social-scientific critics have simply considered time and serious intellectual activity to be too precious to lose oneself in such esoteric activity. Bruce Malina has created a reading theory based on 'scenarios', in part, it would seem, to show either the insignificance or the misguided nature of 'literary' views of reading. For Malina, readers read on the basis of social and cultural scenarios they are able to construct in their minds (Malina 1991e: 3–23). Only when readers learn how to construct strange and foreign scenarios in their minds are they able to start to read New Testament texts from the perspective of the first-century Mediterranean contexts in which they were written. In Malina's words:

> adequate scenario building involves the same steps as getting to understand a group of foreigners with whom we are inevitably and necessarily thrown together, for better or worse. On the one hand, we can choose to ignore the foreigners. . . . In that way we can never find out what those authors said and meant to say. On the other hand . . . we can come to understand our strange and alien biblical ancestors in faith . . . it is the reading process that both enables and facilitates this task.
>
> (Malina 1991e: 23)

Here Malina has articulated a widespread presupposition among social-scientific interpreters: readers understand texts on the basis of social and cultural scenarios they are able to construct in their minds. Most readers, historians included, construct these scenarios on the basis of their own modern social and cultural experiences. Only substantive reconstruction of our social and cultural imaginations, using extensive resources from the disciplines of sociology and anthropology and from multiple foreign societies and cultures, can equip us with insights for reading texts from the perspective of their own social and cultural contexts.

When interpreters function in a highly charged disciplinary mode, they encounter others with statements like the following: 'In order for you to make any kind of significant interpretation of this text you need to take into consideration this phenomenon in the text which we have investigated and interpreted in such and such a manner.' A significant number of both social-scientific and literary critics have responded either to or about one another in this mode during the last two decades, and one of the major reasons is a 'disciplinary' perception of the task of biblical studies, which is the major model of 'serious academic studies' that has been communicated to students and colleagues alike in biblical studies during the twentieth century.

Those who consider disciplinary analysis and interpretation to be the only 'truly responsible' form of biblical study regularly consider the alternative to be 'eclecticism'. Eclecticism is a matter of selecting something here and something there to do the job, because this phenomenon is significantly different from that one. The joy of interpreting a wide range of phenomena overrides the exhilaration of interpreting a more limited range of phenomena systematically, precisely and clearly – in other words, definitively. Some people are born eclectics, it would appear; they simply cannot be bothered with all the concerns of precision and control. They will not 'sell their lives' to disciplinary investigation. In response to criticism that their approach is not truly 'scholarly' or 'academic', their response is that at least it is interesting, creative and liberating.

There is, however, another significant alternative: interdisciplinary analysis and interpretation. An interdisciplinary approach invites data into investigation in the context of boundaries that various disciplines have established. The mood is to ask: 'What phenomena does this particular discipline investigate, how does it investigate it and what conclusions does it draw from the investigation?' Then, however, the interdisciplinary critic redraws the boundaries and asks the same questions of another discipline. The interpreter then develops strategies to place these multiple activities, insights and conclusions in dialogue with one another. The underlying presupposition is that conceptual frameworks are essential for significant analysis and interpretation, yet phenomena are constituted by a complexity that transcends any conceptual frame humans create. In other words, disciplinary approaches create a context for systematic investigation that yields significantly greater results than 'unbounded investigation', yet every disciplinary approach yields a highly insufficient explanation and interpretation of the complex phenomena of the world.

A MODEL FOR INTERDISCIPLINARY INVESTIGATION

You will have perceived that my own mode of choice is an interdisciplinary model, and the diagram on p. 278 (Figure 6) displays a model for interdisciplinary investigation and interpretation that places literary and social-scientific disciplines in dialogue with one another. It is necessary, of course, to have a mode of analysis that guides the interdisciplinary arbitration, and for me it is rhetoric (Bizzell and Herzberg 1990; Robbins 1992, 1994). Rhetoric provides a socially and culturally oriented approach to texts, forming a bridge between the disciplines of social-scientific and literary criticism.

According to this socio-rhetorical model, New Testament interpreters function in the context of their own social, cultural, historical and ideological worlds. Their instinctive social and cultural presuppositions come from their own world rather than the world of the texts they interpret. For the purpose of interpreting texts written in the context of the first-century Mediterranean world, however, they construct a tentative image of the Mediterranean world from a wide range of data. They embed this image of the Mediterranean world into their own world, and they embed New Testament texts in their image of the Mediterranean world. For this reason, there is a rectangle that separates the world of the interpreter from the ancient Mediterranean world, and there is another rectangle that separates the ancient Mediterranean world from a text produced in that world. The activity of interpretation, then, is an on-going project of reinterpreting the Mediterranean world and our modern world on the basis of interpretation of New Testament and other texts. Interpreters who do not consciously construct an image of the Mediterranean world in which to embed New

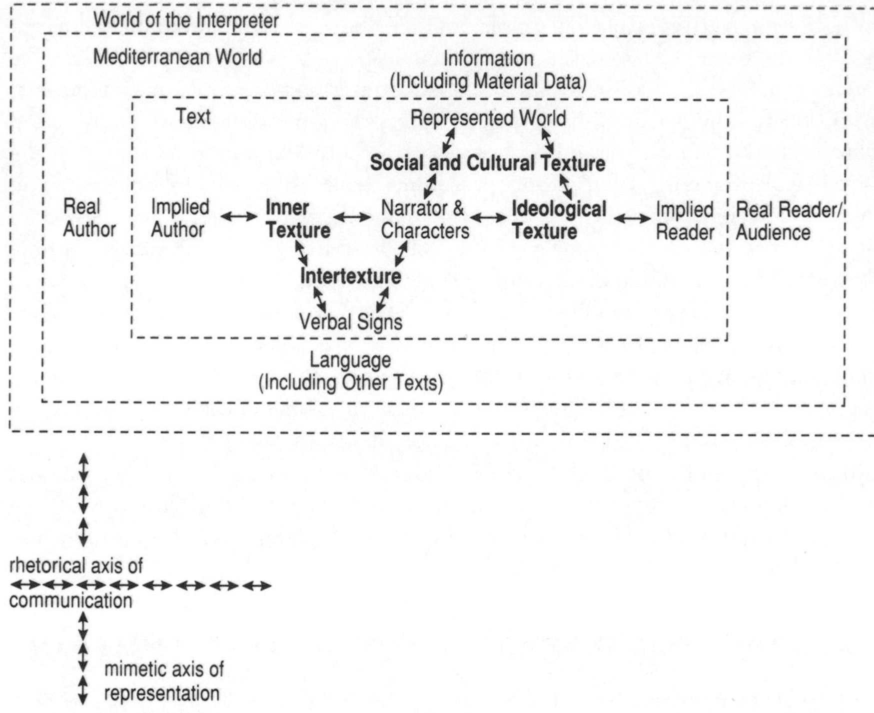

Figure 6 Socio-rhetorical model of textual communication

Testament texts are considered by socio-rhetorical critics, through their indebtedness to social-scientific critics, to be in danger of unexamined ethnocentrism and anachronism. Ethnocentrism arises from an absence of attentiveness to the 'foreign, strange' society and culture in which people produced New Testament texts, and the anachronism arises from an absence of attentiveness to the 'pre-industrial' social and cultural environment in which people lived during the first century CE.

Ethnocentric and anachronistic interpretations misconstrue basic social and cultural meanings and meaning effects of words, phrases, thoughts and actions evoked by texts. In addition, socio-rhetorical readers know that the real author and real reader/audience stood outside texts in the Mediterranean world. The real author, language, information in the world and the real reader/audience stand outside the text, which is represented by the innermost rectangle in the socio-rhetorical model above. Real authors are historical persons. The texts they make somehow are extensions of themselves, but the real author and the text are separate social, cultural and historical phenomena. Thus, the real author is not inside the box, but outside it. Likewise, language is a phenomenon outside of texts which authors use to write texts. Again, a text is a particular manifestation of language, but language itself is a phenomenon outside any particular text. In a related manner, information is also outside the text; some kind of manifestation of this outside information stands inside a text, but not the information itself. Also, readers and audiences to whom the text is read stand outside the text.

The boundary around the text is a broken line, because it is a human-made boundary for the purpose of focusing analysis on a text. Likewise, the boundary around the Mediterranean world is a broken line. All kinds of meanings and meaning effects travel through the gaps in these boundaries. They travelled through the boundary between the Mediterranean world and the text when the author wrote the text, and they travel through the boundaries when any person reads the text. Language and other texts travel through the boundaries just as information and material data travel through the boundaries. Interpreters at least temporarily build boundaries to keep various things out of texts, but since texts are located in the world, were created in it and are related to it, there is no way finally to keep either the Mediterranean world or the world of the interpreter out of them. Texts are in the world and of it.

Literary interpreters have concluded that the inner texture of a narrative text contains a narrator who tells the story and characters who think, act and have their being in the story. The narrator and characters, however, exist in a context of 'images' of the real author, language, information and the real reader/ audience. In other words, the inside of a text is a combination of 'show' and 'tell'. The narrator tells the story. The narratee hears the narrator and sees the characters, who may themselves speak and 'look'. Readers cannot see the real authors of texts, because the real authors are hidden behind their work. But readers see an image of authors in what authors have done. The image 'implies' an author of a certain kind, so literary interpreters regularly call the image of an author in a text the 'implied author'. The implied author is the image created by everything the reader sees in the text (Robbins 1991). Also, readers do not hear language in the text; rather, they 'see' verbal signs, printed letters, to which they give 'voice'. That is, readers turn the signs into sounds that are 'language' among people. Thus, the verbal signs in a text are 'implied language'. In addition, readers cannot hear and see real information and material data in a text but they hear and see 'implied' information and material data. Finally, readers of texts create an image of a reader who can read a particular text with understanding. If they themselves cannot understand the text, they create an image of a reader whom the implied author imagined could read and understand the text. Whether or not all of this is clear to the real reader who is now reading this, literary interpreters have drawn these conclusions about the inner texture of texts. These conclusions guide socio-rhetorical criticism as it approaches the inner texture of a text, and the goal is to create activities for an interpreter that will make it possible to investigate these and other inner phenomena in texts.

At the bottom of the diagram are horizontal and vertical arrows. The horizontal arrows represent what literary interpreters call the rhetorical axis. An axis is an imaginary line through the centre of something, like the imaginary line through the centre of the earth as it spins, as we say, 'on its axis'. Through the centre of a text is an imaginary 'rhetorical' line between the author and the reader. The rhetorical axis is the 'speaking' or 'communicating' line through the centre of the text from the author to the reader. In addition to horizontal arrows there are vertical arrows at the bottom of the diagram. The vertical arrows indicate a 'mimetic' axis. The word mimetic comes from the Greek word *mimesis*, meaning 'imitation'. The written signs in the text 'imitate' the sounds of language, and the narrator, actors and things in the 'textual world' imitate information and material data in the world. Thus, the vertical lines represent an axis of 'imitation'. This axis exists in angles in the diagram, rather than straight up through the centre, since the horizontal movement of the communication causes the vertical axis to run up and down at angles. In other words, the diagram is meant to exhibit action. There is dynamic movement from the author to the reader and from the reader to the author. In the context of this movement words, characters, represented world, implied author and implied reader all 'imitate' the world.

In the midst of all of these phenomena in the text are four arenas of texture printed in bold print: (1) inner texture; (2) intertexture; (3) social and cultural texture; and (4) ideological texture. One of the special features of socio-rhetorical criticism is its identification of these four arenas in a text. Pointing to these arenas, the method gathers practices of interpretation for each arena to enable a person to investigate each arena both on its own terms and in relation to the other arenas. Each arena is given a name for its own particular 'text-ure'. The texture of a text is so 'thick' that no discipline can satisfactorily approach all the aspects of thought, feeling, sight, sound, touch, smell and desire that its signs evoke. At present socio-rhetorical criticism uses four disciplines. In the future it will add psychological texture, but this is an additional task that very few biblical scholars at present are ready to tackle in a disciplinary manner.

THE BEGINNING POINT FOR THE LITERARY AND SOCIAL-SCIENTIFIC CRITIC

The standard lore suggests that a literary critic begins 'inside' the boundaries of a text and a social-scientific critic begins 'outside' the boundaries of a text. But let us test this conventional point of view with a comparison of John Dominic Crossan's interpretation of the parable of the Good Samaritan in his book *Raid on the Articulate* (Crossan 1976) with Richard Rohrbaugh's interpretation of the parable of the Great Supper in *The Social World of Luke–Acts* (Rohrbaugh 1991). I will begin with Crossan's interpretation of the parable of the Good Samaritan in Luke 10. Crossan establishes the context for his interpretation with a discussion of language as play and literature as a system. Language is a game. As people play with language, they create reality. Reality, then, is 'the interplay of worlds created by human imagination' (Crossan 1976: 28). Language creates tragic world and comic world. It breaks and cracks one kind of world with tremors that bring new worlds into being. Language actually functions in a ritual manner – a 'human *interplay* of structure and antistructure . . . which reminds us continually that our structures are both absolutely necessary and completely relative' (Crossan 1976: 36). Literature is a particular manifestation of the game of language. Literature functions as a system that makes and breaks genres. For Crossan, this system is closed. Each new example of literature changes the species itself. In other words:

> It is as if all the chairs and all the space in the auditorium were occupied so that one new arrival involves a total reorganization of those already present. It is of course this new arrival which stops the entire proceedings from becoming static, lifeless, and boring since all those in the audience face not the empty stage but rather the closed door. This subversive advent is necessary because without it the established forms and genres of a period's language and style would become absolutes and their frozen immobility would effectively hide the foundations of play on which and in which they operated.
>
> (Crossan 1976: 61)

For Crossan, then, literature is a closed system created by the game of language that people play. As a result, some of the most vigorous action in literature occurs as 'forms and genres' clash with one another. Here the interpreter sees that literature not only plays with language but, as Crossan says, literature also plays with itself (1976: 61).

From the perspective of the model that is before us, Crossan begins outside any particular text with language as a particular kind of human game, and from this context he approaches literature as a closed system in which forms and genres clash with one another to create new 'literary worlds'. As Crossan explores the arena of the literary system that will inform his interpretation of the parable of the Good Samaritan, he develops a taxonomy of forms and genres which includes law, proverb, beatitude, novel, myth, parable and allegory. This taxonomy informs the model that guides his interpretation of the parable. His beginning point, then, is the construction of a model of literary forms and genres which he perceives to function in a closed system that people create with the game of language.

Now let us turn to Rohrbaugh's interpretation of the parable of the Great Supper in Luke 14. To set the context for his interpretation, he observes that 'fully one half of the references to the "city" in the New Testament are in the Lukan writings' (Rohrbaugh 1991: 125). To understand this phenomenon, Rohrbaugh investigates what he calls 'the urban system'. This system stands in contrast to Crossan's investigation of 'literature as a system'. It stands at the opposite end of the mimetic axis of representation, and it also stands outside any particular text. For Rohrbaugh, within the social world there is a phenomenon he calls 'the urban system'. This system contains 'nucleations' including villages, towns and cities, which link cities and hinterland, and make the specialties in the nucleations intrinsic parts of a single system (Rohrbaugh 1991: 130). A correct understanding of the urban system, then, does not pit 'urban' and 'rural' as 'polar opposites or closed system' but as phenomena in 'a structure of interrelated differentiations' (p. 130).

Within this system there are, however, two opposed systems: the modern urban system and the pre-industrial system of antiquity. In the modern system the labour unit is 'the individual person' who as an aggregate 'constitute a flexible work-force for employers seeking to adapt to changing market conditions at minimum cost' (p. 131). In modern industrial society, therefore, there is a pattern linking city and hinterlands that

> ensures the flow of capital and labour toward the cities. Marketplace and channels of communication/transportation come to include the hinterlands along with the city. . . . By contrast, pre-industrial cities existed in a system which required a socially and geographically fixed labor force. Specialists in the city primarily produced the goods and services needed by the urban elite, who were the only existing consumer market. Since that market was small the labor force needed to supply it was correspondingly small and, as Leeds notes, it thus became 'a major interest to keep others than these out of the towns, fixed in their own agrarian, mining or extractive areas'.
>
> (Rohrbaugh 1991: 131–132, quoting Leeds 1979: 238)

Both Crossan and Rohrbaugh, it will be noticed, begin by constructing a model in their own world that functions as a context for interpretation of texts written in the world of late Mediterranean antiquity. Crossan approaches the text from the bottom of the model with language as a game and literature as a system. Rohrbaugh starts at the top of the model with the social world as a playing field and the urban world as a system. Both interpreters, then, presuppose the value of identifying a system as an overall context for interpreting a text. Crossan uses modern literary theory to define the relation of phenomena in the literary system; Rohrbaugh uses modern social-scientific theory to define the relation of phenomena in the urban system. So far, then, these literary and social-scientific interpreters have a good basis for dialogue. Both presuppose the value of modern theory, of systems within the realm of human activity, of models as contexts for interpretation, of the interrelation and opposition of certain phenomena as articulated in modern theory and of the Mediterranean world as the context in which the text first attained and evoked its meanings and meaning effects. Both start with phenomena outside of texts and create a model as a context for interpretation of a text.

It would be interesting to hear a dialogue between Crossan and Rohrbaugh concerning the nature of human activity in the realm of the literary and the urban system. Crossan emphasizes the activity of 'play' in literature which creates new 'worlds of reality'. Rohrbaugh appears to presuppose that the pre-industrial urban system represents the 'social world of reality' for anyone living in

Mediterranean antiquity. Yet, as Rohrbaugh proceeds, he concludes that the parable presents 'a member of the elite, a host, making a break with the "system" in the most public and radical sort of way' (Rohrbaugh 1991: 145). In Rohrbaugh's approach, does this 'break' create something new? If so, what 'new' phenomenon has been created? Crossan talks about 'new worlds of reality', because he perceives human imagination to be the source of 'reality' as humans can know it. Rohrbaugh does not analyze what occurs when the host 'breaks with the system'. Is it possible that Crossan's analysis picks up where Rohrbaugh's stops? In other words, do their approaches to interpretation stand in a continuum? In the model in Figure 6, narrator and characters represent the meeting ground between the place where Crossan starts and the place where Rohrbaugh starts. It looks like these two interpreters ought to be able to dialogue fruitfully with one another. Before moving on it may be worth our time to notice that the beginning place for Crossan's analysis challenges the conventional lore that literary critics work strictly with phenomena intrinsic to texts while social-scientific critics concern themselves with phenomena extrinsic to texts. Both, it would appear, begin with data extrinsic to texts to create a model for reading a text. Literary critics begin with language and literature to gain entrance into the verbal signs in the text; social-scientific critics begin with social and material data in the world to gain entrance into the represented world in the text. Once they have established a system to guide their interpretations, they start their readings of the text.

THE THINGS LITERARY AND SOCIAL-SCIENTIFIC CRITICS PERSONIFY

As literary and social-scientific critics engage in dialogue, they may discover quite soon that one of the greatest sources of irritation is the different things they personify as they talk. As we interpret, the phenomena we personify exhibit our point of view about reality and truth in the world.

Beginning with information and material data in the world, social-scientific critics personify aspects of human activity in the social world outside of texts and transfer this 'worldly' mode of personification onto aspects of a text. This means that the social-scientific critic is interested primarily in verbal signs in texts that evoke things related to 'persons' and 'their social world'. Other aspects of verbal signs in the text are of little or no importance. Literary critics, in contrast, personify verbal signs in texts and transfer these personified aspects of 'verbal signs' onto texts. I will illustrate by continuing with the interpretations by Crossan and Rohrbaugh.

After constructing a literary context for interpretation, Crossan asks the reader to perform a particular mental act: 'I would ask you to forget everything or anything you know about the story's present setting or editorial interpretation within the Gospel of Luke. Here is the story, the whole story, and nothing but the story' (1976: 101–102). At this point, Crossan prints the entire parable for the reader. The purpose is to get the reader to focus entirely on the story itself as a story. He is interested in the nature of story as story, in other words the nature of this particular form or genre within literature as a system. How does this story function? What makes this story different from other stories? Look, he says, at the story itself and nothing but the story.

As Crossan continues he emphasizes that he is concerned with the 'implicit narrator' rather than the historical author (Jesus) and with an 'implicit hearer or audience' (1976: 102). This language keeps him 'inside' the boundaries of the text in the socio-rhetorical model printed above. Then he distinguishes between an example story and a parable. At this point Crossan personifies forms of literature. As he says: 'The story of Jesus is not an example but a parable. It presents the audience with a paradox involving a double reversal of expectations' (1976: 104). Notice how 'story' has become the subject of a verb of action: the story 'presents the audience with a paradox'. This is a matter of personifying 'story': this story does things to an audience. At this point, then, the literary critic depersonifies the person who tells the story – this person, be it author, implied author, or narrator, is simply the device that brings the story before us, and there are great difficulties trying to talk about that device as a real person. Rather, we have the story, and it is the story that is doing things to us as readers.

I have both heard Bruce Malina object specifically to this kind of personification and I have read comments he has written to me in this regard. Stories do not do anything, he says, people do. The problem, from the literary critic's point of view, is that the 'people' in antiquity who told this story are no longer accessible to us. We have remnants of their language in verbal signs in texts. We activate these signs as we read them. If we are careful with our words, we know we are giving voice and action to verbal signs, not to real people. We cannot give voice and action to the person who told this story; we can only give voice and action to the story itself.

In contrast, Rohrbaugh personifies the author and the audience, both of whom stand outside the text. Rohrbaugh does not talk about an implied author or narrator, or about a narratee or implied hearer of the parable of the Great Supper. He is interested in 'Luke's' version of the parable and in Luke's 'intended audience'. There is nothing 'implicit' either about the author or about the audience in Rohrbaugh's interpretation. Luke is the author and he tells it to a particular audience with specific intentions in mind. As Rohrbaugh says: 'our thesis is that Luke's version of this parable knowingly uses features of the urban system in order to make its point and that these features would have been readily apparent to Luke's intended audience' (1991: 137).

It appears that Rohrbaugh also 'personifies' the parable he interprets, but he embeds that personification in 'Luke' who told it rather than in the nature of language as it functions in 'parable'. In other words, for Crossan this is 'language's' story: for Rohrbaugh this is 'Luke's' story. Crossan is very careful about any talk about anyone's 'intentions' with the story, since the discussion of 'the intentional fallacy' has been an important part of literary theory (Wimsatt 1954: 3–18; Crossan 1976: 90). Rohrbaugh has no such concern. For him, people have intentions, Luke had intentions as he told this story, and therefore there are intentions in this story for an intended audience.

What about the different phenomena Crossan and Rohrbaugh personify in their interpretations? My experience has been that this difference is very difficult to overcome in dialogue. What the literary critic personifies in contrast to the social-scientific critic is the tip of an iceberg with deep roots that evoke emotional and cognitive animosity. For literary critics, neither Luke nor any other person from antiquity is available to us. We cannot bring them to life no matter what we do. We bring their verbal and material signs to life as we read and look, and we can investigate how these verbal and material signs function within language and literature as systems. For social-scientific critics, on the other hand, language and verbal signs do not do anything; people do things with language and verbal signs. Social-scientific critics are not concerned, it appears, with literary critics' discussions of 'mimetic', 'intentional' and 'affective' fallacies. Most social-scientific critics presuppose that language and texts are clear windows to social reality. These windows are 'transparent': what you see is what you get. Here, then, we seem to have an immovable barrier between literary and social-scientific critics. At least I have not found much willingness on either side to give.

There may be one sign of hope. There is very little difference in what is personified as Crossan and Rohrbaugh talk about the characters in the parables they are interpreting. Both interpreters presuppose that the characters function in realms of social and cultural 'realities'. Crossan posits all kinds of social and cultural aspects functioning in and through the story he interprets. In turn, Rohrbaugh posits the nature of the story as parable rather than allegory and posits a significant number of literary aspects in and around the story he interprets. But is this enough of a meeting ground to engage in fruitful dialogue? I think the answer to this question is no. The interpretation of the characters in the story is more of a battleground than a congenial playing field. The reason, I suggest, is the unexplored presuppositions on both sides of the discussion. Let us turn, then, to areas in which literary and social-scientific critics have presupposed they did not need any more refined knowledge.

UNEXAMINED PRESUPPOSITIONS OF LITERARY AND SOCIAL-SCIENTIFIC CRITICS

Given the different arena of focus for the literary and social-scientific critic, the major arena of attention of the one is the major arena of least attention for the other. By this I mean that the literary critic regularly considers the social dynamics of the Mediterranean world to be 'transparent' to any reasonably intelligent historian while the nature of literature is highly complex, requiring extensive investigation. In turn, the social-scientific critic considers literature of any period to be 'transparent' to any reasonably intelligent reader while the nature of social interaction is highly complex, requiring extensive investigation. For the literary critic, it does little good to work out all kinds of theories and models about social systems and institutions if the interpreter does not read the text with intricate care, precision and theoretical guidance. For the social-scientific critic, it does little good to work out all kinds of theories and models about language and literature if the interpreter does not understand the social systems, institutions and dynamics in Mediterranean antiquity with care, precision and theoretical guidance. So is there any beginning place, any hope for cooperation?

The basic hope for serious dialogue and cooperation lies, as I see it, in an admission by both sides that the other side has data that is important for the act of interpretation. Such an approach to each other, given the highly developed nature of each field, calls for an interdisciplinary spirit. If interpreters are 'disciplinary' in their approach to things, in the spirit of nineteenth- and twentieth-century disciplinary investigation, there will be very little gain by either side – both sides will consider the central insights of the other side to be obsessive, irrelevant or simply wrong.

The question about Crossan is whether he could have a deeper interest in the social nature of the Mediterranean world. His recent books on Jesus suggest that he has such an interest (Crossan 1991, 1994). The question for Rohrbaugh is whether he could have a deeper interest in the literary nature of the parable of the Great Supper. Inasmuch as he distinguishes between parable and allegory, he may also find an interest in more detailed literary aspects of the parable.

But I suggest that this overlap of interest is still not enough. In my view, each side needs to have a much more comprehensive conception of the nature of text. This is where rhetorical criticism comes into the discussion, and here I refer to rhetorical criticism based on the tradition of rhetorical analysis and interpretation from its beginnings in pre-Socratic times to its presence today in post-modern criticism (Bizzell and Herzberg 1990). In an appendix to *In Defence of Rhetoric* (Vickers 1988: 491–498), Brian Vickers lists and defines forty-eight rhetorical tropes and figures. Literary criticism pays significant attention to only four of these: metaphor, metonymy, synecdoche and irony. Thus conventional literary criticism investigates a very limited range of phenomena of signification in a text. Social-scientific criticism explores a different range of signification in texts – namely what Aristotle calls the 'common topics'. Social-scientific critics have been exploring those topics that span all sectors of society and culture in the Mediterranean world – the knowledge, conceptions and presuppositions present with any person at any level of society. Aristotle's analysis in his *Ars Rhetorica* makes it clear that the common topics are only one aspect of rhetoric both in speech and in texts. In addition to the common topics are the special or material topics and the final topics (Kennedy 1991: 45–47, 50–52, 187–204; Mack 1989: 38). Social-scientific criticism has the potential to participate fully in a context of comprehensive interpretation of signification in texts if it attends not only to the common social and cultural topics but also the specific and final topics in texts.

Bryan Wilson's typology of sects is the most successful spectrum I can currently find to explore the specific or material topics in texts that evoke a religious view of the world. Through the specific topics in written discourse, a text evokes a response to the world that is conversionist, reformist, revolutionist, introversionist, manipulationist, thaumaturgical or utopian (Wilson 1969, 1973; Robbins 1994: 185–186). James A. Wilde began this kind of analysis with the Gospel of Mark in the 1970s (Wilde 1974, 1978). John H. Elliott included this kind of analysis in *A Home for the Homeless* and has been working hard to refine it in recent years (Elliott 1990b, 1993a, forthcoming). Philip Esler used it in his investigation of the Lukan community (Esler 1987) and has recently applied it to 4 Ezra in a study which also subjects the text to a literary analysis inspired by a central aspect of Russian formalism (Esler 1994a: 110–130 = 1994b). Much more analysis of specific or material topics in texts needs to be undertaken to facilitate dialogue between literary and social-scientific critics.

But also social-scientific critics need to attend to the final or strategic topics. The final topics are those which specific cultures use to deliver their most decisive points of persuasion. The final topics of the rabbis often occur in contexts where brief recitation of a text from Torah contains a particular word with special meaning. The final topics in this kind of rhetoric are distinctive from the final topics at work in the speech and writings of people deeply influenced by Homer and the tragedians. For this kind of analysis, the social-scientific critic needs to use the tools of the sociologist of culture. At present, the most suggestive taxonomy I have been able to find to explore the final topics is to correlate insights into elaboration of the *chreia* (pithy sayings associated with particular persons) with definitions of dominant culture, subculture, counterculture, contraculture and liminal culture (Robbins 1994: 189–190). A beginning place is to explore the cultural nature in which each New Testament text participates both in Jewish culture and in Graeco-Roman culture (Robbins 1993). Burton Mack's work on the Gospel of Mark (Mack 1988a) and Q (Mack 1993) presents the most advanced data currently available for this kind of analysis, but Mack himself does not use the resources of the sociology of culture to analyze and display what he has found. Extensive investigation of the final topics in New Testament texts with the aid of rhetorical criticism working in tandem with sociology of culture will bring a significant advance to dialogue between literary and social-scientific critics.

CONCLUSION

Literary and social-scientific criticism of the Bible emerged in a context where post-modern methods were moving into the humanities and the social sciences. The theoretical consciousness of both approaches is an important part of the new environment. The real antagonists of literary and social-scientific criticism are interpreters who claim to apply tested and proven methods that are free from theory. Approaches that are part of the post-modern era presuppose that every method is not only theoretically grounded but also ideologically driven. Just as no method is free from theory, so no theory is free from the particular interests and view of reality of those who formulate it.

Another characteristic of these approaches is to engage in rigorous, systematic and programmatic investigation, analysis and interpretation in the context of its theoretical and ideological discussions. The contextually limited and subjectively driven nature of its work does not introduce any special concern since that is the nature of all scientific work. Still another characteristic of both literary and social-scientific criticism is that the disciplinary work they do is inherently interdisciplinary. Both literary and social-scientific criticism have been deeply influenced by linguistics and structuralism, which are both richly informed by anthropology, which itself is a rich product of reciprocal exchange between the humanities and the social sciences. This means that the kind of literary and social-scientific criticism that was coming to birth during the last two decades presupposes cross-cultural, pluralistic investigation, analysis and interpretation.

It is natural that both literary and social-scientific approaches began with a disciplinary spirit characteristic of the first half of the twentieth century, since the spirit of historical criticism – the context out of which they emerged – is disciplinary. There is also another reason. Any approach must attain a 'disciplinary' rigour before colleagues in the field of biblical interpretation consider it to be a 'significant' practice in 'serious exegesis'. In other words, there should be no surprise that literary critics started with types of new-critical, structuralist and Russian formalist modes of interpretation that looked as thoroughly scientific as the most rigorous historical practices of interpretation. Social-scientific critics, in turn, could claim to be the practitioners who brought historical criticism to its fullest expression. In other words, while literary critics were imitating the rigour of historical method, social-scientific critics were aspiring to fulfil the grandest dreams of historical method.

The result has been not only the practice of new historicism (Veeser 1989; Thomas 1991) in biblical interpretation but also new rhetoricism (Bizzell and Herzberg 1990: 899–1266; Mack 1988a, 1990, 1993). Socio-rhetorical criticism merges new rhetoricism with new historicism (Robbins 1994). The boundaries established by earlier literary critics have openings through which social, cultural, historical and ideological data freely traffic. The insights of the social-scientific critic are more and more influenced by the textuality of society, culture and reality itself. Language is understood as a social phenomenon and texts are perceived in relation to voices in spoken language. In this new context, both fields become aware of the rhetoric not only of the discourse of the texts they analyze but also of their own discourse. Is there a potential for cooperation? Dialogue and cooperation are already beginning. The only question is who and how various critics undertake the task.

REFERENCES

Abel, E. L. (1970) 'The Genealogies of Jesus *ho Christos*', *NTS* 20: 203–210.

Ackroyd, P. R. and Evans, C. F. (1970) *The Cambridge History of the Bible*, vol. 1, Cambridge: Cambridge University Press.

Adan-Bayewitz, D. (1993) *Common Pottery in Roman Galilee: A Study of Local Trade*, Ramat Gan: Bar Ilan University Press.

Adan-Bayewitz, D. and Perlman, I. (1990) 'The Local Trade of Sepphoris in the Roman Period', *IEJ* 19: 153–172.

Adkins, A. W. (1960) *Merit and Responsibility: A Study in Greek Values*, Oxford: Oxford University Press.

Albertz, R. (1983) 'Die "Antrittspredigt" Jesu im Lukasevangelium auf ihrem alttestamentlichen Hintergrund', *ZNW* 74.3–4: 182–206.

Anderson, Benedict (1983) *Imagined Communities: Reflections on the Origin and Spread of Nationalism*, London: Verso.

Anderson, Janice Capel (1983) 'Matthew: Gender and Reading', in Mary Ann Tolbert, (ed.) *The Bible and Feminist Hermeneutics*, Semeia 28: 3–27.

Anderson, Judith (1987) 'Mary's Difference: Gender and Patriarchy in the Birth Narratives', *JR* 67: 183–202.

Applebaum, S. (1974) 'The Organisation of the Jewish Communities in the Diaspora', in S. Safrai and M. Stern (eds) *The Jewish People in the First Century*, 2 vols, Assen: Van Gorcum, vol. 1, 464–503.

—— (1986) 'Landscape and Pattern: An Archaeological Survey of Samaria 800 B.C.E.–636 C.E.: With a Historical Commentary by Shimon Applebaum', in S. Dar (ed.) *Landscape and Pattern*, Oxford: BAR Publications.

Archer, L. J. (1983) 'The Role of Jewish Women in the Religion, Ritual and Cult of Graeco-Roman Palestine', in A. C. Cameron and A. Kurht (eds) *Images of Women in Antiquity*, Detroit: Wayne State University, 272–287.

Archer, M. (1990) 'Human Agency and Social Structure: A Critique of Giddens', in J. Clark, C. Modgil and S. Modgil (eds) *Anthony Giddens: Consensus and Controversy*, London, New York, Philadelphia: Falmer Press, 73–84, 86–88.

Arthur, Marilyn B. (1977) 'Liberated Women: The Classical Era', in R. Bridenthal and C. Koonz (eds) *Becoming Visible: Women in European History*, Boston: Houghton Mifflin Co., 84–86.

Aune, David E. (1978) 'Septem Sapientium Convivium', in H. D. Betz (ed.) *Plutarch's Ethical Writings and Early Christian Literature*, Leiden: Brill, 51–105.

—— (1987) *The New Testament in its Literary Environment*, Library of Early Christianity, Philadelphia: Westminster.

Aviam, M. (1993) 'Galilee: The Hellenistic and Byzantine Periods', in E. Stern (ed.) *The New Encyclopedia of Archaeological Excavations of the Holy Land*, 4 vols, Jerusalem: The Israel Exploration Society, vol. 2: 452–458.

Avi-Yonah, M. (1966) *The Holy Land from the Persian to the Arab Conquests (536 B.C. to A.D. 64): A Historical Geography*, Grand Rapids: Baker Books.

Bacon, B. W. (1918) ' "The Five Books" of Matthew against the Jews', *The Expositor* 15: 56–66.

—— (1930) *Studies in Matthew*, New York: Henry Holt.

Bahr, Gordon J. (1970) 'The Seder of Passover and the Eucharistic Words', *NovT* 12: 181–202.

Balch, David L. (1986) 'Hellenization/Acculturation in 1 Peter', in Charles H. Talbert (ed.) *Perspectives on First Peter*, Macon, GA: Mercer University Press, 79–101.

—— (1991) (ed.) *Social History of the Matthean Community: Cross-disciplinary Approaches*, Minneapolis: Fortress Press.

Balsdon, J. P. V. D. (1962) *Roman Women: Their History and Habits*, London: Bodley Head.

Banfield, R. G. (1958) *The Moral Basis of a Backward Society*, New York: Free Press.

Banks, Robert (1980) *Paul's Idea of Community: The Early House Churches in their Historical Setting*, Grand Rapids: Wm B. Eerdmans.

Barag, D. (1982–1983) 'Tyrian Currency in Galilee', *Israel Numismatic Journal* 6/7: 7–13.

Barclay, J. M. G. (1992) 'Thessalonica and Corinth: Social Contrasts in Pauline Christianity', *JSNT* 47: 49–74.

—— (1994) 'Who was Considered an Apostate in the Diaspora?', unpublished paper presented to the Conference on Tolerance and its Limits in Early Judaism and Christianity, Jerusalem.

—— (forthcoming 1996) *Jews in the Mediterranean Diaspora from Alexander to Trajan*, Edinburgh: T. and T. Clark.

Bar-Ilan, M. (1988) 'Part Two: Scribes and Books in the Late Second Commonwealth and Rabbinic Period', in H. Sysling and M. Jan Mulder (eds) *Mikra*, Philadelphia: Fortress Press, 21–37.

Barker, G. and Lloyd, J. (eds) (1991) *Roman Landscapes: Archaeological Surveys in the Mediterranean Region*, Archaeological Monographs of the British School at Rome 2, London: British School at Rome.

Barrett, C. K. (1971) *A Commentary on the First Epistle to the Corinthians*, Black's New Testament Commentaries, London: A. and C. Black.

Barrett, L. (1987) *The Way God Fights: War and Peace in the Old Testament*, Scottdale: Herald Press.

Bar Tal, D. (1984) 'The Masada Syndrome: A Case of Central Belief', in N. Milgrom (ed.) *Stress and Coping in Times of War*, New York: Brunner and Mazel, 32–51.

Bartchy, Scott. S. (1973) *'Mallon Chresai': First-century Slavery and the Interpretation of 1.Cor. 7:21*, SBLDS 11, Missoula, Montana: University of Montana.

Barth, M. (1974) *Ephesians 4–6*, Anchor Bible, vol. 34A, Garden City, NY: Doubleday.

Barton, C. A. (1994) 'Savage Miracles: The Redemption of Lost Honor in Roman Society', *Representations* 45.

Barton, Stephen C. (1986) 'Paul's Sense of Place: An Anthropological Approach to Community Formation in Corinth', *NTS* 32: 225–246.

—— (1992) 'The Communal Dimension of Earliest Christianity: A Critical Survey of the Field', *JTS* 43: 399–427.

—— (1993) 'Early Christianity and the Sociology of the Sect', in F. Watson (ed.) *The Open Text: New Directions for Biblical Studies*, London: SCM Press, 140–162.

Barton, Stephen C. and Horsley, G. H. R. (1981) 'A Hellenistic Cult Group and the New Testament Churches', *JAC* 24: 7–41.

Baskin, J. (1985) 'The Separation of Women in Rabbinic Judaism', in Y. Haddad and E. Findly (eds) *Women, Religion and Social Change*, Albany, NY: SUNY.

Batten, A. (1994) 'More Queries for Q: Women and Christian Origins', *BTB* 24: 44 51.

Bauckham, Richard (1993) 'The Apocalypse as a Christian War Scroll', in *The Climax of Prophecy: Studies in the Book of Revelation*, Edinburgh: T. and T. Clark, 210 237.

Baumbach, Gunther (1982) 'Die Anfänge der Kirchwerdung im Urchristentum', *Kairos* 24: 17 30.

Becker, H. S. (1963) *Outsiders: Studies in the Sociology of Deviance*, New York: Free Press.

(1964) (ed.) *The Other Side: Perspectives on Deviance*, New York: Free Press.

Becker, W. A. (1889) *Charicles, or Illustrations of the Private Life of the Athenian Greeks*, London: Longmans Green and Co.

Beckford, James A. (1973) 'Religious Organization', *Current Sociology* 21: 12 18.

(1978) 'Accounting for Conversion', *British Journal of Sociology* 29: 249 262.

Bedale, S. (1954) 'The Meaning of "kephale" in the Pauline Epistles', *JTS* 5: 211 215.

Behm, J. (1964) 'Metamorphoo', *TDNT* IV: 755 759.

Belo, Fernando (1981) *A Materialist Reading of the Gospel of Mark*, Maryknoll, NY: Orbis.

Ben-David, A. (1969) *Jerusalem und Tyros: Ein Beitrag zur Palastinensischen Munz und Wirtschaftsgeschichte*, Basel: Kyklos-Verlag.

Ben-Yehuda, N. (1985) *Deviance and Moral Boundaries*, Chicago: University of Chicago Press.

Berger, Peter L. (1954) 'The Sociological Study of Sectarianism', *Social Research* 21: 467 485.

(1969) *The Sacred Canopy*, Garden City, NY: Doubleday.

Berger, Peter and Luckmann, Thomas (1967) *The Social Construction of Reality*, Harmondsworth: Penguin.

Bernstein, B. (1972) 'Social Class, Language and Socialization', in P. Giglioli (ed.) *Language and Social Context*, Harmondsworth: Penguin Books, 157 178.

Best, Ernest. (1988) *Paul and his Converts*, Edinburgh: T. and T. Clark.

Betz, H. D. (1985) *Essays on the Sermon on the Mount*, Philadelphia: Fortress Press.

Billerbeck, Paul (with Hermann L. Strack) (1926) *Kommentar zum Neuen Testament aus Talmud und Midrasch I*: Das Evangelium Nach Matthäus, Munich: C. H. Beck.

Bizzell, Patricia and Herzberg, Bruce (1990) *The Rhetorical Tradition: Readings from Classical Times to the Present*, Boston: Bedford Books of St Martin's Press.

Blasi, A. J. (1985) *A Phenomenological Transformation of the Social Scientific Study of Religion*, New York: Lang.

(1988) *Early Christianity as a Social Movement*, New York: Lang.

Blenkinsopp, Joseph (1981) 'Interpretation and Tendency to Sectarianism: An Aspect of Second Temple History', in E. P. Sanders (ed.) with A. I. Baumgarten and A. Mendelson, *Jewish and Christian Self-definition*, vol. 2: *Aspects of Judaism in the Graeco-Roman Period*, Philadelphia: Fortress Press, 1 26.

Blidstein, Gerald (1975) *Honour Thy Father and Mother: Filial Responsibility in Jewish Law and Ethics*, New York: KTAV.

Bloch, Maurice (1992) 'What Goes Without Saying: the Conceptualization of Zafimaniry Society', in A. Kuper (ed.) *Conceptualizing Society*, London and New York: Routledge, 127 146.

Boehm, Christopher (1984) *Blood Revenge: The Anthropology of Feuding in Montenegro and Other Tribal Societies*, Lawrence, KS: University Press of Kansas.

Boesen, Willibald (1980) *Jesusmahl, Eucharistisches Mahl, Endzeitmahl: Ein Beitrag zur Theologie des Lukas* (SB 97), Stuttgart: Verlag Katholisches Bibelwerk.

Boissevain, Jeremy (1974) *Friends of Friends: Networks, Manipulators and Coalitions*, New York: St Martin's Press.

Borg, Marcus J. (1984) *Conflict, Holiness and Politics in the Teaching of Jesus*, Studies in the Bible and Early Christianity 5, New York: Edwin Mellen Press.

Boring, M. Eugene (1985) 'Criteria of Authenticity: The Lukan Beatitudes as a Test Case', *Forum* 1/4: 3 38.

Bornkamm, Günther (1963) 'End-expectation and Church in Matthew', in Günther Bornkamm, G. Barth and H. J. Held, *Tradition and Interpretation in Matthew*, trans. P. Scott, Philadelphia: Westminster Press, (original German 1954), 15 51.

(1970) 'The Authority to "Bind" and "Loose" in the Church in Matthew's Gospel: The Problem of Sources in the Gospel', D. G. Miller *et al.* (eds) *Jesus and Man's Hope, Perspective Book 1*, Pittsburgh: Pittsburgh Theological Seminary, 37 50.

Bosen, W. (1985) *Galilee als Lebensraum und Wirkungsfeld Jesu*, Basel and Vienna: Herder.

Bourguignon, Erika (1979) '*Altered States of Consciousness*', *in Psychological Anthropology: An Introduction to Human Nature and Cultural Differences*, New York: Holt, Rinehart and Winston, 233 269.

Bradley, Keith R. (1991) *Discovering the Roman Family: Studies in Roman Social History*, Oxford: Oxford University Press.

Brandes, Stanley (1980) *Metaphors of Masculinity: Sex and Status in Andalusia*, Philadelphia: University of Pennsylvania Press.

(1987) 'Reflections on Honor and Shame in the Mediterranean', D. D. Gilmore (ed.) *Honor and Shame and the Unity of the Mediterranean*, American Anthropological Association Special Publication 22, Washington: American Anthropological Association, 121 134.

Braun, W. (1992) 'Symposium or Anti-Symposium? Reflections on Luke 14: 1 24', *Toronto Journal of Theology* 8/1: 70 84.

Bremen, R. Van (1983) 'Women and Wealth', in A. Cameron and A. Kuhrt (eds) *Images of Women in Antiquity*, Detroit, MI: Wayne State University, 234 245.

Bremmer, J. (1991) 'Walking, Standing and Sitting in Ancient Greek Culture', in J. Bremmer (ed.) *A Cultural History of Gesture*, Ithaca: Cornell University Press, 15 36.

Broer, I. (1986) *Die Seligpreisungen der Bergpredigt: Studien zu ihrer überlieferung und Interpretation*, BBB 61, Bonn: Peter Hanstein Verlag.

Brooks, Stephenson H. (1987) *Matthew's Community: The Evidence of His Special Sayings Source*, JSNTSup 16, Sheffield: JSOT Press.

Brooten, B. J. (1982) *Women Leaders in the Ancient Synagogue*, Brown Judaic Studies 36, Chico: Scholars Press.

(1986) 'Jewish Women's History in the Roman Period: A Task for Christian Theology', *HTR* 79: 22 30.

Broughton, T. R. S. (1938) 'Part IV: Roman Asia', in Tenney Frank (ed.) *An Economic Survey of Ancient Rome*, vol. 4, Baltimore: Johns Hopkins Press, 499 916.

Brown, John Pairman (1976) 'Techniques of Imperial Control: The Background of the Gospel Event', *The Bible and Liberation: Political and Social Hermeneutics*, in Norman K. Gottwald and Antoinette C. Wire (eds), Berkeley, CA: Community for Religious Research and Education, 73 83.

Brown, P. (1987) 'Late Antiquity', in P. Veyne (ed.) *History of Private Life, I: From Pagan Rome to Byzantium*, Cambridge, MA and London: Belknap Press of Harvard University, 241 253.

Brown, Raymond E. (1966, 1970) *The Gospel According to John*, 2 vols, Anchor Bible, Garden City, NY: Doubleday.

(1977) *The Birth of the Messiah*, Garden City, NY: Doubleday.

(1979) *The Community of the Beloved Disciple*, New York: Paulist Press.

(1983) 'Not Jewish Christianity and Gentile Christianity but Types of Jewish/Gentile Christianity', *CBQ* 45: 74 79.

Brown, Raymond E. and Meier, John (1983) *Antioch and Rome*, New York: Paulist Press.

Bruce, F. F. (1984) *The Epistles to the Colossians, to Philemon and to the Ephesians*, NICNT, Grand Rapids, Michigan: Wm B. Eerdmans.

Bryant, J. M. (1993) 'The Sect-church Dynamic and Christian Expansion in the Roman

Empire: Persecution, Penitential Discipline, and Schism in Sociological Perspective', *British Journal of Sociology* 44: 303–339.
Bultmann, Rudolf (1921) *Die Geschichte der synoptischen Tradition*, Göttingen: Vandenhoeck and Ruprecht.
—— (1963) *History of the Synoptic Tradition*, trans. John Marsh, New York: Harper and Row.
—— (1968) *The History of the Synoptic Tradition*, trans. John Marsh, Oxford: Basil Blackwell.
Burgess, T. C. (1902) 'Epideictic Literature', *Studies in Classical Philology* 3: 209–214, 231–233.
Burr, V. (1955) *Tiberius Julius Alexander*, Antiquitas 1, Bonn: Rudolf Habelt.
Burridge, K. (1969) *New Heaven New Earth: A Study of Millenarian Activities*, Oxford: Basil Blackwell.
Busse, U. (1978) *Das Nazareth-Manifest: Eine Einführung in das lukanische Jesusbild nach Lk 4, 16–30*, SBS 91, Stuttgart: Katholisches Bibelwerk.
Byatt, A. (1973) 'Josephus and Population Numbers in First-century Palestine', *PEQ* 105: 51–60.
Cadbury, Henry J. (1979) 'Note XXX: Names for Christians and Christianity in Acts', in F. J. Foakes Jackson and K. Lake (eds) *The Beginnings of Christianity. Part I. The Acts of the Apostles*, vol. 5, Grand Rapids: Baker, 375–392.
Caird, G. B. (1968) 'Towards a Lexicon of the Septuagint, I', *J. T. S.* n.s. 19: 453–475.
Campbell, John K. (1964) *Honour, Family and Patronage in a Greek Mountain Village*, Cambridge: Cambridge University Press.
Cantarella, Eva (1987) *Pandora's Daughters: The Role and Status of Women in Greek and Roman Antiquity*, Baltimore and London: Johns Hopkins University Press.
Carney, Thomas (1975) *The Shape of the Past: Models and Antiquity*, Lawrence, KS: Coronado Press.
Carradice, Ian (1982–1983) 'Coinage in Judaea in the Flavian Period, A. D. 70–96', *Israel Numismatic Journal* 6–7: 14–21.
—— (1993) 'Coin Types and Roman History: The Example of Domitian', in Martin Price, Andrew Burnett and Roger Bland (eds) *Essays in Honour of Robert Carson and Kenneth Jenkins*, London: Spink, 161–175.
Carrithers, Michael (1992) *Why Humans Have Cultures: Explaining Anthropology and Social Diversity*, Oxford: Oxford University Press.
Catchpole, D. R. (1991) 'The Mission Charge in Q', *Semeia* 55: 147–174.
Caulkins, R. Douglas (1995) 'Voluntary Associations', *Encyclopedia of Cultural Anthropology*, Henry Holt Reference Library, New York: Henry Holt.
Chilton, Bruce (1992) 'Transfiguration', *ABD* 6: 640–642.
Chow, J. K. M. (1992) *Patronage and Power*, Sheffield: Sheffield Academic Press.
Christiansen, E. J. (1992) *The Covenant and its Ritual Boundaries in Palestinian Judaism and Pauline Christianity*, Durham University PhD thesis, forthcoming Leiden: Brill.
Cohen, I. J. (1987) 'Structuration Theory and Social Praxis', in A. Giddens and J. H. Turner (eds) *Social Theory Today*, Cambridge: Polity Press, 273–308.
Cohen, Shaye J. D. (1980) 'Women in the Synagogues of Antiquity', *Conservative Judaism* 34: 232–239.
—— (1981) 'Epigraphical Rabbis', *JQR* 72: 1–17.
—— (1986) 'The Political and Social History of the Jews in Greco-Roman Antiquity: The State of the Question', in Robert A. Kraft and George W. E. Nickelsburg, *Early Judaism and its Modern Interpreters*, Atlanta: Scholars Press, 33–56.
—— (1987) *From the Maccabees to the Mishnah*, Philadelphia: The Westminster Press.
—— (1989) 'Crossing the Boundary and Becoming a Jew' *HTR* 82: 13–34.
—— (1990) 'The Rabbinic Conversion Ceremony', *JJS* 41: 177–203.
—— (1993) (ed.) *The Jewish Family in Antiquity*, Atlanta: Scholars Press.
Collins, Marilyn F. (1972) 'The Hidden Vessels in Samaritan Tradition', *JJS* 3: 97–116.
Conzelmann, H. G. (1975) *1 Corinthians*, Philadelphia: Fortress Press.

Cook, Michael J. (1978) *Mark's Treatment of the Jewish Leaders*, Leiden: E. J. Brill.

Cope, O. Lamar (1969) 'Matthew XXV.31–46: The Sheep and Goats Reinterpreted', *NovT* 11: 32–44.

Corley, Kathleen (1987) 'Silence in the Context of Ascent and Liturgy in Gnostic Texts', paper presented in the New Testament Seminar of the Claremont Graduate School.

—— (1989) 'Were the Women Around Jesus Really Prostitutes? Women in the Context of Greco-Roman Meals', *SBLSP*: 487–521.

—— (1993a) *Private Women, Public Meals: Social Conflict in the Synoptic Tradition*, Peabody, MA: Hendrickson.

—— (1993b) 'Jesus' Table Practice: Dining with "Tax Collectors and Sinners", including Women', in Eugene H. Lovering Jr, (ed.) SBLSP: 444–459.

Craffert, Pieter F. (1993) 'The Pauline Movement and First-century Judaism: A Framework for Transforming the Issue', *Neot* 27: 233–263.

Cranford, M. L. (1992) 'Bibliography for the Sermon on the Mount', *South West Journal of Theology* 35: 34–38.

Crosby, Michael H. (1988) *House of Disciples: Church, Economics, and Justice in Matthew*, Maryknoll, NY: Orbis.

Crossan, John Dominic (1976) *Raid on the Articulate: Cosmic Eschatology in Jesus and Borges*, New York: Harper and Row.

—— (1983) *In Fragments: The Aphorisms of Jesus*, San Francisco: Harper and Row.

—— (1991) *The Historical Jesus: The Life of a Mediterranean Jewish Peasant*, Edinburgh: T. and T. Clark, NY: HarperCollins.

—— (1994) *Jesus: A Revolutionary Biography*, San Francisco: Harper San Francisco.

Csillag, P. (1976) *The Augustan Laws on Family Relations*, Budapest: Academiai Kiado.

Cullmann, Oscar (1950) *Baptism in the New Testament*, London: SCM Press.

—— (1980) *The Christology of the New Testament*, London: SCM Press.

Culpepper, Alan R. (1975) *The Johannine School: An Evaluation of the Johannine-school Hypothesis based on an Investigation of the Nature of Ancient Schools*, Missoula: Scholars Press.

Dalman, Gustav (1930) *Die Worte Jesu*, 2nd edn, Leipzig: J. C. Hinrichs.

D'Angelo, Mary Rose (1990) 'Women in Luke–Acts: A Redactional View', *JBL* 109/3: 441–61.

Danielou, Jean (1969) 'Christianity as a Jewish Sect', in Arnold Toynbee (ed.) *The Crucible of Christianity: Judaism, Hellenism and the Historical Background of the Christian Faith*, London: Thames and Hudson, 275–282.

Danker, Fredrick W. (1972) *Jesus and the New Age: A Commentary on the Third Gospel*, St Louis: Clayton.

—— (1982) *Benefactor: Epigraphic Study of a Graeco-Roman and New Testament and Semantic Field*, St Louis: Clayton.

—— (1992) 'Associations, Clubs, Thiasoi', *ABD* 1:501–503.

Dar, S. (ed.) (1986) *Landscape and Pattern*, Oxford: BAR Publications.

Daube, David (1973) *The New Testament and Rabbinic Judaism*, New York: Arno Press.

Davies, Philip R. (1989) 'The Social World of Apocalyptic Writings', in R. E. Clements (ed.) *The World of Ancient Israel: Sociological, Anthropological and Political Perspectives*, Cambridge: Cambridge University Press, 251–271.

Davies, Stevan (1991) 'Women in the Third Gospel and the New Testament Apocrypha', in A. J. Levine (ed.) '*Women Like This*': *New Perspectives on Jewish Women in the Greco-Roman World*, SBL Early Judaism and its Literature, Atlanta, GA: Scholars Press, 185–197.

Davies, W. D. (1964) *The Setting of the Sermon on the Mount*, Cambridge: Cambridge University Press.

Davies, W. D. and Allison, D. C. (1988) *A Critical and Exegetical Commentary on the Gospel According to Saint Matthew*, vol. 1, Edinburgh: T. and T. Clark.

—— (1991) *A Critical and Exegetical Commentary on the Gospel According to Saint Matthew*, vol. 2, Edinburgh: T. and T. Clark.

Davis, E. C. (1967) *The Significance of the Shared Meal in Luke Acts*, Ann Arbor: University Microfilms.

Davis, N. J. (1980) *Sociological Constructions of Deviance: Perspectives and Issues in the Field*, 2nd edn, Dubuque: W. C. Brown.

Dawes, G. (1990) ' "But if you can gain your freedom" (1 Cor. 7:17–24)', *CBQ* 52: 681–697.

Degenhardt, Hans-Joachim (1965) *Lukas: Evangelist der Armen*, Stuttgart: Katholisches Bibelwerk.

Delling, G. (1968) '*Pleonektes*', *TDNT* 6: 266–270.

Delling, K. (1964) '*Baskaino*', *TWNT* 1: 595–596.

Delobel, J. (1966) 'L'onction par la pecheresse', *ETL* 42: 415–475.

Deonna, W. (1965) *Le symbolisme de l'oeil*, Paris: Ecole Fr. d'Athenes, Trav. et Mem.

Derrett, J. D. M. (1977) 'Workers in the Vineyard: A Parable of Jesus', in J. D. M. Derrett, *Studies in the New Testament* 1, Leiden: Brill, 48–75.

—— (1981) 'Mt. 23:8–10: A Midrash on Is. 54:13 and Jer. 31:33–34', *Biblica* 62: 372–386.

—— (1985) *Making of Mark*, Shipston-on-Stour: Drinkwater.

—— (1986) *New Resolutions of Old Conundrums*, Shipston-on-Stour: Drinkwater.

—— (1989) *Ascetic Discourse*, Eilsbrunn: Ko'amar.

—— (1992) 'Koinos, Koinoo', *Filologia Neotestamentica* 5: 69–78.

Descola, Philippe (1992) 'Societies of Nature and the Nature of Society', in A. Kuper (ed.) *Conceptualizing Society*, London and New York: Routledge, 107–126.

Diakonoff, I. M. (1992) 'The Naval Power and Trade of Tyre', *IEJ* 42:168–193.

Dieckmann, H. (1984) 'The Enemy Image', *Quadrant* Fall: 61–69.

Dill, Samuel (1905) *Roman Society from Nero to Marcus Aurelius*, New York: Meridian.

Dillon, Richard J. (1978) *From Eye-witness to Ministers of the Word*, AnBib 82, Rome: Biblical Institute.

Distasio, L. (1981) *Mal Occhio*, San Francisco: North Point.

Dixon, Suzanne (1991) 'The Sentimental Ideal of the Roman Family', in Beryl Rawson (ed.) *Marriage, Divorce and Children in Ancient Rome*, Oxford: Clarendon Press, 99–113.

—— (1992) *The Roman Family*, Baltimore: Johns Hopkins University Press.

Dodds, Eric Robertson (1951) *The Greeks and the Irrational*, Berkeley and Los Angeles: University of California Press.

Donahue, John R. (1986) 'The Parable of the Sheep and Goats: A Challenge to Christian Ethics', *TS* 47: 3–31.

—— (1988) *The Gospel in Parable*, Philadelphia: Fortress Press.

Douglas, Mary (1966) *Purity and Danger*, London: Routledge and Kegan Paul.

—— (1970) *Natural Symbols: Explorations in Cosmology*, London: Routledge and Kegan Paul.

Douglas, R. C. (1992) 'Matthew 18:15–17 and the Hellenistic-Roman Polis', unpublished paper.

Downes, D. and Rock, P. (1988) *Understanding Deviance: A Guide to the Sociology of Crime and Rule-breaking*, 2nd edn, Oxford: Clarendon Press.

Dubisch, J. (ed.) (1986) *Gender and Power in Rural Greece*, Princeton: Princeton University Press.

Duff, P. B. (1992) 'Apostolic Suffering and the Language of Procession', *BTB* 22: 158–165.

Duling, Dennis (1983) 'Matthew and the Problem of Authority: Some Preliminary Observations', *Proceedings 3, Eastern Great Lakes Biblical Society* 3: 59–68; repr. in *Explorations: Journal for Adventurous Thought* 3 (1984) 15–24; and in William P. Frost (ed.) (1984) *New Testament Perspectives*, Dayton, Ohio: College Press, 33–42.

—— (1987) 'Binding and Loosing (Matthew 16:19; Matthew 18:18; John 20:23)', *Forum* 3/4: 3–31.

—— (1990) 'Against Oaths', *Forum* 6/2: 1–45.

—— (1992a) 'Matthew's Plurisignificant "Son of David" in Social Science Perspective: Kinship, Kingship, Magic and Miracle', *BTB* 22/3: 99–116.

—— (1992b) 'Egalitarian Ideology, Leadership, and Factional Conflict in the Matthean Gospel', paper delivered at SBL Synoptic Gospels Section.

—— (1993) 'Matthew and Marginality', *SBLSP*: 642–671; repr. in (1995) Hervormde T St 51:1–30.

—— (1994) 'BTB Readers' Guide: Millennialism', *BTB* 24: 132–142.

Duncan-Jones, R. (1990) *Structure and Scale in the Roman Economy*, Cambridge: Cambridge University Press.

Dundes, A. (1984) *The Evil Eye*, Berkeley: University of California.

Dunn, James D. G. (1990) *Jesus, Paul and the Law*, London: SPCK.

Dupont, J. (1973) *Les Béatitudes*, Paris: Gabalda.

Eagleton, T. (1991) *Ideology: An Introduction*, London and New York: Verso.

Eaton, John H. (1976) *Kingship and the Psalms*, SBT 2/32, Napierville, IL: Allenson.

Edelstein, Emma Jeanette and Edelstein, Ludwig (1975) *Asclepius: A Collection and Interpretation of the Testimonies*, vols 1 & 2, New York: Arno Press (first published 1945).

Edersheim, A. (1906) *The Life and Times of Jesus the Messiah*, London and New York: Longmans Green.

Edwards, D. R. (1988) 'First Century Urban/Rural Relations in Lower Galilee: Exploring the Archaeological and Literary Evidence', in D. J. Lull (ed.) *SBLSP*: 169–182.

—— (1992) 'The Socio-economic and Cultural Ethos of Lower Galilee in the First Century: Implications for the Nascent Jesus Movement', in L. Levine (ed.) *The Galilee in Late Antiquity*, New York: Jewish Theological Seminary of America, 53–73.

Eisenhower, D. D. (1948) *Crusade in Europe*, New York: Doubleday.

Eisenstadt, S. N. (1956) 'Sociological Aspects of the Economic Adaptation of Oriental Migrants in Israel: A Case Study in the Problem of Modernisation', *Economic Development and Cultural Change* 4: 269–78.

Elder, Linda Bennett (1991) *Transformation in the Judith Mythos: A Feminist Critical Analysis*, diss., Florida State University, UMI diss., 3058.

Elliott, John H. (1966) *The Elect and the Holy*, NovTSup 12, Leiden: E. J. Brill.

—— (1981) *A Home for the Homeless: A Sociological Exegesis of 1 Peter, its Situation and Strategy*, Philadelphia: Fortress Press (revised edn 1990).

—— (1986a) 'Social-scientific Criticism of the New Testament: More on Methods and Models', in John H. Elliott (ed.) *Social-scientitific Criticism of the New Testament and its Social World*, Semeia 35, Decatur, GA: Scholars Press, 1–33.

—— (1986b) '1 Peter, its Situation and Strategy: A Discussion with David Balch', in Charles H. Talbert (ed.) *Perspectives on First Peter*, Macon, GA: Mercer University Press, 61–78.

—— (1986c) *Social-scientific Criticism of the New Testament and its Social World*, Semeia 35, Decatur, GA: Scholars Press.

—— (1988) 'The Fear of the Leer: The Evil Eye from the Bible to Li'l Abner', *Forum* 4/4: 42–71.

—— (1989) 'Household and Meals Versus the Temple Purity System: Patterns of Replication in Luke–Acts', *HTS* 47: 386–399.

—— (1990a) 'Paul, Galatians and the Evil Eye', *CurTM* 17: 262–273.

—— (1990b) *A Home for the Homeless: A Social-Scientific Criticism of 1 Peter, its situation and strategy with a New Introduction*, rev. edn, Philadelphia: Fortress Press.

—— (1991a) 'The Evil Eye in the First Testament: The Ecology and Culture of a Pervasive Belief', in N. K. Gottwald (ed.) *The Bible and the Politics of Exegesis*, Cleveland OH: Pilgrim Press, 147–159.

—— (1991b) 'Temple Versus Household in Luke–Acts: A Contrast in Social Institutions', in Jerome H. Neyrey (ed.) *The Social World of Luke–Acts: Models for Interpretation*, Peabody, MA: Hendrickson, 211–240.

—— (1992) 'Matthew 20:1–15: A Parable of Invidious Comparison and Evil Eye Accusation', *BTB* 22/2: 52–65.

—— (1993a) *What is Social-Scientific Criticism?*, Minneapolis: Fortress Press.

—— (1993b) 'The Epistle of James in Rhetorical and Social Scientific Perspective: Holiness–Wholeness and Patterns of Replication', *BTB* 23: 71–81.

—— (1994) 'The Jewish Messianic Movement: From Faction to Sect', unpublished typescript.

—— (forthcoming) 'Phases in the Social Formation of Early Christianity: From Faction to Sect, A Social-scientific Perspective', in P. Bergen, V. K. Robbins and D. Gowler (eds) *Recruitment, Conquest, and Conflict in Judaism, Christianity, and the Greco-Roman World: Emory Studies in Early Christianity 6*, Atlanta: Scholars Press.

Elworthy, F. T. (1895) *Evil Eye*, London: J. Murray.

Engberg-Pedersen, T. (1993) 'Proclaiming the Lord's Death: 1 Corinthians 11:17–34 and the Forms of Paul's Theological Argument', in D. M. Hay (ed.) *Pauline Theology, II: 1 and 2 Corinthians*, Minneapolis: Fortress Press, 103–132.

Erikson, K. T. (1962) 'Notes on the Sociology of Deviance', *Social Problems* 9: 307–314.

—— (1966) *Wayward Puritans: A Study in the Sociology of Deviance*, New York: John Wiley and Sons.

Esler, Philip F. (1987) *Community and Gospel in Luke–Acts: The Social and Political Motivations of Lucan Theology*, SNTSMS 57, Cambridge: Cambridge University Press.

—— (1992) 'Glossolalia and the Admission of Gentiles into the Early Christian Community', *BTB* 22: 136–142.

—— (1993a) 'Political Oppression in Jewish Apocalyptic Literature: A Social-scientific Approach', *Listening: Journal of Religion and Culture* 28: 181–199.

—— (1993b) Review of Neyrey, J. H. (ed.) (1991a) *The Social World of Luke–Acts*, Peabody: Hendrickson, *Biblical Interpretation* 1: 250–255.

—— (1994a) *The First Christians in their Social Worlds: Social-Scientific Approaches to New Testament Interpretation*, London: Routledge.

—— (1994b) 'The Social Function of 4 Ezra', *JSNT* 53: 99–123.

—— (1995) Review of Corley, K. (1993a) *Private Women Public Meals*, Peabody: Hendrickson, *Biblical Interpretation* 3, 125–128.

Evans, Donald (1987) 'Academic Scepticism, Spiritual Reality and Transfiguration', in L. D. Hurst and N. T. Wright (eds) *The Glory of Christ in the New Testament*, Oxford: Clarendon Press, 175–186.

Eyben, Emiel (1991) 'Fathers and Sons', in B. Rawson (ed.) *Marriage, Divorce and Children in Ancient Rome*, Oxford: Clarendon Press, 114–143.

Fee, G. D. (1987) *The First Epistle to the Corinthians*, NICNT, Grand Rapids, MI: Wm B. Eerdmans.

Feldman, L. H. (1960) 'The Orthodoxy of the Jews in Hellenistic Egypt', *JSS* 22: 215–237.

—— (1993) *Jew and Gentile in the Ancient World*, Princeton, NJ: Princeton University.

Ferguson, Everett (1987) *Backgrounds of Early Christianity*, Grand Rapids, MI: Wm B. Eerdmans.

Fiensy, D. (1991) *The Social History of Palestine in the Herodian Period*, Lewiston: Edwin Mellen Press.

Finley, M. I. (1981) 'The Ancient City from Fustel de Coulanges to Max Weber and Beyond', *Comparative Studies in History and Society* 19: 305–327.

—— (1985) *The Ancient Economy*, 2nd edn, London: Chatto and Windus.

Fiorenza, Elizabeth Schüssler (1983) *In Memory of Her*, New York: Crossroad.

—— (1986) 'A Feminist Critical Interpretation for Liberation: Martha and Mary: Luke 10:38–42', *Religion and Intellectual Life* 3: 21–35.

Fishbane, Michael (1985) *Biblical Interpretation in Ancient Israel*, Oxford: Clarendon Press.

(1989) 'From Scribalism to Rabbinism: Perspectives on the Emergence of Classical Judaism', in *The Garments of Torah: Essays in Biblical Hermeneutics*, Bloomington: Indiana University Press, ch. 5; repr. in John G. Gammie and Leo G. Perdue (eds) (1990) *The Sage in Israel and the Ancient Near East*, Winona Lake: Eisenbrauns, 439 456.

Fitzmyer, Joseph. A. (1981) *The Gospel According to Luke (I.I IX)*, The Anchor Bible, 28 Garden City, NY: Doubleday.

(1985) *The Gospel According to Luke (X XXIV)*, The Anchor Bible 28a, New York: Doubleday.

(1989) 'Another Look at "kephale" in 1 Corinthians 11:3', *NTS* 35: 503 511.

(1993) '"Kephale" ' in I Corinthians 11:3', *Int* 47: 52 59.

Flender, Helmut (1967) *St Luke: Theologian of Redemptive History*, Philadelphia: Fortress Press.

Flusser, D. (1989) 'Die Versuchung Jesu und ihr jüdischer Hintergrund', *Judaica* 45/2: 110 128.

Foerster, W. (1935) '*Daimon, daimonia*', *TWNT* 2: 13, 19.

Forbes, Clarence Allen (1933) *Neoi: A Contribution to the Study of Greek Associations*, Philological Monographs of the American Philological Association, 2nd edn, Middleton, CN: American Philological Association.

Forkman, Görin (1972) *The Limits of the Religious Community*, ConBNT 5, Lund: C. W. K. Gleerup.

Forman, Robert K. C. (1993) 'Mystical Knowledge: Knowledge by Identity', *JAAR* 61: 705 738.

Foster, B. O. (1939) *Livy II*, Loeb edn, Cambridge, MA and London: Harvard University Press and William Heinemann.

Foster, George (1965) 'Peasant Society and the Image of Limited Good', *American Anthropologist* 67: 293 315.

Frankel, R. (1992) 'Some Oil Presses from Western Galilee', *BASOR* 286: 39 71.

Fredriksen, P. (1986) 'Paul and Augustine: Conversion Narratives, Orthodox Tradition, and the Retrospective Self', *JTS* 37: 3 34.

Frend, W. H. C. (1984) *The Rise of Christianity*, Philadelphia: Fortress Press.

Frey, J. B. (1936) *Corpus Inscriptionum Iudaicarum*, 2 vols, Rome and Paris.

Freyne, Sean (1980) *Galilee from Alexander the Great to Hadrian: A Study of Second Temple Judaism*, Wilmington DE: Glazier/Notre Dame University Press.

(1985) 'Vilifying the Other and Defining the Self: Matthew's and John's Anti-Jewish Polemic in Focus', in Jacob Neusner and E. Frerichs (eds) *'To See Ourselves as Others See Us': Christians, Jews, 'Others' in Late Antiquity*, Chico, CA: Scholars Press, 117 144.

(1987) 'Galilee Jerusalem Relations in the Light of Josephus' *Vita*', *NTS* 33: 600 609.

(1988) *Galilee, Jesus and the Gospels: Literary Approaches and Historical Investigations*, Dublin: Gill and Macmillan.

(1992) 'Urban Rural Relations in First Century Galilee: Some Suggestions from the Literary Sources', in L. Levine (ed.) *The Galilee in Late Antiquity*, New York: Jewish Theological Seminary of America, 75 91.

Friedrich, Paul (1977) 'Sanity and the Myth of Honor: The Problem of Achilles', *Journal of Psychological Anthropology* 5: 281 305.

Fuchs, A. (1984) 'Versuchung Jesu', *Studien zum Neuen Testament und seiner Unwelt* 9: 95 159.

Funk, Robert W., Hoover, Roy W. and the Jesus Seminar (1993) *The Five Gospels: The Search for the Authentic Words of Jesus*, New York: Macmillan.

Füssel, Kuno (1987) *Drei Tage mit Jesus im Tempel: Einführung in die materialistische Lektüre der Bibel*, Münster: Edition Liberaciün.

Gabriel, R. and Metz, K. (1991) *From Sumer to Rome: The Military Capabilities of Ancient Armies*, Westport, CT: Greenwood Press.

Gager, John G. (1975) *Kingdom and Community: The Social World of Early Christianity*, Englewood Cliffs: Prentice Hall.

Gallagher, E. V. (1993) 'Conversion and Community in Late Antiquity', *JR* 73: 1 15.

Gallas, S. (1990) '"Fünfmal vierzig weiger einen . . ." Die an Paulus vollzogenen Synagogalstrafen nach 2Kor 11, 24', *ZNW* 81: 178–191.

Gammie, John G. (1990) 'The Sage in Sirach', in John G. Gammie and Leo G. Perdue (eds) *The Sage in Israel and the Ancient Near East*, Winona Lake: Eisenbrauns, 355–372.

Gamson, W. A. (1992) 'The Social Psychology of Collective Action', in A. D. Morris and C. M. Mueller (eds) *Frontiers in Social Movement Theory*, New Haven and London: Yale University Press, 53–76.

Gardner, Jane F. and Wiedemann, Thomas (1991) *The Roman Household: A Sourcebook*, London and New York: Routledge.

Garland, David E. (1979) *The Intention of Matthew 23*, Leiden: E. J. Brill.

Garnsey, Peter (1970) *Social Status and Legal Privilege in the Roman Empire*, Oxford: Clarendon Press.

—— (1988) *Famine and Food Supply in the Graeco-Roman World*, Cambridge: Cambridge University Press.

Garnsey, Peter, Hopkins, K. and Whittaker, C. R. (1983) *Trade in the Ancient Economy*, Cambridge: Cambridge University Press.

Garnsey, P. and Saller, R. P. (1987) *The Roman Empire: Economy, Society and Culture*, London: Duckworth.

Garrett, Susan (1992) 'Sociology of Early Christianity', *ABD* 6: 89–99.

Geertz, Clifford (1962) 'The Rotating Credit Association: A Middle Rung in Development', *Economic Development and Cultural Change* 10: 241–263.

—— (1976) 'From the Natives' Point of View: On the Nature of Anthropological Understanding', in K. H. Basso and H. A. Selby (eds) *Meaning in Anthropology*, Albuquerque NM: University of New Mexico, 221–237.

—— (1988) *Works and Lives: The Anthropologist as Author*, Stanford: Stanford University Press.

Gerhardsson, Birger (1966) *The Testing of God's Son*, Lund: Gleerup.

Germani, Gino (1980) *Marginality*, New Brunswick, NJ: Transaction Books.

Gibbs, J. P. (1966) 'Conceptions of Deviant Behaviour: The Old and the New', *Pacific Sociological Review* 9: 9–14.

Giddens, A. (1976) *New Rules of Sociological Method: A Positive Critique of Interpretative Sociologies*, London: Hutchinson.

—— (1979) *Central Problems in Social Theory*, London: Macmillan.

—— (1982) *Profiles and Critiques in Social Theory*, London: Macmillan.

—— (1984) *The Constitution of Society: Outline of the Theory of Structuration*, Cambridge: Polity Press.

—— (1991) 'Structuration Theory: Past, Present and Future', in C. G. A. Bryant and D. Jary (eds) *Giddens' Theory of Structuration: A Critical Appreciation*, London and New York: Routledge, 201–221.

Gilmore, David D. (1982) 'Anthropology of the Mediterranean Area', *Annual Review of Anthropology* 11: 175–205.

—— (1987) *Honor and Shame and the Unity of the Mediterranean*, American Anthropological Association Special Publication 22, Washington: American Anthropological Association.

—— (1991) *Manhood in the Making: Cultural Concepts of Masculinity*, New Haven: Yale University Press.

Gilmore, D. D. and Gilmore, M. (1979) 'Machismo: A Psychodynamic Approach' *Journal of Psycho-analytical Anthropology* 2: 281–300.

Gilmore, D. D. and Uhl, S. (1987) 'Further Notes on Andalusian Machismo', *Journal of Psycho-analytical Anthropology* 10: 341–360.

Gliddon, C. P. (1971) 'The Gospel Basis for Pacifism', in R. Jones (ed.) *The Gospel, Church and War*, New York: Garland, 16–40.

Gnilka, J. (1963) 'Die Kirche des Matthäus und die Gemeinde von Qumran', *BZ* 7: 43–63.

Goodman, Felicitas D. (1972) *Speaking in Tongues: A Cross-cultural Study of Glossolalia*, Chicago: University of Chicago Press.

Goodman, Martin (1983) *State and Society in Roman Galilee, A.D. 132–212*, Totowa, NJ: Rowman and Allanheld.

——(1987) *The Ruling Class of Judaea: The Origins of the Jewish Revolt Against Rome A.D. 66–70*, New York: Cambridge University Press.

——(1994) *Mission and Conversion*, Oxford: Clarendon Press.

Goody, Jack (1968) 'Introduction', in J. Goody (ed.) *Literacy in Traditional Societies*, Cambridge: Cambridge University Press, 1–26.

Gordon, Colin (ed.) (1981) *Michel Foucault: Power/Knowledge: Selected Interviews and Other Writings*, London: Harvester Press.

Gordon, C. H. (1977) 'Paternity at Two Levels', *JBL* 96: 101.

Gove, W. R. (ed.) (1975) *The Labelling of Deviance: Evaluating a Perspective*, New York: John Wiley and Sons.

Graf, F. (1991) 'Gestures and Coventions: The Gestures of Roman Actors and Orators', in J. Bremmer (ed.) *A Cultural History of Gesture*, Ithaca: Cornell University Press, 36–58.

Grant, F. C. (1923) *The Economic Background to the Gospels*, Oxford: Clarendon Press.

Gray, J. G. (1959) *The Warriors: Reflections of Men in Battle*, New York: Harper and Row.

Gray, Sherman W. (1989) '*The Least of My Brothers: Matthew 25:31–46: A History of Interpretation*, Atlanta: Scholars Press.

Grudem, W. (1985) 'Does "kephale" ("Head") Mean "Source" or "Authority Over" in Greek Literature? A Survey of 2,336 Examples', *Trinity Journal* 6: 38–59.

——(1990) 'The Meaning of "kephale" ("Head"): A Response to Recent Studies', *Trinity Journal* 11: 3–72.

Guelich, R. A. (1976a) 'The Antitheses of Matthew 5:21–48: Traditional and/or Redactional?', *NTS* 22: 444–457.

——(1976b) 'The Matthean Beatitudes: Entrance Requirements or Eschatological Blessings?', *JBL* 95: 415–434.

——(1982) *The Sermon on the Mount: A Foundation for Understanding*, Waco, TX:

Gundry, Robert H. (1982) *Matthew: A Commentary on his Literary and Theological Art*, Grand Rapids: Eerdmans.

——(1994) 'On True and False Disciple in Matthew 8:18–22', *NTS* 40: 433–441.

Gutman, Joseph (1981) 'Synagogue Origins: Theories and Facts', in Joseph Gutman (ed.) *Ancient Synagogues: The State of Research*, Chico, CA: Scholars Press, 1–6.

Hachlili, Rachael (1992) 'Synagogue (Diaspora Synagogues)', in D. N. Freedman (ed.) *The Anchor Bible Dictionary*, vol. 6, Garden City, NY: Doubleday, 260–263.

Hadas-Lebel, M. (1973) *De Providentia I et II: Les oeuvres de Philon d'Alexandrie*, Paris: Cerf.

Hallett, Judith (1984) *Fathers and Daughters in Roman Society: Women and the Elite Family*, Princeton, NJ: Princeton University.

Halliday, Michael A. K. (1978) *Language as Social Semiotic: The Social Interpretation of Language and Meaning*, Baltimore: University Park Press.

Hamel, Gildas (1990) *Poverty and Charity in Roman Palestine, First Three Centuries C.E.*, Berkeley, CA: University of California Press.

Hands, A. R. (1968) *Charities and Social Aid in Greece and Rome*, Ithaca, NY: Cornell University Press.

Hankoff, L. D. (1991) 'Religious Healing in First-century Christianity', *Journal of Psychohistory* 19: 387–407.

Hanks, T. D. (1992) 'Poor', *Anchor Bible Dictionary* 5: 414–424.

Hanson, K. C. (1989) 'The Herodians and Mediterranean Kinship. Part I: Genealogy and Descent', *BTB* 19: 75–84.

Hanson, R. (1980) *Tyrian Influence in the Upper Galilee*, Cambridge: American Schools of Oriental Research.

Hanson, V. D. (1989) *The Western Way of War: Infantry Battle in Ancient Greece*, New York: A. Knopf.

Hare, Douglas R. A. (1967) *The Theme of Jewish Persecution of Christians in the Gospel According to St Matthew*, SBLMS 6, Cambridge: Cambridge University Press.

Harnack, A. (1981) *Militia Christi: The Christian Religion and the Military in the First Three Centuries*, trans. D. McInnes Gracie, Philadelphia: Fortress Press.

Harper, R. F. (1901) *Assyrian and Babylonian Literature: Selected Translations*, New York: Appleton.

Harrington, Daniel (1991) *The Gospel of Matthew*, Collegeville, MN: Michael Glazier/Liturgical Press.

Harris, William V. (1979) *War and Imperialism in Republican Rome*, Oxford: Clarendon Press.

(1989) *Ancient Literacy*, Cambridge, MA and London: Harvard University Press.

Hart, H. St. J. (1952) 'Judaea and Rome: The Official Commentary', *JTS*, n. s. 3: 172 198.

Harvey, A. E. (1985) 'Forty Strokes Save One: Social Aspects of Judaizing and Apostasy', in A. E. Harvey (ed.) *Alternative Approaches to New Testament Study*, London: SPCK, 79 96.

Hatch, E. (1889) *Essays in Biblical Greek*, Oxford: Clarendon Press.

Hauck, Friedrich (1968a) '*Ekballo*', *TDNT* 1: 527 528.

(1968b) '*Ptochos*', *TDNT* 6: 886 887.

Heaton, E. W. (1994) *The School Tradition of the Old Testament*, Bampton Lectures 1994, Oxford and New York: Oxford University Press.

Hefner, R. W. (1993) 'World-building and the Rationaltiy of Conversion', in R. W. Hefner (ed.) *Conversion to Christianity*, Berkeley CA: University of California, 3 44.

Heichelheim, F. M. (1938) 'Part II: Roman Syria', in Tenney Frank (ed.) *An Economic Survey of Ancient Rome*, vol. 4, Baltimore: Johns Hopkins University Press, 121 257.

Heirich, M. (1977) 'Change of Heart: A Test of Some Widely Held Theories about Religious Conversion', *American Journal of Sociology* 83: 653 680.

Hengel, Martin (1966) 'Die Synagogeninschrift von Stobi', *ZNW* 57: 145 183.

(1974) *Judaism and Hellenism*, 2 vols, trans. John Bowden, Philadelphia: Fortress Press.

Hennessey, L. R. (1993) 'Sexuality, Family and the Life of Discipleship: Some Early Christian Perspectives', *Chicago Studies* 32: 19 31.

Herzfeld, M. (1980) 'Honor and Shame: Problems in Comparative Analysis of Moral Systems', *Man* 15: 399 350.

Hill, David (1965) 'DIKAIOI as a Quasi-technical Term', *NTS* 11: 296 302.

(1971) 'The Rejection of Jesus at Nazareth (Luke 4: 16 30)', *NovT* 13: 161 180.

(1976) 'False Prophets and Charismatics: Structure and Interpretation in Mt. 7:15 23', *Biblica* 57: 327 348.

Hill, George Francis (1914) *Catalogue of the Greek Coins of Palestine (Galilee, Samaria, and Judaea)*, London: British Museum

Hill, Michael (1987) 'Sect', *Encyclopedia of Religion* 13: 154 159.

Hirschfeld, Y. and Birger-Calderon, R. (1991) 'Early Roman and Byzantine Estates near Caesarea', *IEJ* 41:81 111.

Hobbs, T. R. (1989a) *A Time for War: A Study of Warfare in the Old Testament*, Wilmington: Glazier.

(1989b) 'Reflections on "The Poor" and the Old Testament', *ExpTim* 100: 291 294.

Hobbs, T. R. and Jackson, P. K. (1991) 'The Enemy in the Psalms', *BTB* 21: 22 29.

Hock, R. (1982) 'The Will of God and Sexual Morality: 1 Thessalonians 4:8 in its Social and Intellectual Context', paper presented at the Annual Meeting of the SBL, New York.

Hoehner, H. (1972) *Herod Antipas*, SNTSMS 17, Cambridge: Cambridge University Press.

Hoekstra, Hidde (1990) *Rembrandt and the Bible: Stories from the Old and New Testament, Illustrated by Rembrandt in Paintings, Etchings and Drawings*, Utrecht: Magna Books.

Hofius, Otfried (1967) *Jesu Tischgemeinschaft mit den Sündern*, Stuttgart: Calwer.

Hoh, J. (1926) 'Der christliche *grammateus* (GK) (Mt 13, 52)', *BZ* 17: 265–269.

Hollenbach, Paul W. (1983) 'Jesus, Demoniacs, and Public Authorities: A Socio-historical Study', *JAAR* 49: 567–588.

—— (1987) 'Defining Rich and Poor Using Social Sciences', *SBLSP*: 50–63

Holmberg, Bengt (1980) *Paul and Power: The Structure of Authority in the Primitive Church as Reflected in the Pauline Epistles*, Philadelphia: Fortress Press.

—— (1990) *Sociology and the New Testament: An Appraisal*, Minneapolis: Fortress Press.

Holmes, A. F. (1976) *War and Christian Ethics*, Grand Rapids: Baker Book House.

Hood, R. T. (1961) 'The Genealogies of Jesus', in A. Wikgren (ed.) *Early Christian Origins: Studies in Honor of H. R. Willoughby*, Chicago: Quadrangle Books.

Hopkins, K. (1978) 'Economic Growth and Towns in Classical Antiquity', in P. Abrams and E. Wrigley (eds) *Towns in Societies: Essays in Economic History and Historical Sociology*, Cambridge: Cambridge University Press, 35–37.

—— (1980) 'Taxes and Trade in the Roman Empire (200 BC–AD 400)', *JRS* 70: 101–125.

Horbury, W. (1985) 'Extirpation and Excommunication', *VT* 35: 13–38.

Horrell, D. G. (1993) 'Converging Ideologies: Berger and Luckmann and the Pastoral Epistles', *JSNT* 50: 85–103.

—— (1994) *The Social Ethos of Pauline Christianity: Interests and Ideology in the Corinthian Correspondence from 1 Corinthians to 1 Clement*, unpublished PhD thesis, Cambridge University.

Horsley, G. H. R. (ed.) (1982) 'Reclining at the Passover Meal', in *New Documents Illustrating Early Christianity*, Macquarie University, Australia: Ancient History Documentary Research Centre, 2: 75.

Horsley, Richard A. (1987) *Jesus and the Spiral of Violence: Popular Jewish Resistance in Roman Palestine*, San Francisco: Harper and Row.

—— (1989a) 'Questions about Redactional Strata and the Social Relations Reflected in Q', *SBLSP*: 186–203.

—— (1989b) *Sociology and the Jesus Movement*, New York: Crossroad.

—— (1991) 'Q and Jesus: Assumptions, Approaches, and Analysis', *Semeia* 55: 175–209.

Horsley, Richard A. and Hanson, John S. (1985) *Bandits, Prophets, and Messiahs: Popular Movements at the Time of Jesus*, Minneapolis: Winston.

Hsu, Francis L. K. (ed.) (1972) *Psychological Anthropology*, Cambridge, MA: Schenkman.

Hummel, Reinhart (1963) *Die Auseinandersetzung zwischen Kirche und Judentum im Matthäus-Evangelium*, Munich: Kaiser Verlag.

Hurd, J. C. (1965) *The Origin of 1 Corinthians*, London: SPCK.

Inglis, B. (1977) *Natural and Supernatural: A History of the Paranormal from Earliest Times to 1914*, London: Hodder and Stoughton.

—— (1989) *A Natural History of Altered States of Mind*, London: Grafton Books.

Jacobs-Malina, Diane (1993) *Beyond Patriarchy: The Images of Family in Jesus*, New York: Paulist Press.

Jahn, O. (1855) cited at *TWNT* 1: 595.

James, Paul (1992) 'Forms of Abstract "Community": From Tribe and Kingdom to Nation and State', *Philosophy of the Social Sciences* 22: 313–336.

Janner, G. (1993) cited in *Sunday Telegraph* 24 Oct.

Jeffreys, Elizabeth, Jeffreys, Michael and Scott, Roger (1986) *The Chronicle of John Malalas*, Melbourne: Australian Association for Byzantine Studies.

Jeremias, Joachim (1931) 'Zöllner und Sünder', *ZNW* 30: 293–300.

—— (1957–1965) *Die Religion in Geschichte und Gegenwart*, 3rd edn, K. Galling (ed.), Tübingen: Mohr (Siebeck).

—— (1963) *The Parables of Jesus*, trans. S. H. Horke, New York: Scribner's.

—— (1966) *The Eucharistic Words of Jesus*, 3rd edn London: SCM Press.

—— (1969) *Jerusalem in the Time of Jesus*, trans. F. H. Cave and C. H. Cave, Philadelphia: Fortress Press.

—— (1971) *New Testament Theology: The Proclamation of Jesus*, New York: Scribner's.
Johannes (1675) *Tractatus de fascinatione novus et singularis*, Nuremberg.
Johnson, Allan Chester, Coleman-Norton, Paul Robinson and Bourne, Frank C. (1961) *Ancient Roman Statutes*, vol. 2, Austin: University of Texas Press.
Johnson, L. T. (1981) *Sharing Possessions*, OBT, Philadelphia: Fortress Press.
Johnson, M. D. (1969) *The Purpose of the Biblical Genealogies with Special Reference to the Setting of the Genealogies of Jesus*, *SNTSMS* 8, Cambridge: Cambridge University Press.
Johnson, Thomas F. (1986) 'Sectarianism and the Johannine Community', paper read at the Society of Biblical Literature annual meeting, Atlanta, Georgia, Nov. 26.
Joubert, Stephan J. (1992) 'Behind the Mask of Rhetoric: 2 Corinthians 8 and 9 and the Intra-textual Relation between Paul and the Corinthians', *Neot* 26: 101–112.
Judge, Edwin A. (1960a) 'The Early Christians as a Scholastic Community', *JRH* 1:4–15, 125–137.
—— (1960b) *The Social Pattern of the Christian Groups in the First Century: Some Prolegomena to the Study of New Testament Ideas of Social Obligation*, London: Tyndale.
—— (1982) *Rank and Status in the World of the Caesars and St Paul*, Christchurch: University of Canterbury.
Jung, C. G. (1976) *The Symbolic Life: Miscellaneous Writings*, Collected Works 18, Princeton, NJ: Princeton University Press.
Kalluveettil, Paul (1982) *Declaration and Covenant: A Comprehensive Review of Covenant Formulae from the Old Testament and the Ancient Near East*, AnBib 88, Rome: Biblical Institute.
Kampen, John (1994) 'The Sectarian Form of the Antitheses within the Social World of the Matthean Community', *Dead Sea Discoveries* 1:338–363.
Karris, Robert J. (1985) *Luke: Artist and Theologian*, Studies in Contemporary Biblical and Theological Problems, New York: Paulist.
—— (1990) *The Gospel According to Luke*, *NJBC*, Englewood Cliffs, NJ: Prentice Hall.
Käsemann, Ernst (1969) 'Sentences of Holy Law in the New Testament', in Ernst Kasemann, *New Testament Questions of Today*, trans. W. J. Montague, Philadelphia: Fortress Press, 66–81.
Kasher, A. (1985) *The Jews in Hellenistic and Roman Egypt: The Struggle for Equal Rights*, Tübingen: J. C. B. Mohr (Paul Siebeck).
Katz, D. and Kahn R. (1966) *The Social Psychology of Organizations*, New York: Wiley.
Kautsky, John H. (1982) *The Politics of Aristocratic Empires*, Chapel Hill, NC: University of North Carolina Press.
Kee, Howard C. (1974) 'The Linguistic Background of Shame in the New Testament', in M. Black and W. A. Smalley (eds) *On Language, Culture and Religion*, Hague: Mouton, 133–148.
—— (1986) *Medicine, Miracle and Magic in New Testament Times*, SNTSMS 55, Cambridge: Cambridge University Press.
—— (1990) 'The Transformation of the Synagogue after 70 CE: Its Import for Early Christianity', *NTS* 36: 1–24.
Kennedy, George A. (1991) *Aristotle, On Rhetoric: A Theory of Civic Discourse*, New York: Oxford University Press.
Kent, J. (1986) *The Unacceptable Face: The Modern Church in the Eyes of the Historian*, London: SCM Press.
Kerr, Graham B. (1978) 'Voluntary Associations in West Africa: "Hidden" Agents of Social Change', in P. Stevens, Jr (ed.) *The Social Sciences and African Development Planning*, Waltham, MA: Crossroads Press, 87–100.
Kerri, J. N. (1976) 'Studying Voluntary Associations as Adaptive Mechanisms: A Review of Anthropological Perspectives', *Current Anthropology* 17: 23–47.
Kiilunen, J. (1991) 'Der nachfolgewillige Schriftgelehrte: Matthäus 8.19–20 im Verständnis des Evangelisten', *NTS* 37: 268–279.

Kilbourne, B. and Richardson, J. T. (1988) 'Paradigm Conflict, Types of Conversion, and Conversion Theories', *Sociological Analysis* 50: 1–21.

Kilgallen, J. J. (1989) 'Provocation' in Lk 4, 23–24', *Biblica* 70/4: 511.

Kilpatrick, G. D. (1950) *The Origins of the Gospel According to St Matthew*, Oxford: Clarendon Press.

Kingsbury, Jack D. (1975) *Matthew: Structure, Christology, and Kingdom*, Minneapolis: Fortress Press.

—— (1978) 'The Verb *Akolouthein* ("to follow") as an Index of Matthew's View of his Community', *JBL* 97: 56–73.

—— (1988) *Matthew as Story*, 2nd edn, Philadelphia: Fortress Press.

—— (1991) 'Conclusion: Analysis of a Conversation', in D. L. Balch (ed.) *Social History of the Matthean Community: Cross-disciplinary Approaches*, Minneapolis: Fortress Press, 259–269.

Kissinger, W. S. (1975) *The Sermon on the Mount: A History of Interpretation and Bibliography*, American Theological Library Association Bibliography Series 3, Metuchen, NJ: Scarecrow Press.

Kitsuse, J. I. (1962) 'Societal Reaction to Deviant Behaviour: Problems of Theory and Method', *Social Problems* 9: 247–256.

Klauck, Hans-Joseph (1992) *Gemeinde zwischen Haus und Stadt: Kirche bei Paulus*, Freiburg: Herder.

Kleijwegt, M. (1994) ' "Voluntarily, But Under Pressure": Voluntarity and Constraint in Greek Municipal Politics', *Mnemosyne* 47: 64–78.

Klijn, A. F. J. (1983) '2 (Syriac Apocalypse of) BARUCH: A New Translation and Introduction', in James H. Charlesworth (ed.) *The Old Testament Pseudepigrapha: Vol. 1 Apocalyptic Literature and Testaments*, London: Darton, Longman and Todd, 615–652.

Kloppenborg, John S. (1986) 'Blessing and Marginality: The "Persecution Beatitude" in Q, Thomas, and Early Christianity', *Forum* 2/3: 36–56.

—— (1987) *The Formation of Q: Trajectories in Ancient Wisdom Collections*, Philadelphia: Fortress Press.

—— (1989) 'The Formation of Q Revisited: A Response to Richard Horsley', SBLSP: 204–215.

—— (1991) 'Literary Convention, Self-Evidence and the Social History of the Q People', *Semeia* 55: 77–102.

Klosinski, Lee E. (1988) *Meals in Mark*, PhD dissertation, Claremont Graduate School.

Knutsson, J. (1977) *Labeling Theory: A Critical Examination*, Stockholm: Scientific Research Group.

Kohler, K. (1901) 'Abba, Father: Title of Spiritual Leader and Saint', *JQR* 13: 567–580.

Kopas, Jane (1986) 'Jesus and Women: Luke's Gospel', *TToday* 42: 192–202.

Kornemann, Ernst (1900) '*Koinon*; Collegium', *PW* 4.1, cols 380–479, suppl. 4, 915ff.; suppl. 5, 453ff.

Kraabel, A. Thomas (1981a) 'Social Systems of Six Diaspora Synagogues', Joseph Gutman (ed.) *Ancient Synagogues: The State of Research*, Chico, CA: Scholars Press, 79–91.

—— (1981b) 'The Disappearance of the "God-Fearers" ', *Numen* 28: 113–126.

—— (1987) 'Unity and Diversity Among Diaspora Synagogues', in Lee I. Levine (ed.) *The Synagogue in Late Antiquity*, Philadelphia, PA: American Schools of Oriental Research, 49–60.

Kraemer, R. S. (1986a) 'Non-literary Evidence for Jewish Women in Rome and Egypt', in M. B. Skinner (ed.) *Rescuing Creusa: New Methodological Approaches to Women in Antiquity*, *Helios* 2, 85–101.

—— (1986b) 'Hellenistic Jewish Women: The Epigraphical Evidence', *SBLSP*: 183–200.

—— (1989) 'Monastic Jewish Women in Greco-Roman Egypt: Philo on the Therapeutrides', *Signs: Journal of Women in Culture and Society* 1: 343–344.

Krentz, Edgar (1987) 'Community and Character: Matthew's Vision of the Church', in Kent Harold Richards (ed.) *SBLSP*: 565–573.

Kroll, W. (1916) '*Iobakchoi*', PW 9, cols 1828–1832.

Kugel, J. S. (1987) 'On Hidden Hatred and Open Reproach: Early Exegesis of Leviticus 19:17', *HTR* 28: 43–61.

Kuper, Adam (1982) 'Lineage Theory: A Critical Retrospective', *Annual Review of Anthropology* 11: 71–95.

—— (ed.) (1992) *Conceptualizing Society*, London and New York: Routledge.

Kürzinger, J. (1978) 'Mann und Frau nach 1 Kor 11, 11f.', *BZ* 22: 270–275.

Lacey, W. K. (1987) 'Patria Potestas', in Beryl Rawson (ed.) *The Family in Ancient Rome: New Perspectives*, Ithaca: Cornell University Press, 121–144.

LaHurd, C. S. (1994) 'Rediscovering the Lost Women in Luke 15', *BTB* 24: 66–75.

Lambek, Michael (1981) *Human Spirits: A Cultural Account of Trance in Mayotte*, New York: Cambridge University Press.

Lapin H. (1992) 'Rabbi', in D. N. Freedman (ed.) *The Anchor Bible Dictionary*, vol. 5, New York: Doubleday, 600–601.

Leach, Edmund (1974) *Dramas, Fields and Metaphors*, Ithaca and London: Cornell University Press.

—— (1976) *Culture and Communication*, Cambridge: Cambridge University Press.

Leeds, Anthony (1979) 'Forms of Urban Integration: Social Urbanization in Comparative Perspective', *Urban Anthropology* 8: 227–247.

Lefkowitz, Mary R. (1981) *Heroines and Hysterics*, London: Duckworth.

Lefkowitz, Mary R. and Fant, Maureen B. (1982) *Women's Life in Greece and Rome*, London: Duckworth.

Lemaire, André (1990) 'The Sage in School and Temple', in J. G. Gammie and L. G. Perdue (eds) *The Sage in Israel and the Ancient Near East*, Winona Lake: Eisenbrauns, 165–181.

—— (1992) 'Writing and Writing Materials', in D. N. Freedman (ed.) *The Anchor Bible Dictionary*, vol. 6, New York: Doubleday, 999–1008.

Lemert, E. M. (1951) *Social Pathology*, New York: McGraw-Hill.

—— (1972) *Human Deviance, Social Problems, and Social Control*, 2nd edn, Englewood Cliffs: Prentice Hall.

Lenski, Gerhard (1984) *Power and Privilege: A Theory of Social Stratification*, Chapel Hill: University of North Carolina Press.

Lenski, Gerhard, and Lenski, Jean (1987) *Human Societies: An Introduction to Macrosociology*, 5th edn, New York: McGraw-Hill.

Lentzen-Deis, Fritzleo (1970) *Die Taufe Jesu nach den Synoptikern: Literarkritische und Gattungsgeschichtliche Untersuchungen*, Frankfurt am Main: Josef Knecht.

Levine, L. I. (ed.) (1992) *The Galilee in Late Antiquity*, New York: Jewish Theological Seminary of America.

Leon, Harry J. (1960) *The Jews of Ancient Rome*, Philadelphia: Jewish Publication Society of America.

Licht, H. (1953) *Sexual Life in Ancient Greece*, New York: Barnes and Noble.

Lightfoot, J. (1823) *Whole Works*, IX, London: Hatchard, 150–151.

Lincoln, Andrew T. (1990) *Ephesians*, WBC 42, Dallas, TEX: Word Books.

Lindars, Barnabas (1961) *New Testament Apologetic*, Philadelphia: Fortress Press.

Lindbeck, George A. (1984) *The Nature of Doctrine: Religion and Theology in a Postliberal Age*, London: SPCK.

von Lips, Hermann (1979) *Glaube – Gemeinde – Amt: Zum Verständnis der Ordination in den Pastoralbriefen*, Göttingen: Vandenhoeck & Ruprecht.

Little, Kenneth (1957) 'The Role of Voluntary Associations in West African Urbanization', *American Anthropologist* 59/4: 579–596.

Lloyd-Jones, H. (1987) 'Ehre und Schande in der griechishen Kultur', *Antike und Abendland* 33:1–28.

Lofland, J. (1969) *Deviance and Identity*, Englewood Cliffs: Prentice Hall.

Lofland, J. and Skonovd, N. (1981) 'Conversion Motifs', *JSSR* 20: 373–385.

Lofland, J. and Stark, R. (1965) 'Becoming a World-saver: A Theory of Conversion to a Deviant Perspective', *American Sociological Review* 30: 862–875.

Lohse, Eduard (1971) *Colossians and Philemon: A Commentary on the Epistle to the Colossians and to Philemon*, trans. William R. Poehlmann and Robert J. Karris, Hermeneia Commentary, Philadelphia, PA: Fortress.

Long, T. F. and Hadden, J. K. (1983) 'Religious Conversion and the Concept of Socialization: Integrating the Brainwashing and the Drift Models', *JSSR* 22: 1–14.

Love, Stuart (1993) 'The Household: A Major Social Component for Gender Analysis in the Gospel of Matthew', *BTB* 23: 21–31.

—— (1994) 'The Place of Women in Public Settings in Matthew's Gospel: A Sociological Inquiry', *BTB* 24: 52–65.

Luck, George (1989) 'Theurgy and Forms of Worship in Neoplatonism', in J. Neusner, E. S. Frerichs and P. V. McCracken Flesher (eds) *Religion, Science and Magic: In Concert and in Conflict*, New York: Oxford University Press, 185–225.

Luz, Ulrich (1983) 'The Disciples in the Gospel According to Matthew', in Graham Stanton (ed.) *The Interpretation of Matthew*, IRT 3. Philadelphia: Fortress Press, 98–128.

—— (1989) *Matthew 1–7. A Commentary*, trans. Wilhelm C. Linss, vol. 1, Minneapolis: Augsburg.

—— (1990) *Das Evangelium nach Matthaus*, vol. 2, Zürich: Benziger/Neukirchen-Vluyn: Neukirchener Verlag.

McCarthy, John D. and Zald, Mayer N. (1987) 'Resource Mobilization and Social Movements: A Partial Theory', in Mayer N. Zald and John D. McCarthy (eds) *Social Movements in an Organizational Society*, New Brunswick: Transactions Books, 15–42.

MacDonald, D. R. (1987) *There is No Male and Female: The Fate of a Dominical Saying in Paul and Gnosticism*, HDR 20, Philadelphia: Fortress Press.

MacDonald, M. Y. (1988) *The Pauline Churches: A Socio-historical Study of Institutionalization in the Pauline and Deutero-Pauline Writings*, SNTSMS 60; Cambridge: Cambridge University Press.

Macfarlane, A. (1985) 'The Root of All Evil', in D. Parkin (ed.) *The Anthropology of Evil*, Oxford: Blackwell, 56–91.

McGuire, Meredith B. (1981) *Religion: The Social Context*, 3rd edn 1992, Belmont, CA: Wadsworth.

Mack, Burton L. (1988a) *A Myth of Innocence: Mark and Christian Origins*, Philadelphia: Fortress Press.

—— (1988b) 'The Kingdom That Didn't Come: A Social History of the Q Tradents', *SBLSP*: 608–635.

—— (1989) 'Elaboration of the Chreia in the Hellenistic School', in Burton L. Mack and Vernon K. Robbins, *Patterns of Persuasion in the Gospels*, Sonoma, CA: Polebridge Press, 31–67.

—— (1990) *Rhetoric and the New Testament*, Minneapolis: Fortress Press.

—— (1993) *The Lost Gospel: The Book of Q and Christian Origins*, San Francisco: Harper.

McKnight, S. (1991) *A Light among the Gentiles*, Minneapolis, IA: Fortress Press.

Maclagan, R. C. (1902) *Evil Eye in the Western Highlands*, London: Nutt.

McMahan, Thomas Craig (1987) *Meals as Type Scenes in the Gospel of Luke*, PhD dissertation, Southern Baptist Theological Seminar.

MacMullen, Ramsey (1974) *Roman Social Relations 50 B.C. to A.D. 284*, New Haven, CN: Yale University Press.

—— (1980) 'Women in Public in the Roman Empire', *Historia* 29: 208–218.

—— (1981) *Paganism in the Roman Empire*, New Haven, CN: Yale University Press.

—— (1984) *Christianizing the Roman Empire*, New Haven, CN: Yale University Press.

McVann, Mark (1991) 'Rituals of Status-transformation in Luke–Acts: The Case of Jesus the Prophet', in J. Neyrey (ed.) *The Social World of Luke–Acts: Models for Interpretation*, Peabody: Hendrickson, 333–360.

Malherbe, Abraham J. (1989) *Paul and the Popular Philosophers*, Minneapolis, MN: Fortress Press.

Malina, Bruce J. (1978) 'What are the Humanities: A Perspective for the Scientific American', in William L. Blizek (ed.) *The Humanities and Public Life*, Lincoln, NE: Pied Publications, 33–47.

—— (1979) 'The Individual and the Community: Personality in the Social World of Early Christianity', *BTB* 9: 126–138.

—— (1981) *The New Testament World*, London: SCM Press.

—— (1983) 'The Social Sciences and Biblical Interpretation', in Norman K. Gottwald (ed.) *The Bible and Liberation: Political and Social Hermeneutics*, Maryknoll, NY: Orbis Books, 11–35.

—— (1985) *The Gospel of John in Sociolinguistic Perspective*, Berkeley, CA: Center for Hermeneutical Studies in Hellenistic and Modern Cutlure.

—— (1986a) 'The Received View and What it Cannot Do: III John and Hospitality', in John. H. Elliott (ed.) *Social-scientific Criticism of the New Testament and its Social World*, Semeia 35, Decatur, GA: Scholars Press, 171–189.

—— (1986b) 'Interpreting the Bible with Anthropology: The Case of the Poor and the Rich', *Listening: Journal for Culture and Religion* 21: 148–159.

—— (1986c) *Christian Origins and Cultural Anthropology: Practical Models for Interpretation*, Atlanta: John Knox.

—— (1986d) 'Religion in the World of Paul', *BTB* 16: 92–101.

—— (1987) 'Wealth and Poverty in the New Testament and its World', *Int* 41: 354–367.

—— (1988a) 'Patron and Client: The Analogy Behind Synoptic Theology', *Forum* 4/1: 2–32.

—— (1988b) 'A Conflict Approach to Mark 7', *Forum* 4: 3–30.

—— (1990) 'Mary – Mediterranean Woman: Mother and Son', *BTB* 20: 54–64.

—— (1991a) 'Conflict in Luke–Acts: Labelling and Deviance Theory', in J. H. Neyrey (ed.) *The Social World of Luke–Acts: Models for Interpretation*, Peabody: Hendrickson, 97–122.

—— (1991b) 'First-century Personality: Dyadic, not Individual', in Jerome H. Neyrey (ed.) *The Social World of Luke–Acts: Models for Interpretation*, Peabody: Hendrickson, 67–96.

—— (1991c) 'Honour and Shame in Luke–Acts: Pivotal Values of the Mediterranean World', in J. Neyrey (ed.) *The Social World of Luke–Acts: Models for Interpretation*, Peabody: Hendrickson, 25–26.

—— (1991d) 'Interpretation: Reading, Abduction, Metaphor', in D. Jobling *et. al.* (eds) *The Bible and the Politics of Exegesis*, Cleveland, OH: Pilgrim Press.

—— (1991e) 'Reading Theory Perspective: Reading Luke–Acts', in Jerome Neyrey (ed.) *The Social World of Luke–Acts: Models for Interpretation*, Peabody: Hendrickson, 1–23.

—— (1992) 'Is there a Circum-Mediterranean Person: Looking for Stereotypes?', *BTB* 11: 66–87.

—— (1993a) *The New Testament World: Insights from Cultural Anthropology*, rev. edn, Louisville: Westminster/John Knox.

—— (1993b) 'Patronage', in Bruce J. Malina and John J. Pilch (eds) *Biblical Social Values and their Meaning: A Handbook*, Peabody: Hendrickson, 133–137.

—— (1993c) *Windows on the World of Jesus: Time Travel to Ancient Judea*. Louisville: Westminster/John Knox.

—— (1994) ' "Let Him Deny Himself" (Mark 8: 34): A Social Psychological Model of Self-Denial', *BTB* 24: 106–119.

Malina, Bruce J. and Neyrey, Jerome H. (1988) *Calling Jesus Names: The Social Value of Labels in Matthew*, Sonoma: Polebridge Press.

—— (1991a) 'Honor and Shame in Luke–Acts: Pivotal Values of the Mediterranean World', in J. H. Neyrey (ed.) *The Social World of Luke–Acts: Models for Interpretation*, Peabody: Hendrickson, 25–65.

—— (1991b) 'First-century Personality: Dyadic, not Individualistic', in J. H. Neyrey (ed.) *The Social World of Luke–Acts: Models for Interpretation*, Peabody: Hendrickson, 67–96.

Malina, Bruce J. and Rohrbaugh, Richard L. (1992) *Social-Science Commentary on the Synoptic Gospels*, Minneapolis: Fortress Press.

Mantel, H. (1976) 'Sanhedrin', in Keith Crim (ed.) *The Interpreter's Dictionary of the Bible*, supp. vol., Nashville: Abingdon, 784–786.

Marcus, G. E. and Fischer, M. M. J. (1986) *Anthropology as Cultural Critique*, Chicago: University of Chicago Press.

Markus, R. A. (1980) 'The Problem of Self-definition: From Sect to Church', in E. P. Sanders (ed.) *Jewish and Christian Self-definition*, vol. 1: *The Shaping of Christianity in the Second and Third Centuries*. Philadelphia: Fortress Press, 1–15.

Marshall, Bruce D. (ed.) (1990) *Theology and Dialogue: Essays in Conversation with George Lindbeck*, Notre Dame, IN: University of Notre Dame Press.

Marshall, I. H. (1978) *The Gospel of Luke: A Commentary on the Greek Text*, Grand Rapids, MI: Eerdmans.

Marshall, P. (1983) 'A Metaphor of Social Shame: Thriambevein', *NT* 25: 302–317.

Martin, Josef (1931) *Symposion: Die Geschichte einer literarischen Form*, Studien zur Geschichte und Kultur des Altertums 17.1–2, Paderborn: F. Schoningh.

Martin, R. P. (1986) *2 Corinthians*, WBC 40, Waco: Word Inc.

Martyn, J. Louis (1978) 'Glimpses into the History of the Johannine Community', in *The Gospel of John in Christian History*, New York: Paulist Press, 90–121.

Marx, K. and Engels, F. (1957) *On Religion*, Moscow: Foreign Languages Publishing House.

Mason, Steve (1992) *Josephus and the New Testament*, Peabody, MA: Hendrickson.

Matthews, Victor H. and Benjamin, Don C. (1991) 'The Stubborn and the Fool', *Bible Today* 29: 222–226.

Mattingly, D. J. (1988) 'Oil for Export? A Comparison of Libyan, Spanish and Tunisian Olive Oil Production in the Roman Empire', *JRA* 1: 33–56.

Mattingly, Harold (1930) *Coins of the Roman Empire in the British Museum, Volume 2 Vespasian to Domitian*, London: British Museum.

Matza, D. (1969) *Becoming Deviant*, Englewood Cliffs, NJ: Prentice Hall.

Mead, G. H. (1934) *Mind, Self and Society*, Chicago: Chicago University Press.

Mealand, David L. (1980) *Poverty and Expectation in the Gospels*, London: SPCK.

Meeks, Wayne A. (1972) 'The Man From Heaven in Johannine Sectarianism', *JBL* 91: 44–72.

—— (1974) 'The Image of the Androgyne: Some Uses of a Symbol in Earliest Christianity', *HR* 13: 165–208.

—— (1975) 'Am I a Jew? Johannine Christianity and Judaism', in J. Neusner (ed.) *Christianity, Judaism and Other Greco-Roman Cults*, vol. 1, SJLA 12, Leiden: Brill, 163–186.

—— (1983a) *The First Urban Christians: The Social World of the Apostle Paul*, New Haven: Yale University Press.

—— (1983b) 'Social Functions of Apocalyptic Language in Pauline Christianity', in D. Hellholm (ed.) *Apocalypticism in the Mediterranean World and the Near East*, Tübingen: Mohr (Siebeck), 687–705.

—— (1985) 'Breaking Away: Three New Testament Pictures of Christianity's Separation from the Jewish Communities', in J. Neusner and E. S. Frerichs (eds) '*To See Ourselves as Others See Us': Christians, Jews, 'Others' in Late Antiquity*, Chico, CA: Scholars Press, 93–115.

—— (1986a) *The Moral World of the First Christians*, Philadelphia: Westminster.

—— (1986b) 'A Hermeneutics of Social Embodiment', *HTR* 79: 1–3, 176–186.

—— (1993) *The Origins of Christian Morality: The First Two Centuries*, New Haven: Yale University Press.

Meeus, X. de (1961) 'Composition de Luc XIV et genre symposiaque', *ETL* 37: 847–870.

Meier, John P. (1992) 'Matthew, Gospel of', in D. N. Freedman (ed.) *The Anchor Bible Dictionary*, vol. 4. New York: Doubleday, 622–641.

Meshorer, Y. (1967) *Jewish Coins of the Second Temple Period*, Tel Aviv: Am Hassefer.

Messick, D. M. and Mackie, D. M. (1989) 'Intergroup Relations', *Annual Review of Psychology* 40: 45–81.

Meyers, Eric M. (1986) 'Sepphoris, Ornament of all Galilee', *BA* 49: 4–19.

—— (1992) 'Roman Sepphoris in Light of New Archaeological Evidence and Recent Research', in L. I. Levine (ed.) *The Galilee in Late Antiquity*, New York: Jewish Theological Seminary of America, 321–338.

Meyers, Eric M. and Strange, James F. (1981) *Archaeology, the Rabbis, and Early Christianity*, Nashville: Abingdon Press.

Meyers, Eric M., Strange, James and Groh, D. (1978) 'The Meiron Excavation Project: Archaeological Survey in Galilee and Golan, 1976', *BASOR* 230: 1–24.

Michaelis, W. (1964) 'Horao', *TDNT* 5: 325–382.

Michalson, Gordon E. (1988) 'The Response to Lindbeck', *Modern Theology* 4: 107–120.

Michel, O. (1967) '*Miseo*', *TDNT* 4: 683–694.

Milgrom, N. (ed.) (1986) *Stress and Coping in Time of War*, New York: Bruner and Mazel.

Millard, Alan R. (1985) 'An Assessment of the Evidence for Writing in Ancient Israel (and Responses)', in *Biblical Archaeology Today: Proceedings of the International Congress on Biblical Archaeology*, Jerusalem: Israel Exploration Society and American Schools of Oriental Research, 301–370.

Miller, Donald E. (1979) 'Sectarianism and Secularization: The Work of Bryan Wilson', *RSR* 5: 161–174.

Mitchell, M. (1989) 'Concerning *peri de* in 1 Corinthians', *NovT* 31: 229–256.

Moessner, David P. (1989) *Lord of the Banquet: The Literary and Theological Significance of the Lukan Travel Narrative*, Minneapolis: Fortress Press.

—— (1983) 'Luke 9:1–50: Luke's Preview of the Journey of the Prophet Like Moses of Deuteronomy', *JBL* 102: 575–605.

Moir, Alfred (1982) *Caravaggio*, New York: Harry N. Abrams.

Moreau, H. I. (1956) *A History of Education in Antiquity*, trans. George Lamb, New York: Sheed and Ward.

Moreland, Richard L. and Levine, John M. (1988) 'Group Dynamics Over Time: Development and Socialization in Small Groups', in J. E. McGrath (ed.) *The Social Psychology of Time: New Perspectives*, Newbury Park: Sage Publications, 151–181.

Morgan, Robert and Barton, John (1988) 'Theology and the Social Sciences', in *Biblical Interpretation*, Oxford University Press, 133–166.

Morgenthaler, R. (1958) *Statistik des neutestamentliches Wortschatzes*, Zürich: Gotthelf Verlag.

Moxnes, Halvor (1988) *The Economy of the Kingdom: Social Conflict and Economic Relations in Luke's Gospel*, Philadelphia: Fortress Press.

—— (1991) 'Patron–Client Relations and the New Community in Luke–Acts', in Jerome Neyrey (ed.) *The Social World of Luke–Acts: Models for Interpretation*, Peabody: Hendrickson, 241–268.

Munck, J. (1959) *Paul and the Salvation of Mankind*, London: SCM Press.

Murdock, G. P. (1980) *Theories of Illness*, Pittsburgh: University of Pittsburgh Press.

Murphy, Frederick J. (1987) 'The Temple in the Syriac *Apocalypse of Baruch*', *JBL* 106: 671–683.

Murphy-O'Connor, Jerome (1980) 'Sex and Logic in 1 Corinthians 11:2–16', *CBQ* 42: 482–500.

—— (1983) *St Paul's Corinth: Texts and Archaeology*, Wilmington: Michael Glazier.

—— (1987) 'What Really Happened at the Transfiguration?', *BR* 3: 8–21.

Murray, Robert (1985) 'Disaffected Judaism and Early Christianity: Some Predisposing Factors', in Jacob Neusner and E. Frerichs (eds) *'To See Ourselves as Others See Us': Christians, Jews, 'Others' in Later Antiquity*, Chico, CA: Scholars Press, 263–281.

Mussner, F. (1975) 'Das Wesen des Christentums ist *sunesthiein*', in Heribert Bossman and Joseph Ratzinger (eds) *Mysterium Der Gnade: Festschrift f. Johann Auerus*, Regensburg: Pustet.

Navone, John (1979) *Themes of St Luke*, Rome: Gregorian University.

Neusner, Jacob (1960) 'The Fellowship (*Haburah*) in the Second Jewish Commonwealth', *HTR* 53/2: 125–142.

—— (1978) 'From Scripture to Mishnah: The Origins of Tractate Niddah', *JJS* 29: 135–148.

—— (1979a) 'Thematic or Systemic Description: The Case of Mishnah's Division of Women', in Jacob Neusner, *Method and Meaning in Ancient Judaism*, Missoula, MT: Scholars Press.

—— (1979b) *The Tosefta: The Order of Women*, New York: Ktav.

—— (1980) *A History of the Mishnaic Law of Women*, Leiden: E. J. Brill.

Neusner, J. and Frerichs, E. S. (eds) (1985) *'To See Ourselves as Others See Us': Christians, Jews, 'Others' in Late Antiquity*, Chico, CA: Scholars Press.

Neusner, Jacob, Frerichs, E. S. and McCracken Flesher, P. V. (eds) (1989) *Religion, Science and Magic: In Concert and in Conflict*, New York: Oxford University Press.

Neyrey, Jerome. H. (1985) *The Passion According to Luke: A Redaction Study of Luke's Soteriology*, New York: Paulist.

—— (1986) 'The Idea of Purity in Mark's Gospel', in John H. Elliott (ed.) *Social-scientific Criticism of the New Testament and its Social World*, Semeia 35, Decatur, GA: Scholars Press, 91–128.

—— (1988a) *An Ideology of Revolt: John's Christology in Social-Science Perspective*, Philadelphia: Fortress Press.

—— (1988b) 'A Symbolic Approach to Mark 7', *Forum*, 4: 63–91.

—— (1990) *Paul in Other Words: A Cultural Reading of his Letters*, Louisville: Westminster/John Knox Press.

—— (1991a) (ed.) *The Social World of Luke–Acts: Models for Interpretation*, Peabody: Hendrickson.

—— (1991b) 'Ceremonies in Luke–Acts: The Case of Meals and Table Fellowship', in J. H. Neyrey (ed.) *The Social World of Luke–Acts: Models for Interpretation*, Peabody: Hendrickson, 361–387.

—— (1991c) 'The Symbolic Universe of Luke–Acts: "They Turn the World Upside Down" ', in J. H. Neyrey (ed.) *The Social World of Luke–Acts: Models for Interpretation*, Peabody: Hendrickson, 271–304.

—— (1993a) 'Clothing', in J. Pilch and B. Malina (eds) *Biblical Social Values and their Meanings*, Peabody: Hendrickson, 20–25.

—— (1993b) 'Nudity', in J. Pilch and B. Malina (eds) *Biblical Social Values and their Meanings*, Peabody: Hendrickson, 119–125.

—— (1993c) *2 Peter, Jude: A New Translation with Introduction and Commentary*, Anchor Bible 37C, New York: Doubleday.

—— (1994) 'What's Wrong With This Picture? John 4: Cultural Stereotypes of Women, Public and Private Space', *BTB* 24: 77–91.

Nickelsburg, George, and Stone, Michael (1983) *Faith and Piety in Early Judaism: Texts and Documents*, Philadelphia: Fortress Press.

Niebuhr, H. Richard (1928) *The Social Sources of Denominationalism*, New York: Henry Holt.

Nisbet, R. A. (1953) *The Quest for Community*, New York: Oxford University Press.

—— (1991) 'The Countryside in Luke–Acts', in J. H. Neyrey (ed.) *The Social World of Luke–Acts: Models for Interpretation*, Peabody: Hendrickson, 151–179.

Nissen J. (1982) 'Den urkristne daab som Kirche-sociologisk faktor', in S. Pedersen (ed.) *Daaben i Ny Testamente*, Aarhus: Aros, 202–229.

Nock, A. D. (1924) 'The Historical Importance of Cult Associations', *Classical Review* 38: 105–109.

—— (1933) *Conversion*, New York: Oxford University Press.

Nun, M. (1988) *Ancient Anchorages and Harbours around the Sea of Galilee*, Kibbuz Ein Gev: Kinnereth Sailing.

Oakman, Douglas E. (1986) *Jesus and the Economic Questions of His Day*, Lewiston, NY: Edwin Mellen Press.

—— (1991) 'The Countryside in Luke–Acts', in J. H. Neyrey (ed.) *The Social World of Luke–Acts: Models for Interpretation*, Peabody: Hendrickson.

Obeyesekere, G. (1977) 'Psychocultural Exegesis of a Case of Spirit Possession in Sri Lanka', in V. Crapanzano and V. Garrison (eds) *Case Studies in Spirit Possession*, New York: Wiley and Sons.

O'Brien, P. T. (1982) *Colossians, Philemon*, WBC 44, Milton Keynes: Word Books.

O'Dea, Thomas F. (1968) 'Sects and Cults', in D. L. Sills (ed.) *International Encyclopedia of the Social Sciences*, vol. 14, New York: Macmillan, 130–136.

O'Fearghail, Fearghus (1985) 'Rejection at Nazareth: Lk 4:22', *ZNW* 75/1–2: 60–72.

Oliver, P. E. (1993) 'Formal Models of Collective Action', *Annual Review of Sociology* 19: 271–300.

Orton, David E. (1989) *The Understanding Scribe: Matthew and the Apocalyptic Ideal*, JSNTSupp 25, Sheffield: JSOT Press.

Osborne, R. (1991) 'Pride and Prejudice, Sense and Subsistence: Exchange and Society in the Greek City', in J. Rich and A. Wallace-Hadrill (eds) *City and Country in the Ancient World*, London and New York: Routledge, 119–146.

Overman, A. J: (1988) 'Who were the First Urban Christians? Urbanisation in Galilee in the First Century', in D. Lull (ed.) *SBLSP*: 160–168.

—— (1990) *Matthew's Gospel and Formative Judaism: The Social World of the Matthean Community*, Minneapolis: Fortress Press.

Park, Robert E. (1928) 'Human Migration and the Marginal Man', *American Journal of Sociology* 33: 892.

—— (1931) 'Personality and Cultural Conflict', *Publications of the American Sociological Society* 25: 95–110.

Parrucci, D. J. (1968) 'Religious Conversion: A Theory of Deviant Behavior', *Sociological Analysis* 29: 144–154.

Parsons, Talcott (1960) *Structure and Process in Modern Societies*, New York: Free Press.

Parvey, C. F. (1974) 'The Theology and Leadership of Women in the New Testament', in Rosemary R. Reuther (ed.) *Religion and Sexism: Images of Woman in the Jewish and Christian Traditions*, New York: Simon and Schuster, 117–149.

Patai, Raphael (1983) *The Arab Mind*, New York: Charles Scribner's Sons.

Pax, Elpidius Wolfgang (1955) *EPIPHANEIA: Ein religionsgeschichtlicher Beitrag zur biblischen Theologie*, Munich: Karl Zink Verlag.

Payer, L. (1990) *Medicine and Culture*, London: Gollancz.

Peacock, D. P. S. and Williams, D. F. (1986) *Amphorae and the Roman Economy*, London and New York: Longman.

Peacock, J. L. (1986) *The Anthropological Lens: Harsh Light, Soft Focus*, Cambridge: Cambridge Universigy Press.

Pelling, Christopher (1990) 'Childhood and Personality in Greek Biography', in C. Pelling (ed.) *Characterization and Individuality in Greek Literature*, Oxford: Clarendon Press, 213–244.

Peristiany, J. G. (1966) *Honor and Shame: The Values of Mediterranean Society*, Chicago: Chicago University Press.

Peristiany, J. G. and Pitt-Rivers, Julian (1992) *Honor and Grace in Anthropology*, Cambridge: Cambridge University Press.

Perkins, J. (1992) 'The "Self" as Sufferer', *HTR* 85: 245–272.

Perkins, Pheme (1991) 'Gender Analysis: A Response to Antoinette Clark Wire', in David L. Balch (ed.) *Social History of the Matthean Community*, Minneapolis: Fortress Press, 122–126.

Perrin, Norman (1967) *Rediscovering the Teaching of Jesus*, New York: Harper and Row.

Perrow, C. (1961) 'The Analysis of Goals in Complex Organizations', *American Sociological Review* 26: 854–866.

Peters, Lawrence and Price-Williams, David (1983) 'A Phenomenological View of Trance', *Transcultural Psychiatric Research Review* 20: 5–39.

Petersen, Norman R. (1985) *Rediscovering Paul: Philemon and the Sociology of Paul's Narrative World*, Philadelphia: Fortress Press.

Pfisterer Darr, K. (1994) 'Two Unifying Female Images in the Book of Isaiah', in L. M. Hopfet (ed.) *Uncovering Ancient Stones: Essays in Memory of H. Neil Richardson*, Winona Lake: Eisenbrauns, 17–30.

Pfohl, S. J. (1985) *Images of Deviance and Social Control: A Sociological History*, New York: McGraw-Hill.

Pfuhl, Edwin H. (1980) *The Deviance Process*, New York: Van Nostrand Reinhold.

Phillips, D. Z. (1988) 'Lindbeck's Audience', *Modern Theology* 4: 133–154.

Pilch, John J. (1988) 'A Structural Analysis of Mark 7', *Forum* 4/3: 31–62.

—— (1991) *Introducing the Cultural Context of the New Testament*, New York and Mahwah: Paulist Press.

—— (1993a) 'Visions in Revelation and Alternate Consciousness: A Perspective from Cultural Anthropology', *Listening: Journal of Religion and Culture* 28: 231–244.

—— (1993b) ' "Beat his Ribs While he is Young" (Sir 30:12): A Window on the Mediterranean World', *BTB* 23: 101–113.

Pilch, John J. and Malina, Bruce J. (eds) (1993) *Biblical Social Values and their Meaning: A Handbook*, Peabody: Hendrickson.

Pilgrim, W. E. (1981) *Good News to the Poor*, Minneapolis: Augsburg.

Pitt-Rivers, Julian (1968) 'Pseudo-Kinship', in D. L. Sills (ed.) *International Encyclopedia of the Social Sciences*, vol. 8, New York: Macmillan, 408–413.

—— (1977) *The Fate of Shechem or the Politics of Sex: Essays in the Anthropology of the Mediterranean*, Cambridge Studies in Social Anthropology 19, Cambridge: Cambridge University Press.

Plank, K. A. (1988) *Paul and the Irony of Affliction*, Atlanta: Scholars Press.

Plevnik, Joseph (1993) 'Honor/Shame', in John J. Pilch and Bruce J. Malina (eds) *Biblical Social Values and their Meaning: A Handbook*, Peabody: Hendrickson, 95–104.

Plummer, A. (1903) *The Gospel According to St Luke*, ICC, New York: Scribner.

Pokorny, P. (1974) 'The Temptation Stories and their Intention', *NTS* 20: 115–127.

Pomeroy, S. (1975) *Goddesses, Whores, Wives and Slaves: Women in Classical Antiquity*, New York: Schocken Books.

Praet, Danny (1992–1993) 'Explaining the Christianization of the Roman Empire: Older Theories and Recent Developments', *Sacris Erudiri* 33: 5–119.

Qedar, S. (1986–1987) 'Two Lead Weights of Herod Antipas and Agrippa II and the Early History of Tiberias', *Israel Numismatic Journal* 9: 29–35.

Rabinow, Paul (ed.) (1986) *The Foucault Reader: An Introduction to Foucault's Thought*, London: Penguin.

Räisänen, H. (1985) 'Galatians 2:16 and Paul's Break with Judaism', *NTS* 31: 543–553.

Rambo, L. R. (1993) *Understanding Religious Conversion*, New Haven: Yale University Press.

Ramsey, Arthur Michael (1949) *The Glory of God and the Transfiguration of Christ*, London: Longmans, Green and Co.

Rathbone, D. (1991) *Economic Rationalism and Rural Society in Third-century A.D. Egypt: The Heroninos Archive and the Appianus Estate*, Cambridge: Cambridge University Press.

Rawson, Beryl (1987) 'The Roman Family', in Beryl Rawson (ed.) *The Family in Ancient Rome: New Perspectives*, Ithaca: Cornell University Press, 1–57.

—— (1991) (ed.) *Marriage, Divorce and Children in Ancient Rome*, Oxford: Clarendon Press.

Raynor, J. and Meshorer, Y. (1988) *The Coins of Ancient Meiron*, Winona Lake: Eisenbrauns and American Schools of Oriental Research.

Reicke, B. (1973) 'Jesus in Nazareth: Lk 4:16–30', in H. Balz and S. Schulz (eds) *Das Wort und die Wörter: Festscrift G. Friedrich*, Stuttgart: Kohlhammer.

Reid, Barbara P. (1993) *The Transfiguration: A Source- and Redaction-critical Study of Luke 9:28–26*, Cahiers de la Revue Biblique 32. Paris: Gabaldas.

Remus, H. E. (1982) 'Sociology of Knowledge and the Study of Early Christianity' *Studies in Religion* 11: 45–56.

Rensberger, David (1988) *Johannine Faith and Liberating Community*, Philadelphia: Westminster.

Rheubottom, D. (1985) 'The Seed of Evil Within', in D. Parkin (ed.) *The Anthropology of Evil*, Oxford: Blackwell, ch. 5.

Rich, J. and Wallace-Hadrill, A. (eds) (1991) *City and Country in the Ancient World*, London and New York: Routledge.

Riches, John K. (1991) 'Apocalyptic: Strangely Relevant', in William Horbury (ed.) *Templum Amicitiae: Essays on the Second Temple Presented to Ernst Bammel*, JSNTSup 48, Sheffield: Sheffield Academic Press, 237–263.

Richlin, A. (1981) 'Sources on Adultery at Rome', in H. P. Foley (ed.) *Reflections of Women in Antiquity*, New York: Gordon and Breach Science Publishers, 379–404.

Rieu, E. V. (1950) *Homer: Iliad*, Harmondsworth: Penguin Books.

Robbins, Vernon K. (1985) 'Pragmatic Relations as a Criterion for Authentic Sayings', *Forum* 1/3: 35–63.

—— (1991) 'The Social Location of the Implied Author of Luke–Acts', in J. H. Neyrey (ed.) *The Social World of Luke–Acts: Models for Interpretation*, Peabody: Hendrickson, 305–332.

—— (1992) *Jesus the Teacher: A Socio-rhetorical Interpretation of Mark*, Minneapolis: Fortress Press.

—— (1993) 'Rhetoric and Culture: Exploring Types of Cultural Rhetoric in a Text', in Stanley E. Porter and Thomas H. Olbricht (eds) *Rhetoric and the New Testament: Essays from the 1992 Heidelberg Conference*, Sheffield: Sheffield Academic Press.

—— (1994) 'Socio-rhetorical Criticism: Mary, Elizabeth, and the Magnificat as a Test Case', in Elizabeth Struthers Malbon and Edgar V. McKnight (eds) *The New Literary Criticism and the New Testament*, JSNTSup 109, Sheffield: Sheffield Academic Press, 164–209.

Robertson, D. B. (ed.) (1966) *Voluntary Associations: A Study of Groups in Free Societies: Essays in Honour of James Luther Adams*, Richmond: John Knox.

Rock, P. (1973) *Deviant Behaviour*, London: Hutchinson and Co.

Rohrbaugh, Richard L. (1991) 'The Pre-industrial City in Luke–Acts', in J. H. Neyrey (ed.) *The Social World of Luke–Acts: Models for Interpretation*, Peabody: Hendrickson, 125–149.

Rolfe, E. N. and Ingleby, H. (1888) *Naples in 1888*, London: Trubner.

Rolfe, J. C. (1927) *The Attic Nights of Aulus Gellius*, Loeb edn, vol. 1, Cambridge MA and London: Harvard University Press.

Rosaldo, Michael Z. and Lamphere, Louise (eds) (1974) *Women, Culture, and Society*, Stanford: Stanford University Press.

Ross, Robert and Staines, Graham L. (1972) 'The Politics of Analyzing Social Problems', *Social Problems* 20: 18–40.

Rostovtzeff, M. (1957) *Economic and Social History of the Roman Empire*, 2 vols, Oxford: Clarendon Press.

Rouselle, A. (1988) *Porneia: On Desire and the Body in Antiquity*, Oxford: Basil Blackwell.

Rowland, Christopher (1985) *Christian Origins: An Account of the Setting and Character of the Most Important Messianic Sect of Judaism*, London: SPCK.

Rudolf, Kurt (1979a) 'Wesen und Struktur der Sekte: Bemerkungen zum Stand der Diskussion in Religionswissenschaft und Religionssoziologie', *Kairos* 21: 241–254.

—— (1979b) 'Gnosis: Weltreligion oder Sekte (Zur Problematik sachgemässer Terminologie in der Religionswissenschaft)', *Kairos* 21: 255–263.

Ryan, Rosalie (1985) 'The Women from Galilee and Discipleship in Luke', *BTB* 15: 56–59.

Safrai, Z. (1994) *The Economy of Ancient Palestine*, London: Routledge.

Sage, Evan T. (1935) *Livy: Books XXXV–XXXVI*, Loeb edn, London and Cambridge, MA: Heinemann and Harvard University Press.

Saldarini, Anthony J. (1988) *Pharisees, Scribes, and Sadducees in Palestinian Society: A Sociological Approach*, Wilmington, DE: Michael Glazier.

—— (1991) 'The Gospel of Matthew and Jewish–Christian Conflict', in David L. Balch (ed.) *Social History of the Matthean Community*, Minneapolis: Fortress Press, 38–61.

—— (1992a) 'Delegitimation of Leaders in Matthew 23', *CBQ* 54: 659–680.

—— (1992b) 'Pharisees', in D. N. Freedman (ed.) *The Anchor Bible Dictionary*, vol. 5, New York: Doubleday, 289–303.

—— (1994) *Matthew's Christian–Jewish Community*, Chicago: University of Chicago Press.

Saler, Benson (1977) 'Supernatural as a Western Category', *Ethos* 5: 31–53.

Saller, Richard (1990) 'Patronage and Friendship in Early Imperial Rome: Drawing the Distinction', in A. Wallace-Hadrill (ed.) *Patronage in Ancient Society*, London: Routledge, 49–62.

Sanders, H. A. (1913) 'The Genealogies of Jesus', *JBL* 32: 184–193.

Sanders, James A. (1974) 'The Ethic of Election in Luke's Great Banquet Parable', in J. L. Crenshaw and J. T. Willis (eds) *Essays in Old Testament Ethics: J. Philip Hyatt, In Memoriam*, New York: Ktav, 247–271.

Sanders, J. T. (1993) *Schismatics, Sectarians, Dissidents, Deviants: The First One Hundred Years of Jewish–Christian Relations*, London: SCM Press.

Schalit, A. (1969) *König Herodes: der Mann und sein Werk*, Berlin: Walter de Gruyter and Co.

Schaps, D. (1977) 'The Women Least Mentioned: Etiquette and Women's Names', *Classical Quarterly* 27: 323–330.

Schiffman, Lawrence H. (1983) *Sectarian Law in the Dead Sea Scrolls*, Chico, CA: Scholars Press.

Schlier, Heinrich (1964) 'Haireomai etc', *TDNT* 1: 180–186.

Schmidt, K. L. (1967) 'Aphorizô', *TDNT* 5: 454–455.

Schneider, J. (1968) 'Oneidismos', *TDNT* 5: 238–242.

Schöttgen, C. (1733) *Horae Hebraicae et Talmudicae*, Dresden and Leipzig: Hekelius.

Schottroff, L. and Stegemann, W. (1986) *Jesus and the Hope of the Poor*, Maryknoll, NY: Orbis Books.

Schrage, W. (1974–1975) 'Zur Ethik der neutestamentlichen Haustafeln', *NTS* 21: 1–22.

Schulz, Fritz (1992) *Classical Roman Law*, Aalen: Scientia Verlag.

Schur, E. M. (1971) *Labeling Deviant Behaviour: Its Sociological Implications*, New York: Harper and Row.

—— (1980) *The Politics of Deviance: Stigma Contests and the Uses of Power*, Englewood Cliffs: Prentice Hall.

Schürer, Emil, Vermes, Geza, Millar, Fergus and Black, Matthew (1979) *The History of the Jewish People in the Age of Christ (175 B.C.–A.D. 135)*, vol. 2, Edinburgh: T. and T. Clark.

Schutz, A. and Luckmann, T. (1974) *The Structures of the Life-world*, London: Heinemann.

Schwartz, Gary (1970) *Sect Ideologies and Social Status*, Chicago: University of Chicago Press.

Schweizer, E. (1970) 'Observance of the Law and Charismatic Activity in Matthew', *NTS* 16: 213–230.

—— (1974a) 'The "Matthaean" Church', *NTS* 20: 216.

—— (1974b) *Matthäus and seine Gemeinde*, SBS 71, Stuttgart: Katholisches Bibelwerk Verlag.

—— (1975) *The Good News According to Matthew*, trans. D. E. Green, Atlanta: John Knox Press.

—— (1982) *The Letter to the Colossians: A Commentary*, trans. A. Chester, London: SPCK.

Scroggs, R. (1972) 'Paul and the Eschatological Woman', *JAAR* 40: 283–303.

—— (1975) 'The Earliest Christian Communities as Sectarian Movement', in J. Neusner (ed.) *Christianity, Judaism and Other Greco-Roman Cults*, Part 2: *Early Christianity*, Leiden: E. J. Brill, 1–23.

Seethaler, P. (1972) 'Eine kleine Bermerkung zu den Stammbäumen Jesu nach Matthäus und Lukas', *BZ* 16: 256–257.

Segal, A. F. (1990) *Paul the Convert: The Apostolate and Apostasy of Saul the Pharisee*, New Haven: Yale University Press.

Seland, Torrey (1987) 'Jesus as a Faction Leader: On the Exit of the Category Sect', in P. W. Bøckman and R. E. Kristiansen (eds) *Context*, Trondheim: TAPIR, 197–211.

Seligmann, S. (1910) *Der Böse Blick und Verwandtes: Ein Beitrag zur Geschichte des Aberglaubens alter Zeiten und Völker*, 2 vols, Berlin: Hermann Barsdorf.

Seltman, C. T. (ed.) (1939) *The Cambridge Ancient History, Volume of Plates, 5* Cambridge: Cambridge University Press.

Setzer, Claudia J. (1992) 'Rulers of the Synagogue', in D. N. Freedman (ed.) *The Anchor Bible Dictionary*, vol. 5, New York: Doubleday, 841–842.

Siker, Jeffrey S. (1992) 'First to the Gentiles': A Literary Analysis of Luke 4:16–30', *JBL* 111/1: 73–90.

Simmons, J. (1986) *Winning Wars: The Spiritual Dimension of the Military Art*, New York: University Press of America.

Simon, Marcel (1967) *Jewish Sects at the Time of Jesus*, Philadelphia: Fortress Press.

Skehan, Patrick W. and DiLella, Alexander A. (1987) *The Wisdom of Ben Sira*, Anchor Bible, New York: Doubleday.

Smallwood, E. Mary (1976) *The Jews Under Roman Rule: From Pompey to Diocletian*, Leiden: E. J. Brill.

Smith, Dennis E. (1980) *Social Obligation in the Context of Communal Meals*, ThD dissertation, Harvard University.

—— (1987) 'Table Fellowship as a Literary Motif in the Gospel of Luke', *JBL* 106: 613–638.

Smith, Jonathan Z. (1976) 'A Pearl of Great Price and a Cargo of Yams: A Study in Situational Incongruity', *HR* 16: 1–19.

Smith, Morton (1951) *Tannaitic Parallels to the Gospels*, JBL Monograph 6. Philadelphia: Society of Biblical Literature.

—— (1956) 'Palestinian Judaism in the First Century', in Mosher Davis (ed.) *Israel: Its Role in Civilization*, New York: Jewish Theological Seminary of America, 67–81.

Smyth-Florentin, F. (1973) 'Jésu, le Fils du Père, vainqueur de Satan: Mt 4,1–11; Mc 1,12–15; Lc 4,1–13', *Assemblées du Seigneur* 14: 56–75.

Snow, D. A. and Machalek, R. (1983) 'The Convert as a Social Type', in R. Collins (ed.) *Sociological Theory 1983*, San Francisco: Jossey Bass, 259–289.

von Soden, H. F. (1964) 'Adelphos, etc.', *TDNT* 1: 144–146.

Soskice, Janet Martin (1985) *Metaphor and Religious Language*, Oxford: Clarendon Press.

Spilka, B., Shaver, P. and Kirkpatrick, L. A. (1985) 'A General Attribution Theory for the Psychology of Religion', *JSSR* 24: 1–20.

Staden, Piet Van (1991) *Compassion – the Essence of Life: A Social-scientific Study of the Religious Symbolic Universe Reflected in the Ideology/Theology of Luke*, Hervormde Teologiese Studies Supplementum 4, Pretoria: University of Pretoria.

Stanley, John E. (1986) 'The Apocalypse and Contemporary Sect Analysis', in H. Richards (ed.) *SBLSP*: 412–421.

Stanton, Graham N. (1977) '5 Ezra and Matthean Christianity in the Second Century', *JTS* 28: 67–83.

—— (1985) 'The Origin and Purpose of Matthew's Gospel: Matthean Scholarship from 1945–1980', *ANRW* II.25/3: 1889–1951.

—— (1992a) 'The Communities of Matthew', *Int* 46: 379–391.

—— (1992b) *A Gospel for a New People: Studies in Matthew*, Edinburgh: T. and T. Clark.

Staples, C. L. and Mauss, A. (1987) 'Conversion or Commitment? A Reassessment to the Snow and Machalek Approach to the Study of Conversion', *JSSR* 26: 133–147.

Stark, Rodney (1986) 'The Class Basis of Early Christianity: Inferences from a Sociological Model', *Sociological Analysis* 47: 216–25.

Stark, Rodney and Bainbridge, William Sims (1985) *The Future of Religion: Secularization, Revival and Cult Formation*, Berkeley: University of California Press.

—— (1987) *A Theory of Religion*, Toronto Studies in Religion 2, New York: Peter Lang.

Stark, Werner (1967) *The Sociology of Religion: A Study of Christendom*, vol. 2: *Sectarian Religion*, London: Routledge and Kegan Paul.

Ste. Croix, G. E. M. de (1975) 'Early Christian Attitudes to Property and Slavery', in D. Baker (ed.) *Studies in Church History*, vol. 12: *Church, Society and Politics*, Oxford: Blackwell, 1–38.

—— (1981) *The Class Struggle in the Ancient Greek World: From the Archaic Age to the Arab Conquests*, London: Duckworth.

Steele, E. Springer III (1981) *Jesus' Table-fellowship with Pharisees: An Editorial Analysis of Luke 7:36–50 (sic); 11:37–54; and 14:1–24*, PhD dissertation, Notre Dame.

—— (1984) 'Luke 11:37–54: A Modified Hellenistic Symposium?', *JBL* 103/3: 379–394.

Stegemann, Wolfgang (1991) *Zwischen Synagoge und Obrigkeit: Zur historischen Situation der lukanischen Christen*, FRLANT 152, Göttingen: Vandenhoeck und Ruprecht.

Stegner, W. R. (1990) 'The Temptation Narrative: A Study in the Use of Scripture by Early Jewish Christians' *Biblical Research* 35: 5–17.

Stein, S. (1957) 'The Influence of Symposia Literature on the Literary Form of the Pesah Haggadah', *JJS* 8: 13–44.

Stein, Robert H. (1976) 'Is the Transfiguration (Mark 9:2–8) a Misplaced Resurrection Account?', *JBL* 95: 79–95.

Stendahl, Krister (1968) *The School of St Matthew and its Use of the Old Testament*, 2nd edn, Philadelphia: Fortress Press (first published 1954).

Sterling, G. E. (1992) *Historiography and Self-definition: Josephus, Luke–Acts and Apologetic Historiography*, Leiden: E. J. Brill.

Stern, M. (1974) 'The Reign of Herod and the Herodian Dynasty', in S. Safrai and M. Stern (eds) *The Jewish People in the First Century*, CRINT I/i, Assen: van Gorcum.

Stone, Michael Edward (1981) 'Reactions to the Destruction of the Second Temple', *JJS* 12:195–204.

—— (1990) *Fourth Ezra: A Commentary on the Book of Fourth Ezra*. Minneapolis: Fortress Press.

Stonequist, E. V. (1937) *The Marginal Man*, New York: Charles Scribner's Sons.

Story, W. W. (1877) *Castle St Angelo and the Evil Eye*, London: Chapman and Hall.

Strack, H. and Billerbeck, P. (1969) *Kommentar zum Neuen Testament aus Talmud und Midrasch*, 4 vols, Munich: C. H. Beck'sche Verlagsbuchhandlung.

Strange, J. (1992) 'Some Implications of Archeology for New Testament Studies', in J. Charlesworth and W. Weaver (eds) *What has Archaeology to do with Faith?*, Philadelphia: Trinity Press International, 23–59.

Straus, R. A. (1979) 'Religious Conversion as a Personal and Collective Accomplishment', *Sociological Analysis* 40: 158–65.

Strecker, Georg (1966) *Der Weg der Gerechtigkeit: Untersuchung zur Theologie des Matthäusevangelium*, Göttingen: Vandenhoeck and Ruprecht.

—— (1970) 'Die Makarismen der Bergpredigt', *NTS* 17: 255–275.

Suggs, M. Jack (1970) *Wisdom, Christology, and Law in Matthew's Gospel*, Cambridge MA: Harvard University Press.

Swanston, H. (1966) 'The Lucan Temptation Narrative', *JTS* 17: 71.

Swatos, William H. (1976) 'Weber or Troeltsch? Methodology, Syndrome, and the Development of Church–sect Theory', *JSSR* 15: 129–144.

Swidler, L. (1976) *Women in Judaism: The Status of Women in Formative Judaism*, Metuchen, NJ: Scarecrow.

Syreeni, Kari (1990) 'Between Heaven and Earth: On the Structure of Matthew's Symbolic Universe', *JSNT* 40: 3–13.

Talbert, Charles H. (1974) *Literary Patterns, Theological Themes and the Genre of Luke–Acts*, Missoula, MT: SBL and Scholars.

—— (1986) *Reading Luke, A Literary and Theological Commentary on the Third Gospel*, New York: Crossroad.

Tannehill, Robert L. (1986) *The Narrative Unity of Luke–Acts: A Literary Interpretation*, Philadelphia: Fortress Press.

Tate, M. E. (1990) *Psalms 51–100*, WBC 20. Waco, TX: Word.

Taylor, A. B. (1960) 'Decision in the Desert: The Temptation of Jesus in the Light of Deuteronomy', *Int* 14: 300–309.

Taylor, N. H. (1992) *Paul, Antioch and Jerusalem*, Sheffield: Sheffield Academic Press.

—— (1993) 'Paul's Apostolic Legitimacy: Autobiographical Reconstruction in Galatians 1:11–2:14', *Journal of Theology for Southern Africa* 83: 65–77.

Tcherikover, Victor (1937) *Palestine under the Ptolemies: A Contribution to the Study of the Zenon Papyri, Muzraim IV-V*, New York: G. E. Stechert.

—— (1970) *Hellenistic Civilization and the Jews*, trans. S. Applebaum, New York: Atheneum.

Tetlow, Elizabeth (1980) *Women and Ministry in the New Testament*, New York: Paulist.

Theissen, Gerd (1973) 'Wanderradikalismus: Literatursoziologische Aspekte der Überlieferung von Worten Jesu im Urchristentum', *ZTK* 70: 245–271

—— (1978) *Sociology of Early Palestinian Christianity*, trans. J. Bowden, Philadelphia: Fortress Press (German edn 1977).

—— (1982) *The Social Setting of Pauline Christianity*, ed. and trans. J. Schutz, Edinburgh: T. and T. Clark.

—— (1987) *Psychological Aspects of Pauline Theology*, trans. J. Galvin, Edinburgh: T. and T. Clark.

—— (1991) *The Gospels in Context: Social and Political History in the Synoptic Tradition*, Minneapolis: Fortress Press.

Thibeaux, Evelyn Rose (1990) *The Narrative Rhetoric of Luke 7:36–50: A Study of Context, Text, and Interpretation*, PhD dissertation, Graduate Theological Union.

Thomas, Brook (1991) *The New Historicism and Other Old-fashioned Topics*, Princeton: Princeton University Press.

Thompson, Henry O. (1992) 'Dura-Europos', in D. N. Freedman (ed), *The Anchor Bible Dictionary*, vol. 2, New York: Doubleday, 241–243.

Thompson, J. B. (1984) *Studies in the Theory of Ideology*, Cambridge: Polity Press.

Thompson, William (1970) *Matthew's Advice to a Divided Community: Mt. 17:22–18, 35*, AnBib 44, Rome: Biblical Institute Press.

Tilborg, Sjef Van (1972) *The Jewish Leaders in Matthew*, Leiden: E. J. Brill.

Tomber, R. (1993) 'Quantitative Approaches to the Investigation of Long-Distance Exchange', *JRA* 6: 142–166.

Townsend, John T. (1961) 'Matthew XXIII.9', *JTS* 12: 56–59.

—— (1971) 'Ancient Education in the Time of the Early Roman Empire', in Stephen Benko and John J. O'Rourke (eds) *The Catacombs and the Colosseum*, Valley Forge: Judson Press, 139–163.

—— (1992) 'Education (Greco-Roman)', in D. N. Freedman (ed.), *The Anchor Bible Dictionary*, vol. 2, New York: Doubleday, 312–317.

Travisano, R. V. (1981) 'Alternation and Conversion as Qualitatively Different Transformations', in G. P. Stone and H. A. Farberman (eds) *Social Psychology through Symbolic*

Interaction, Waltham MA: Ginn-Blaisdell, 237–248.
Triandis, H. C. (1989) 'Cross-cultural Studies of Individualism and Collectivism', in R. A. Dienstbier *et al.* (eds) *Nebraska Symposium on Motivation 1989*, Lincoln: University of Nebraska Press, 41–133.
Trilling, Wolfgang (1964) *Das Wahre Israel*, 3rd edn, Munich: Kössel Verlag.
Troeltsch, Ernst (1960) *The Social Teaching of the Christian Churches*, 2 vols, New York: Harper and Brothers, trans. of *Die Soziallehren der christlichen Kirchen und Gruppen, Gesammelte Schriften I*, Tübingen: Mohr (Siebeck), 1912, 2nd edn 1919.
Trummer, P. (1975) 'Die Chance der Freiheit: Zur Interpretation des mallon chresai in 1 Kor 7,21', *Bib* 56: 344–368.
Tuckman, B. W. (1965) 'Developmental Sequence in Small Groups', *Psychological Bulletin* 63: 384–399.
Turner, E. G. (1954) 'Tiberius Julius Alexander', *JRS* 44: 54–64.
Turner, Jonathan H. (1984) *Societal Stratification: A Theoretical Analysis*, New York: Columbia University Press.
Tyler, Stephen (1986) 'Post-modern Ethnography: From Document of the Occult to Occult Document', in James Clifford and George E. Marcus (eds) *Writing Culture: The Poetics and Politics of Ethnography: A School of American Research Advanced Seminar*, Berkeley, CA: University of California Press, 122–140.
Urbach, E. E. (1975) *The Sages*, Jerusalem: Magnes Press.
—— (1987) *The Sages: Their Concepts and Beliefs*, trans. I. Abrahams, Cambridge, MA: Harvard University Press.
Urman, D. (1985) *The Golan: A Profile of a Region during the Roman and Byzantine Periods*, Oxford: BAR International Series 269.
Veeser, H. Aram (ed.) (1989) *The New Historicism*, London: Routledge.
Vermes, Geza (1987) *The Dead Sea Scrolls in English*, 3rd edn, London: Penguin Books.
Vickers, Brian (1988) *In Defence of Rhetoric*, Oxford: Clarendon Press.
Vitto, F. (1983–1984) 'A Look into the Workshop of a Late Roman Galilean Potter', *Bulletin of the Anglo-Israel Archaeological Society*, 3:19–22.
Viviano, Benedict V. (1990) 'Social World and Community Leadership: The Case of Matthew 23:1–12, 34', *JSNT* 39: 3–21.
Wachsmann, S. (1990) *The Excavation of an Ancient Boat in the Sea of Galilee (Lake Kinneret), Atiqot 19*, Jerusalem: Israel Antiquities Authority.
Walker, Rolf (1967) *Die Heilsgeschichte im ersten Evangelium*, Göttingen: Vandenhoeck and Ruprecht.
Wallace-Hadrill, Andrew (ed.) (1989) *Patronage in Ancient Society*, Leicester–Nottingham Studies in Ancient Society 1, London and New York: Routledge.
—— (1991) 'Elites and Trade in the Roman Town', in J. Rich and A. Wallace-Hadrill (eds) *City and Country in the Ancient World*, London and New York: Routledge, 241–272.
Walsh, Roger (1993) 'Phenomenological Mapping and Comparisons of Shamanic, Buddhist, Yogic, and Schizophrenic Experiences', *JAAR* 61: 739–769.
Waltzing, J.-P. (1895) *Étude historique sur les corporations professionelles chez les Romains*, vol. 1, Louvain: Peeters.
Wanamaker, C. A. (1989) 'Like a Father Treats His Own Children': Paul and the Conversion/Resocialization of the Thessalonians' (unpublished).
—— (1990) *The Epistles to the Thessalonians*, Grand Rapids, MI: Eerdmans.
Ward, S. (1987) 'Consumer Behavior', in C. R. Berger and S. H. Chaffee (eds) *Handbook of Communication Science*, Newbury Park: Sage, 651–674.
Watson, Francis (1986) *Paul, Judaism and the Gentiles: A Sociological Approach*, SNTSMS 56, New York and Cambridge: Cambridge University Press.
—— (1992) 'Strategies of Recovery and Resistance: Hermeneutical Reflections on Genesis 1–3 and its Pauline Reception', *JSNT* 45: 79–103.

—— (1994) *Text, Church and World: Biblical Interpretation in Theological Perspective*, Edinburgh: T. and T. Clark.

Weber, Max (1952) *Ancient Judaism*, New York: The Free Press (German edn 1917–1919).

—— (1955) *The Protestant Ethic and the Spirit of Capitalism*, trans. Talcott Parsons, New York: Charles Scribner's Sons, 1955 (German edn 1904–1905).

—— (1964) *The Sociology of Religion*, Boston: Beacon Press; trans. of 'Religionssoziologie', *Wirtschaft und Gesellschaft*, 4th edn 1956.

—— (1978) *Economy and Society*, Guenther Roth and Claus Wittich (eds), 2 vols, Berkeley: University of California Press; trans. of *Wirtschaft und Gesellschaft*, 4th edn 1956.

Wedderburn, A. J. M. (1993) 'The Theology of Colossians', in A. J. M. Wedderburn and A. T. Lincoln, *The Theology of the Later Pauline Epistles*, New Testament Theology, Cambridge: Cambridge University Press, 3–71.

Wegner, Judith (1988) *Chattel or Person? The Status of Women in the Mishnah*, New York and Oxford: Oxford University Press.

Weigert, A. J., Teitge, J. S. and Teitge, D. W. (1986) *Society and Identity*, Cambridge: Cambridge University Press.

White, Leland J. (1986) 'Grid and Group in Matthew's Community: The Righteousness/ Honor Code in the Sermon', in J. H. Elliott (ed.) *Social-scientific Criticism of the New Testament and its Social World*, Semeia 35, Decatur, GA: Scholars Press, 61–88.

White, L. Michael (1987) 'Scaling the Strongman's "Court" (Luke 11:21)', *Forum* 3/3: 3–28.

—— (1988) 'Shifting Sectarian Boundaries in Early Christianity', *Bulletin of the John Rylands University Library of Manchester* 70/3: 7–24.

Whittaker, C. R. (1990) 'The Consumer City Revisited: The *vicus* and the City', *JRA* 3: 110–118.

Wilde, James A. (1974) *A Social Description of the Community Reflected in the Gospel of Mark*, Ann Arbor, MI: Xerox University Microfilms.

—— (1978) 'The Social World of Mark's Gospel: A Word About Method', in Paul J. Achtemeier, (ed.) *SBLSP*: 47–70.

Wilken, Robert L. (1971) 'Collegia, Philosophical Schools, and Theology', in Stephen Benko and John J. O'Rourke (eds) *The Catacombs and the Colosseum: The Roman Empire as the Setting of Primitive Christianity*, Valley Forge: Judson, 268–291.

—— (1984) *The Christians as the Romans saw them*, New Haven, CN: Yale University Press.

Wilkins, Michael J. (1992) 'Brother, Brotherhood', D. N. Freedman (ed.) *The Anchor Bible Dictionary*, vol. 1, Garden City, NY: Doubleday, 782–783.

Willis, W. L. (1985) *Idol Meat in Corinth*, Chico: Scholars Press.

Wilson, Bryan R. (1959) 'An Analysis of Sect Development', *American Sociological Review* 24: 3–15.

—— (1961) *Sects and Society: A Sociological Study of the Elim Tabernacle, Christian Science, and Christadelphians*, Berkeley: University of California Press.

—— (1967) *Patterns of Sectarianism: Organization and Ideology in Social and Religious Movements*, London: Heinemann.

—— (1969) 'A Typology of Sects', in Roland Robertson (ed.) *Sociology of Religion*, Baltimore: Penguin Books, 361–383.

—— (1970) *Religious Sects: A Sociological Study*, London: Weidenfeld and Nicolson.

—— (1973) *Magic and the Millennium: A Sociological Study of Religious Movements of Protest among Tribal and Third-world Peoples*, New York: Harper and Row.

—— (1982) 'The Sociology of Sects', in B. R. Wilson, *Religion in Sociological Perspective*, Oxford: Oxford University Press, 89–120.

—— (1988) 'Methodological Perspectives in the Study of Religious Minorities', *Bulletin of the John Rylands University Library of Manchester* 70: 225–240.

Wilson, R. R. (1975) 'The Old Testament Genealogies in Recent Research', *JBL* 94: 168–189.

Wimsatt, W. K. (1954) *The Verbal Icon*, Lexington: University of Kentucky Press.
Winter, Bruce (1991) 'The Messiah as the Tutor: The Meaning of *kathegetes* in Matthew 23:10', *Tyndale Bulletin* 42/1: 152–157.
Wire, Antoinette (1991) 'Gender Roles in a Scribal Community', in David L. Balch (ed.) *Social History of the Matthean Community*, Minneapolis: Fortress Press, 87–121.
Witherington, B. III (1979) 'On the Road with Mary Magdalene, Joanna, Susanna, and Other Disciples: Luke 8:1–3', *ZNW* 70: 243–248.
—— (1984) *Women in the Ministry of Jesus*, Cambridge: Cambridge University Press.
—— (1988) *Women in the Earliest Churches* SNTSMS 59, Cambridge: Cambridge University Press.
Wright, N. T. (1986) *Colossians and Philemon*, Tyndale New Testament Commentary, Leicester: IVP.
Yinger, J. Milton (1970) *The Scientific Study of Religion*, New York: Macmillan.
Yoder, J. H. (1972) *The Politics of Jesus*, Grand Rapids, Michigan: Wm B. Eerdmans.
Zald, M. N. and McCarthy, J. D. (1987) 'Religious Groups as Crucibles of Social Movements', in M. N. Zald and J. D. McCarthy (eds) *Social Movements in an Organizational Society*, New Brunswick: Transaction Books, 67–95.
Zander, Alvin (1971) *Motives and Goals in Groups*, Orlando: Academic Press.
—— (1985) *The Purposes of Groups and Organizations*, San Francisco: Jossey-Bass.
Zanker, P. (1988) *The Power of Images in the Age of Augustus*, Ann Arbor: University of Michigan Press.
Ziebarth, Erich (1896) *Das griechische Vereinswesen*, Wiesbaden: Martin Sändig (repr. 1969).

INDEX OF ANCIENT SOURCES

Apocrypha and Pseudepigrapha

Other Ancient Sources

Rabbinic Literature

INDEX OF MODERN AUTHORS